ONE-PUNCH MAN 03

ONE + YUSUKE MURATA

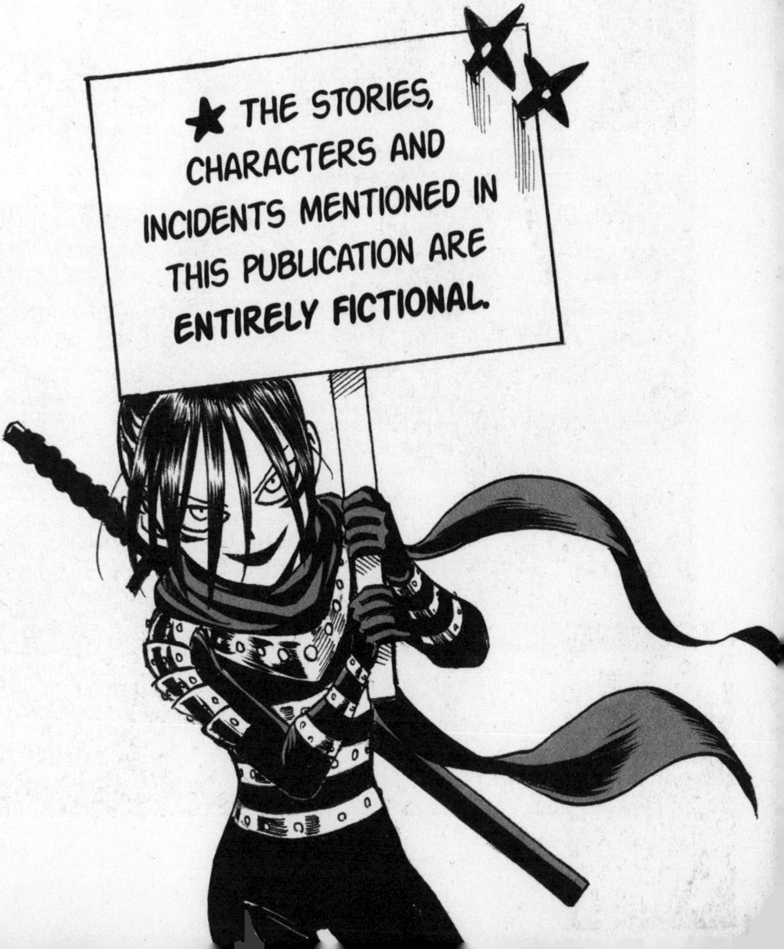
★ THE STORIES, CHARACTERS AND INCIDENTS MENTIONED IN THIS PUBLICATION ARE ENTIRELY FICTIONAL.

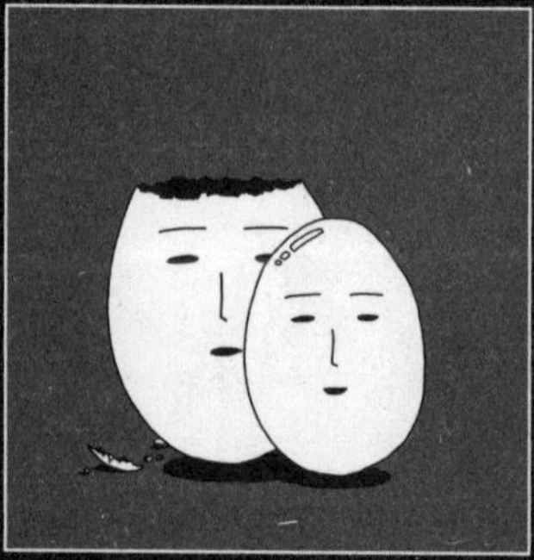

O N E

Every single positive comment from every reader is encouraging.

—ONE

Manga creator ONE began *One-Punch Man* as a webcomic, which quickly went viral, garnering over 10 million hits. In addition to *One-Punch Man*, ONE writes and draws the series *Mob Psycho 100* and *Makai no Ossan*.

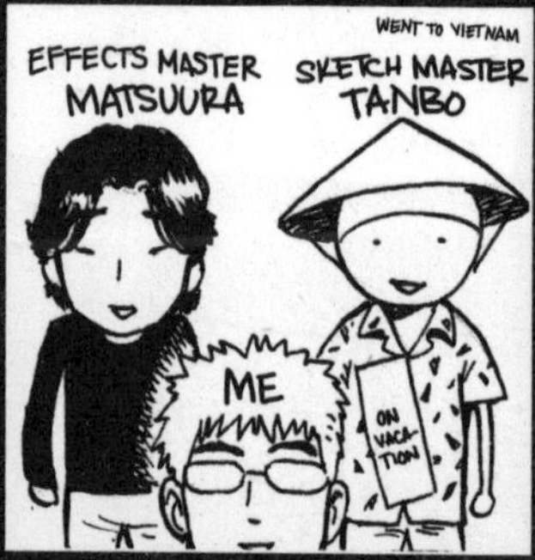
WENT TO VIETNAM
EFFECTS MASTER MATSUURA
SKETCH MASTER TANBO
ME
ON VACATION

Y U S U K E M U R A T A

(AND THE CURRENT MEMBERS OF VILLAGE STUDIO)

Try sliding up the dust cover on the Japanese graphic novel version. Sonic will form one picture together with the inside illustration (page 208 in English version).

—Yusuke Murata

A highly decorated and skilled artist best known for his work on *Eyeshield 21*, Yusuke Murata won the 122nd Hop Step Award (1995) for *Partner* and placed second in the 51st Akatsuka Award (1998) for *Samui Hanashi*.

ONE-PUNCH MAN

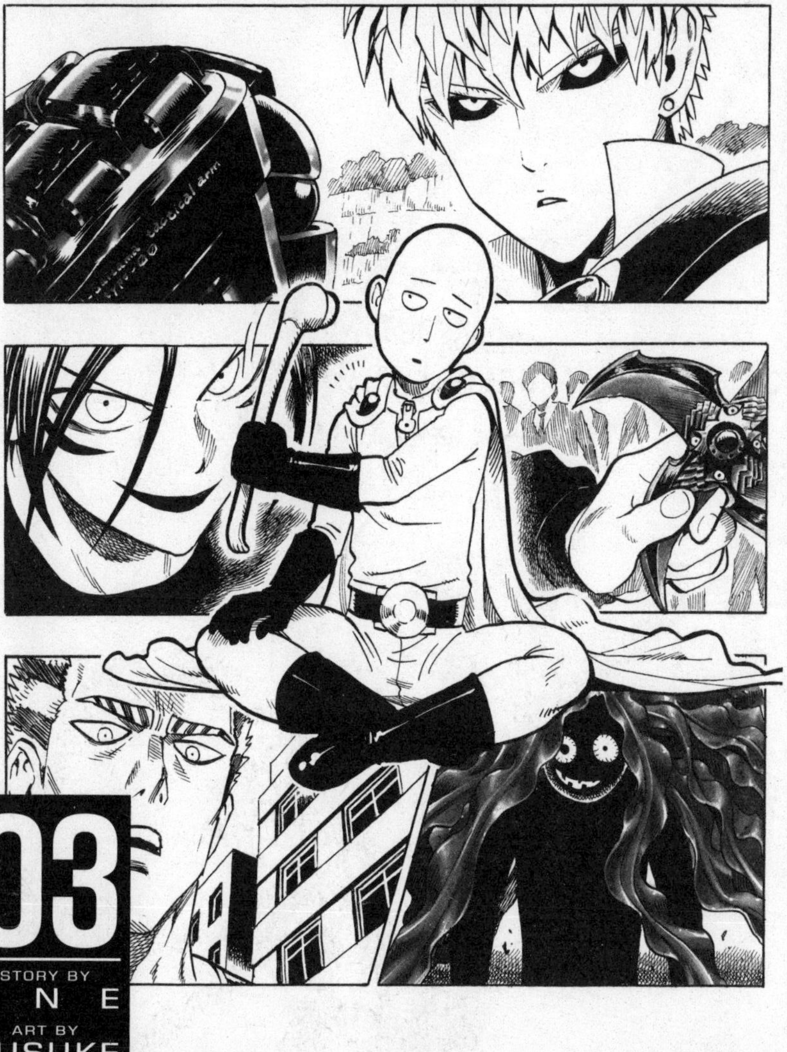

03

STORY BY
O N E

ART BY
YUSUKE
MURATA

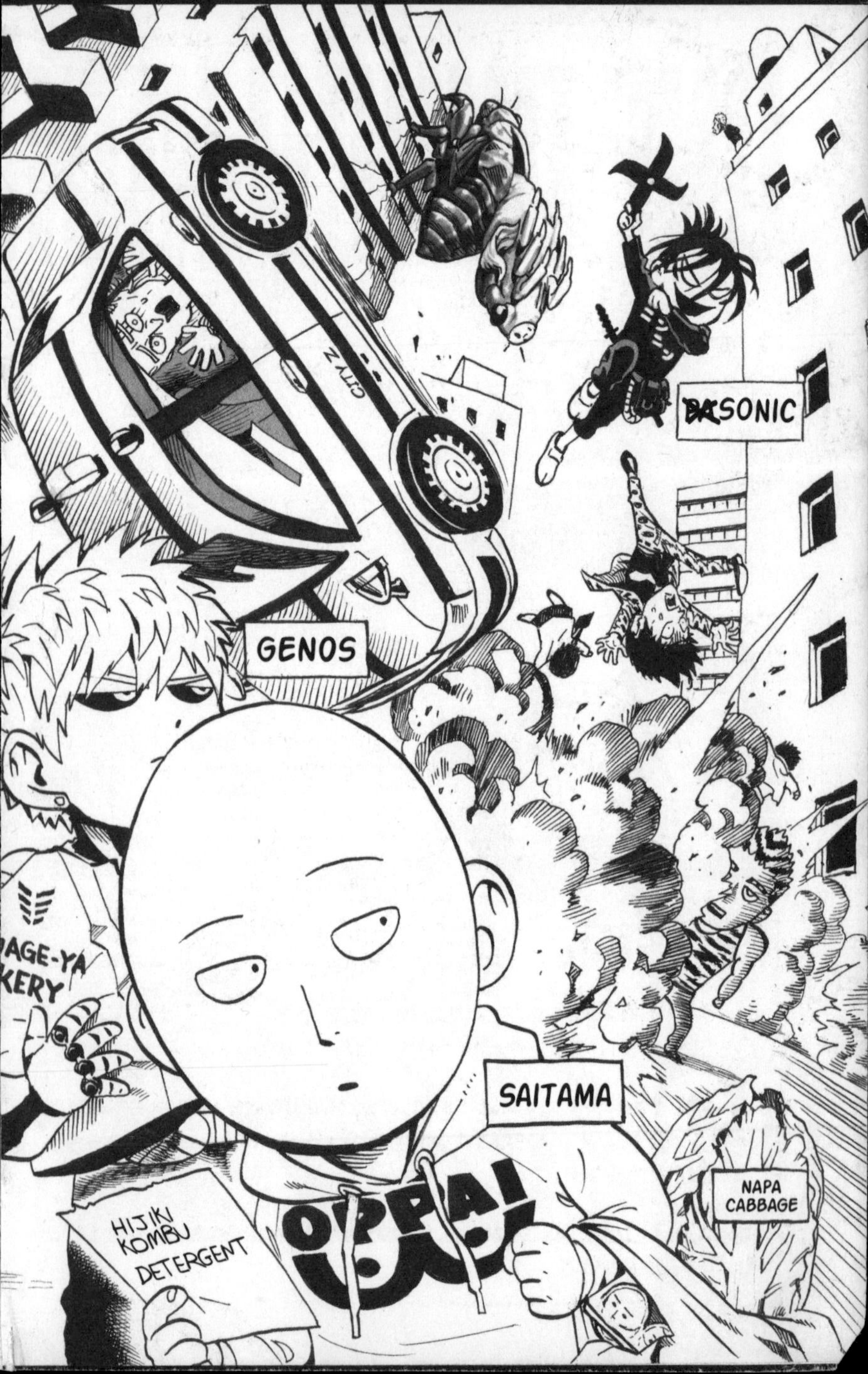
SONIC
CITY Z
GENOS
AGE-YA
KERY
SAITAMA
NAPA CABBAGE
OPPAI
HIJIKI
KOMBU
DETERGENT

ONE-PUNCH MAN

vol. 3 CHARACTERS

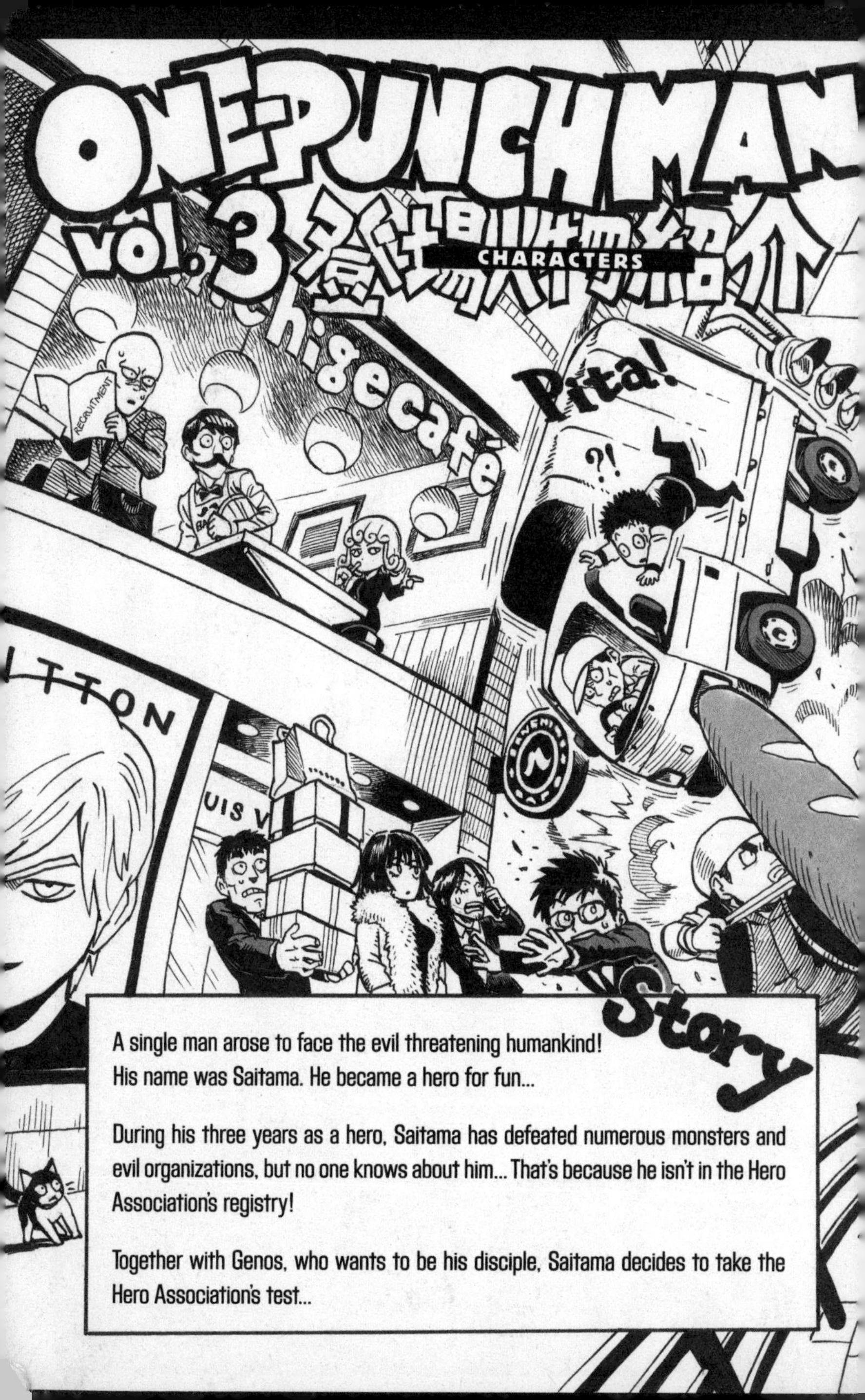
RECRUITMENT
Shigecafé
Pita!
?!
ITTON
UIS V

Story

A single man arose to face the evil threatening humankind!
His name was Saitama. He became a hero for fun...

During his three years as a hero, Saitama has defeated numerous monsters and evil organizations, but no one knows about him... That's because he isn't in the Hero Association's registry!

Together with Genos, who wants to be his disciple, Saitama decides to take the Hero Association's test...

ONE-PUNCH MAN
INDEX

CONTENTS

ONE-PUNCH MAN VOLUME THREE

ONE-PUNCH MAN
ONE + YUSUKE MURATA

My name is Saitama. I am a hero. My hobby is heroic exploits. I got too strong. And that makes me sad. I can defeat any enemy with one blow. I lost my hair. And I lost all feeling. I want to feel the rush of battle. I would like to meet an incredibly strong enemy. And I would like to defeat it with one blow. That's because I am One-Punch Man.

03

THE RUMOR

PUNCH 16: I PASSED

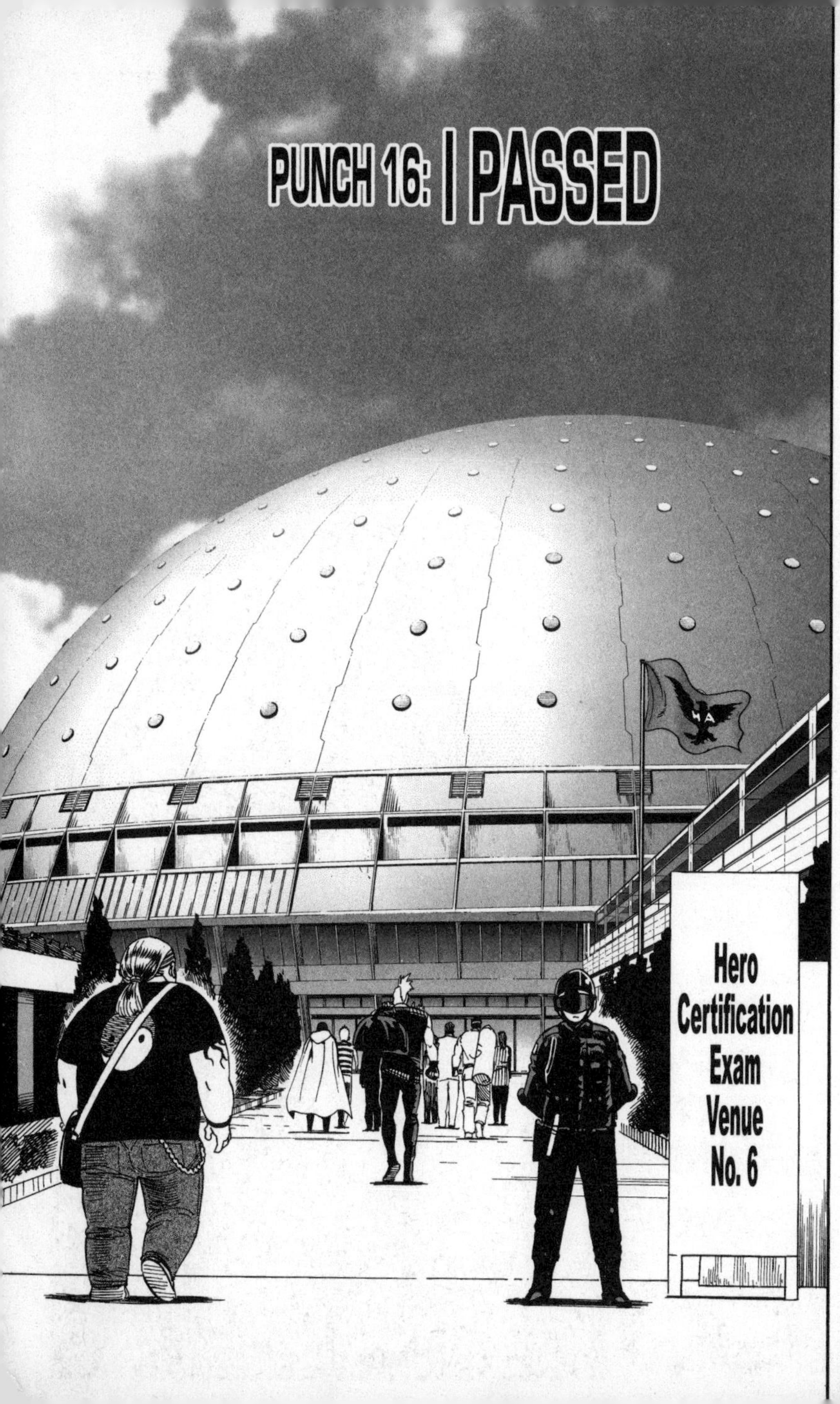
Hero Certification Exam Venue No. 6

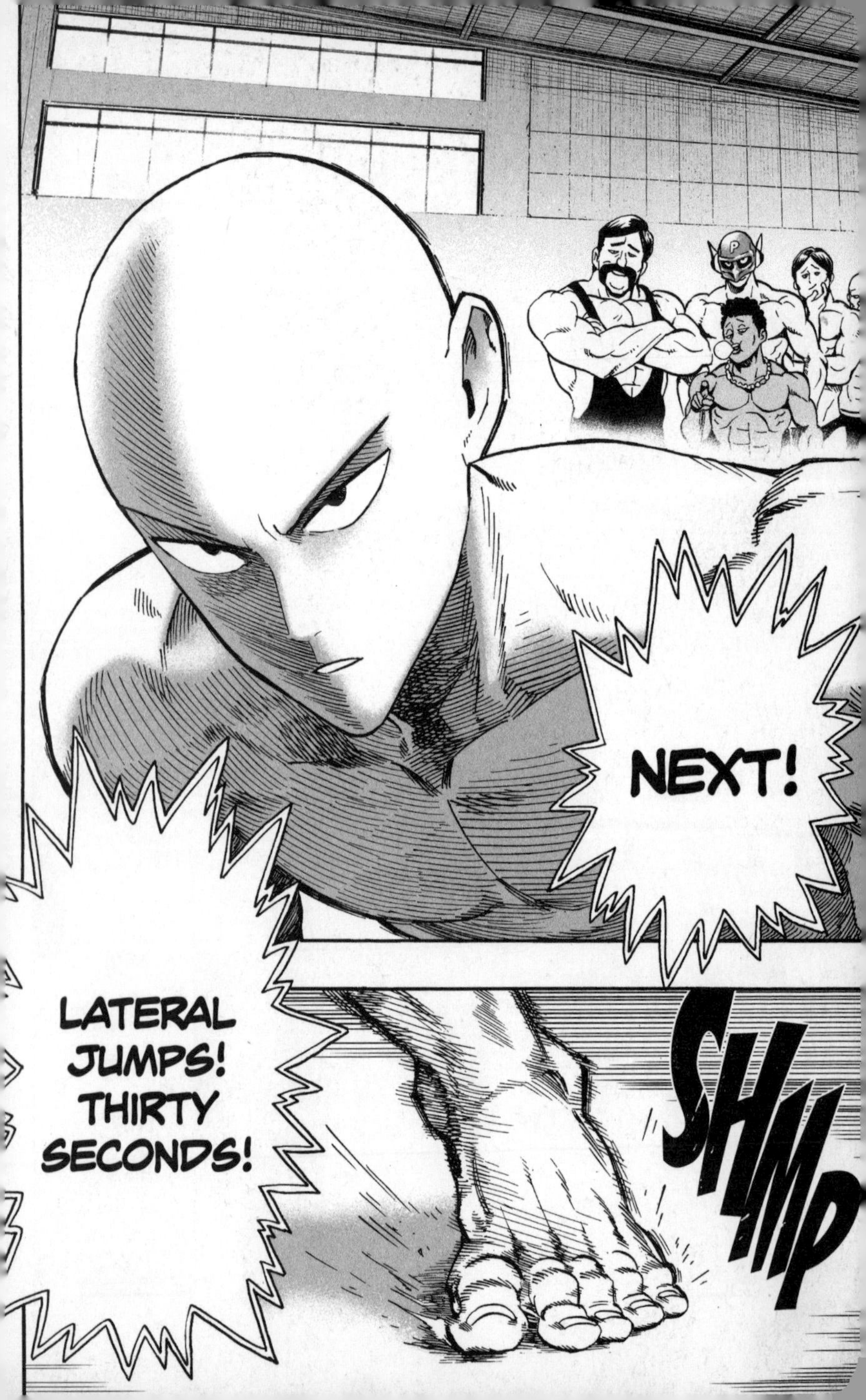
NEXT!
LATERAL JUMPS! THIRTY SECONDS!
SHMP

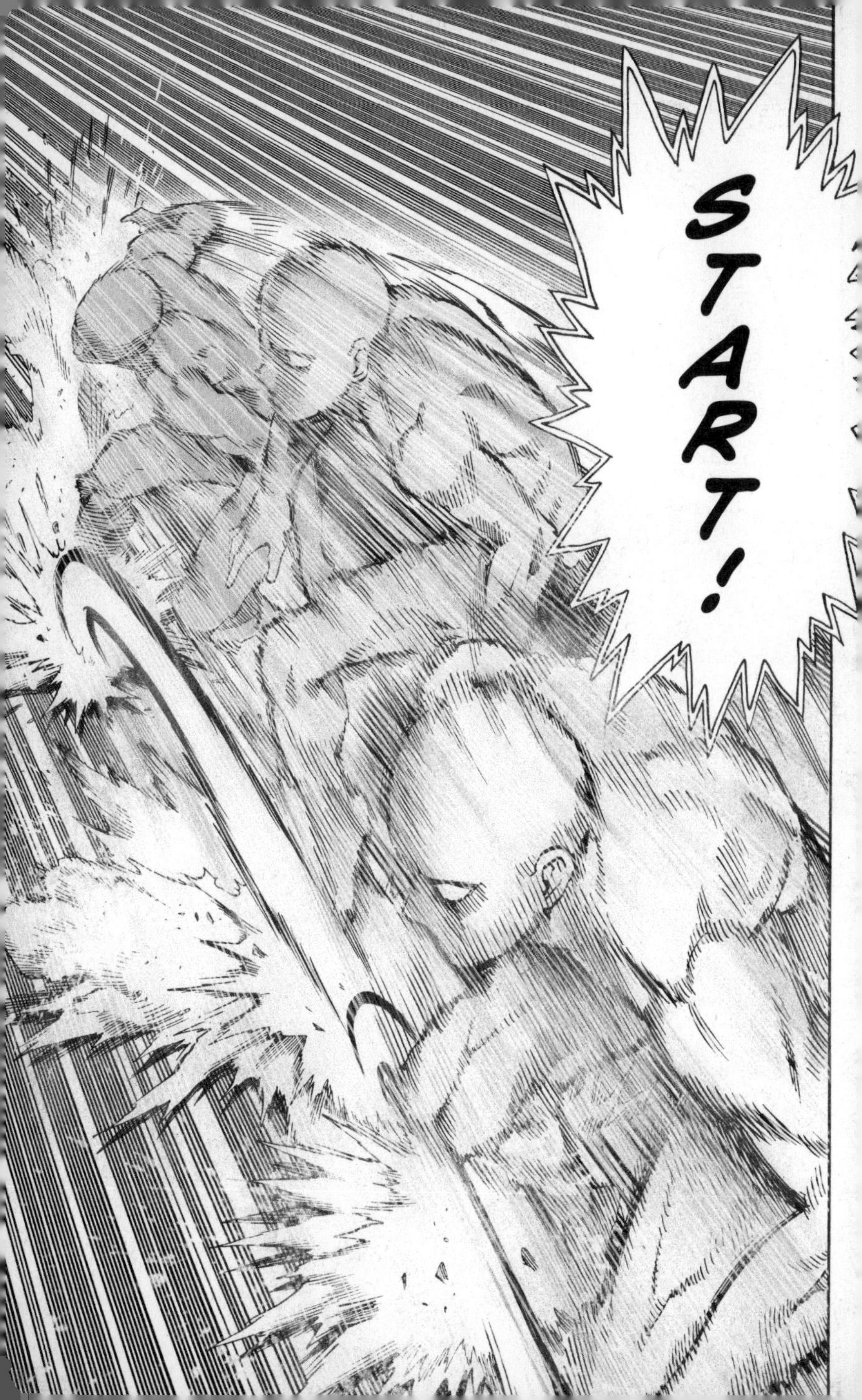
START!!

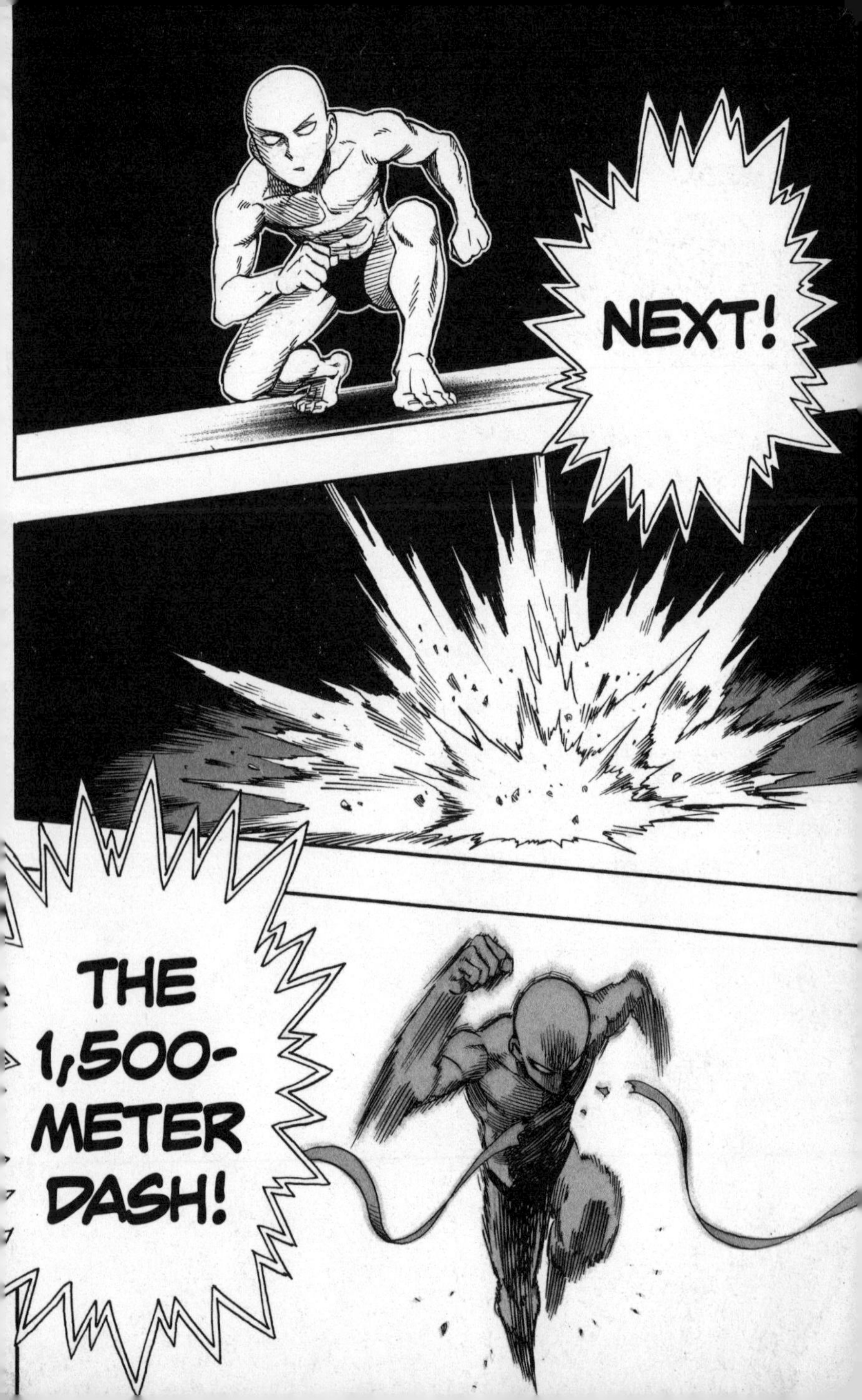
NEXT!
THE 1,500-METER DASH!

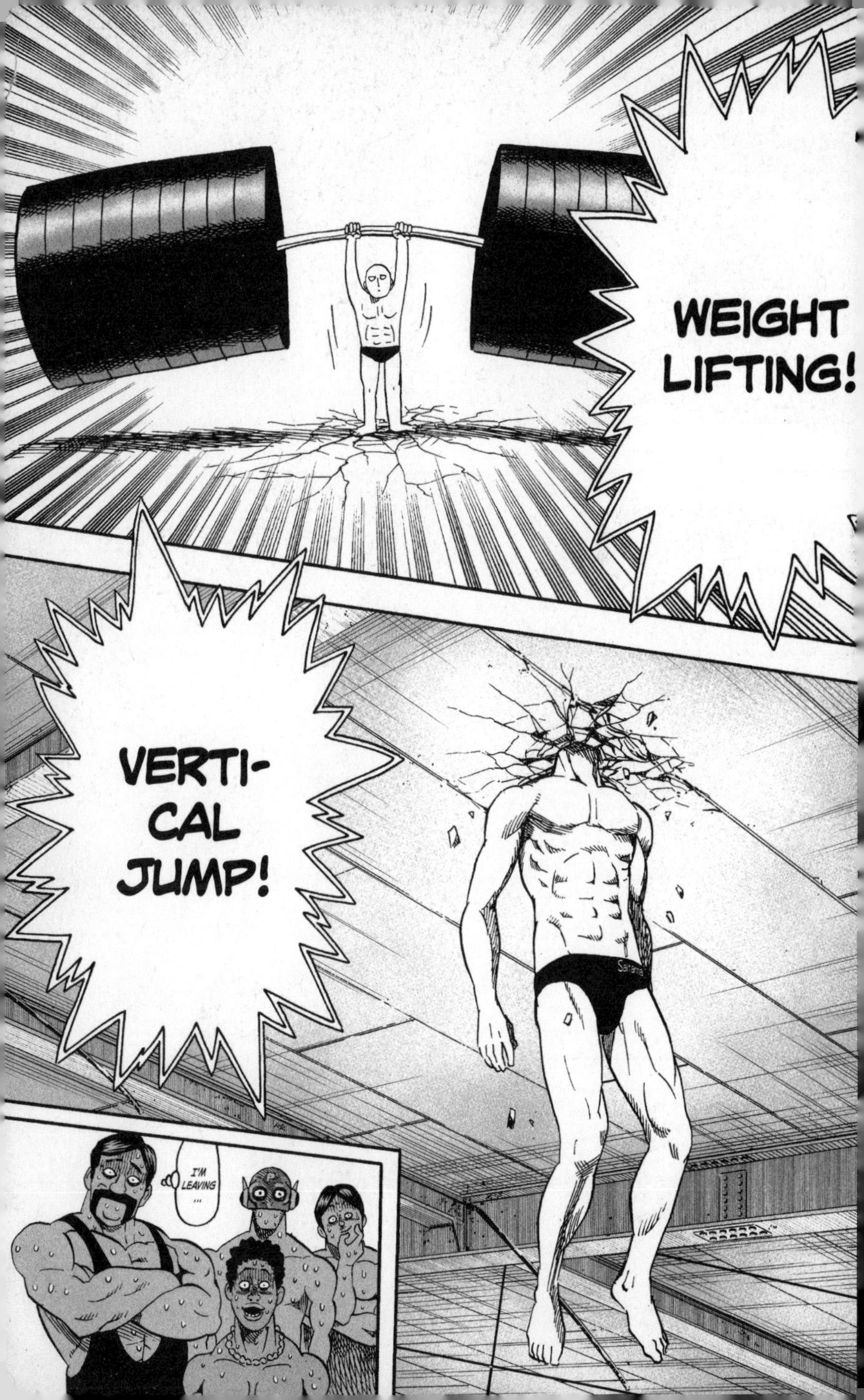
WEIGHT LIFTING!
VERTI-CAL JUMP!
Saitama
I'M LEAVING ...

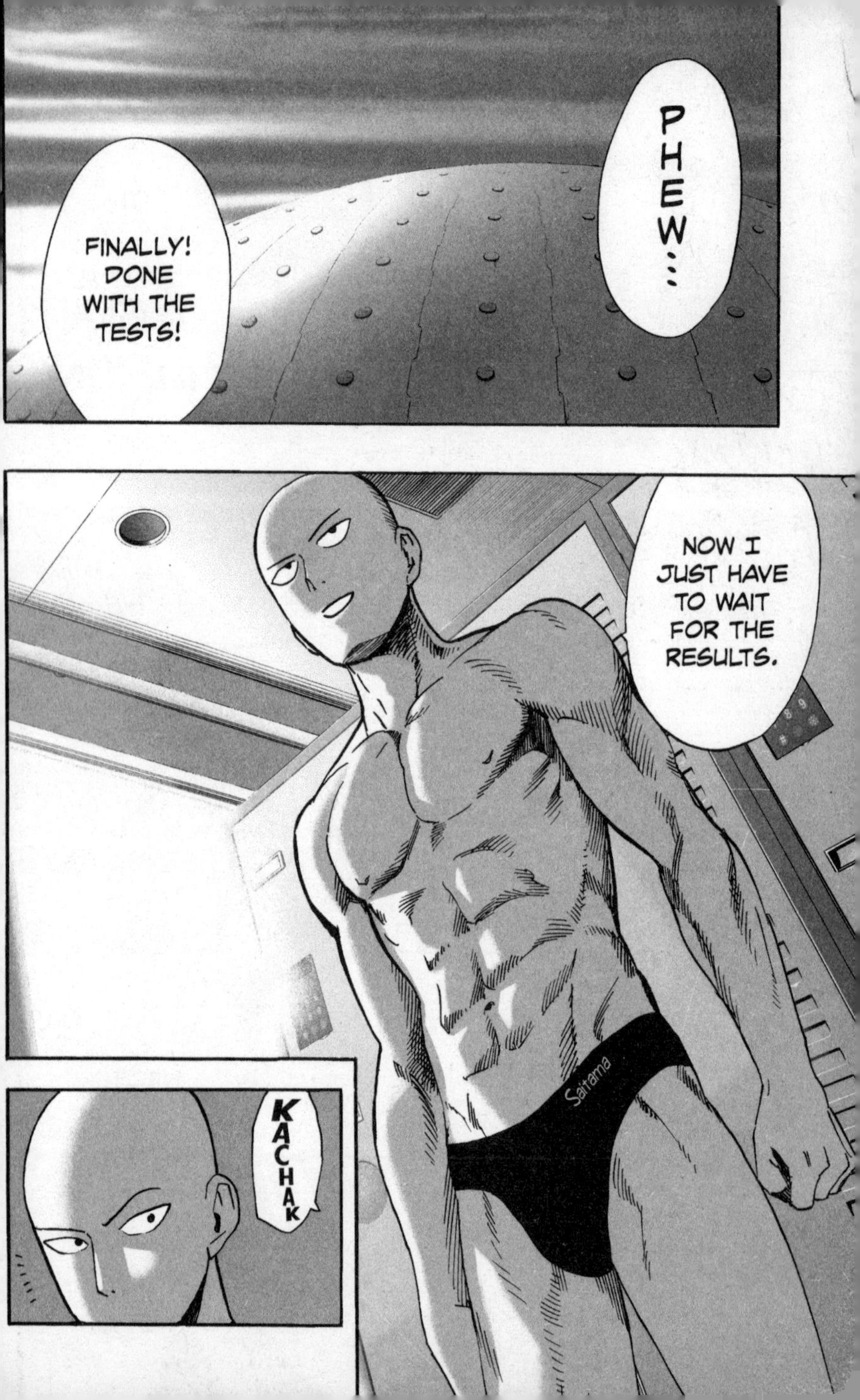
PHEW...
FINALLY! DONE WITH THE TESTS!
NOW I JUST HAVE TO WAIT FOR THE RESULTS.
Saitama
KACHAK

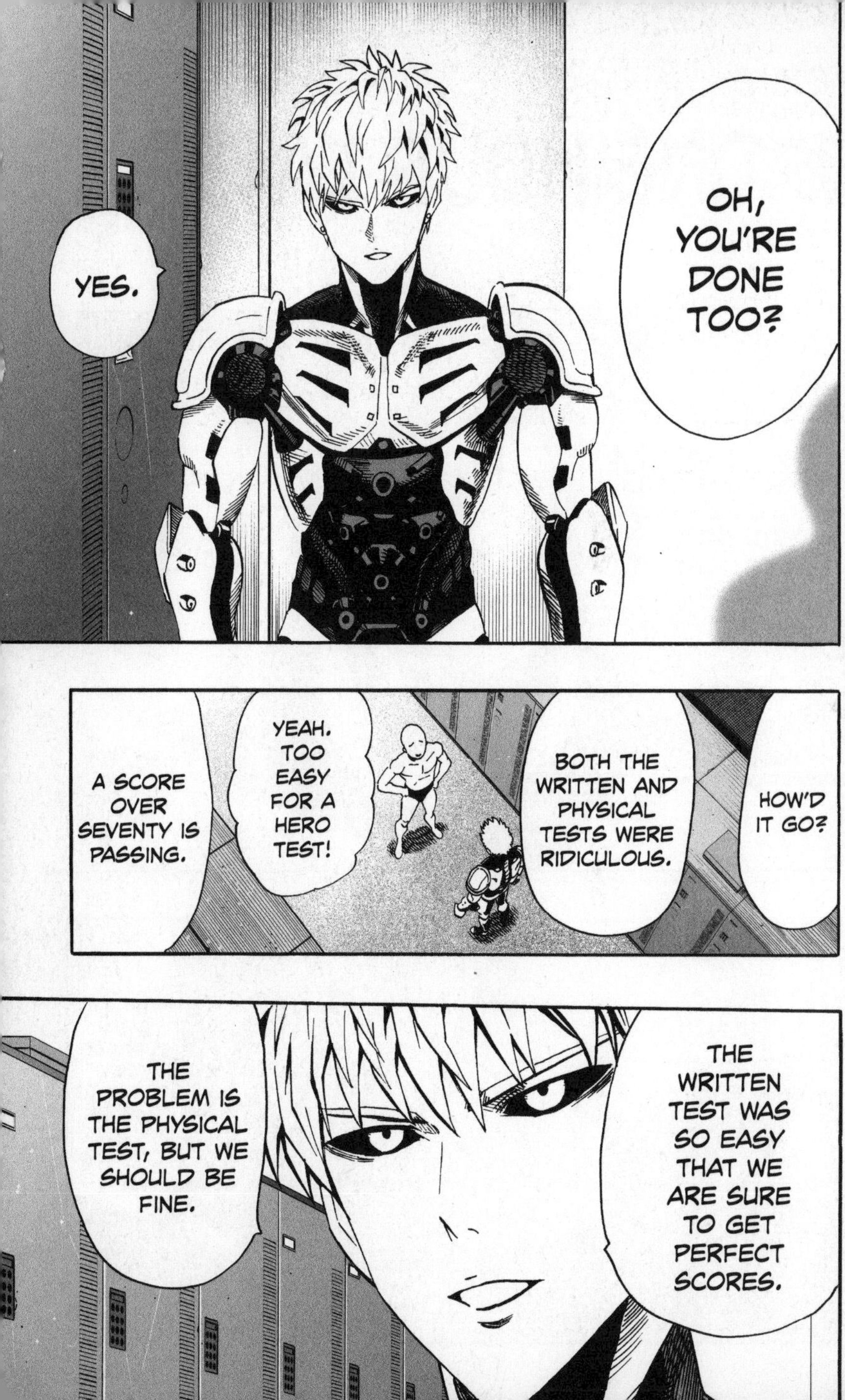
OH, YOU'RE DONE TOO?
YES.
HOW'D IT GO?
BOTH THE WRITTEN AND PHYSICAL TESTS WERE RIDICULOUS.
YEAH. TOO EASY FOR A HERO TEST!
A SCORE OVER SEVENTY IS PASSING.
THE WRITTEN TEST WAS SO EASY THAT WE ARE SURE TO GET PERFECT SCORES.
THE PROBLEM IS THE PHYSICAL TEST, BUT WE SHOULD BE FINE.

ONE HOUR LATER

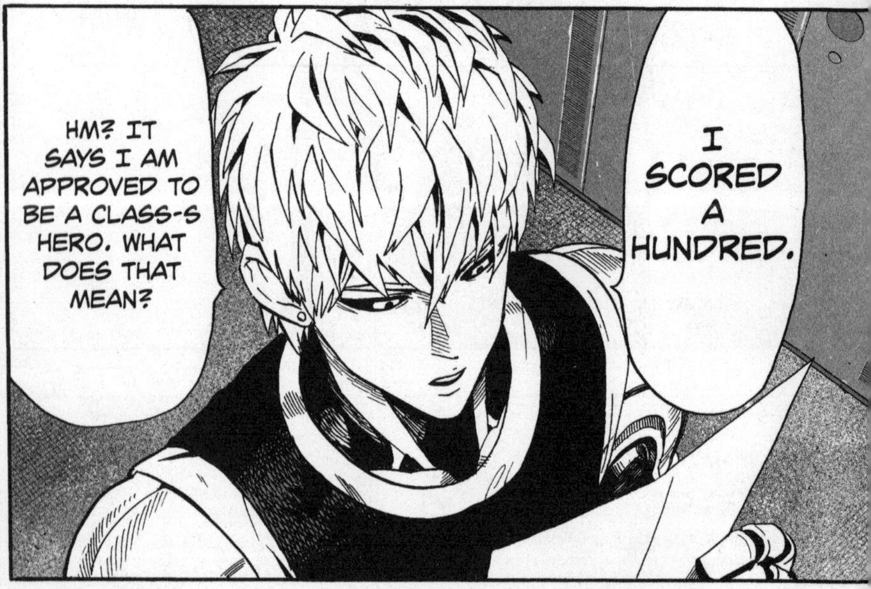
I SCORED A HUNDRED.
HM? IT SAYS I AM APPROVED TO BE A CLASS-S HERO. WHAT DOES THAT MEAN?

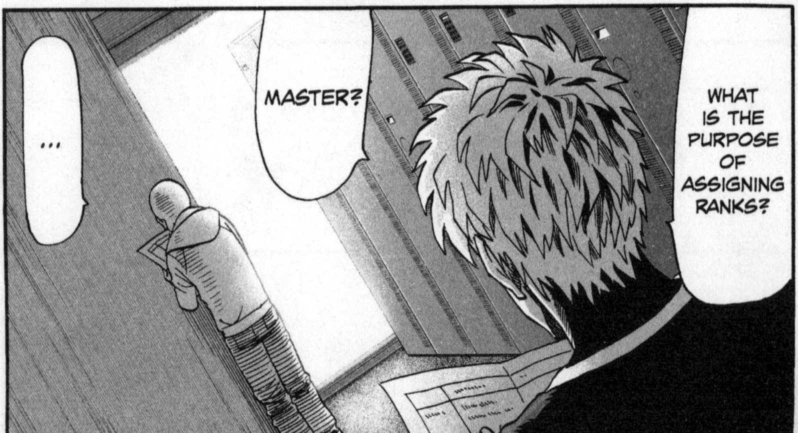
WHAT IS THE PURPOSE OF ASSIGNING RANKS?
MASTER?
...

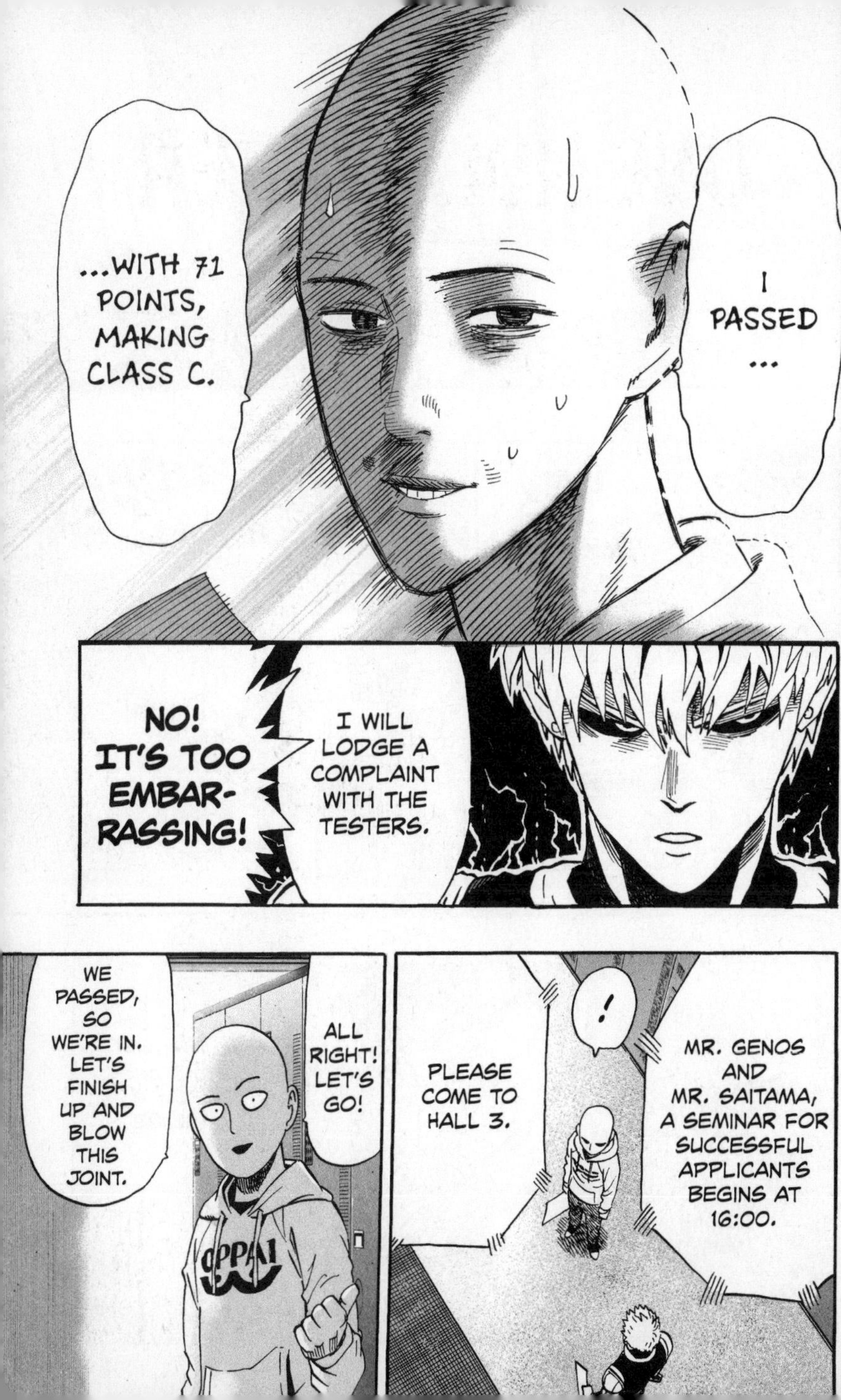
I PASSED ...
...WITH 71 POINTS, MAKING CLASS C.
I WILL LODGE A COMPLAINT WITH THE TESTERS.
NO! IT'S TOO EMBARRASSING!
MR. GENOS AND MR. SAITAMA, A SEMINAR FOR SUCCESSFUL APPLICANTS BEGINS AT 16:00.
PLEASE COME TO HALL 3.
!
WE PASSED, SO WE'RE IN. LET'S FINISH UP AND BLOW THIS JOINT.
ALL RIGHT! LET'S GO!
OPPAI

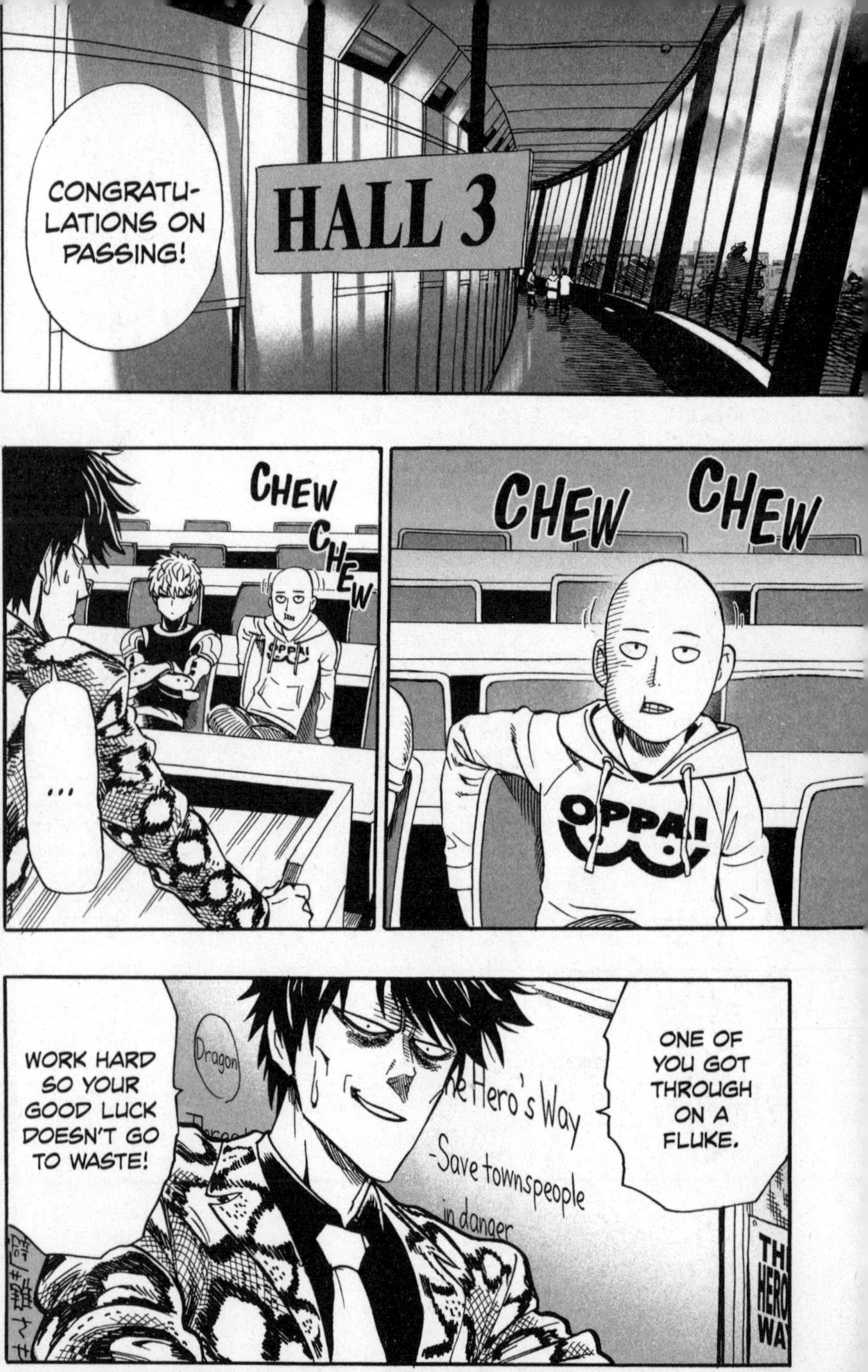
HALL 3
CONGRATULATIONS ON PASSING!
CHEW CHEW
CHEW CHEW
...
ONE OF YOU GOT THROUGH ON A FLUKE.
WORK HARD SO YOUR GOOD LUCK DOESN'T GO TO WASTE!
Dragon
he Hero's Way
-Save townspeople
in danger

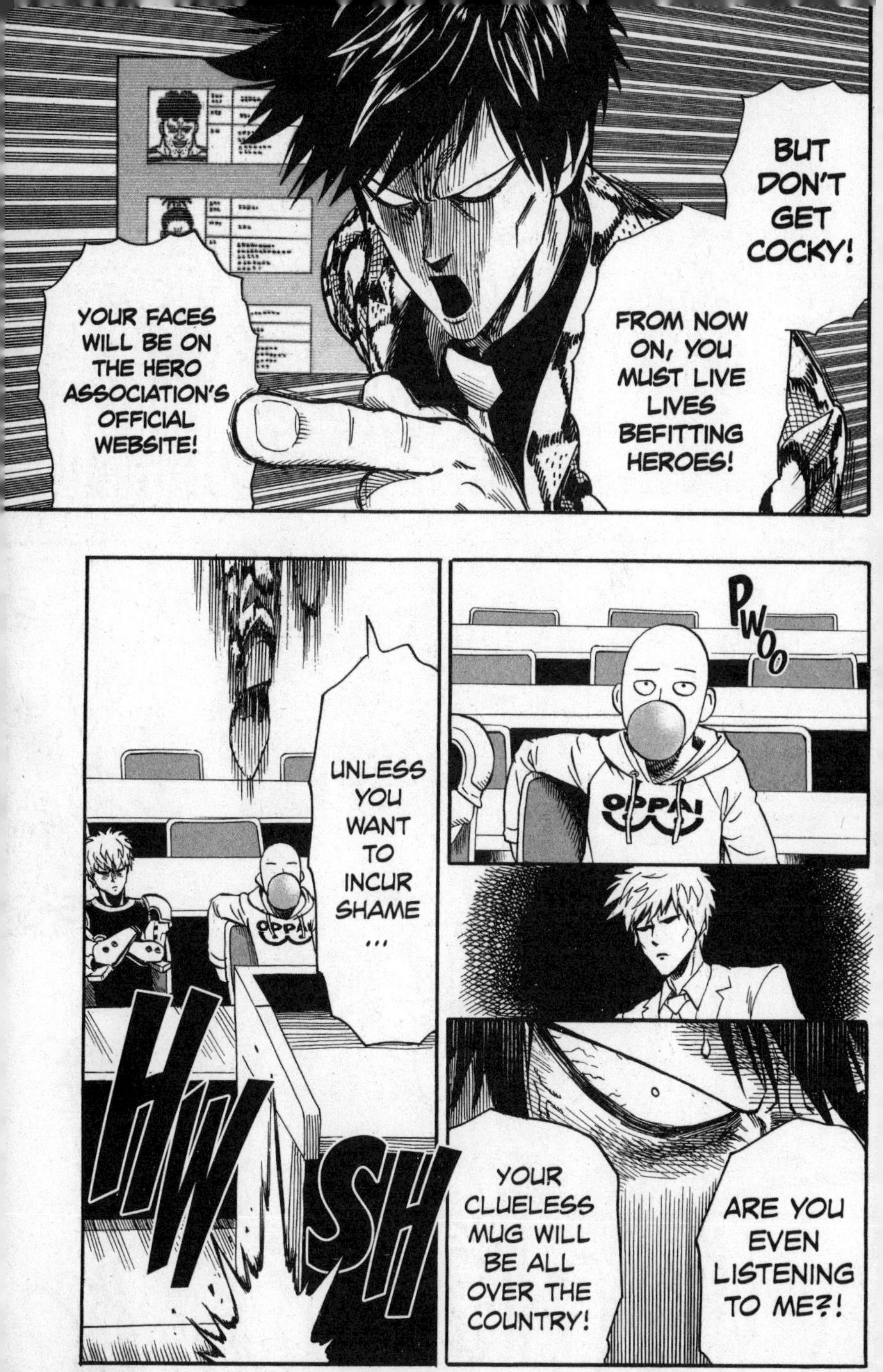

BUT DON'T GET COCKY!
FROM NOW ON, YOU MUST LIVE LIVES BEFITTING HEROES!
YOUR FACES WILL BE ON THE HERO ASSOCIATION'S OFFICIAL WEBSITE!
PWOO
ARE YOU EVEN LISTENING TO ME?!
YOUR CLUELESS MUG WILL BE ALL OVER THE COUNTRY!
UNLESS YOU WANT TO INCUR SHAME...
HWSH

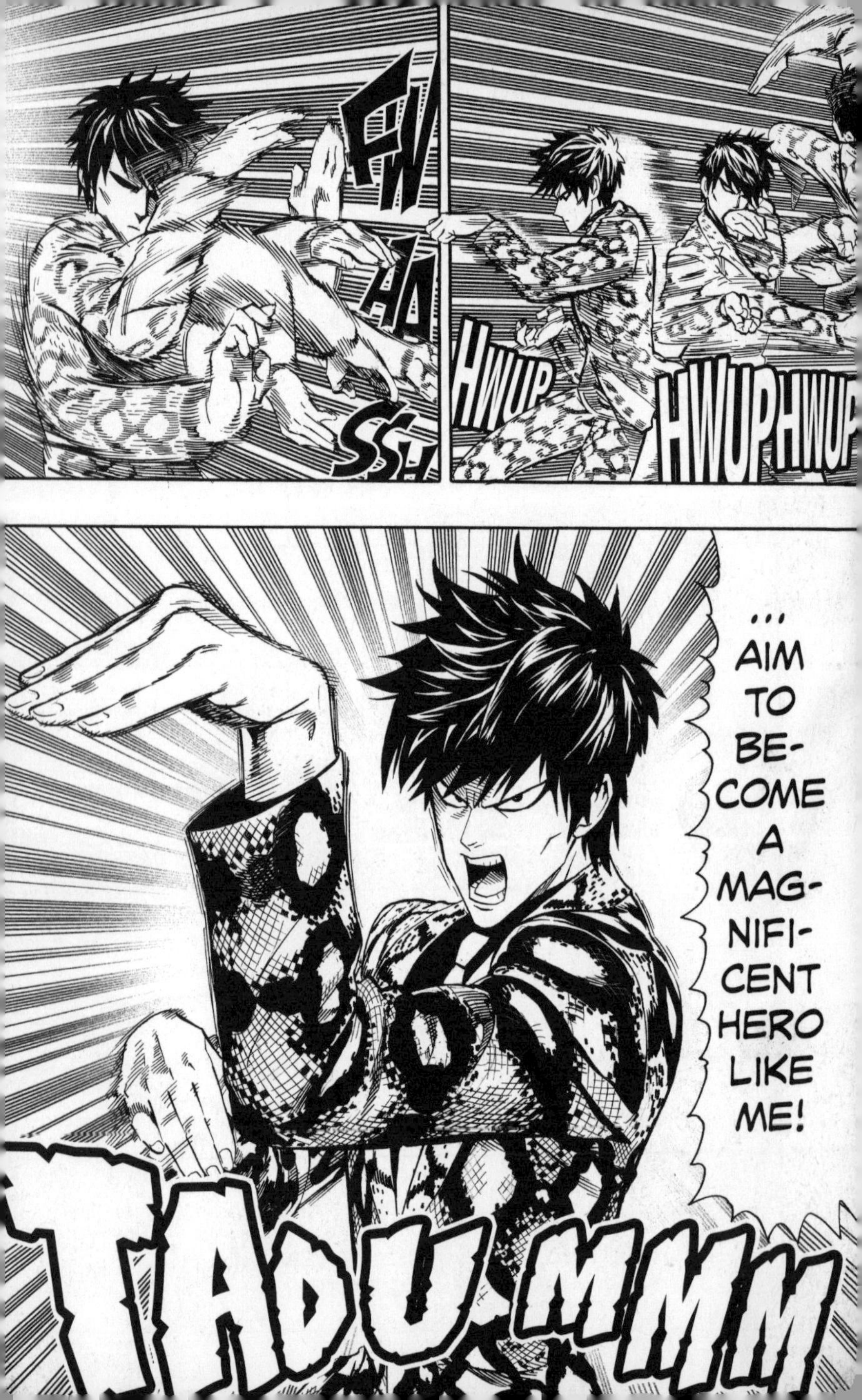
HWUPHWUP
HWUP
... AIM TO BE-COME A MAG-NIFI-CENT HERO LIKE ME!
TADU-MMM

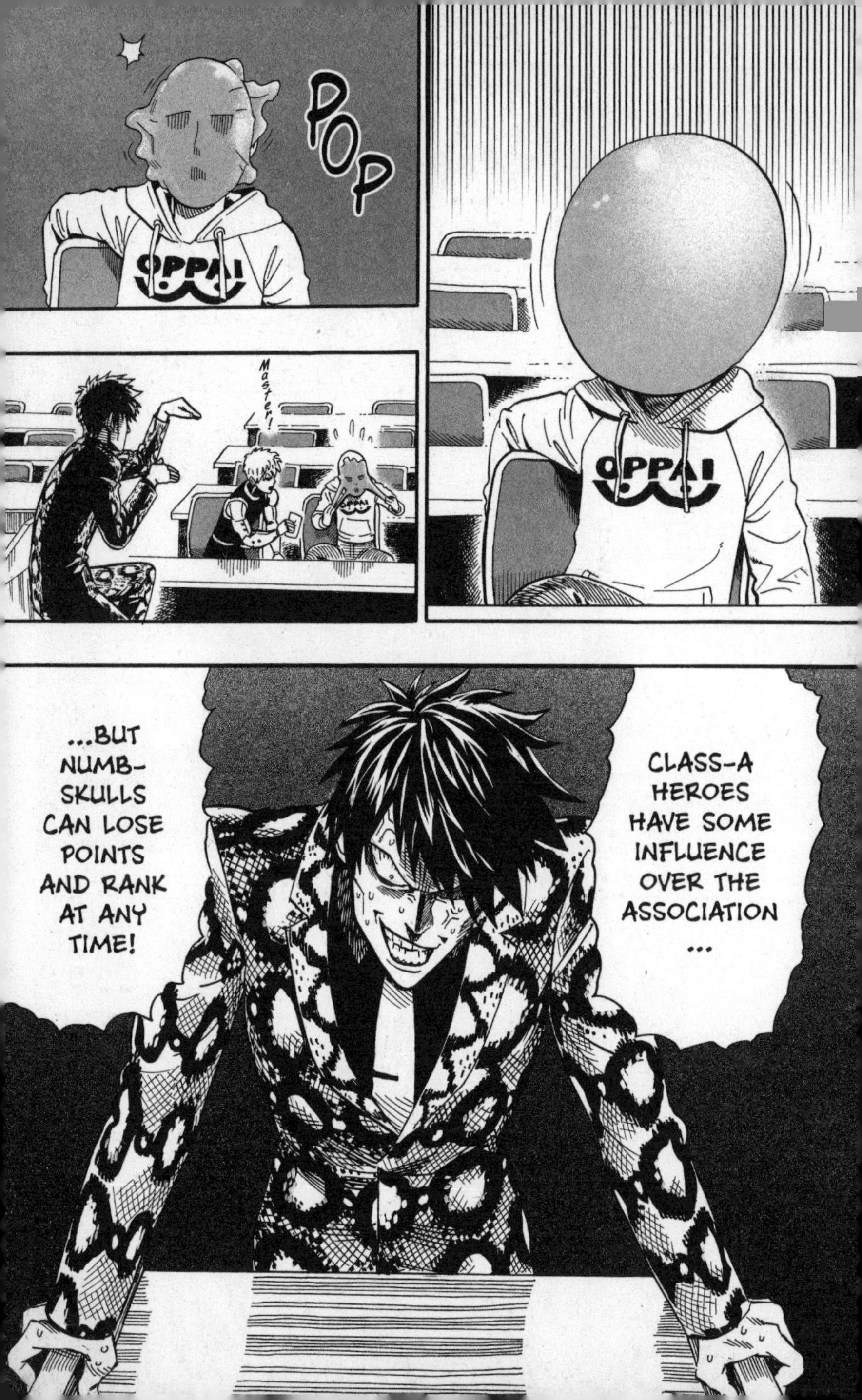
POP
Master!
CLASS-A HEROES HAVE SOME INFLUENCE OVER THE ASSOCIATION...
...BUT NUMB-SKULLS CAN LOSE POINTS AND RANK AT ANY TIME!

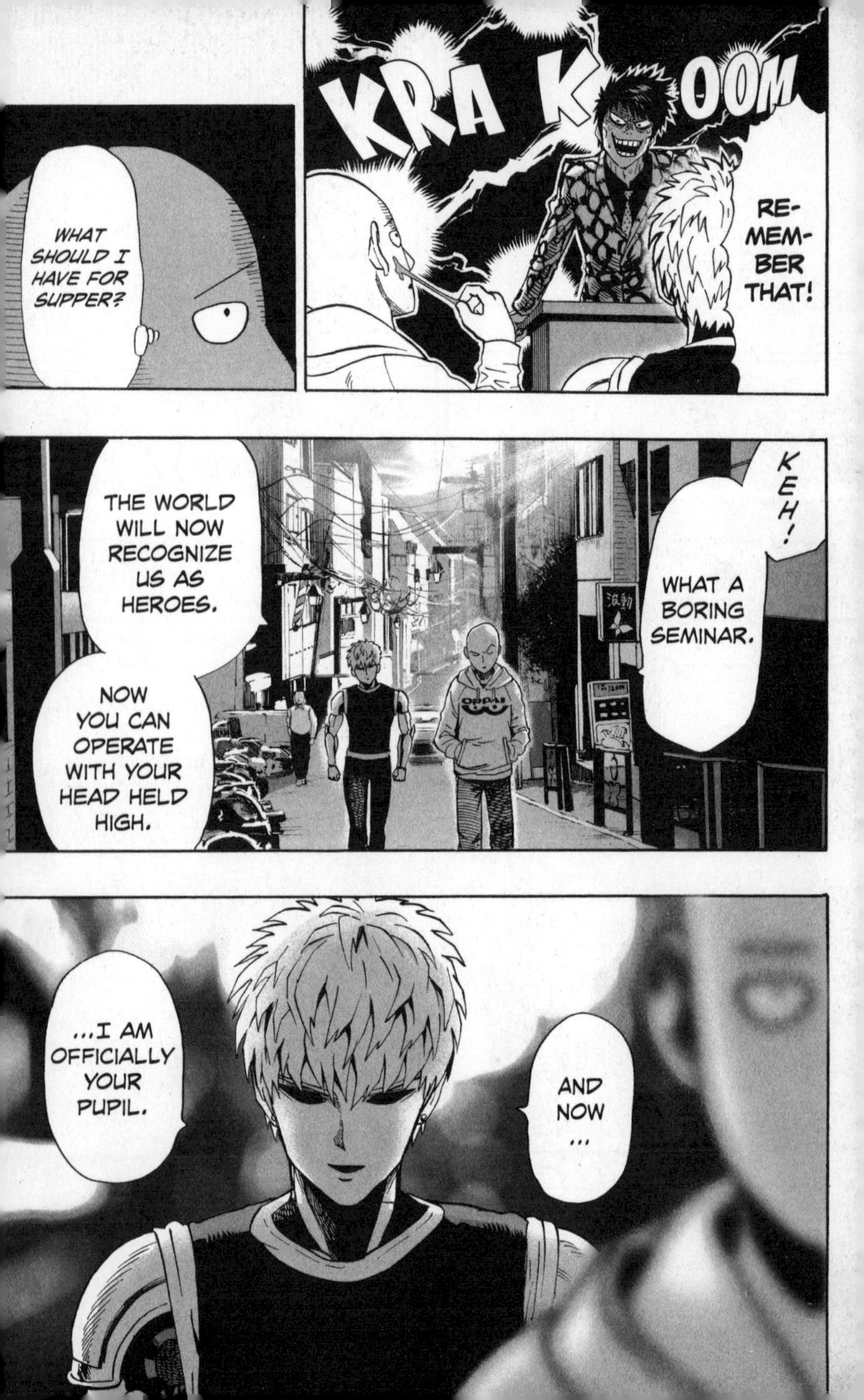
KRA KOOM
RE-MEM-BER THAT!
WHAT SHOULD I HAVE FOR SUPPER?
KEH!
WHAT A BORING SEMINAR.
THE WORLD WILL NOW RECOGNIZE US AS HEROES.
NOW YOU CAN OPERATE WITH YOUR HEAD HELD HIGH.
AND NOW ...
...I AM OFFICIALLY YOUR PUPIL.

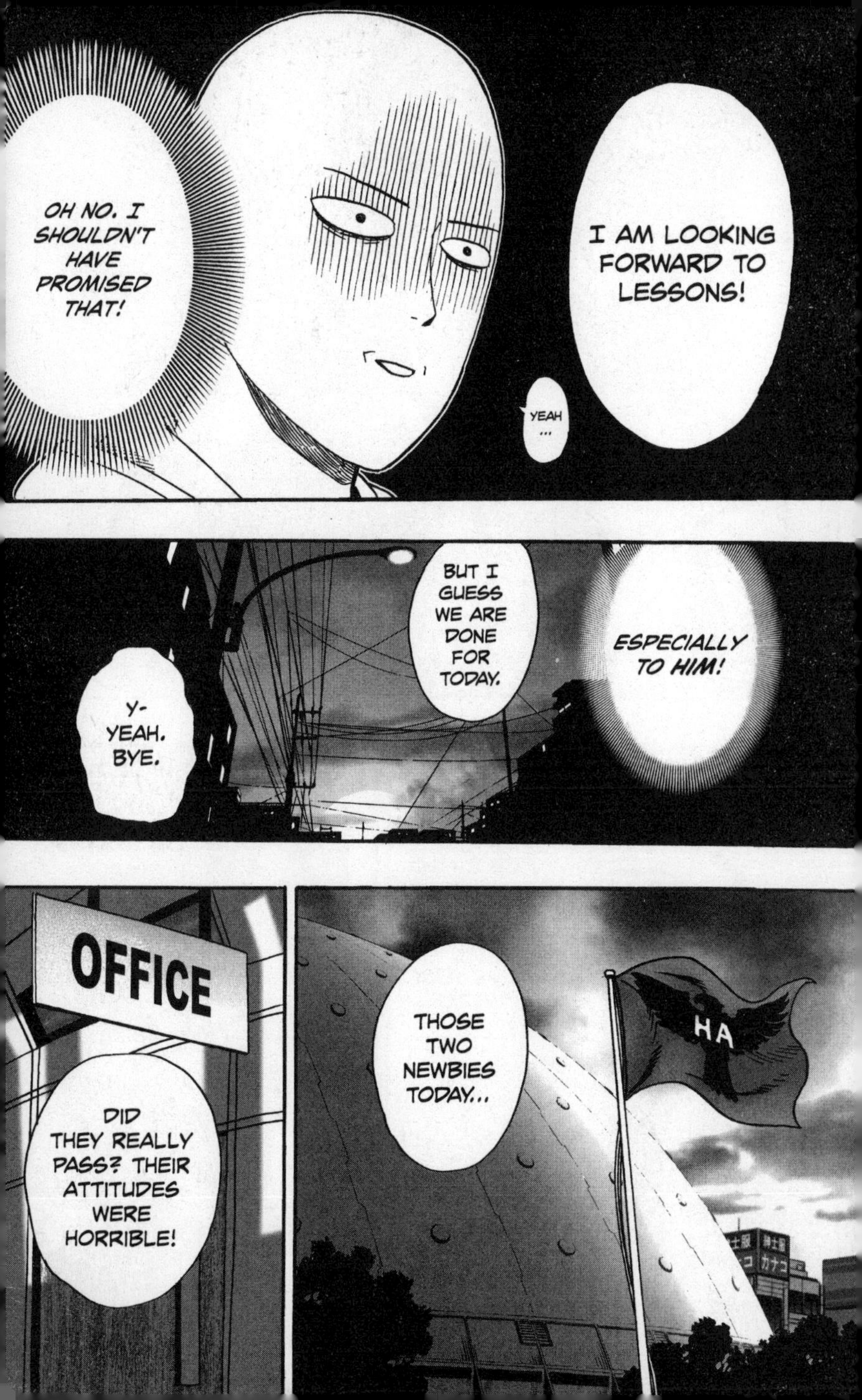
I AM LOOKING FORWARD TO LESSONS!
YEAH ...
OH NO. I SHOULDN'T HAVE PROMISED THAT!
ESPECIALLY TO HIM!
BUT I GUESS WE ARE DONE FOR TODAY.
Y- YEAH. BYE.
HA
THOSE TWO NEWBIES TODAY...
OFFICE
DID THEY REALLY PASS? THEIR ATTITUDES WERE HORRIBLE!

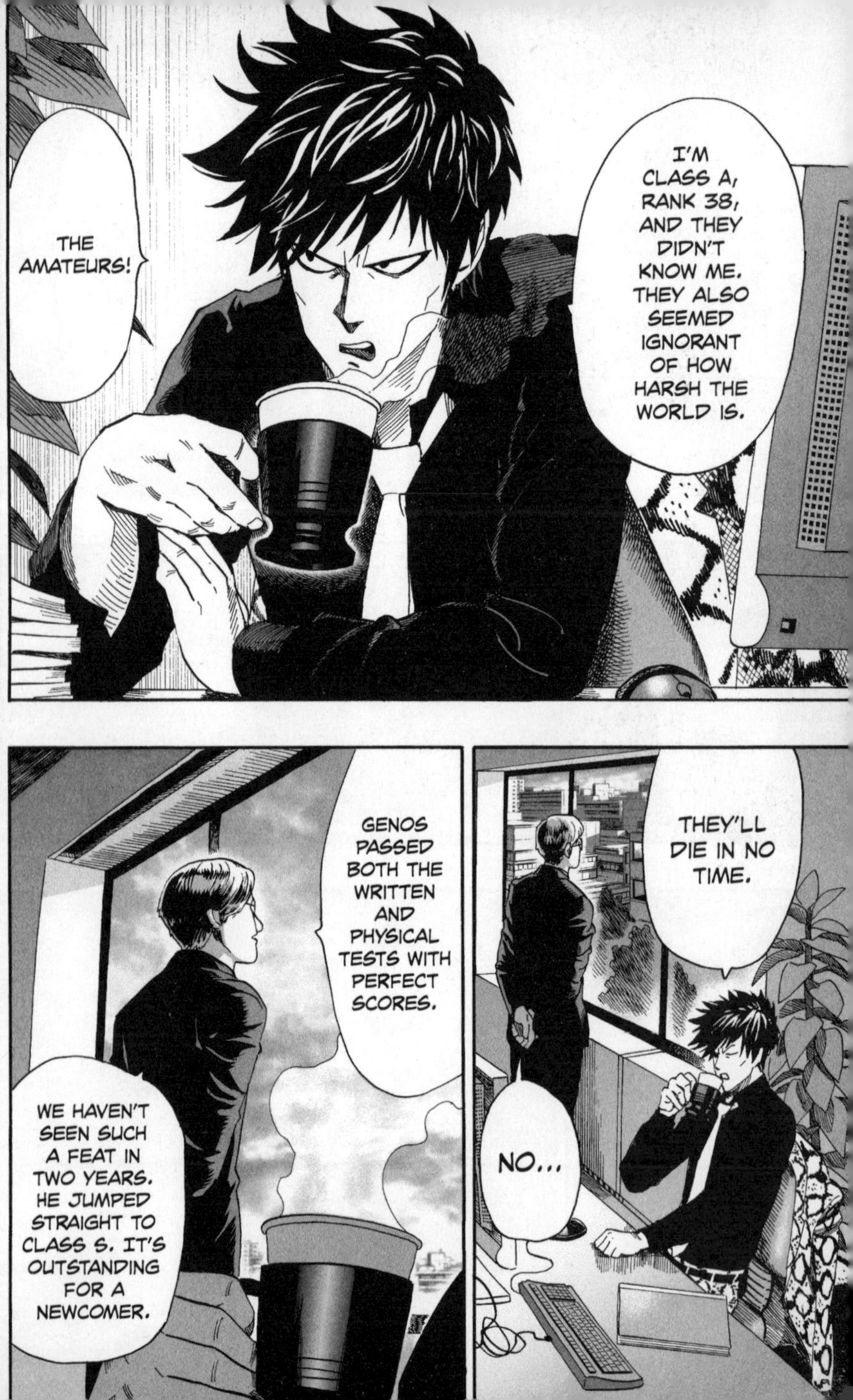
I'M CLASS A, RANK 38, AND THEY DIDN'T KNOW ME. THEY ALSO SEEMED IGNORANT OF HOW HARSH THE WORLD IS.
THE AMATEURS!
THEY'LL DIE IN NO TIME.
NO...
GENOS PASSED BOTH THE WRITTEN AND PHYSICAL TESTS WITH PERFECT SCORES.
WE HAVEN'T SEEN SUCH A FEAT IN TWO YEARS. HE JUMPED STRAIGHT TO CLASS S. IT'S OUTSTANDING FOR A NEWCOMER.

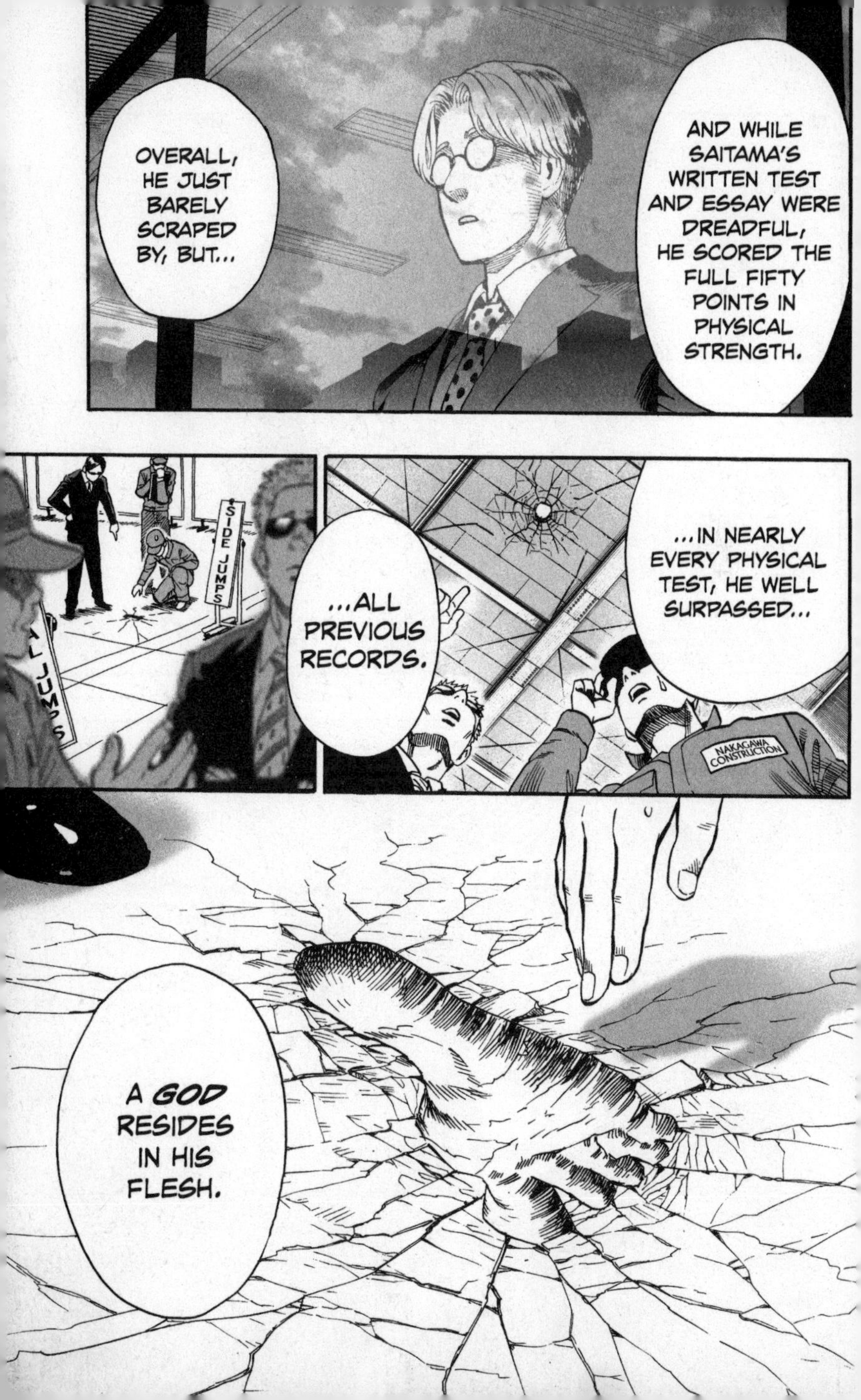

AND WHILE SAITAMA'S WRITTEN TEST AND ESSAY WERE DREADFUL, HE SCORED THE FULL FIFTY POINTS IN PHYSICAL STRENGTH.
OVERALL, HE JUST BARELY SCRAPED BY, BUT...
...IN NEARLY EVERY PHYSICAL TEST, HE WELL SURPASSED...
...ALL PREVIOUS RECORDS.
SIDE JUMPS
NAKAGAWA CONSTRUCTION
A *GOD* RESIDES IN HIS FLESH.

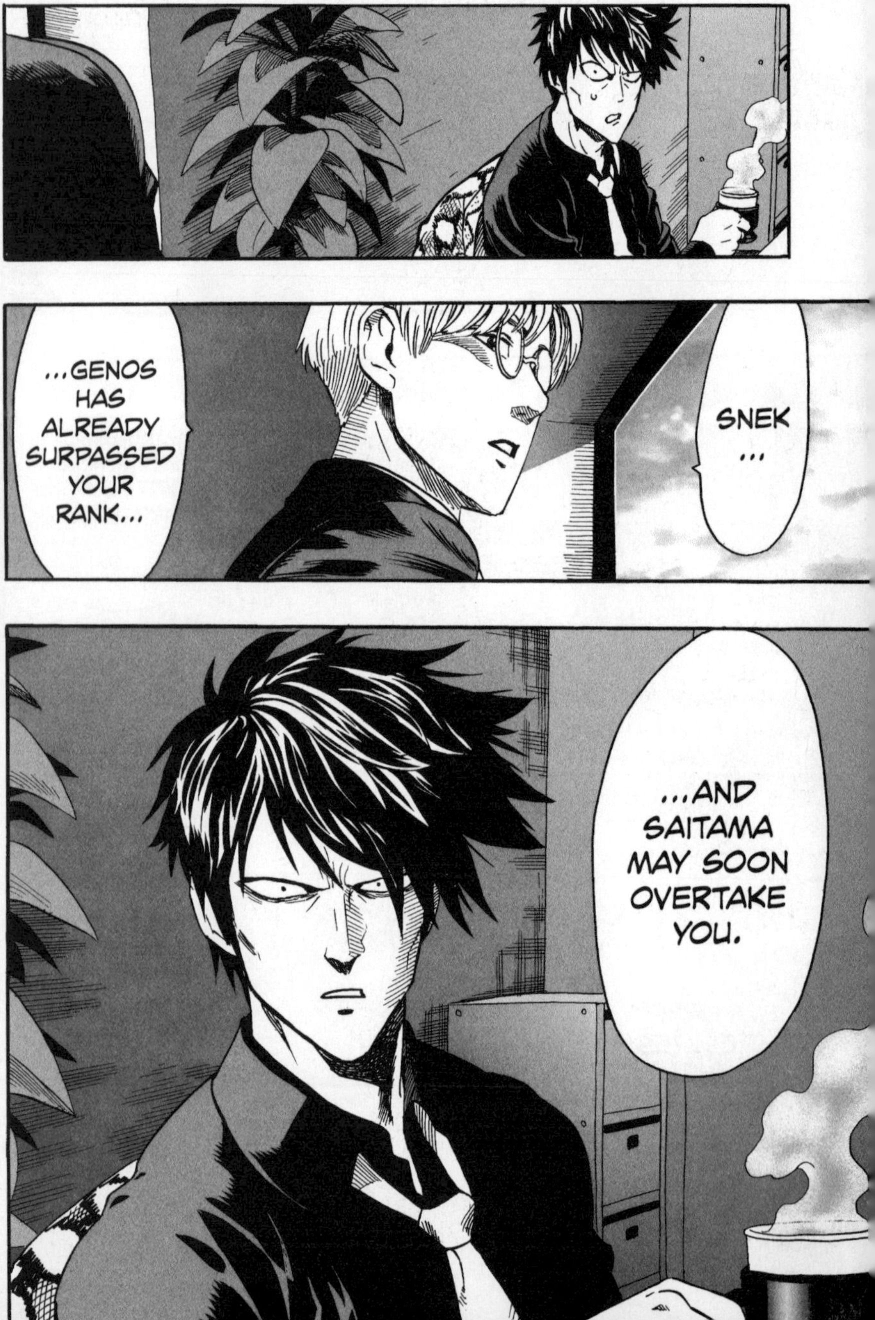
SNEK ...
...GENOS HAS ALREADY SURPASSED YOUR RANK...
...AND SAITAMA MAY SOON OVERTAKE YOU.

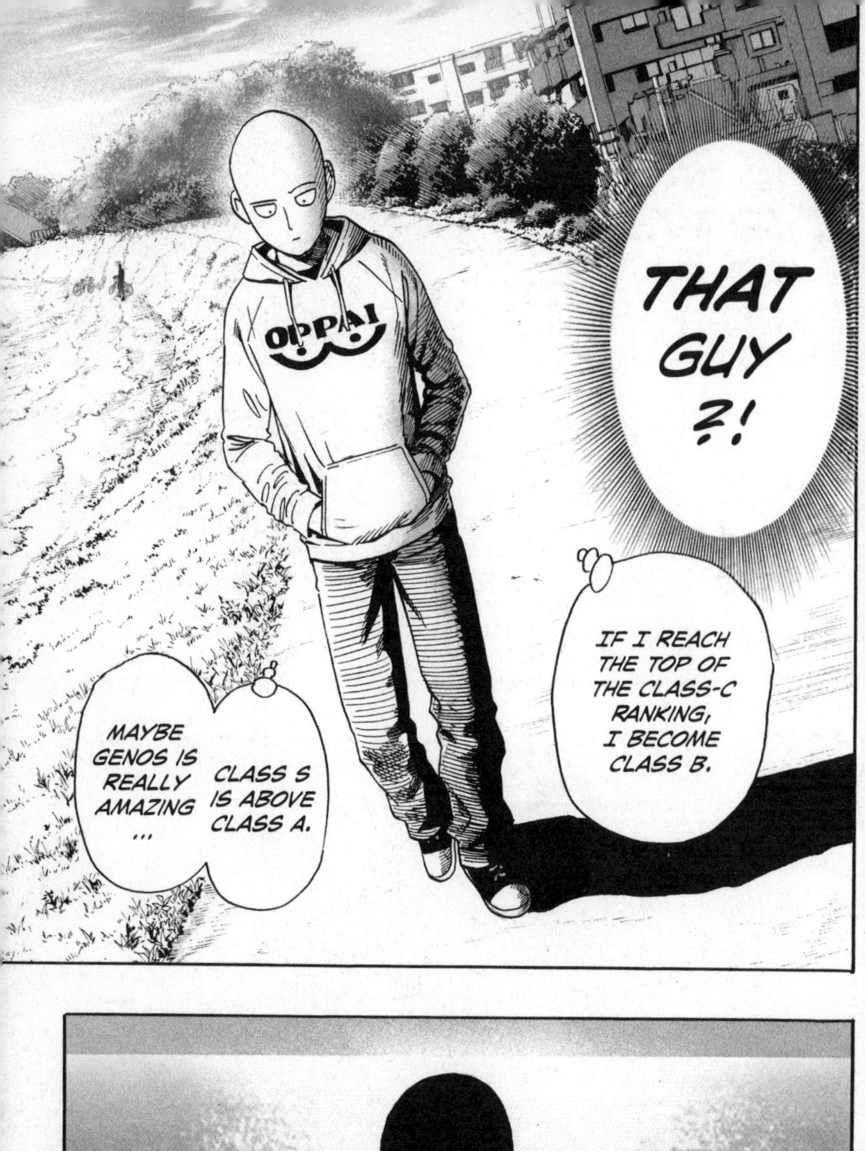
OPPAI
IF I REACH THE TOP OF THE CLASS-C RANKING, I BECOME CLASS B.
CLASS S IS ABOVE CLASS A.
MAYBE GENOS IS REALLY AMAZING ...
THAT GUY ?!

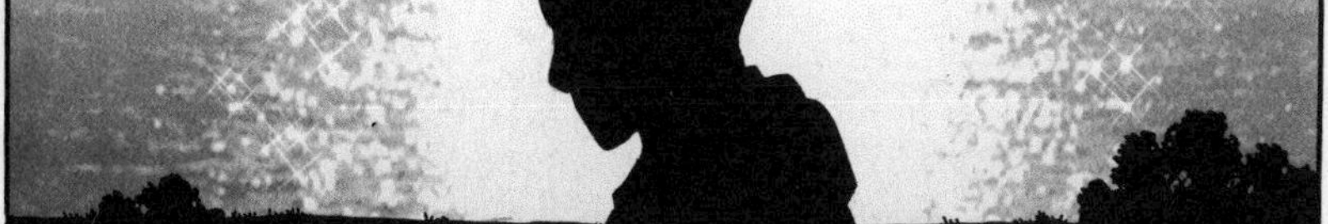

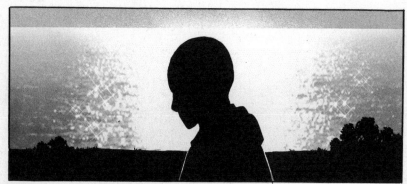

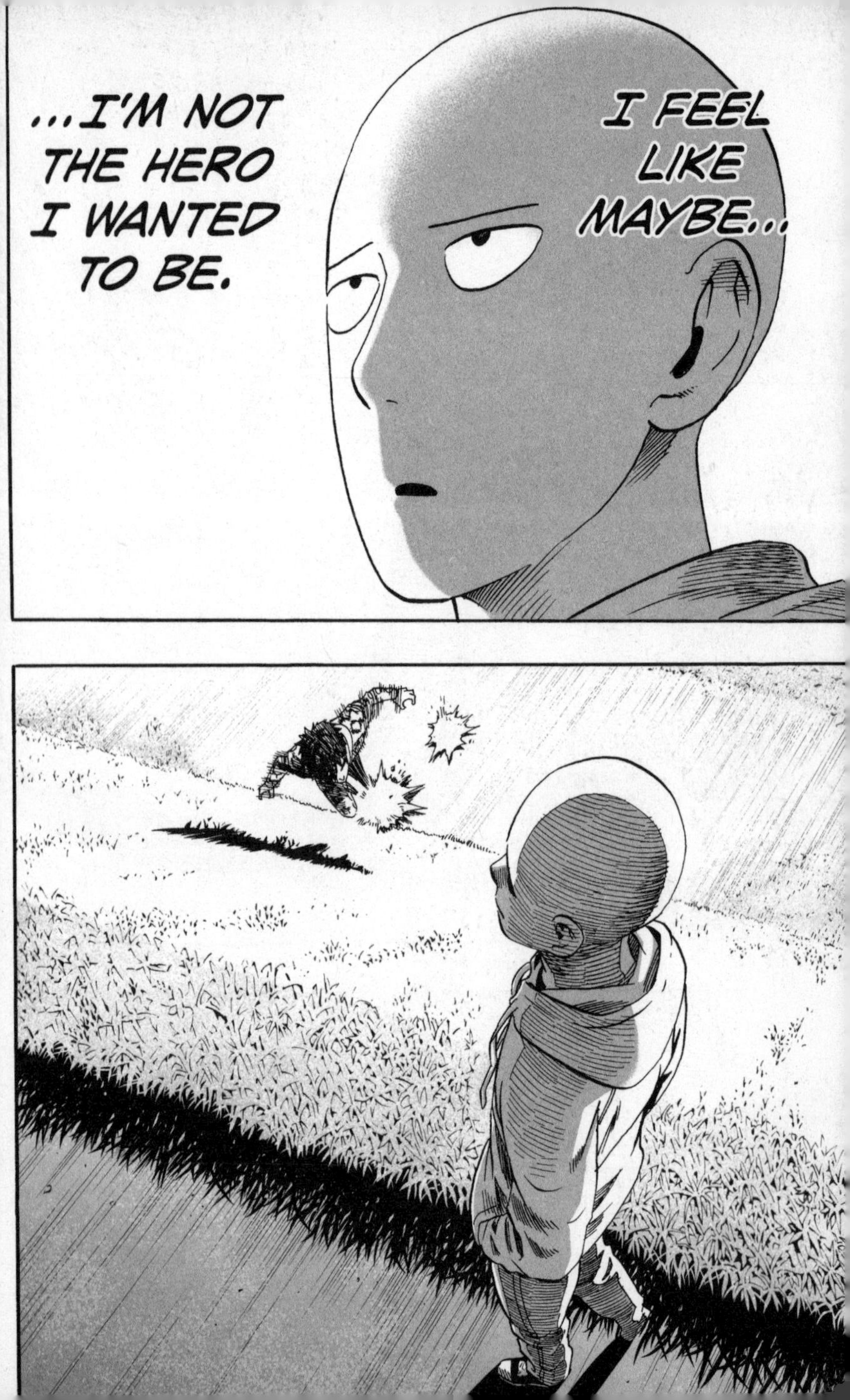
I FEEL LIKE MAYBE...
...I'M NOT THE HERO I WANTED TO BE.

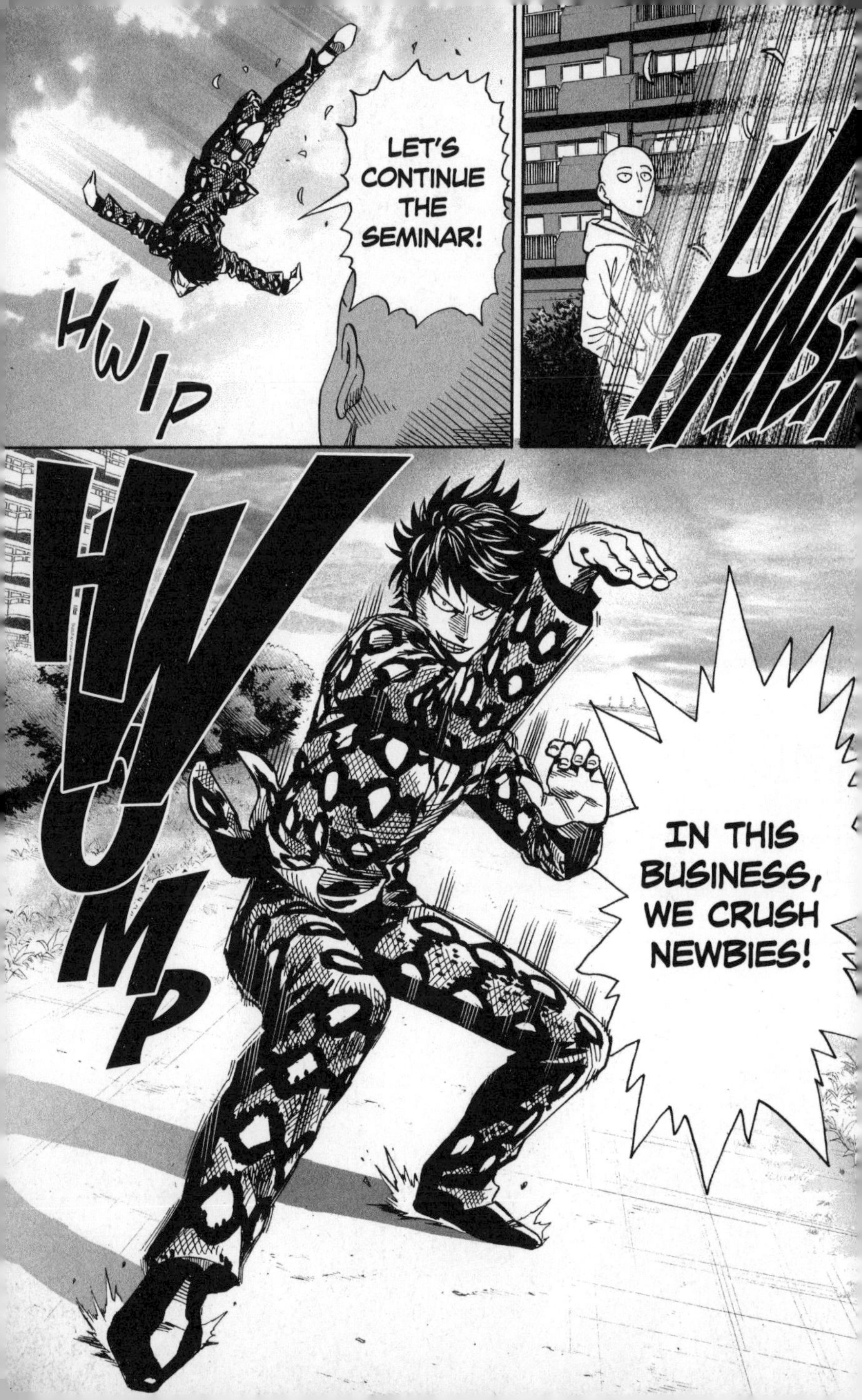
LET'S CONTINUE THE SEMINAR!
HWIP
HWUMP
IN THIS BUSINESS, WE CRUSH NEWBIES!

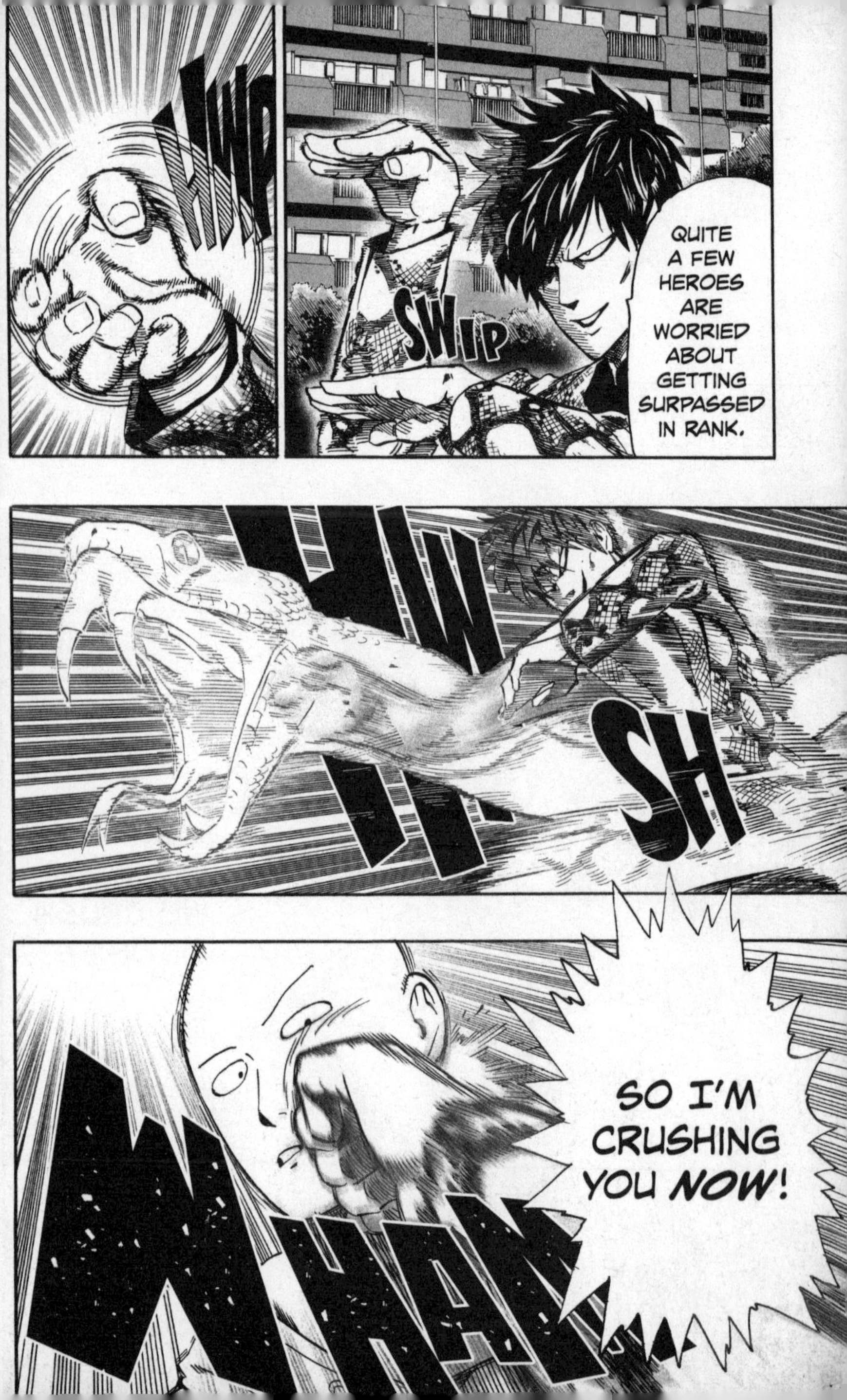
SWIP
QUITE A FEW HEROES ARE WORRIED ABOUT GETTING SURPASSED IN RANK.
SH
SO I'M CRUSHING YOU *NOW*!

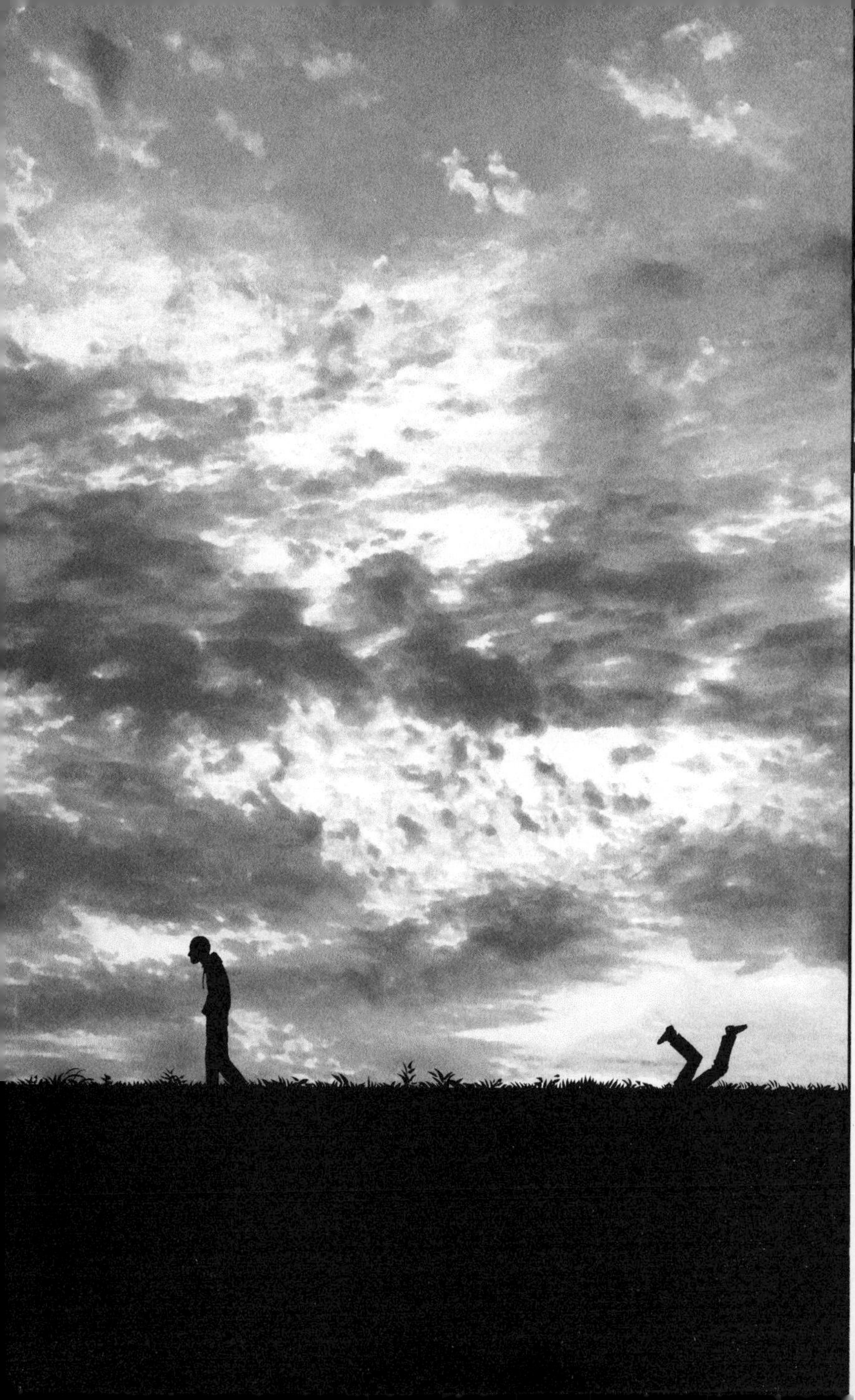

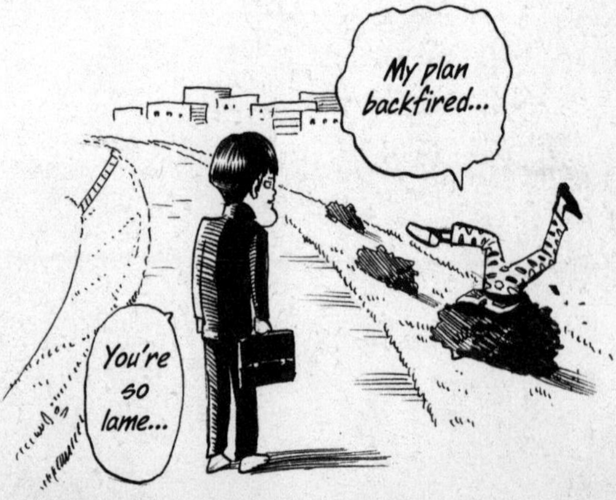
My plan backfired...
You're so lame...

PUNCH 17: SPARRING

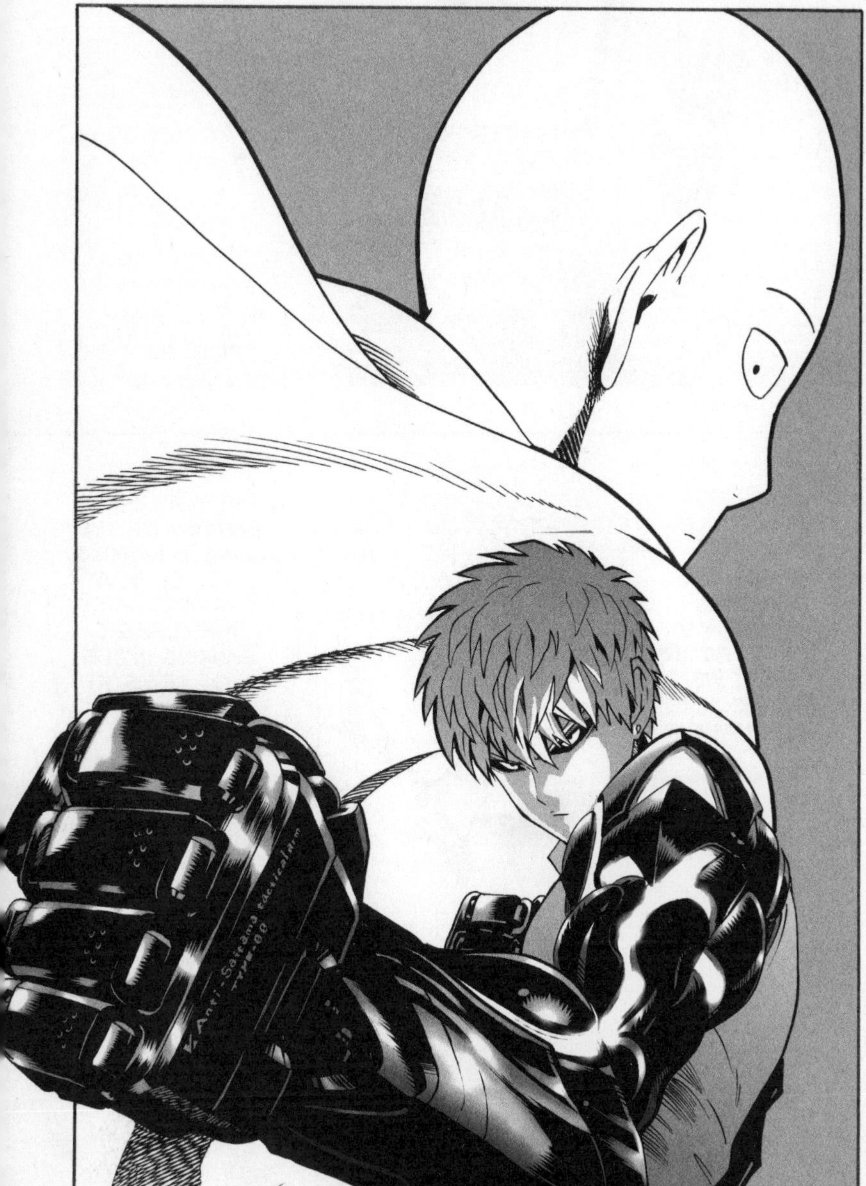
Anti-Saitama tactical arm

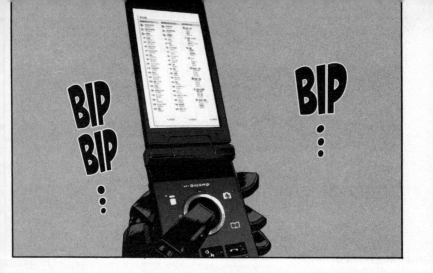

BIP
BIP
⋮

BIP
⋮

I'M AT THE BOTTOM OF THE CLASS-S RANKING, AND YOU'RE AT THE BOTTOM OF THE CLASS-C RANKING IN THE HERO REGISTRY.

FOR NOW, IT LISTS US AS GENOS AND SAITAMA, BUT AT SOME POINT WE WILL ACQUIRE HERO NAMES.

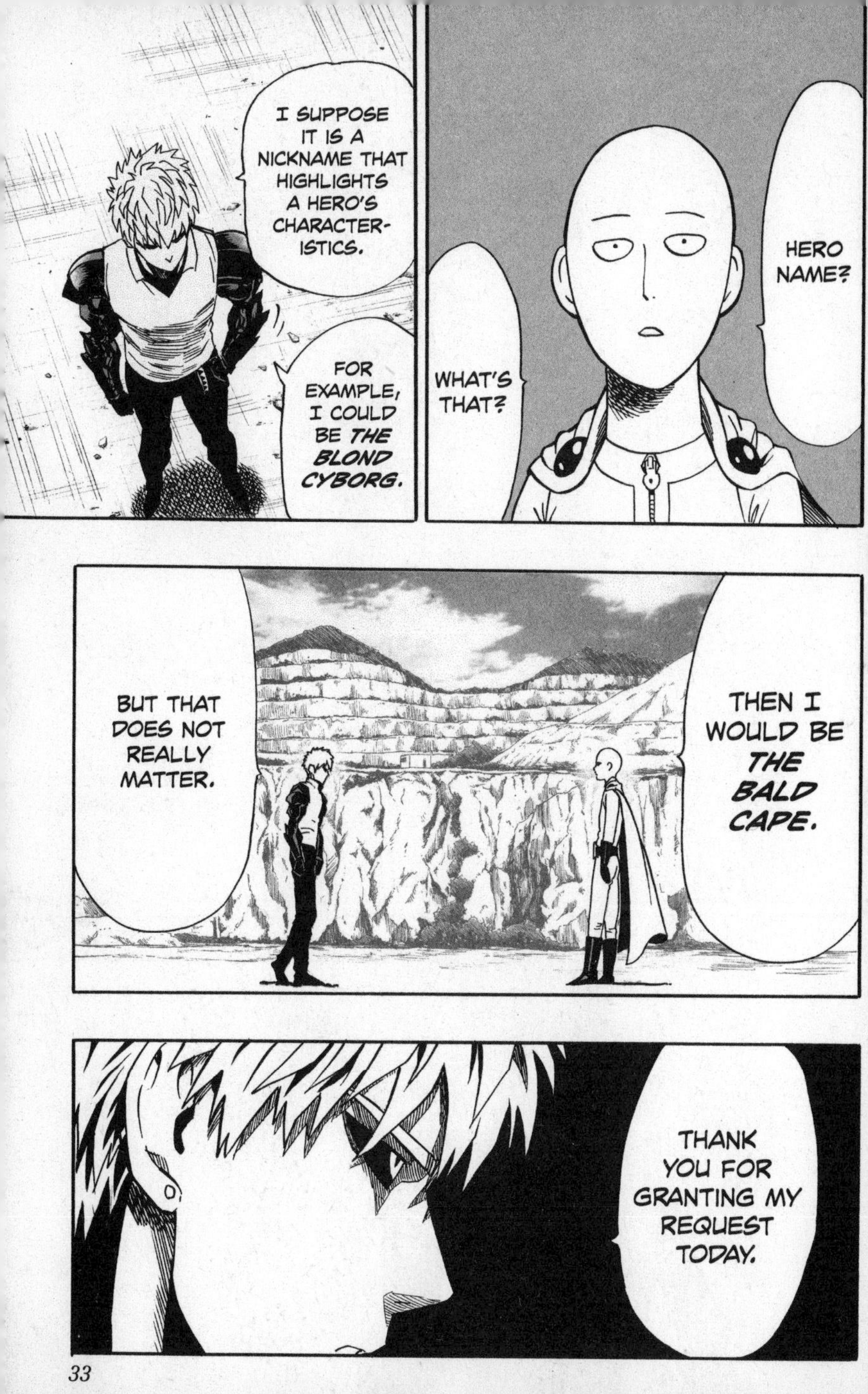
HERO NAME?
WHAT'S THAT?
I SUPPOSE IT IS A NICKNAME THAT HIGHLIGHTS A HERO'S CHARACTER-ISTICS.
FOR EXAMPLE, I COULD BE *THE BLOND CYBORG*.
THEN I WOULD BE *THE BALD CAPE*.
BUT THAT DOES NOT REALLY MATTER.
THANK YOU FOR GRANTING MY REQUEST TODAY.

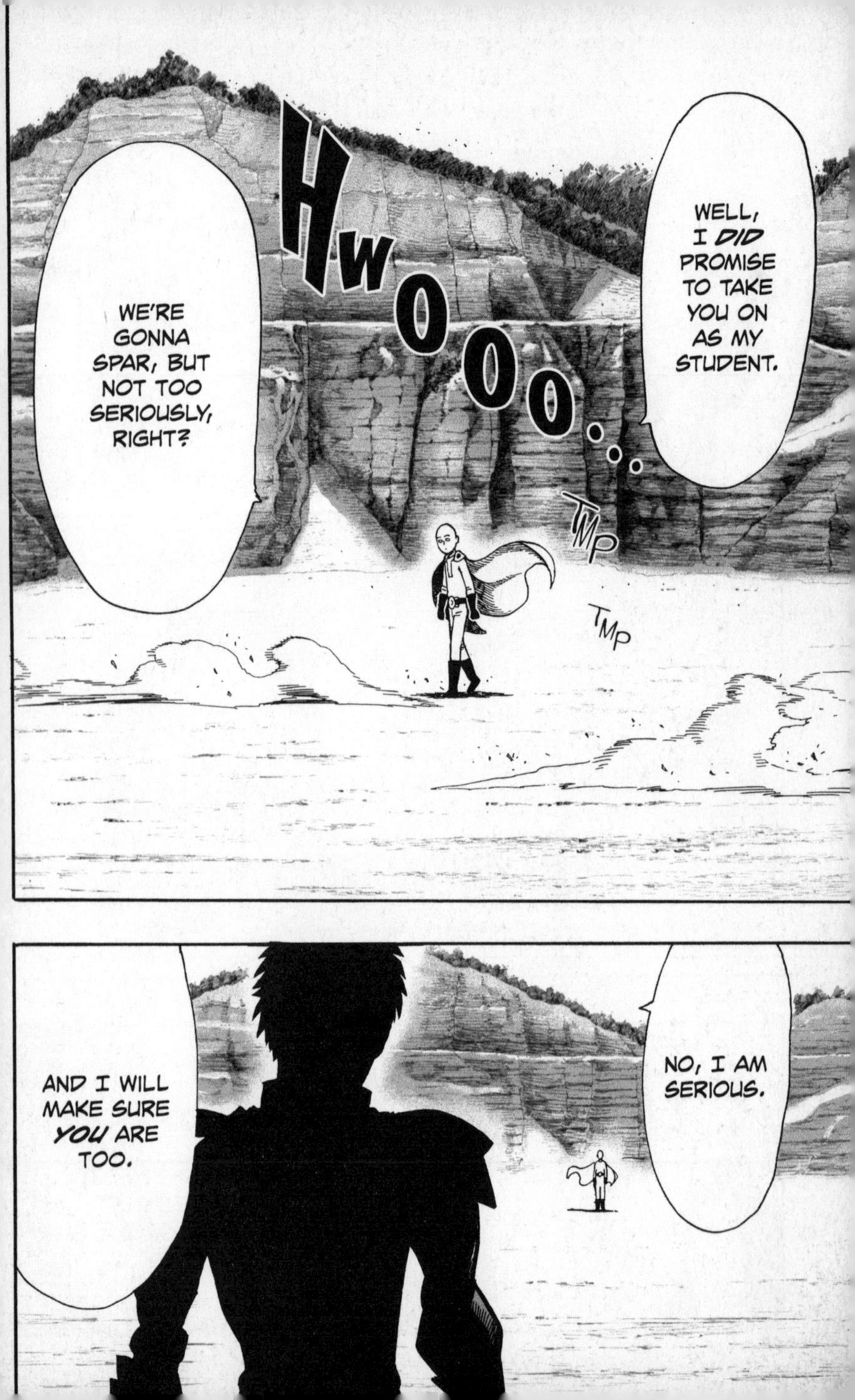
WELL, I *DID* PROMISE TO TAKE YOU ON AS MY STUDENT.
HWOOO...
WE'RE GONNA SPAR, BUT NOT TOO SERIOUSLY, RIGHT?
TMP
TMP
NO, I AM SERIOUS.
AND I WILL MAKE SURE *YOU* ARE TOO.

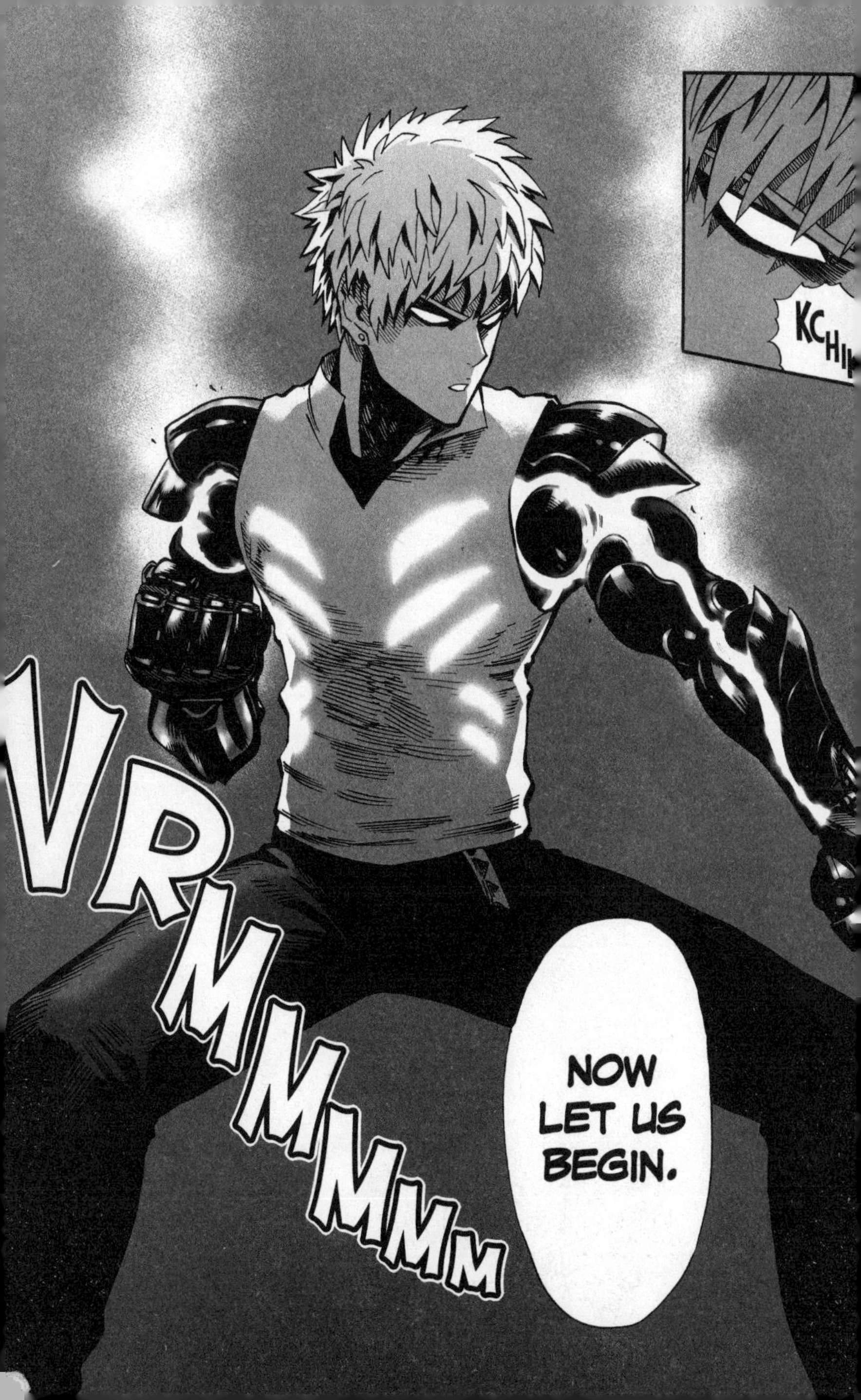
KCHIP
NOW LET US BEGIN.
VRMMMMMM

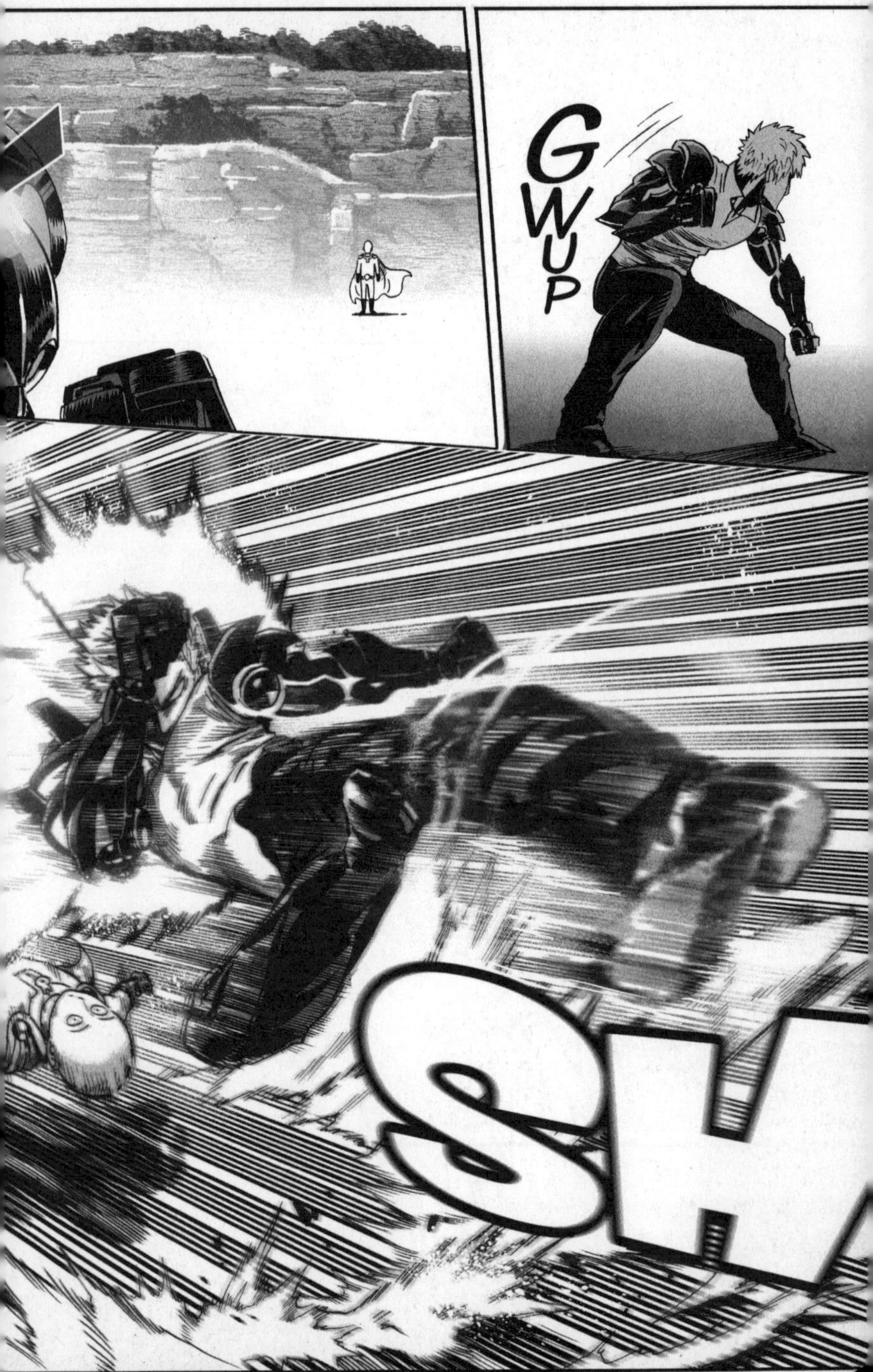
GWUP
SH

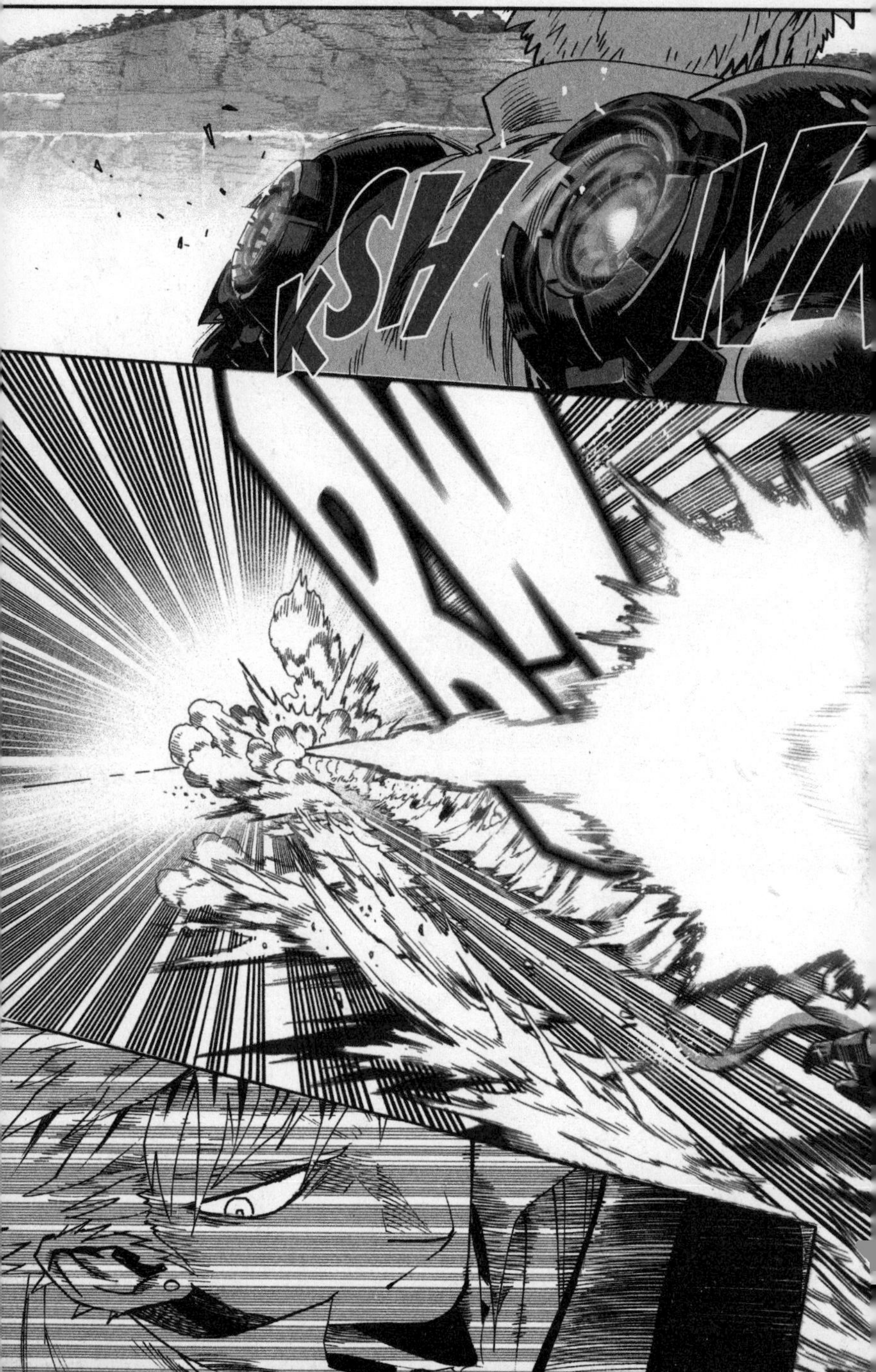
KSH

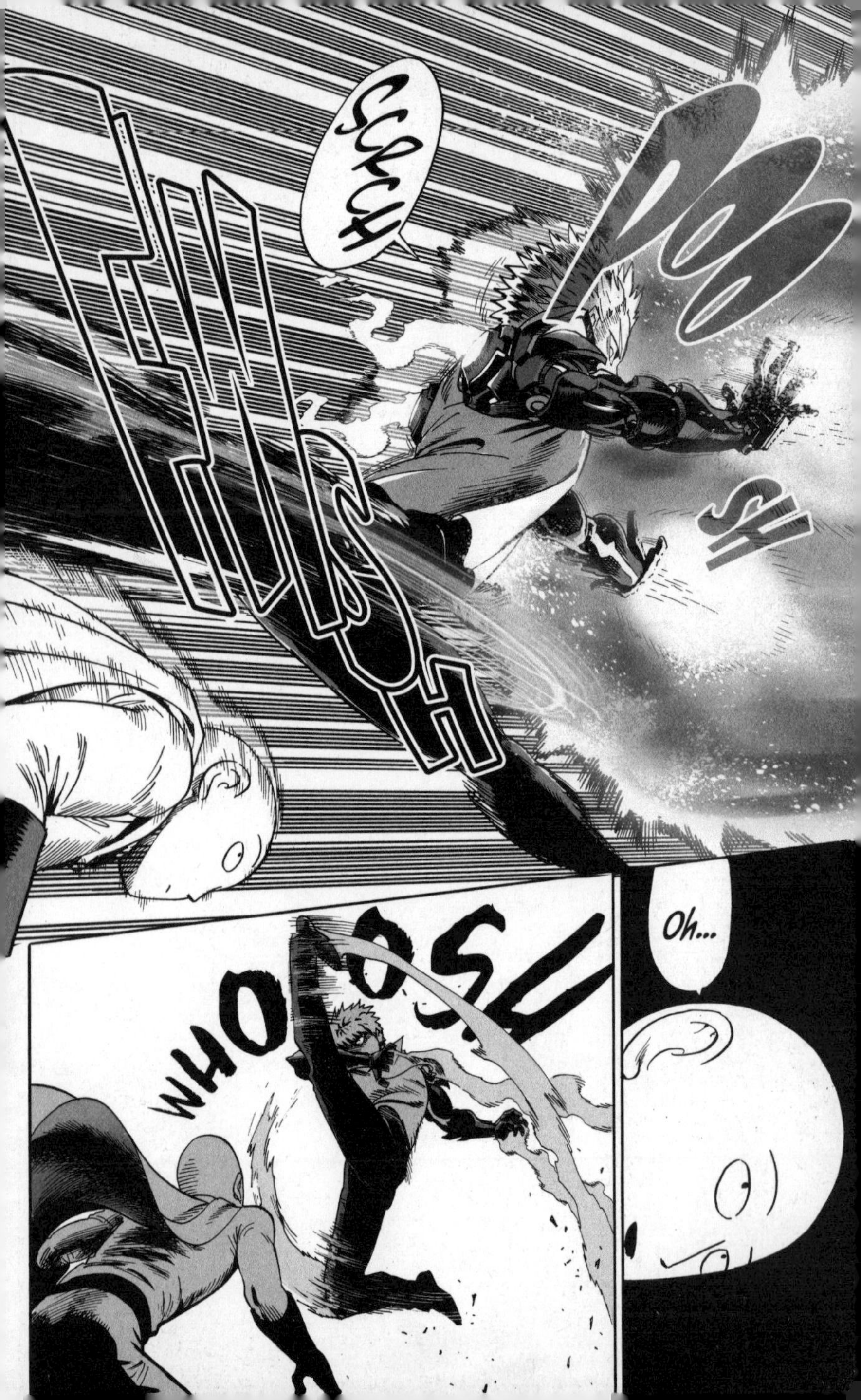

SCRCH
Oh...
WHOOSH

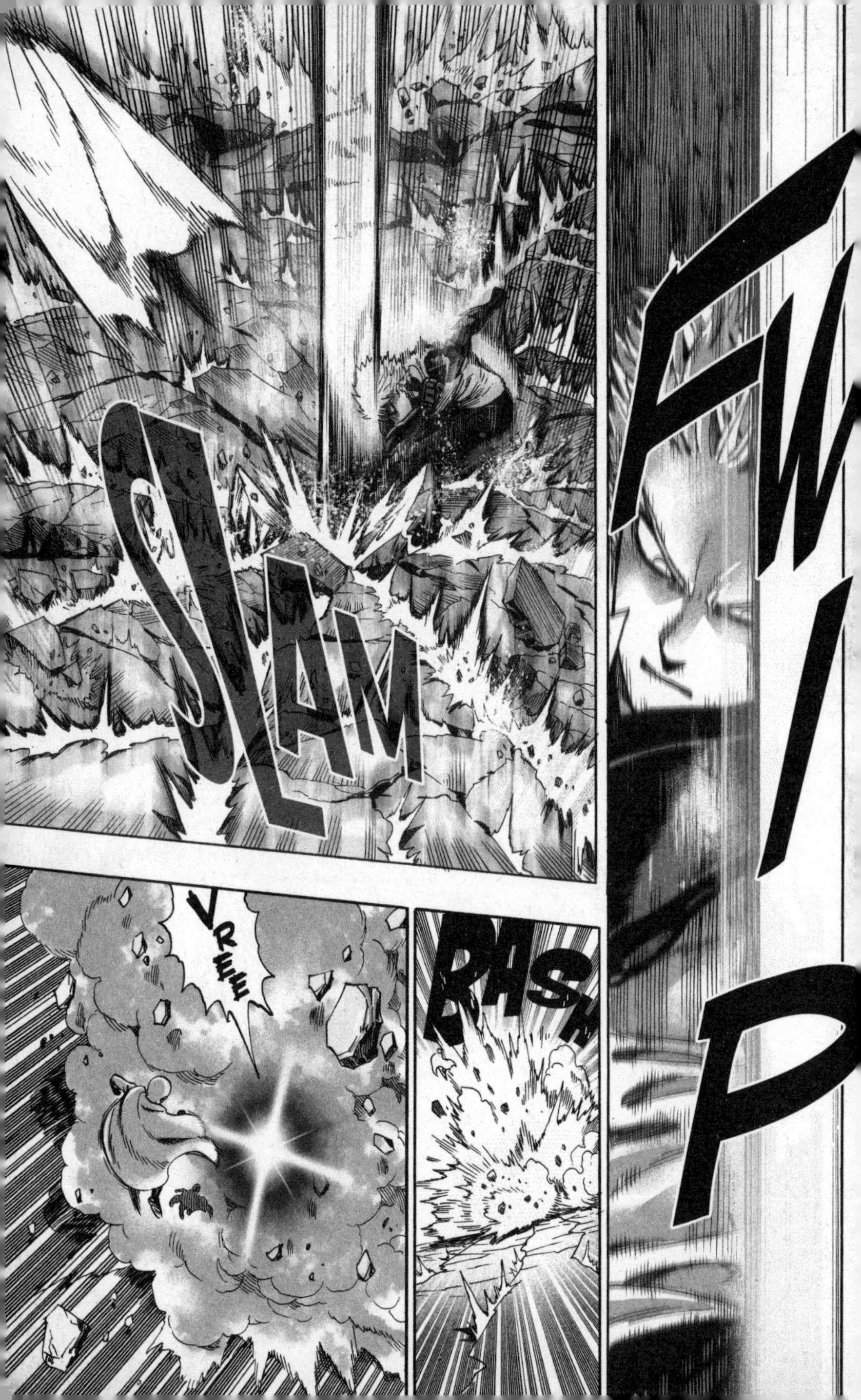
FWIP
SLAM
VREEE
BASH

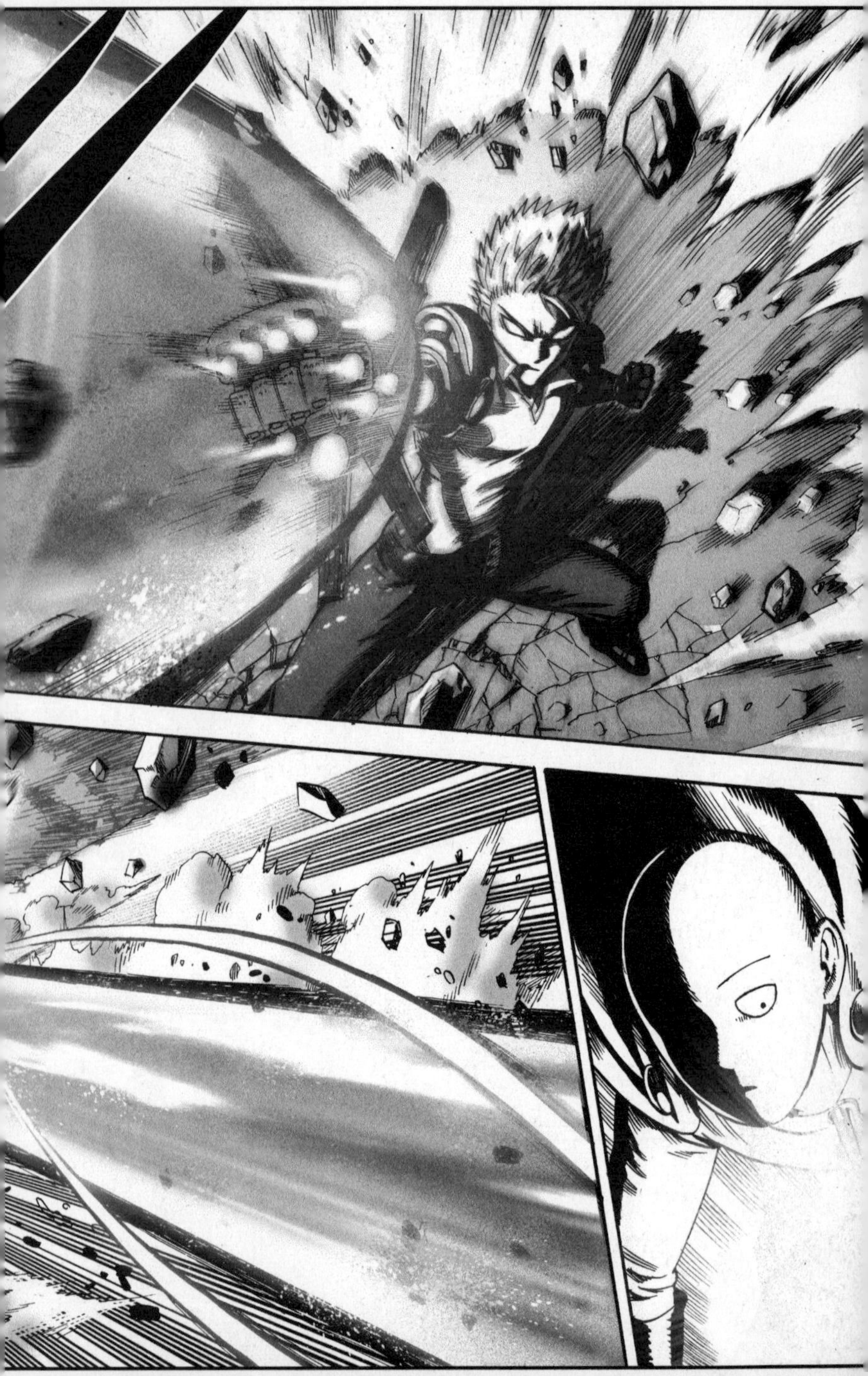

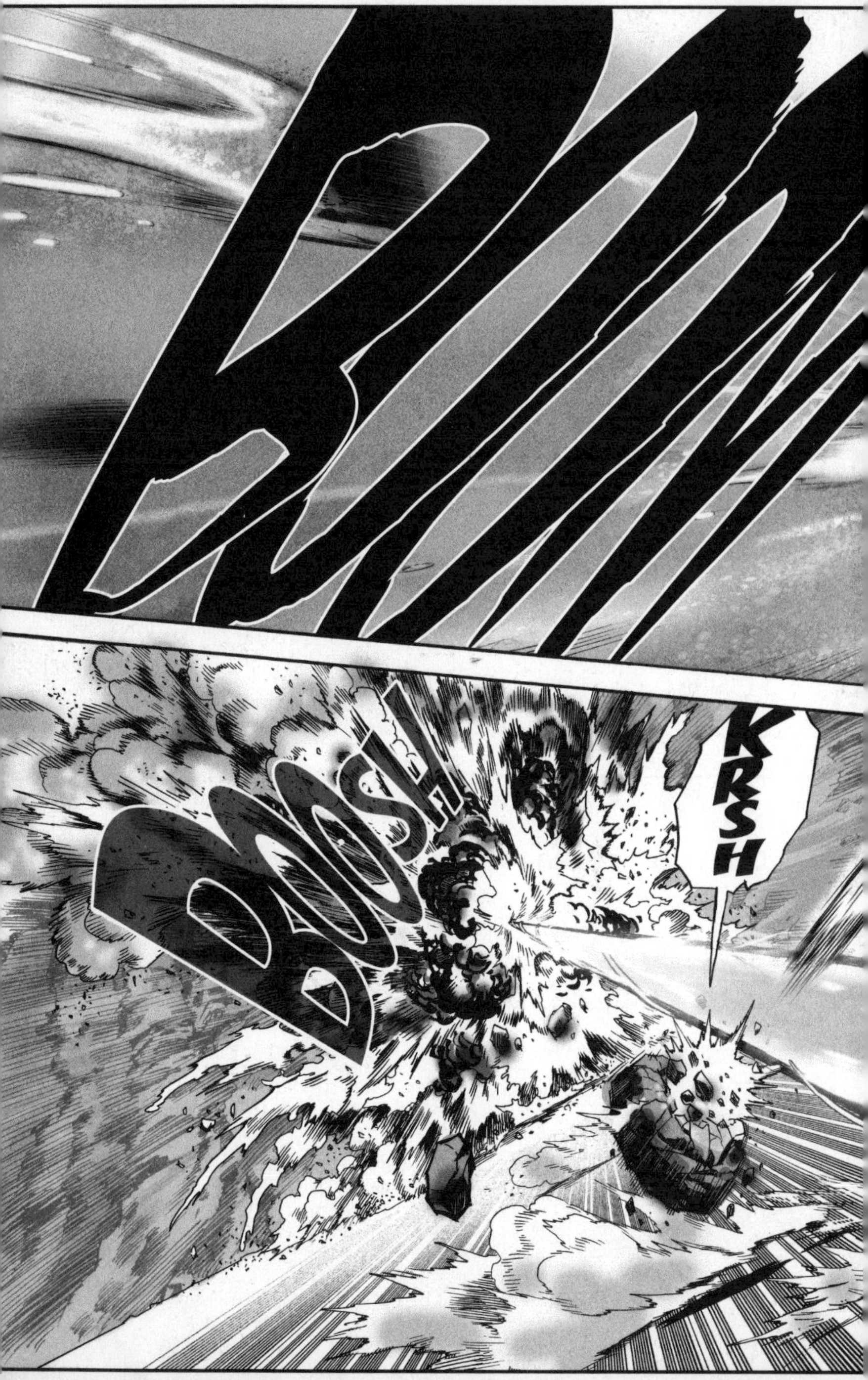
KRSH
BOOSH!

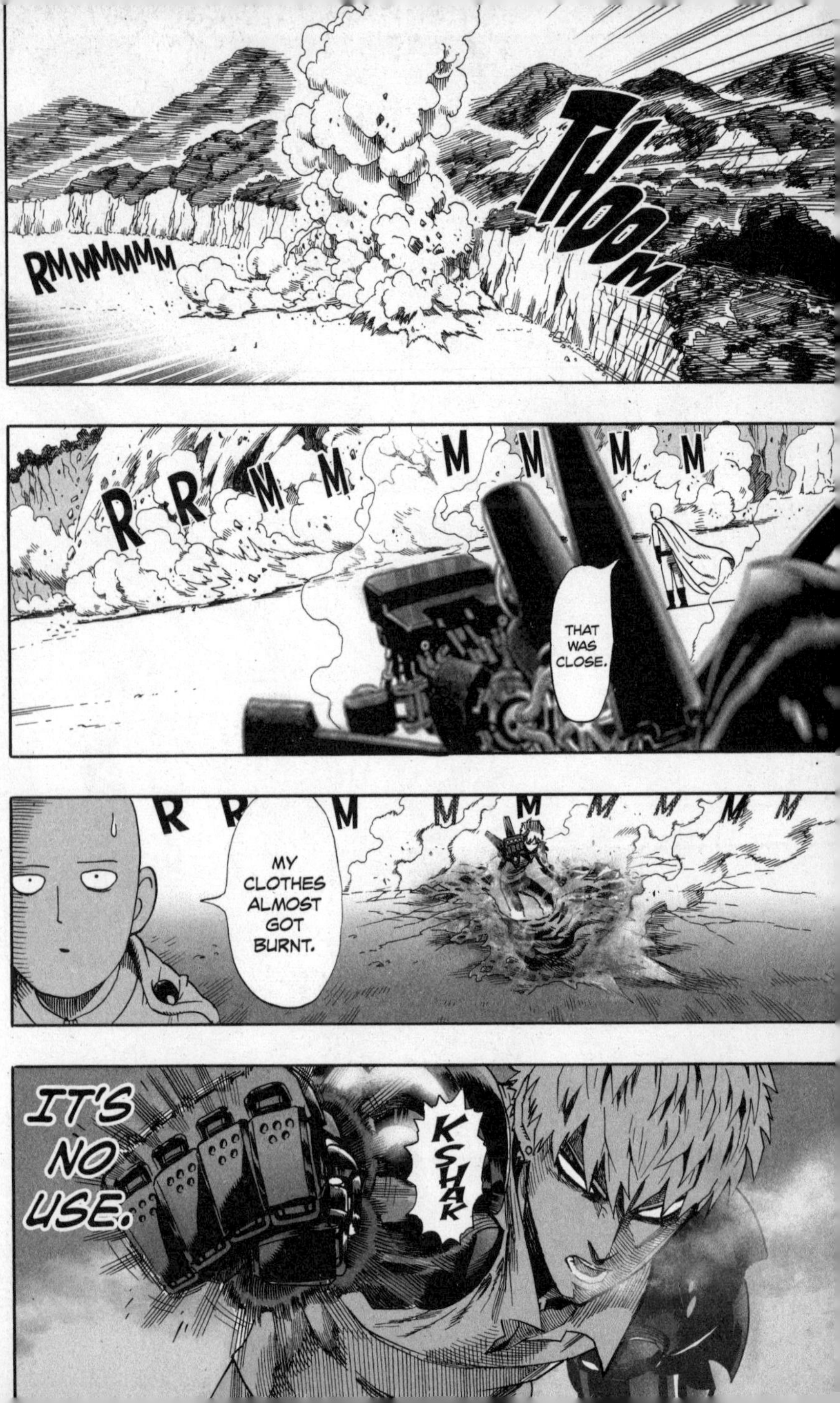
THOOM
RMMMMMM
RRMMMMMM
THAT WAS CLOSE.
RRMMMMMMMM
MY CLOTHES ALMOST GOT BURNT.
KSHAK
IT'S NO USE.

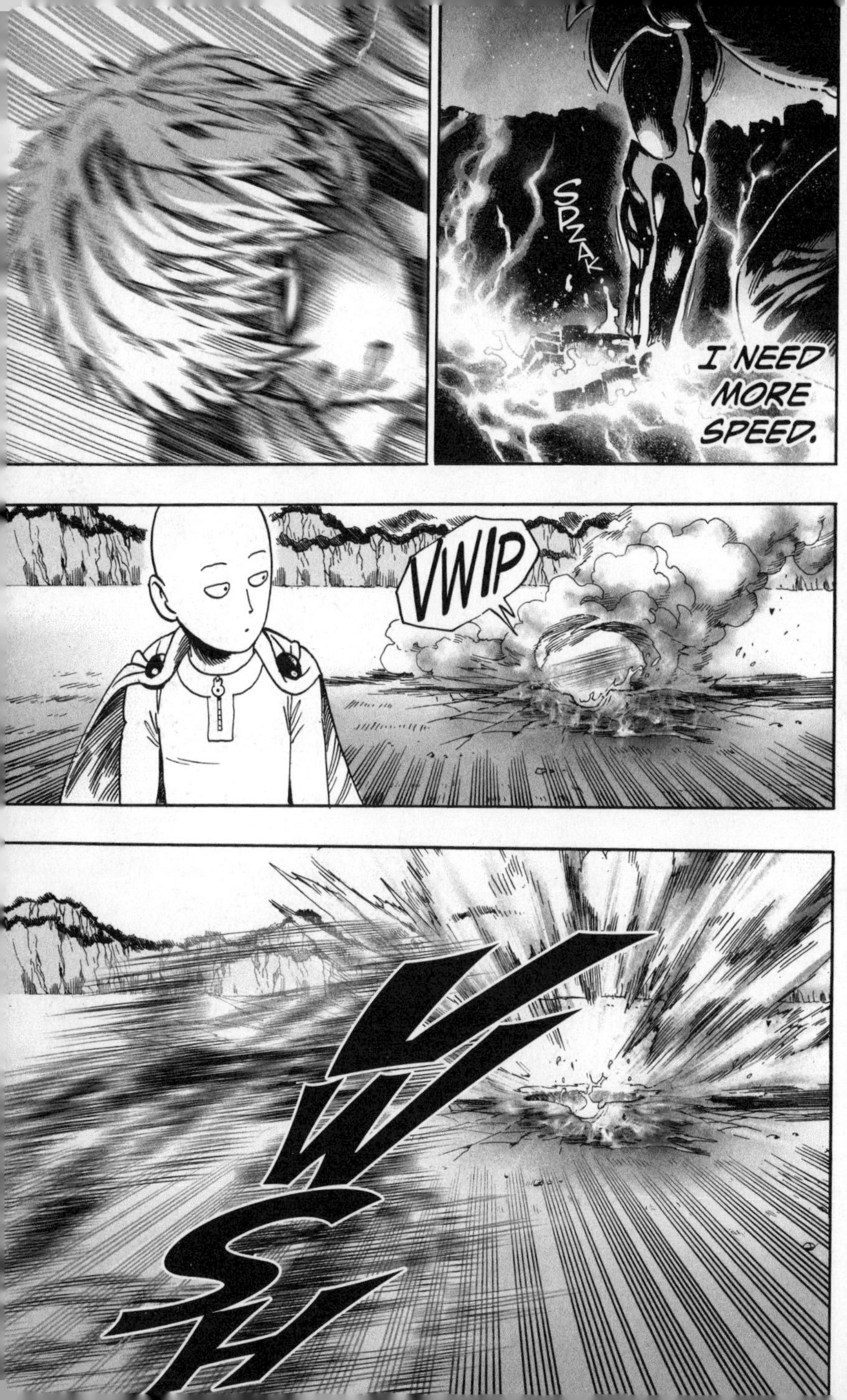
SPZAK
I NEED MORE SPEED.
VWIP
VWSH

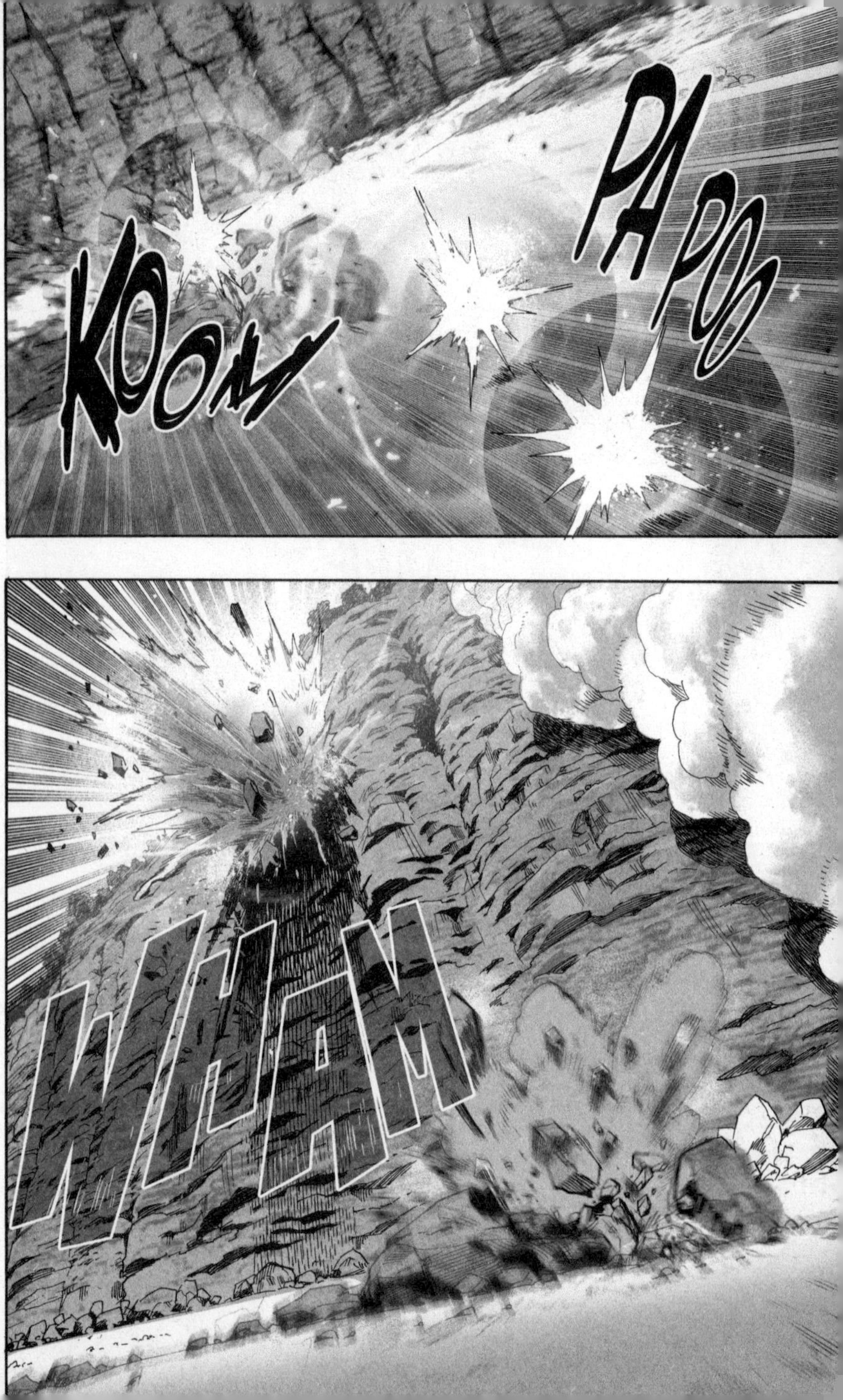
PAPOW
KOOM
WHAM

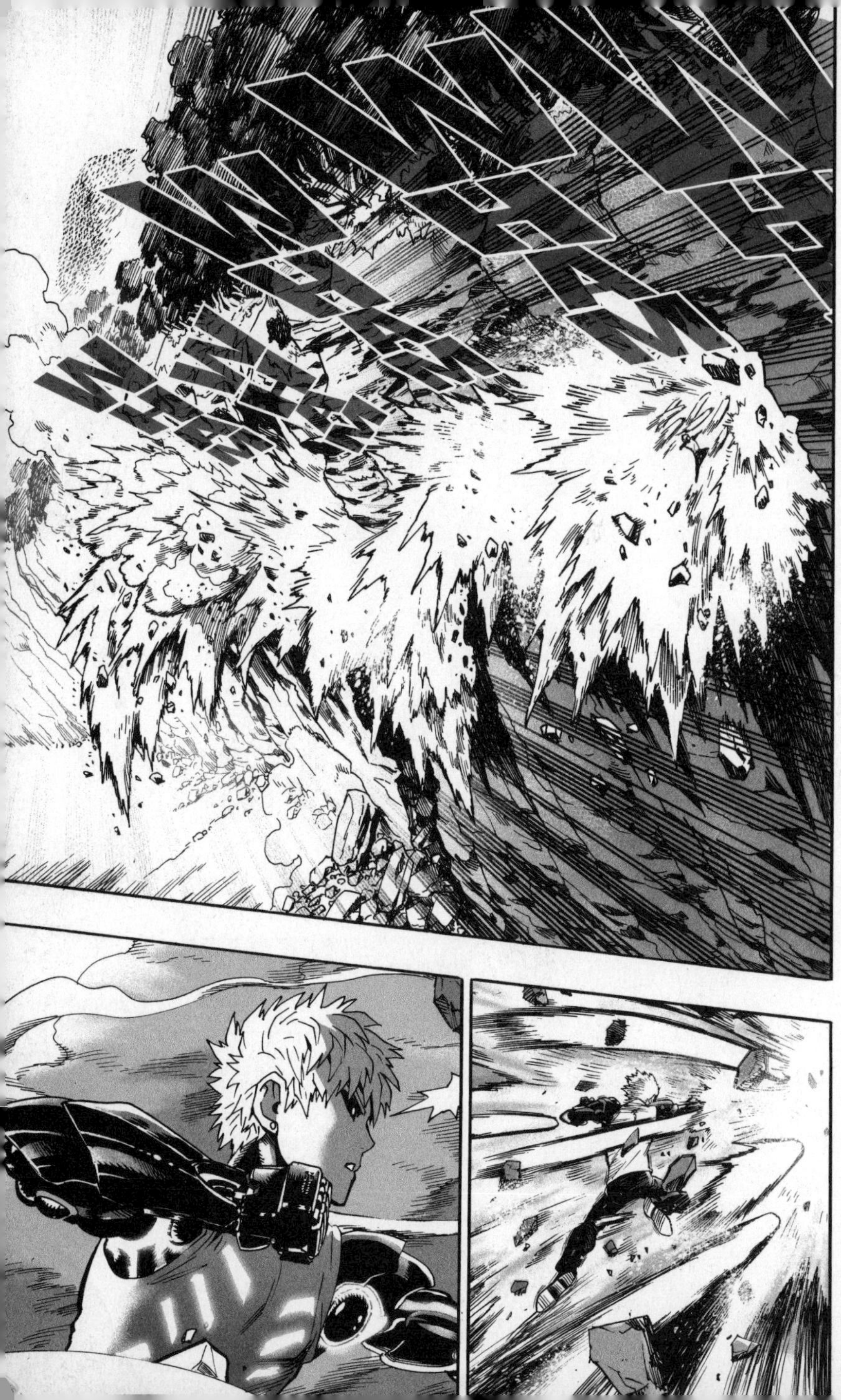

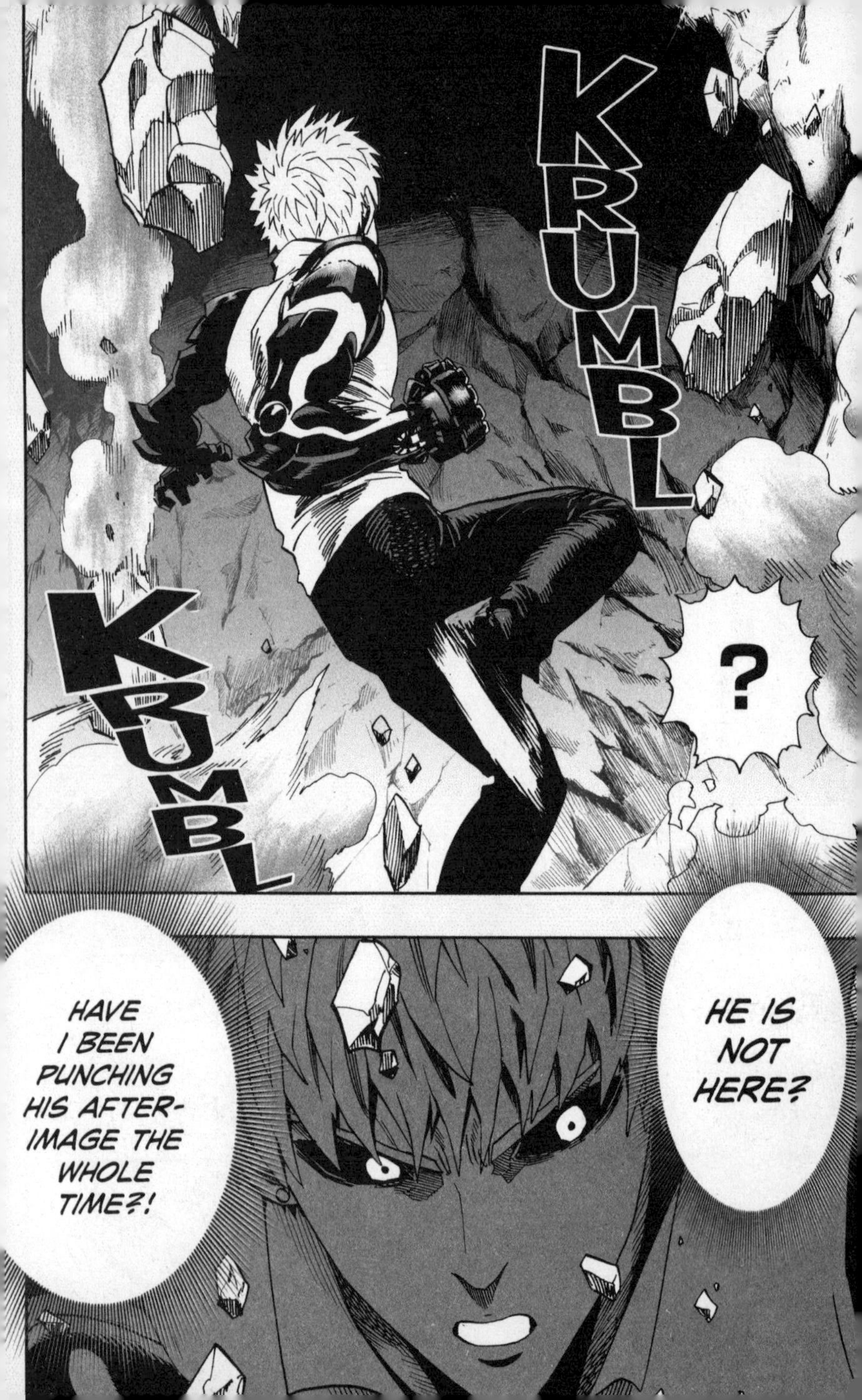
KRUMBL
KRUMBL
?
HE IS NOT HERE?
HAVE I BEEN PUNCHING HIS AFTER-IMAGE THE WHOLE TIME?!

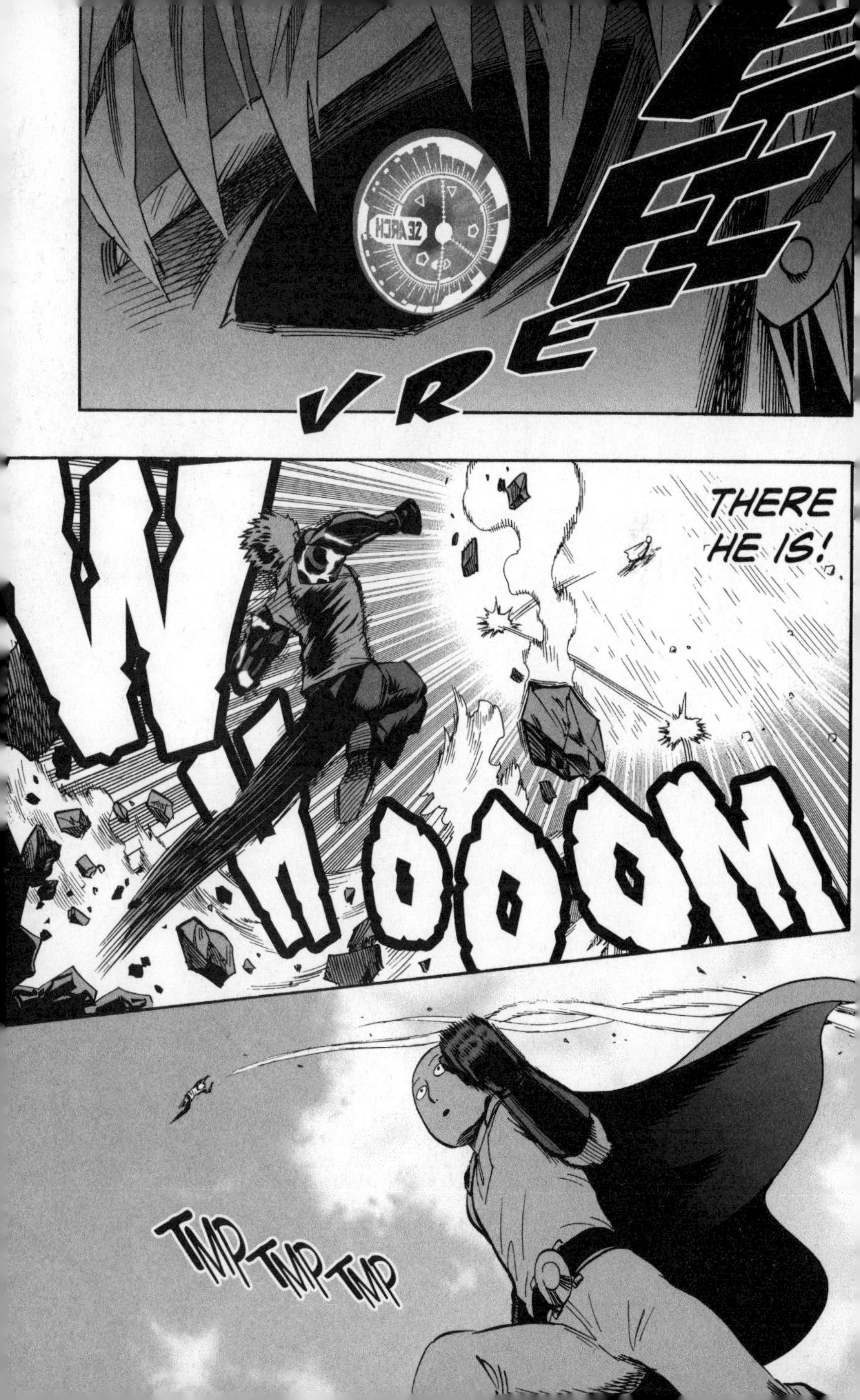
SEARCH
VREEEEE
THERE HE IS!
WHOOOM
TMP TMP TMP

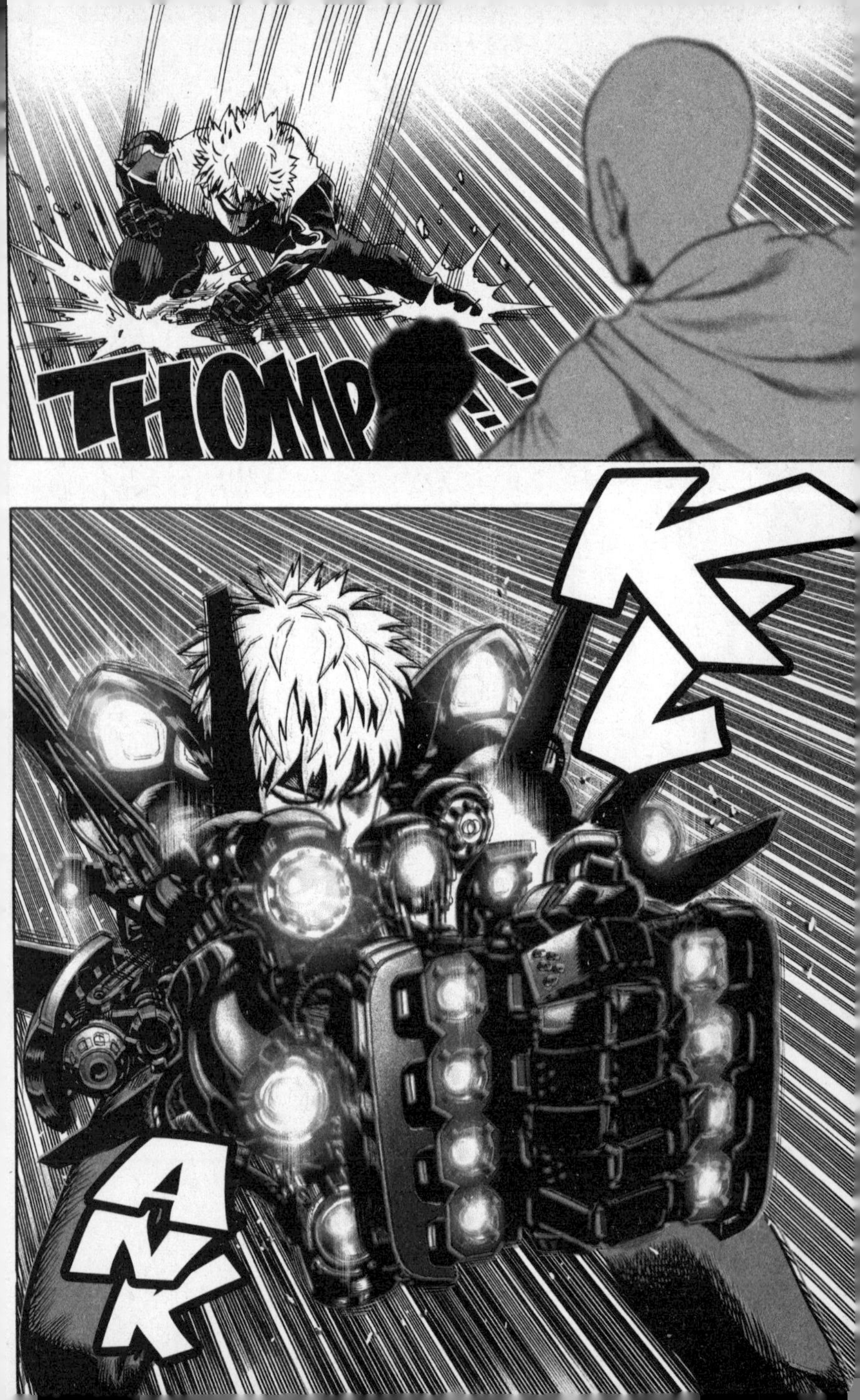
THOMP
ANK

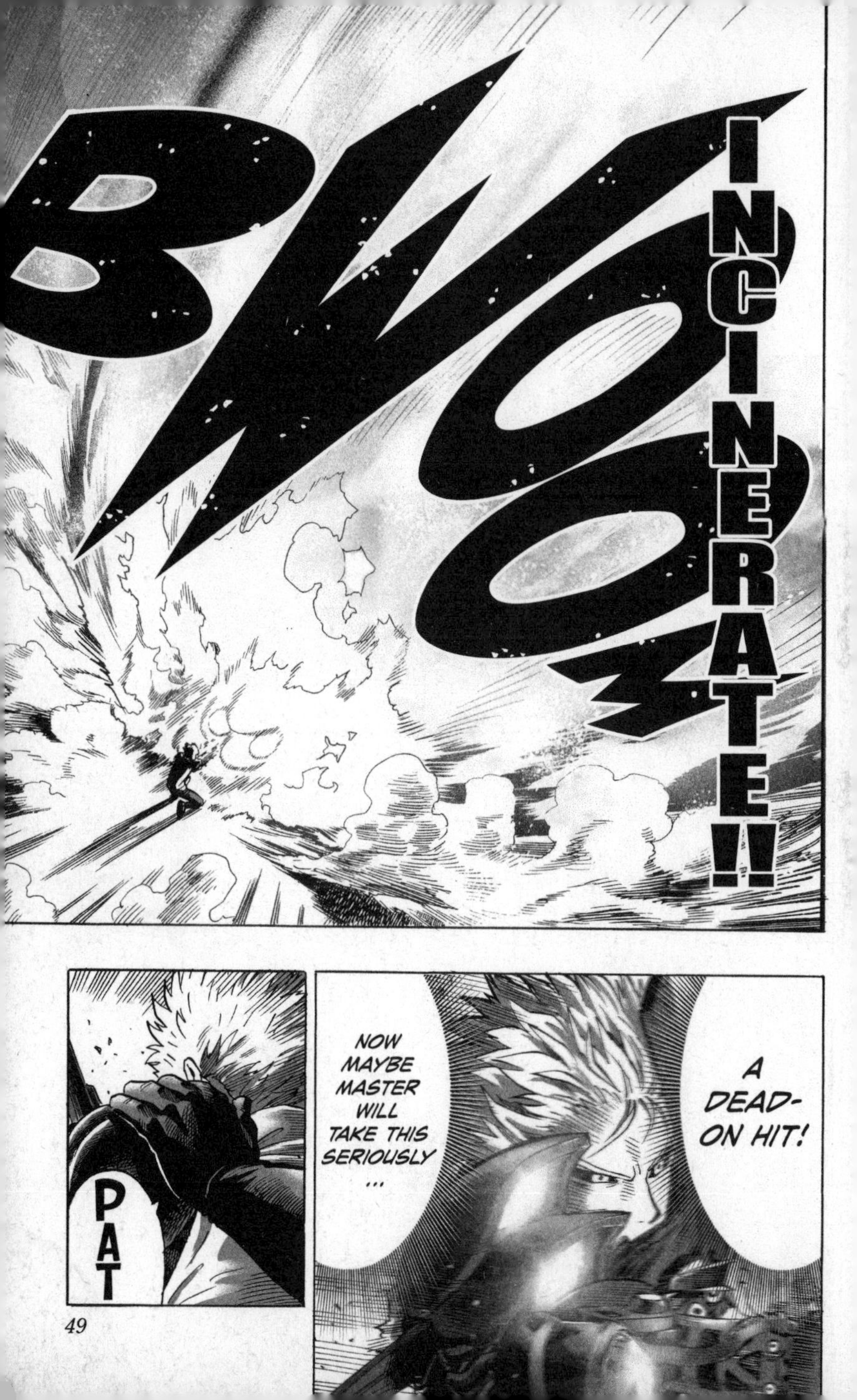
BWOO
INCINERATE!!
A DEAD-ON HIT!
NOW MAYBE MASTER WILL TAKE THIS SERIOUSLY ...
PAT

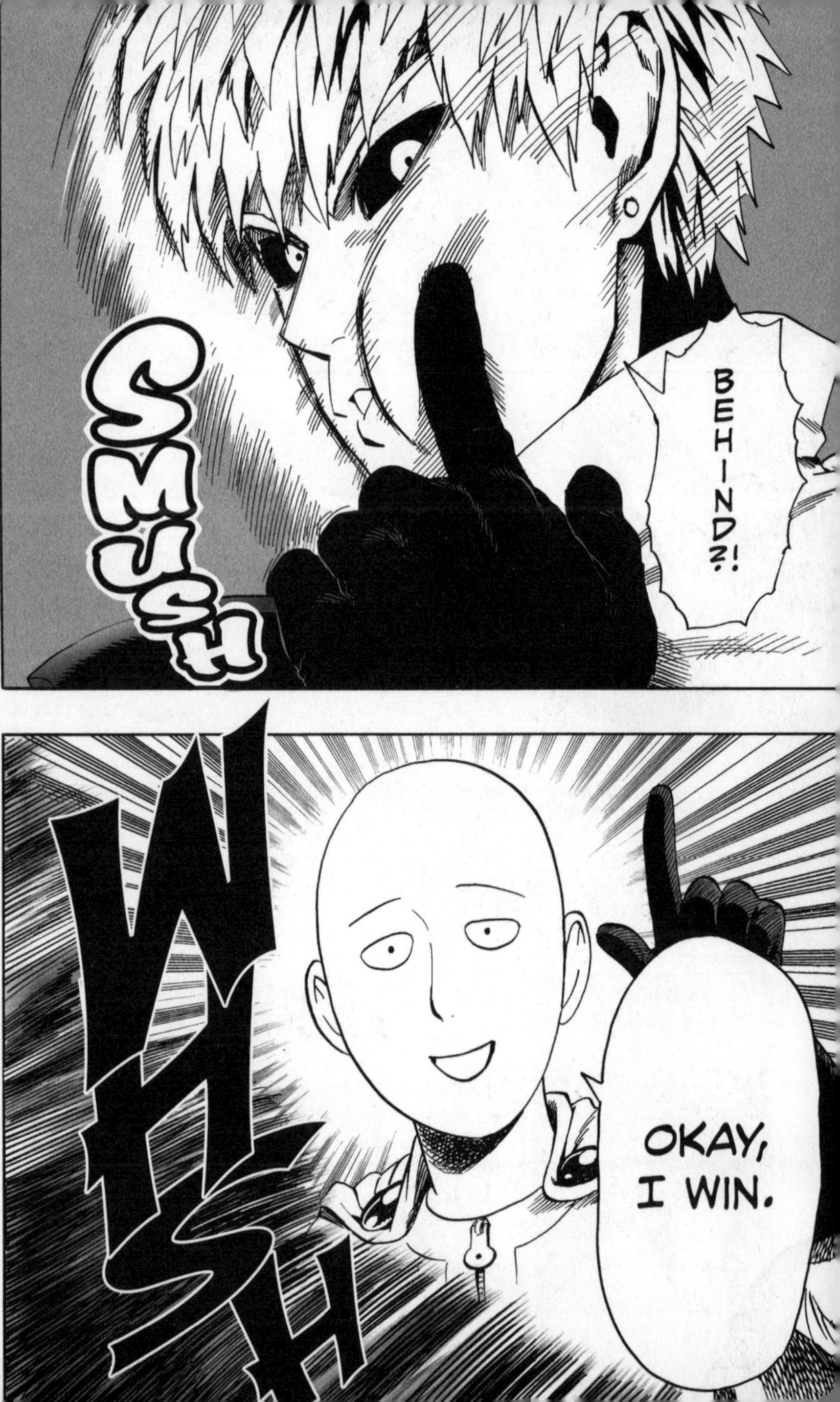
BEHIND?!
SMUSH
WHSH
OKAY, I WIN.

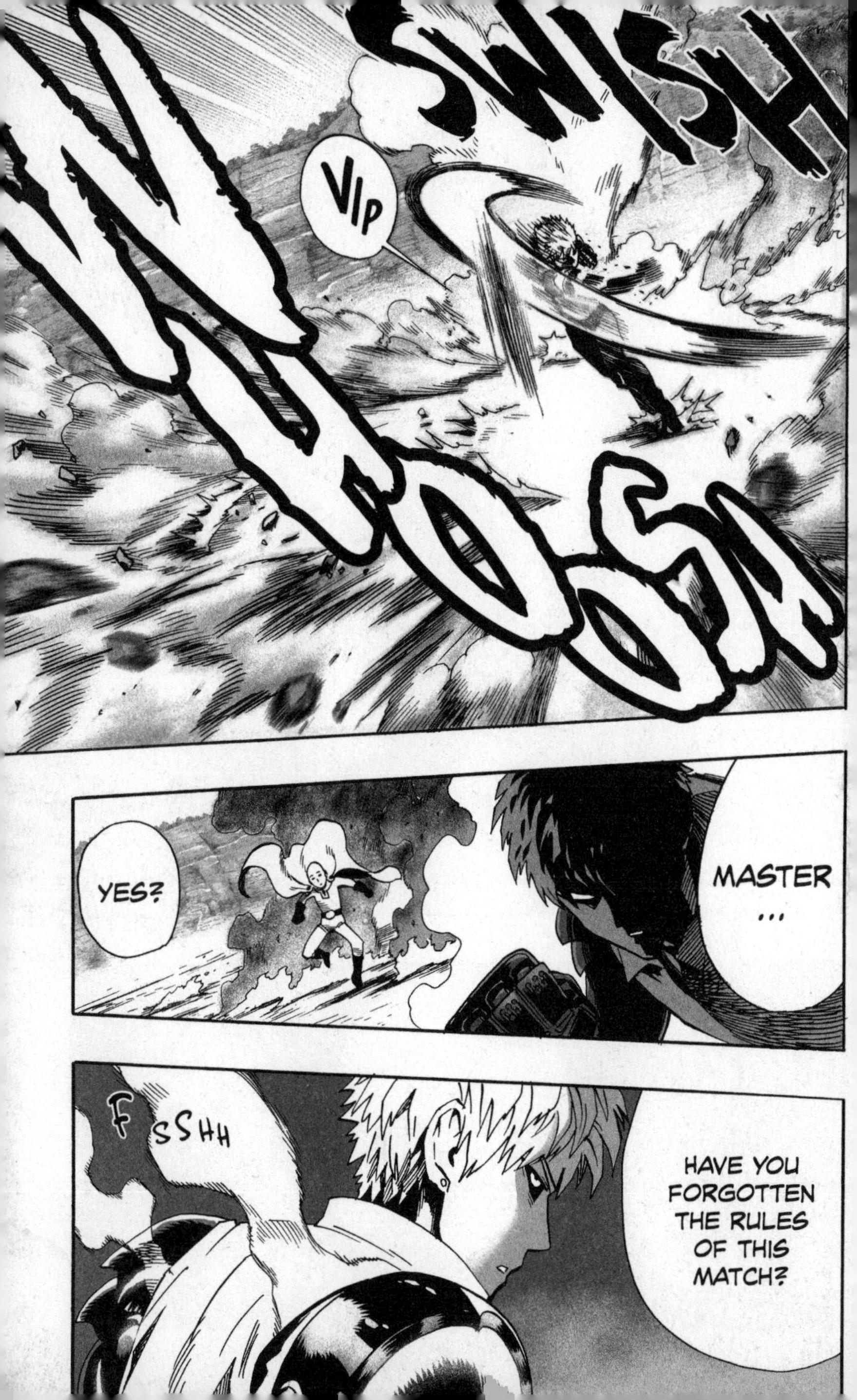
SWISH
VIP
WHOOSH
MASTER
...
YES?
HAVE YOU FORGOTTEN THE RULES OF THIS MATCH?
FSSHH

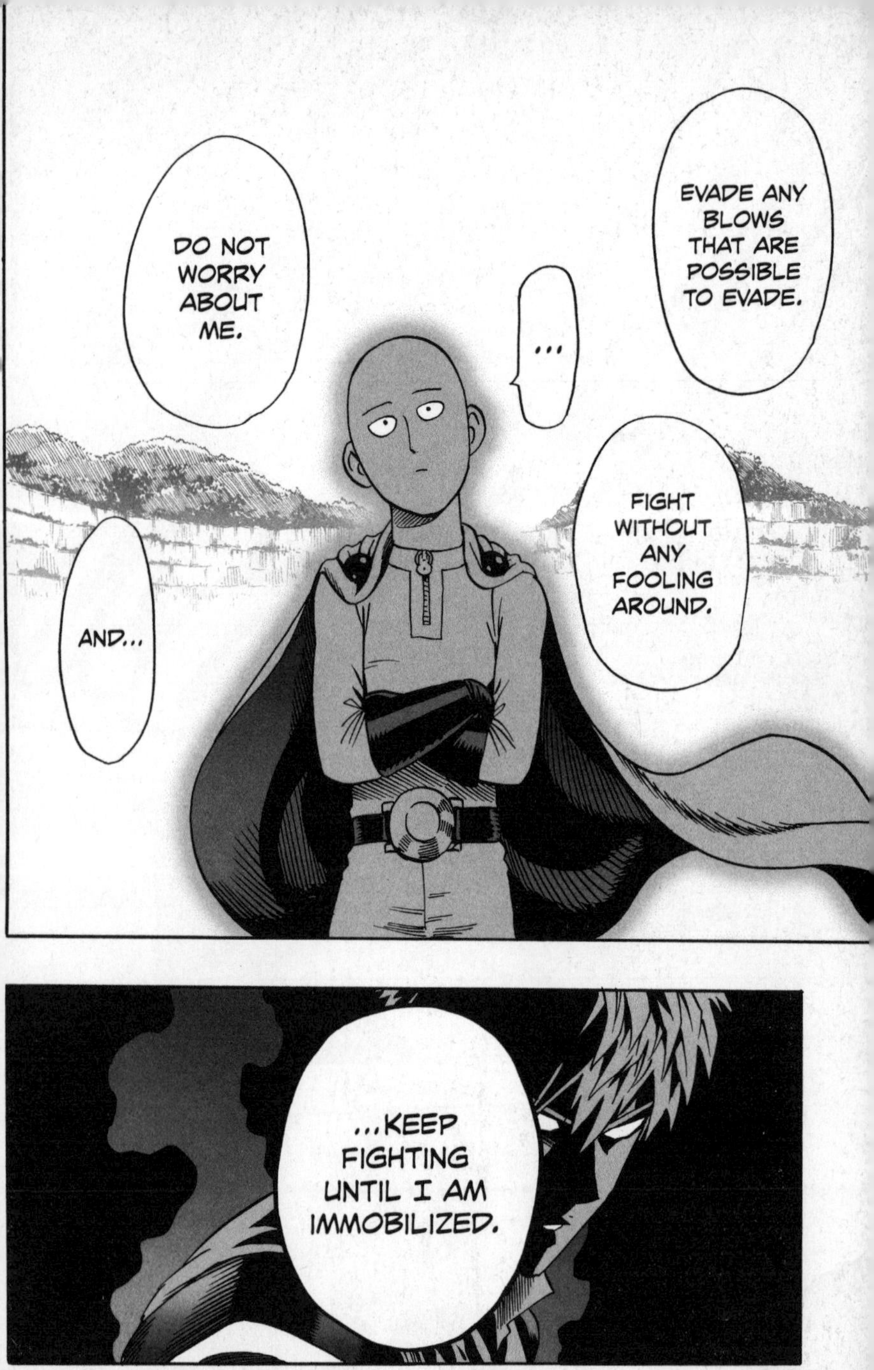
EVADE ANY BLOWS THAT ARE POSSIBLE TO EVADE.
...
DO NOT WORRY ABOUT ME.
FIGHT WITHOUT ANY FOOLING AROUND.
AND...
...KEEP FIGHTING UNTIL I AM IMMOBILIZED.

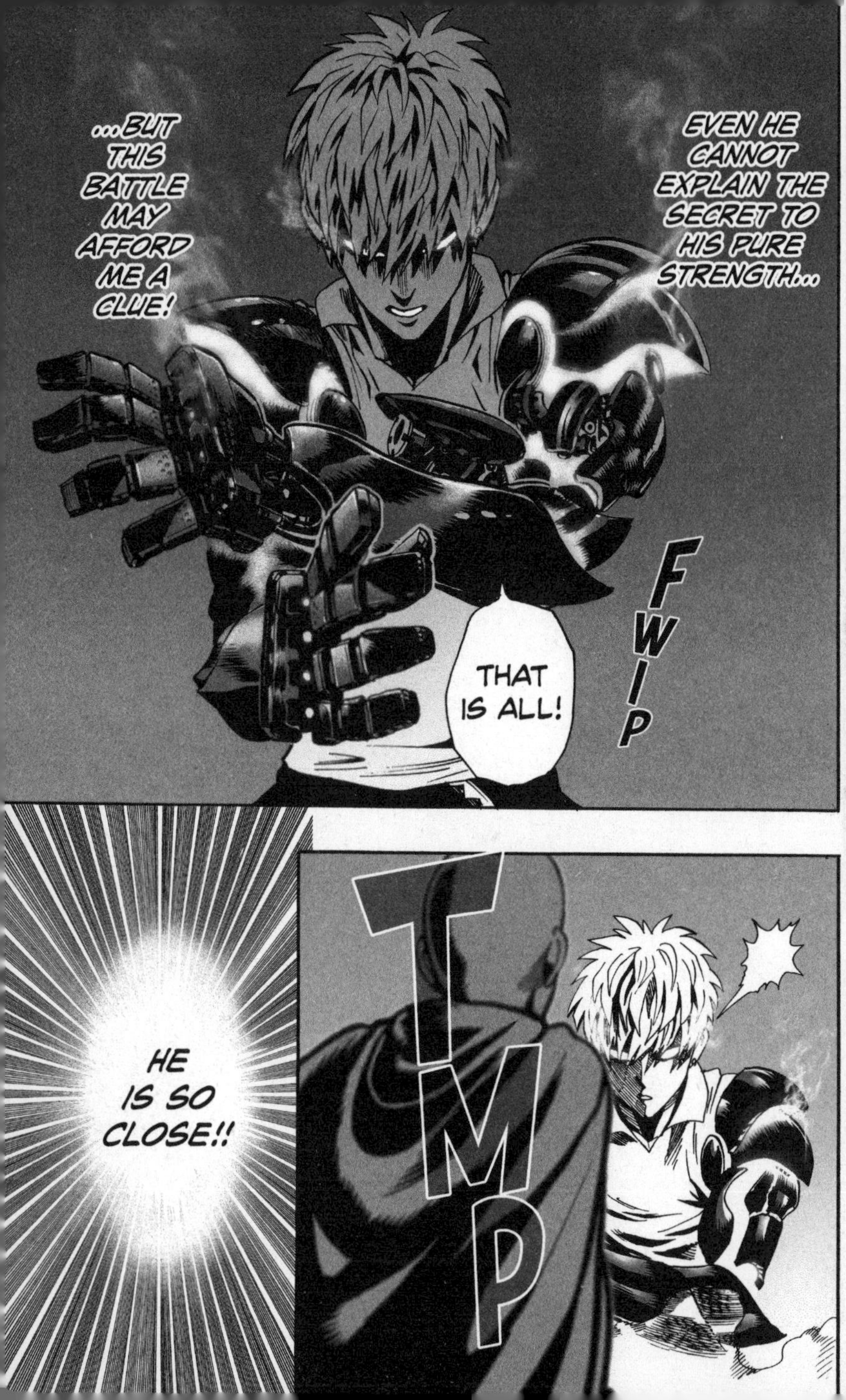
EVEN HE CANNOT EXPLAIN THE SECRET TO HIS PURE STRENGTH...
...BUT THIS BATTLE MAY AFFORD ME A CLUE!
THAT IS ALL!
FWIP
TMP
HE IS SO CLOSE!!

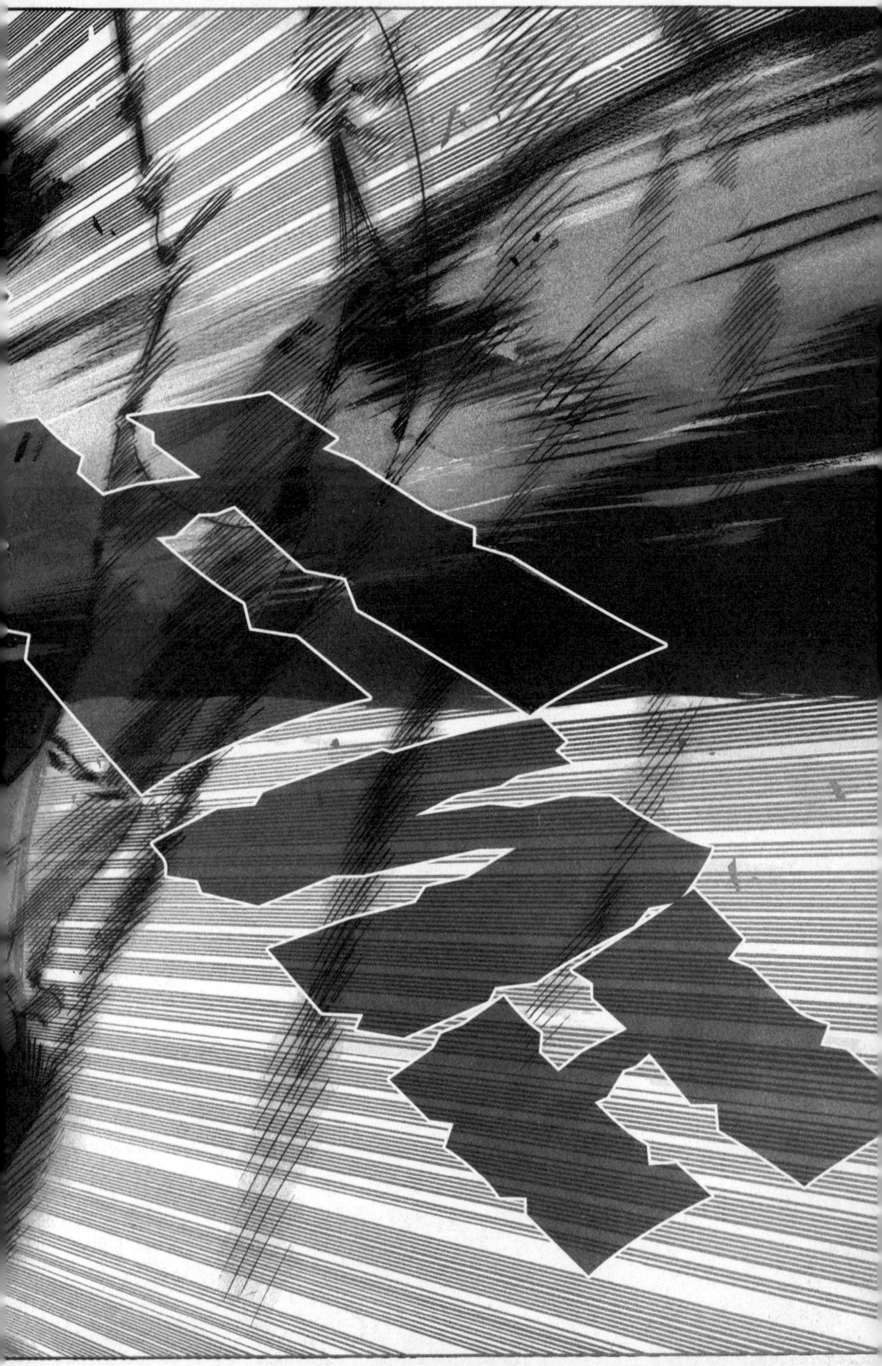

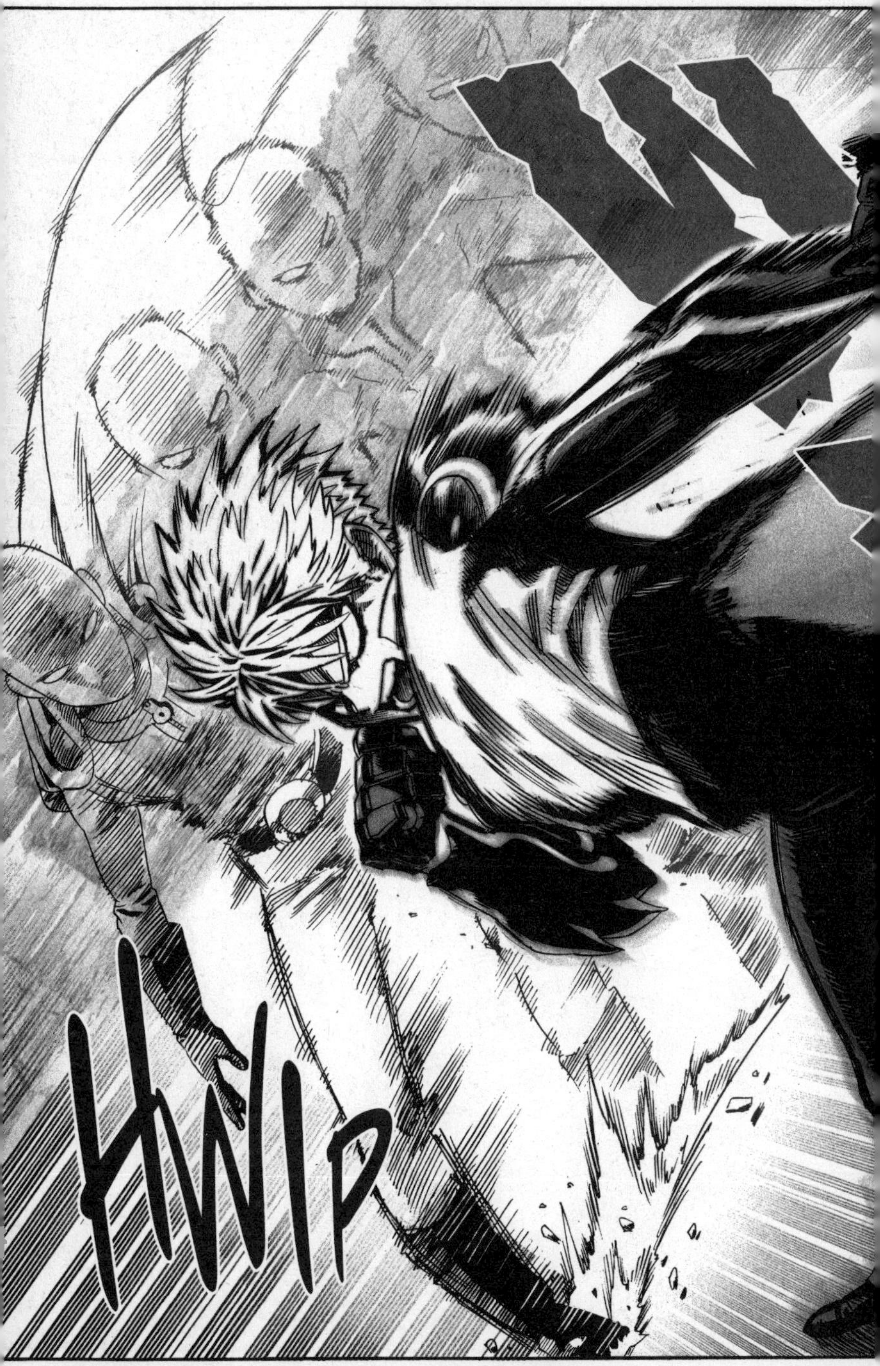
HWIP

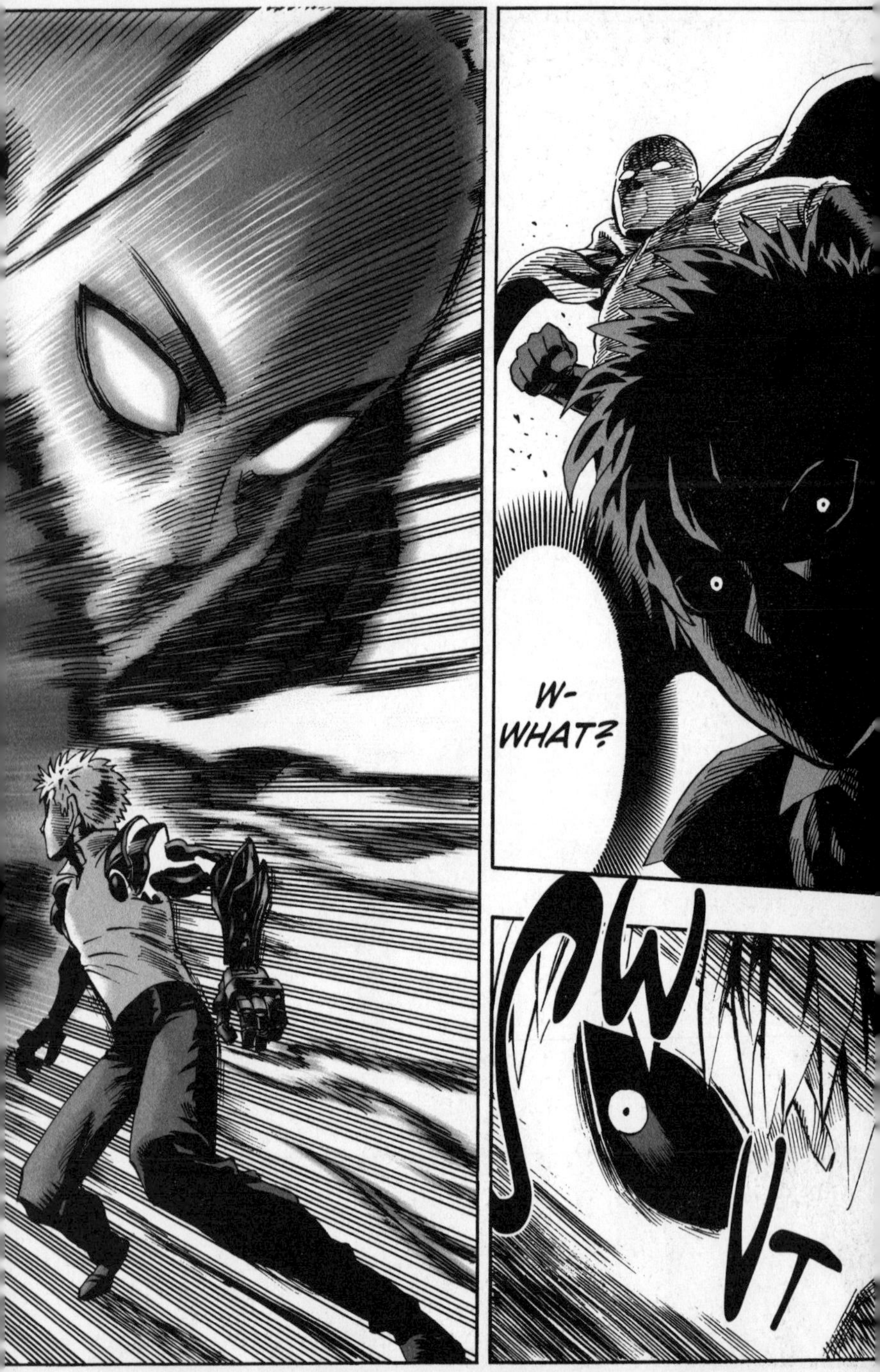
W-
WHAT?

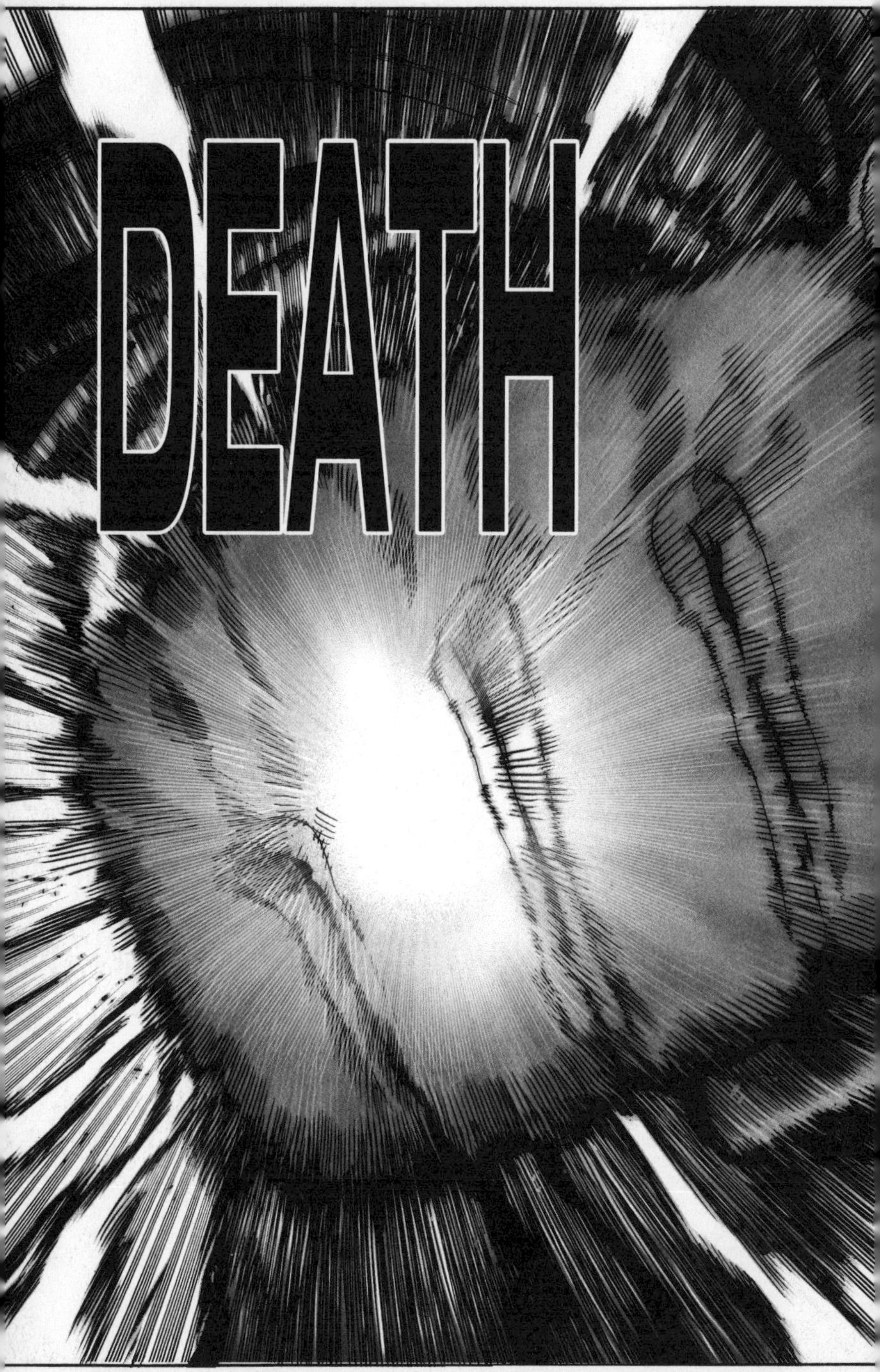
DEATH

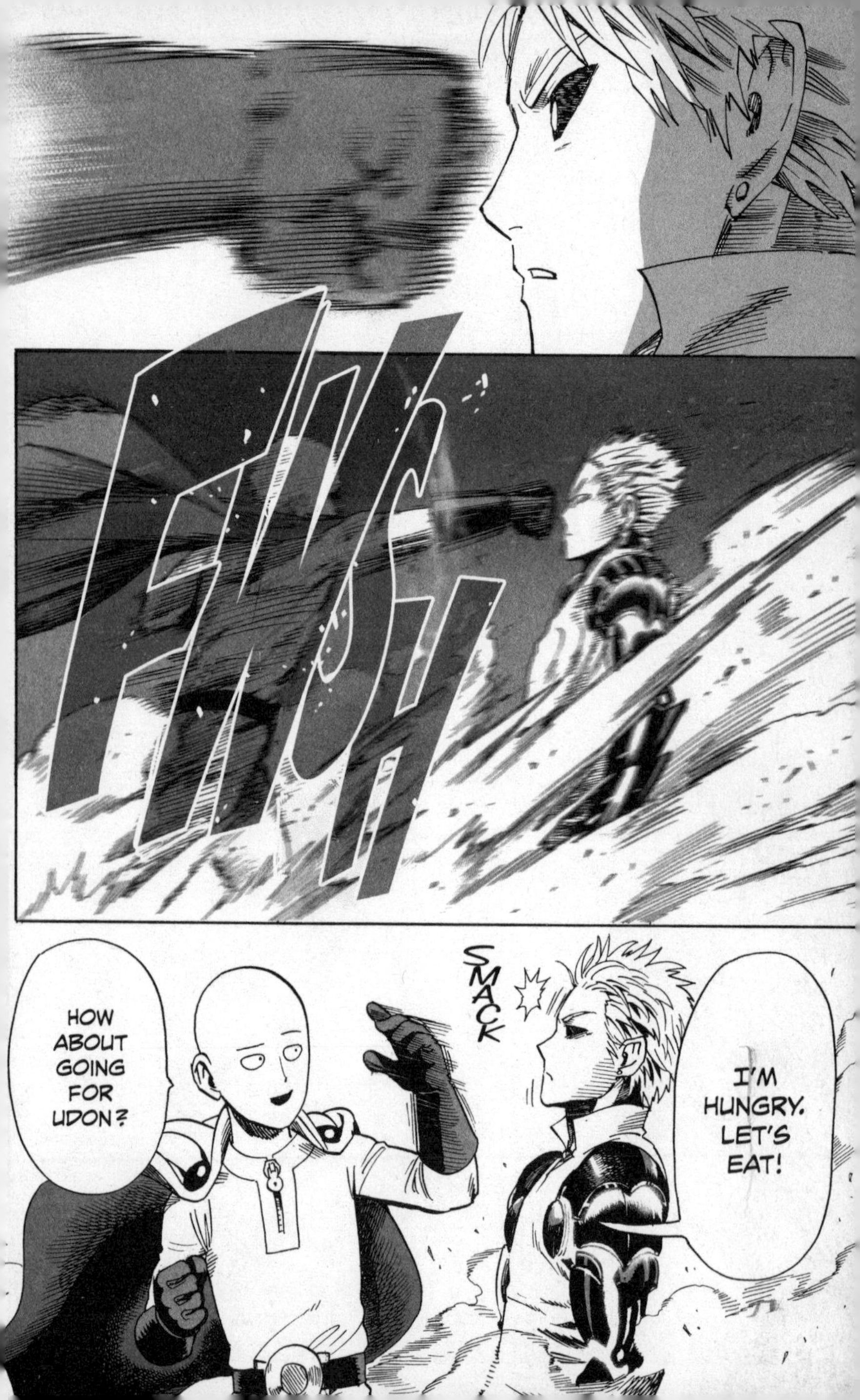
FWSH
SMACK
I'M HUNGRY. LET'S EAT!
HOW ABOUT GOING FOR UDON?

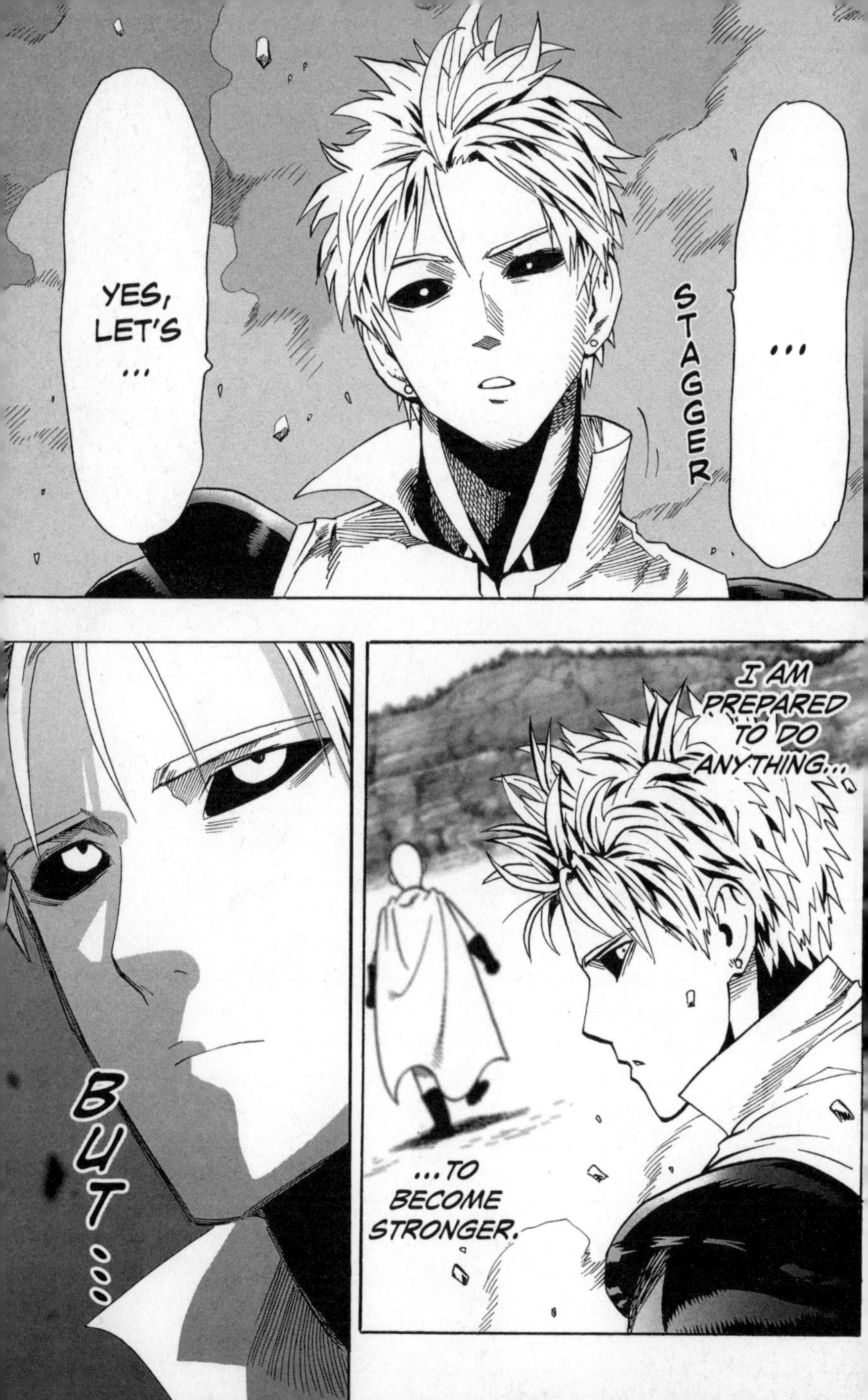
...
STAGGER
YES, LET'S ...
I AM PREPARED TO DO ANYTHING...
...TO BECOME STRONGER.
BUT...

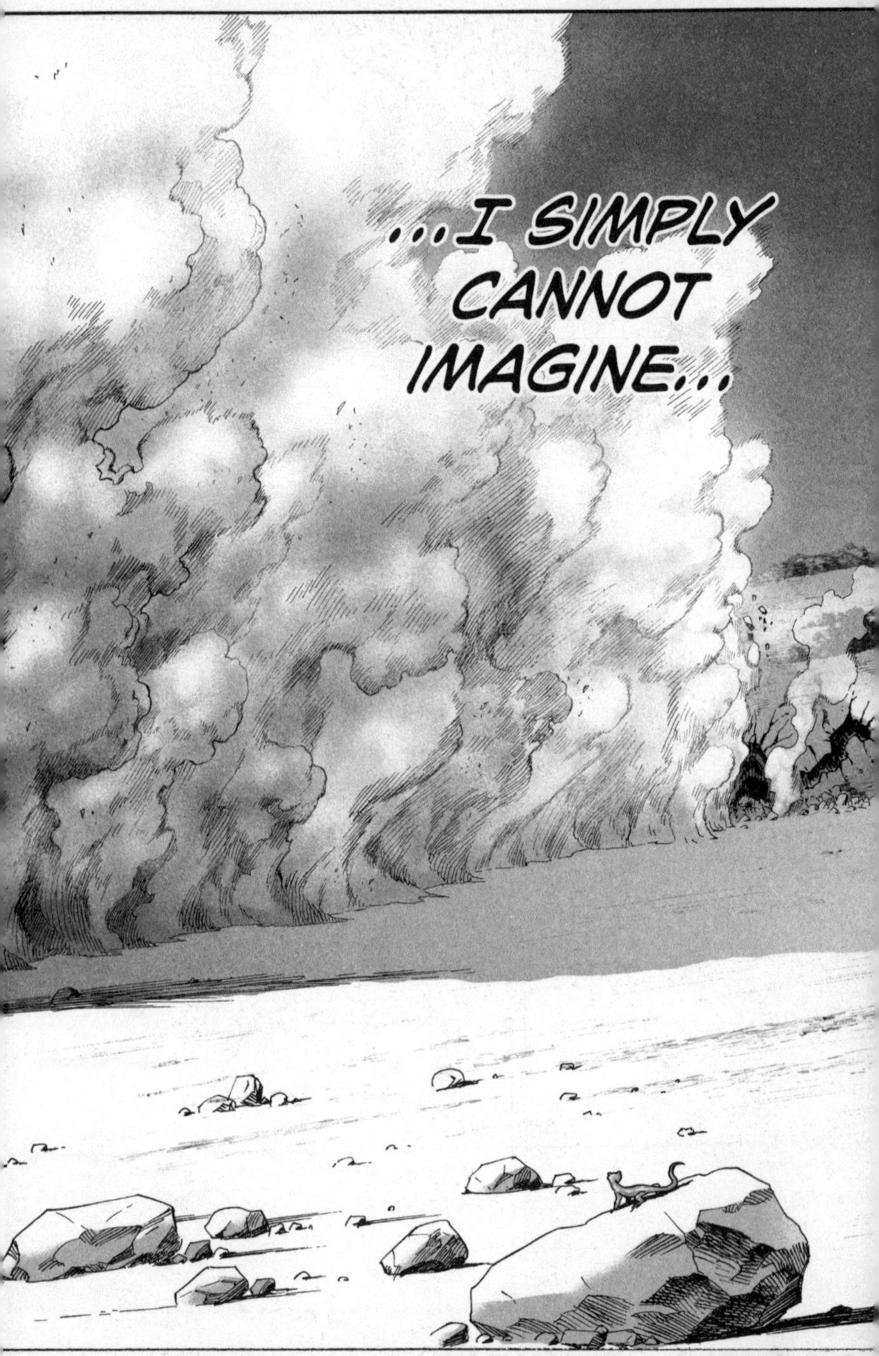
...I SIMPLY CANNOT IMAGINE...

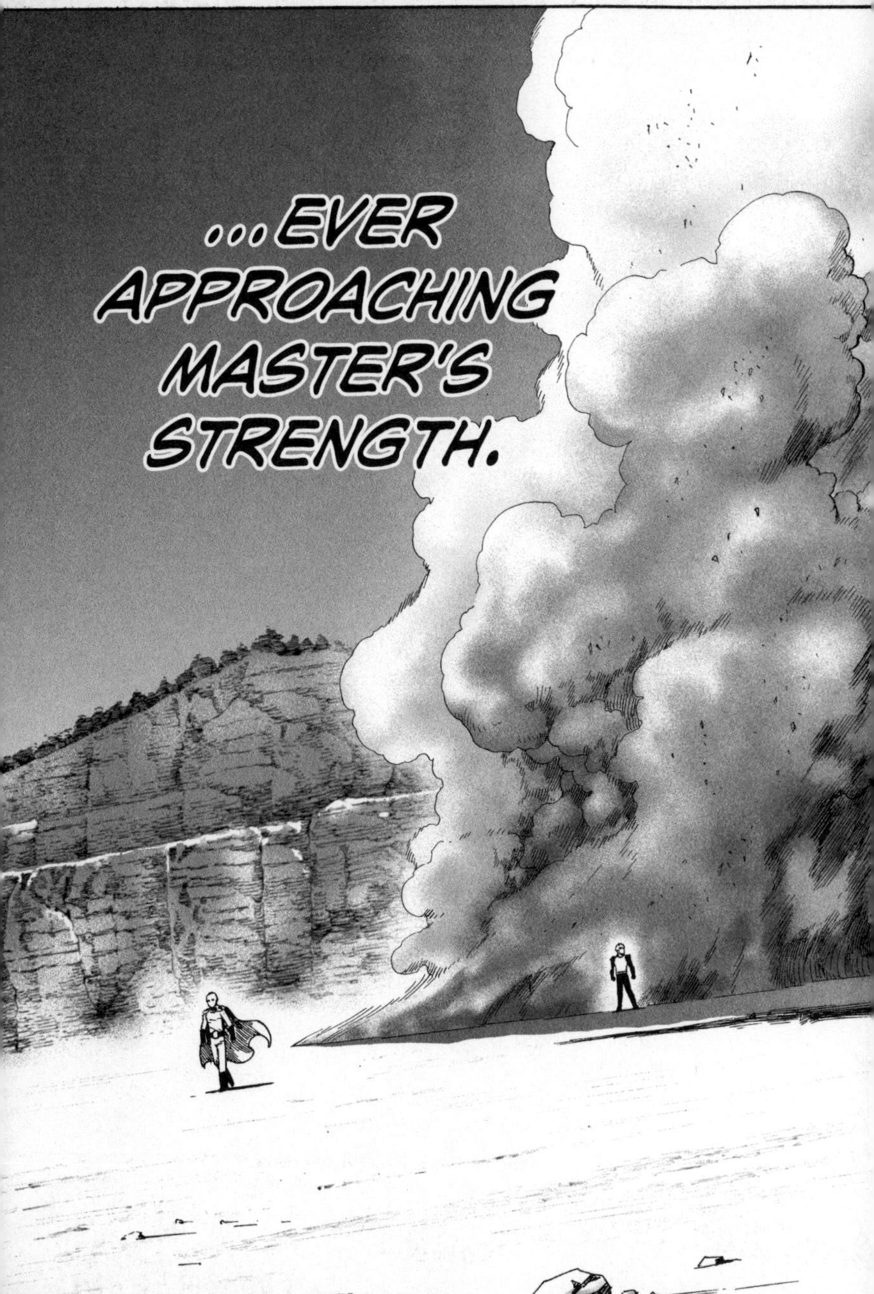
...EVER APPROACHING MASTER'S STRENGTH.

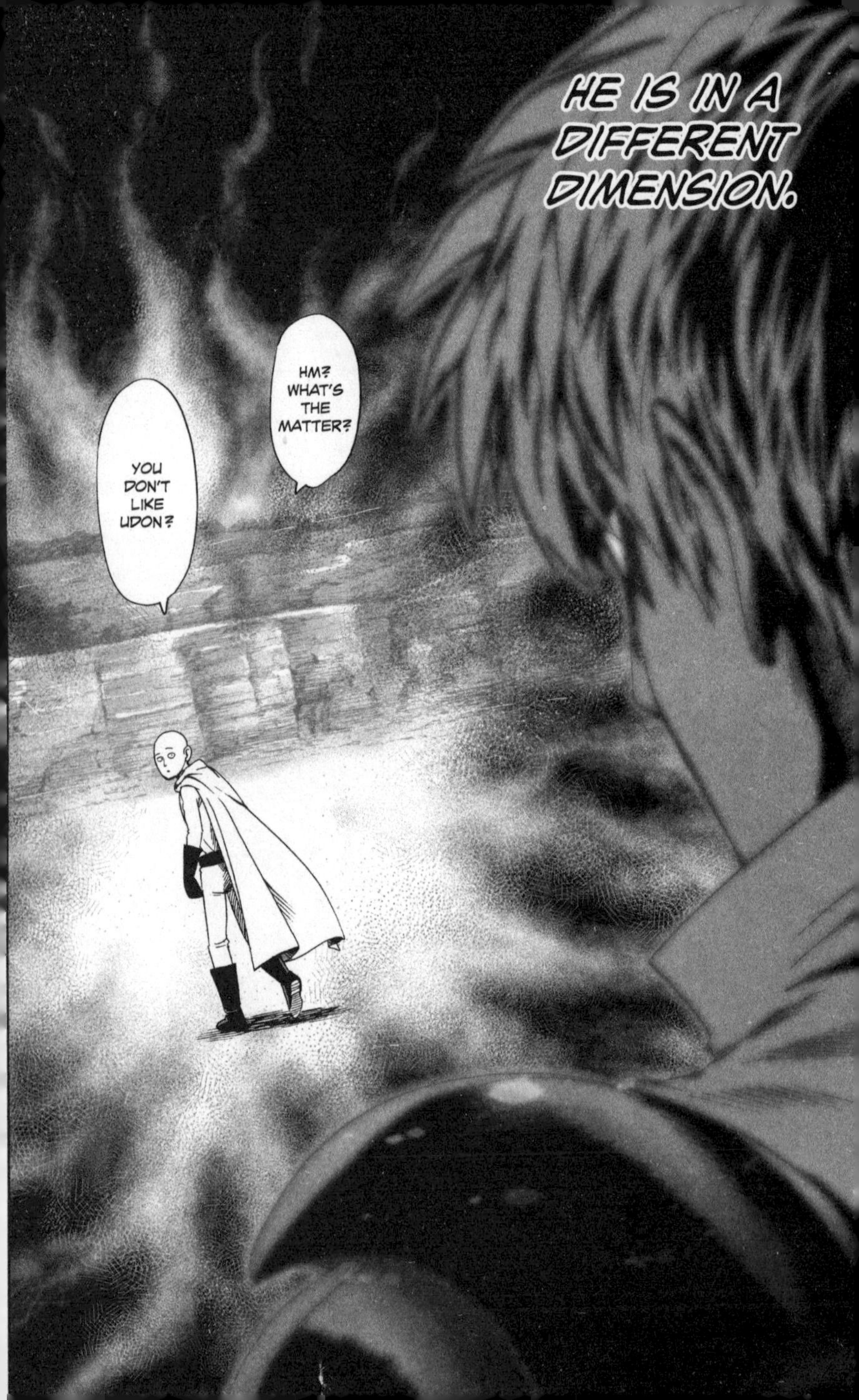
HE IS IN A DIFFERENT DIMENSION.
HM? WHAT'S THE MATTER?
YOU DON'T LIKE UDON?

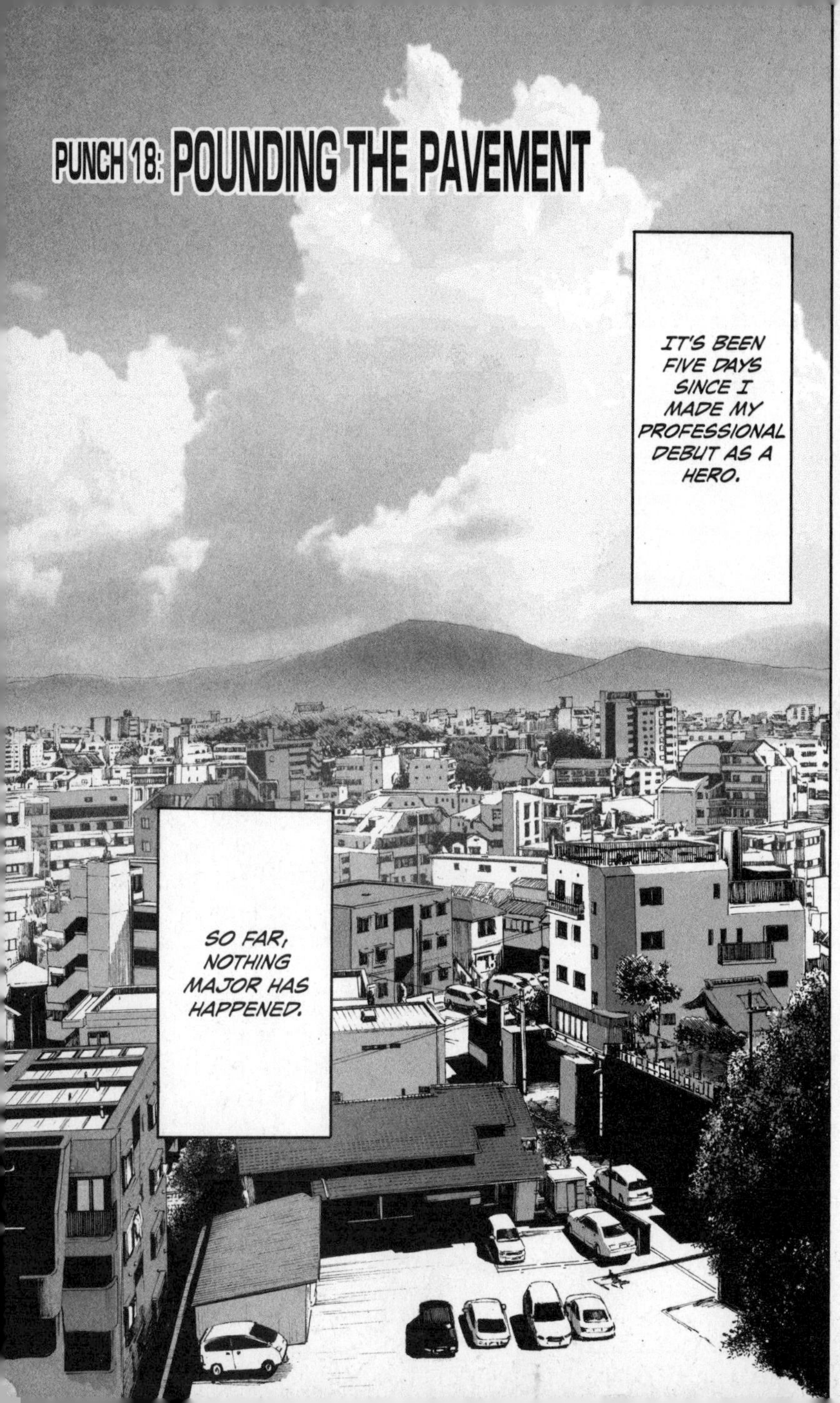
PUNCH 18: POUNDING THE PAVEMENT
IT'S BEEN FIVE DAYS SINCE I MADE MY PROFESSIONAL DEBUT AS A HERO.
SO FAR, NOTHING MAJOR HAS HAPPENED.

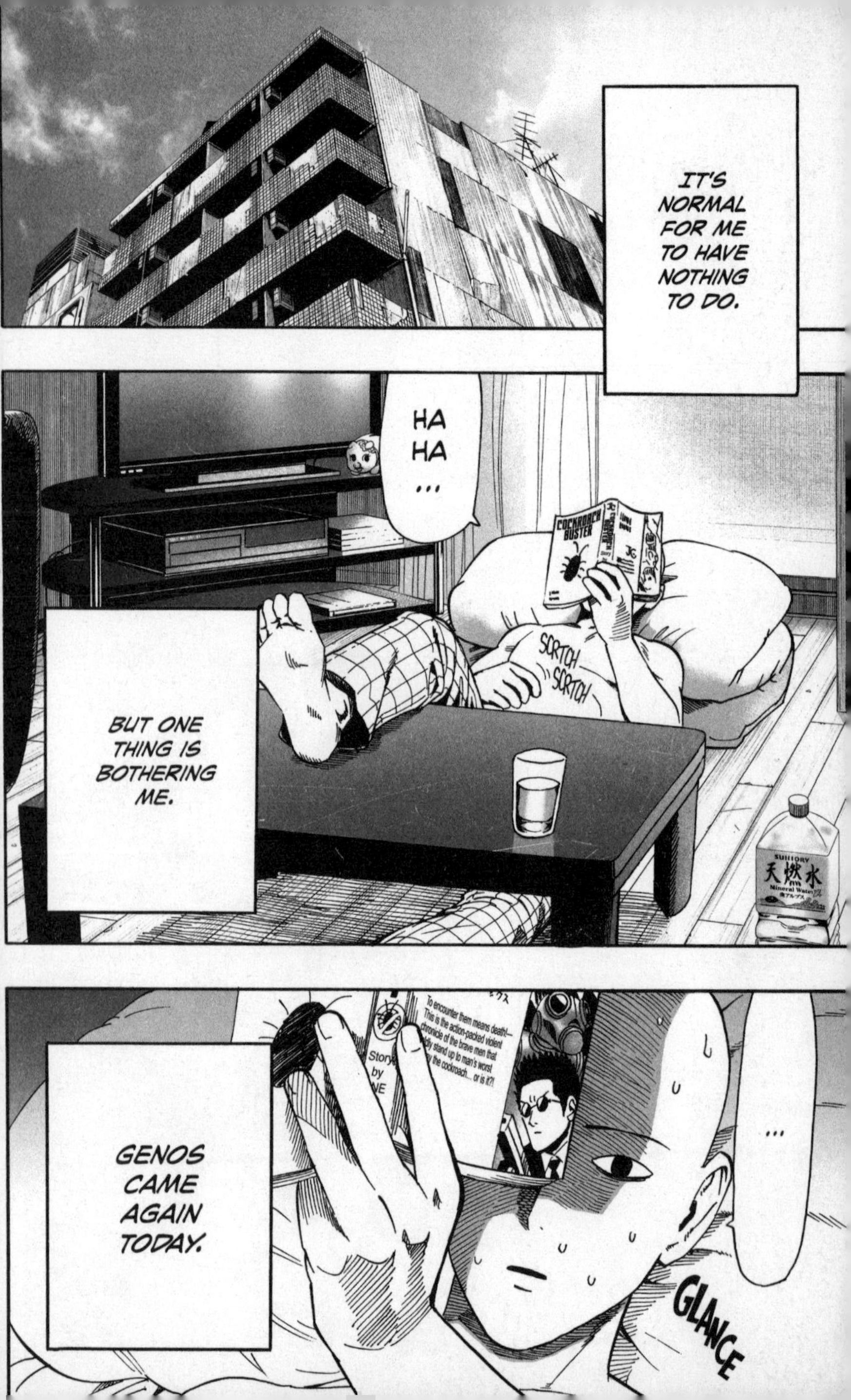
IT'S NORMAL FOR ME TO HAVE NOTHING TO DO.
HA HA ...
COCKROACH BUSTER
SCRTCH SCRTCH
BUT ONE THING IS BOTHERING ME.
...
GENOS CAME AGAIN TODAY.
GLANCE

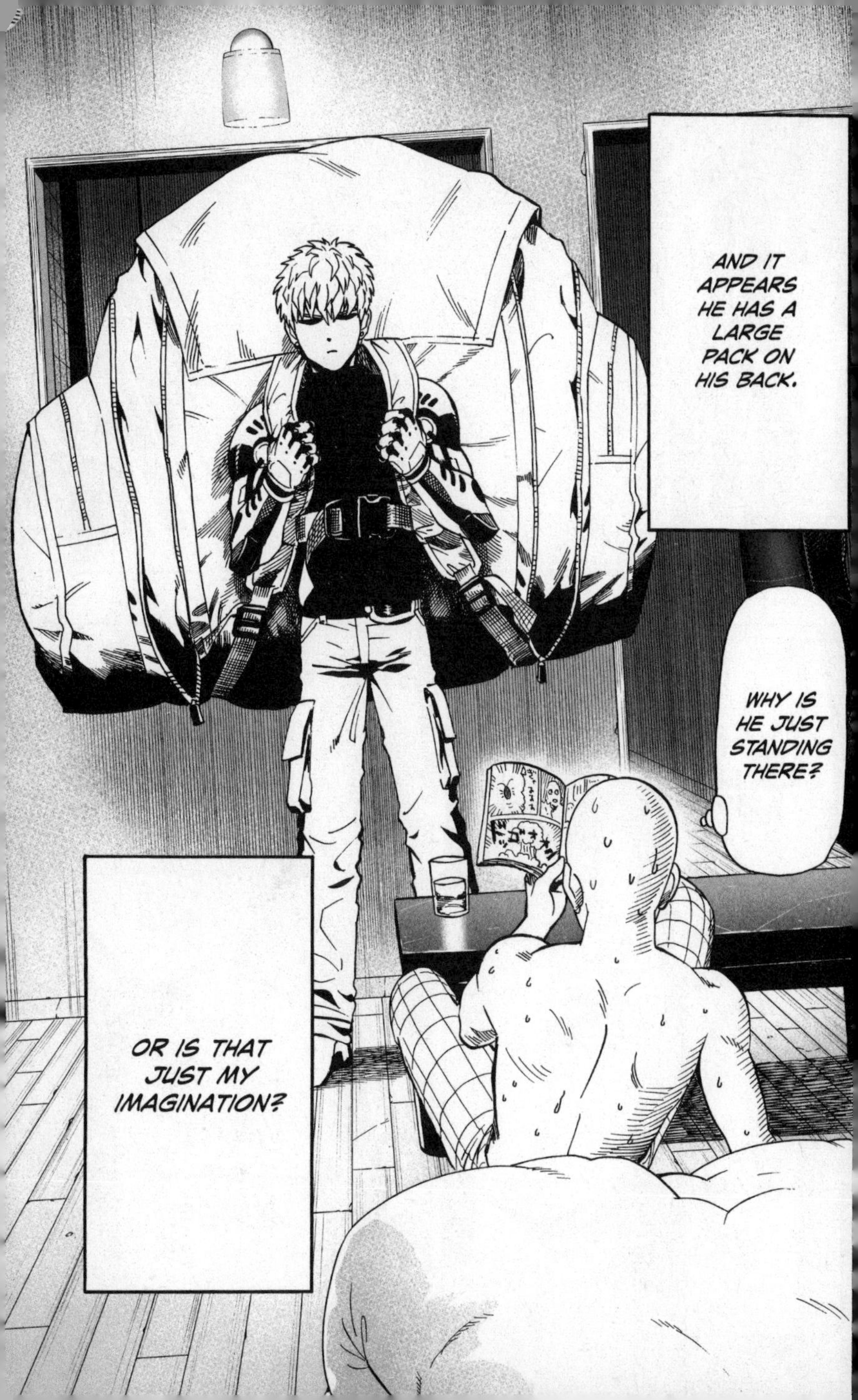
AND IT APPEARS HE HAS A LARGE PACK ON HIS BACK.
WHY IS HE JUST STANDING THERE?
OR IS THAT JUST MY IMAGINATION?

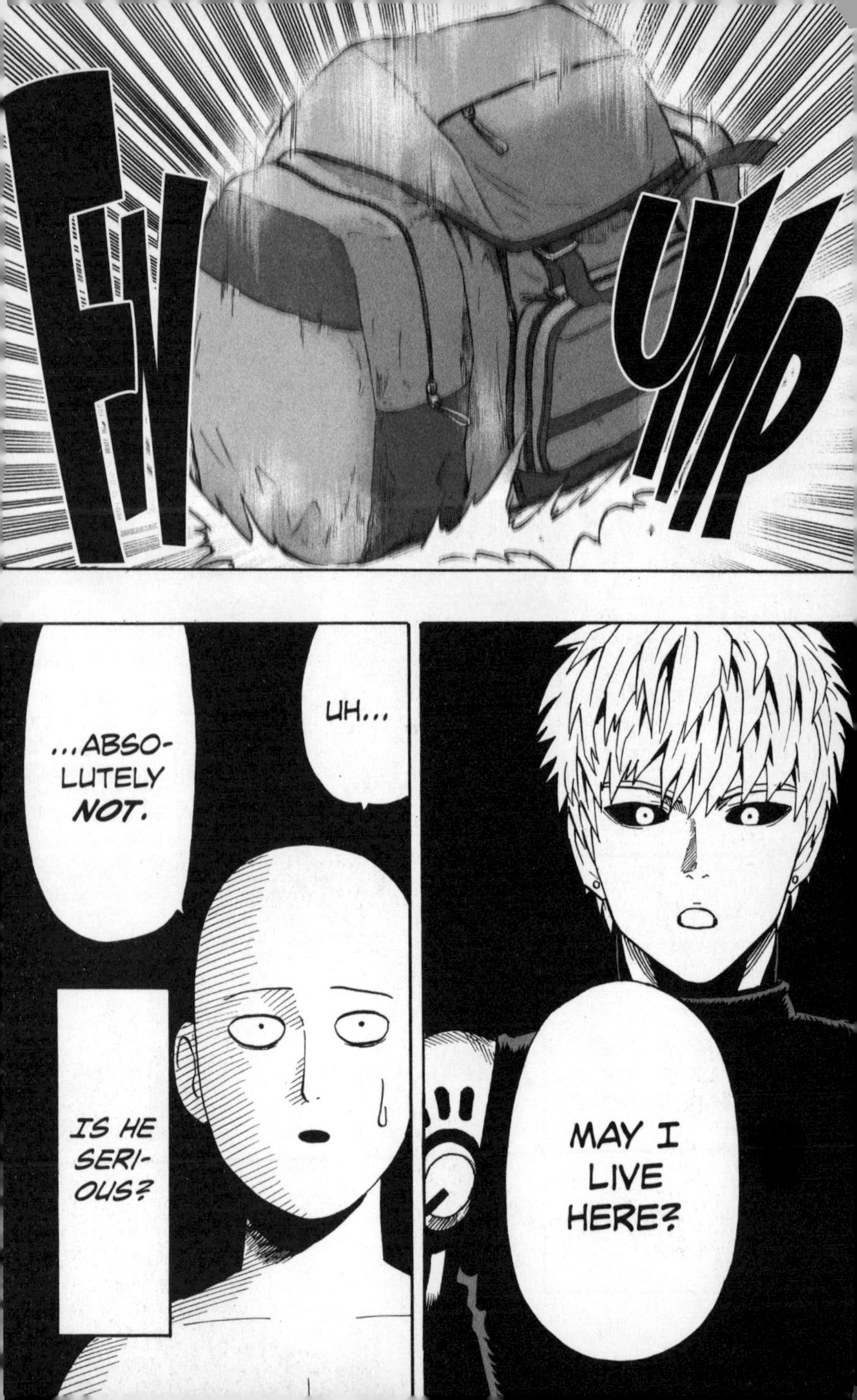
MAY I LIVE HERE?
UH...
...ABSOLUTELY NOT.
IS HE SERIOUS?

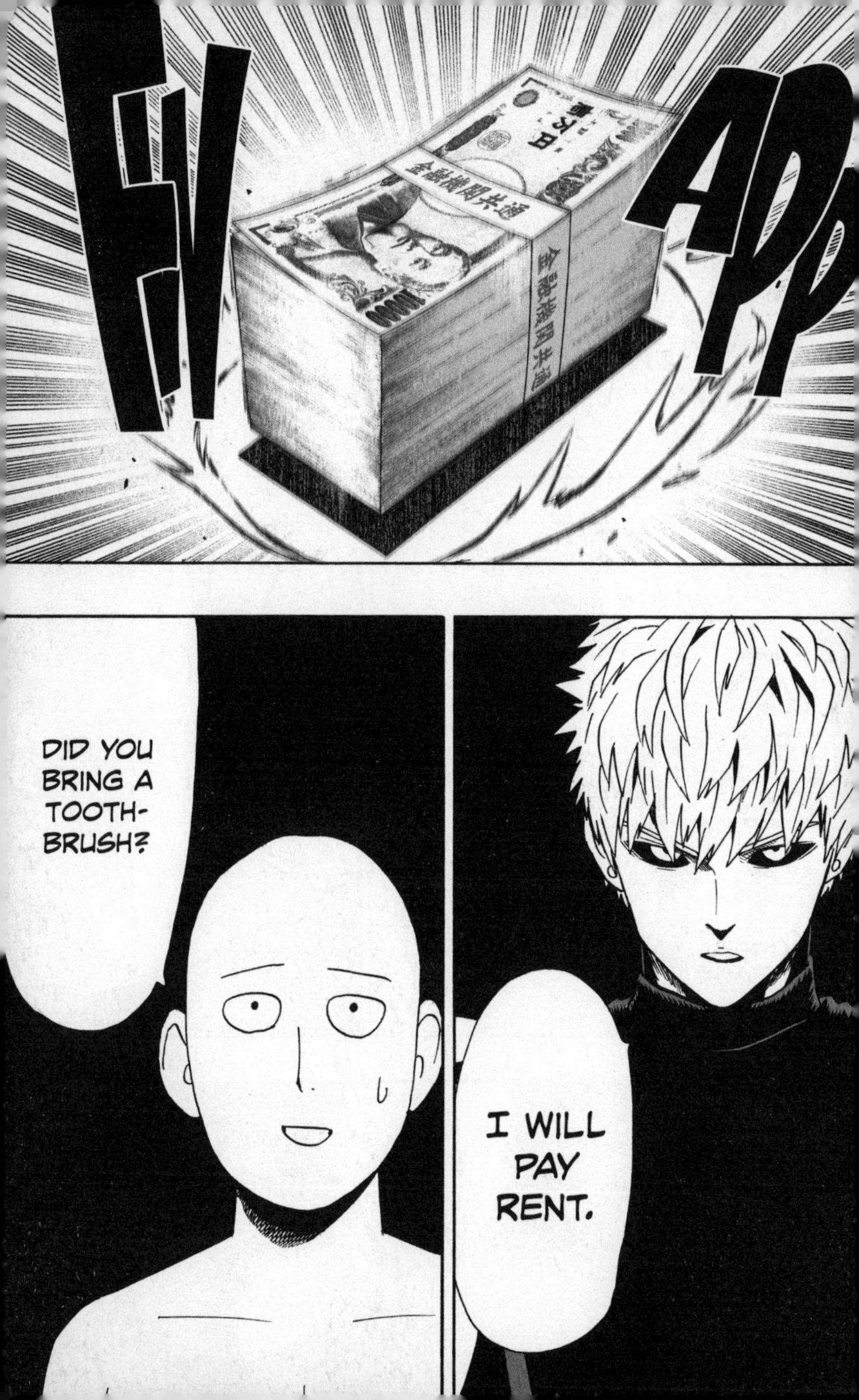
I WILL PAY RENT.
DID YOU BRING A TOOTH-BRUSH?

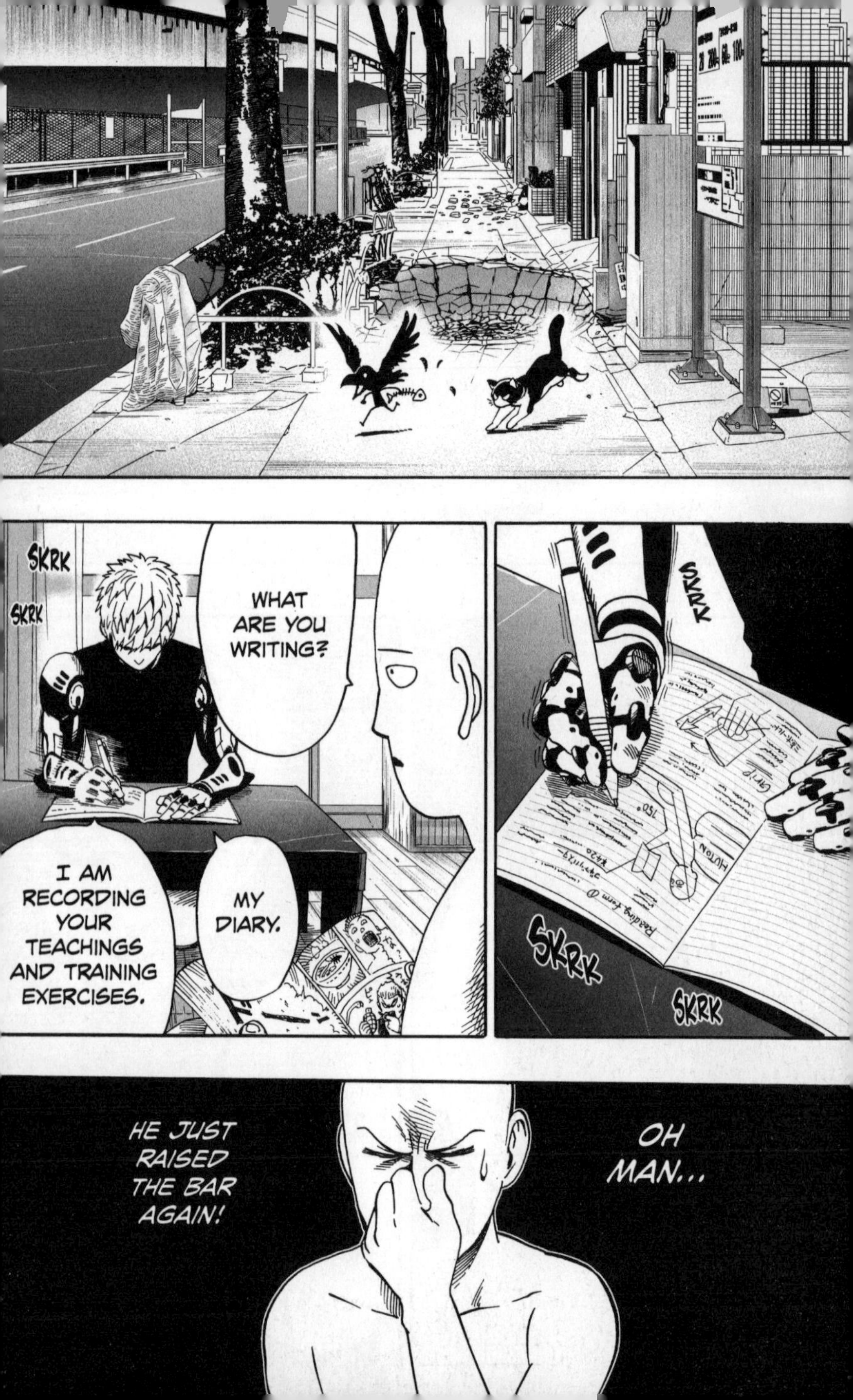
SKRK
SKRK
WHAT ARE YOU WRITING?
MY DIARY.
I AM RECORDING YOUR TEACHINGS AND TRAINING EXERCISES.
SKRK
SKRK
SKRK
OH MAN...
HE JUST RAISED THE BAR AGAIN!

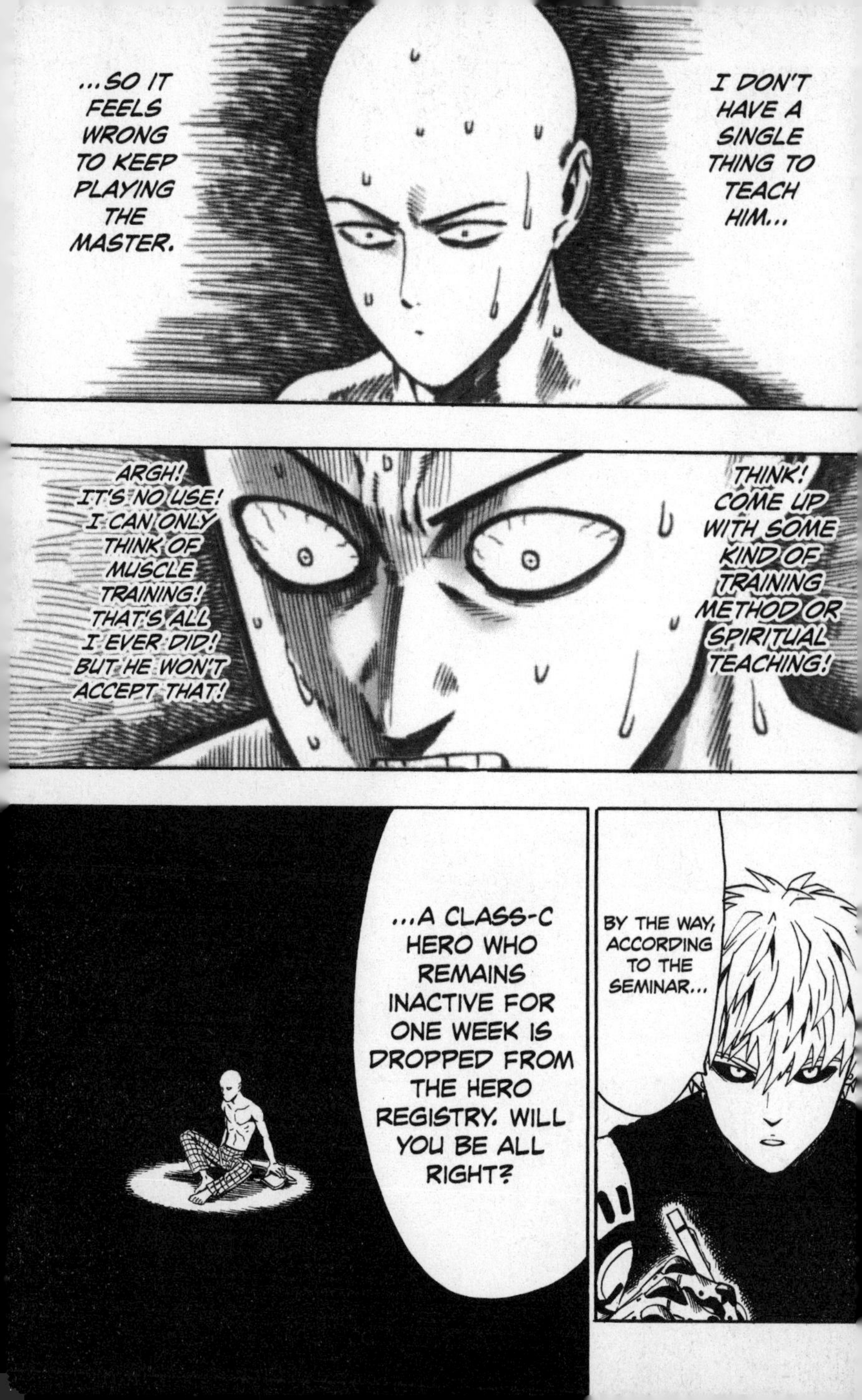
I DON'T HAVE A SINGLE THING TO TEACH HIM...
...SO IT FEELS WRONG TO KEEP PLAYING THE MASTER.
THINK! COME UP WITH SOME KIND OF TRAINING METHOD OR SPIRITUAL TEACHING!
ARGH! IT'S NO USE! I CAN ONLY THINK OF MUSCLE TRAINING! THAT'S ALL I EVER DID! BUT HE WON'T ACCEPT THAT!
BY THE WAY, ACCORDING TO THE SEMINAR...
...A CLASS-C HERO WHO REMAINS INACTIVE FOR ONE WEEK IS DROPPED FROM THE HERO REGISTRY. WILL YOU BE ALL RIGHT?

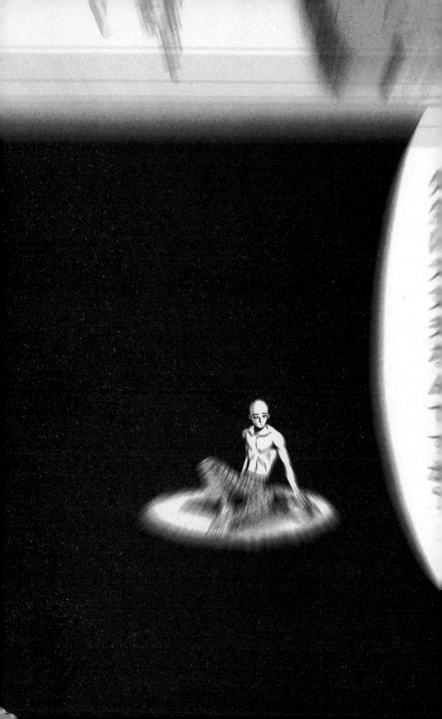

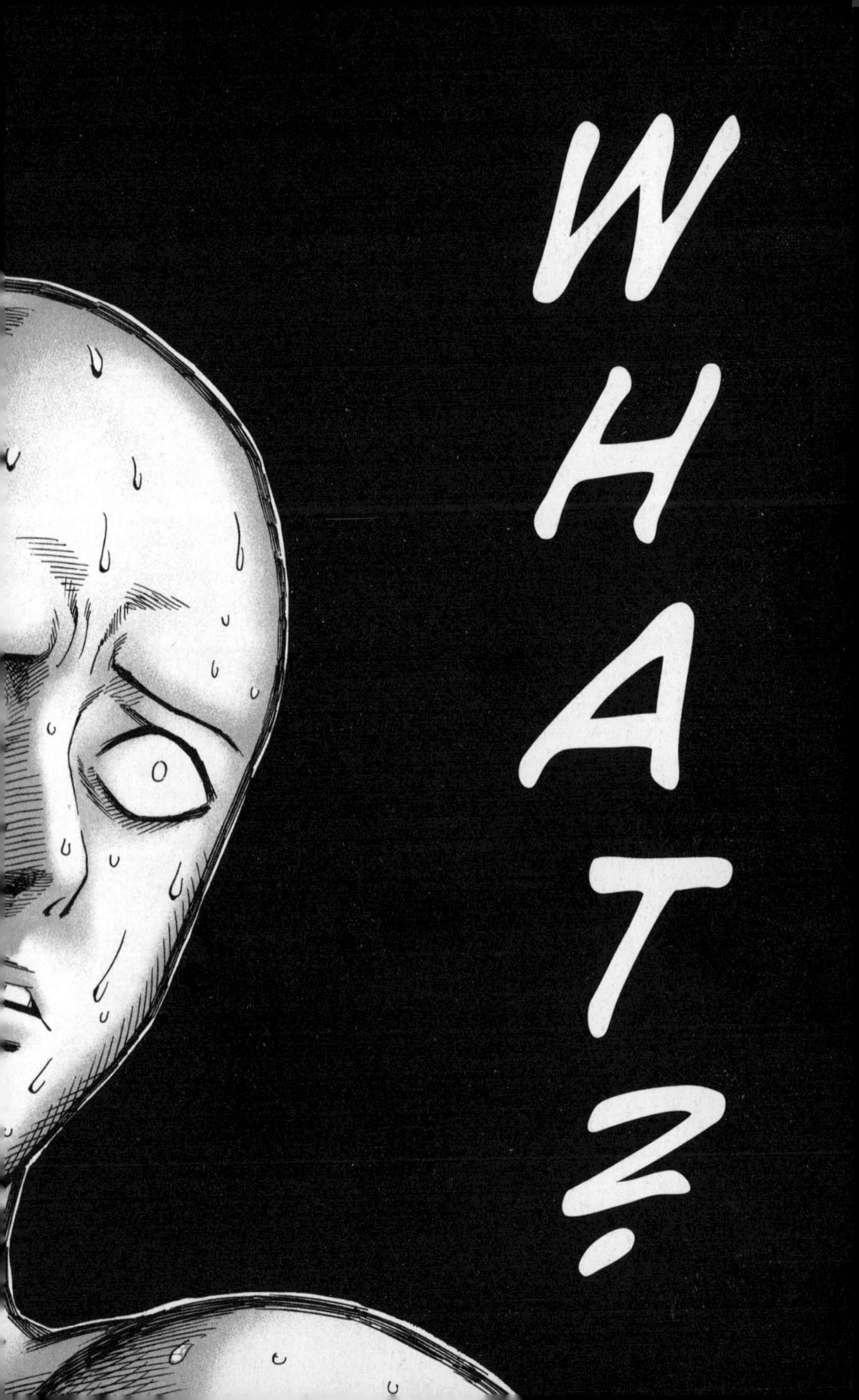
WHAT?

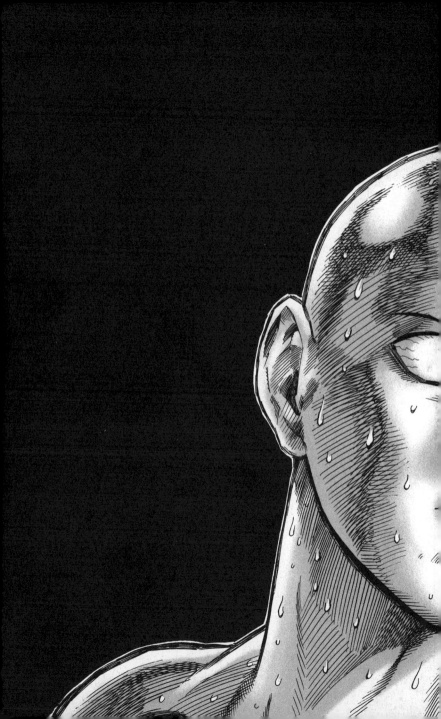

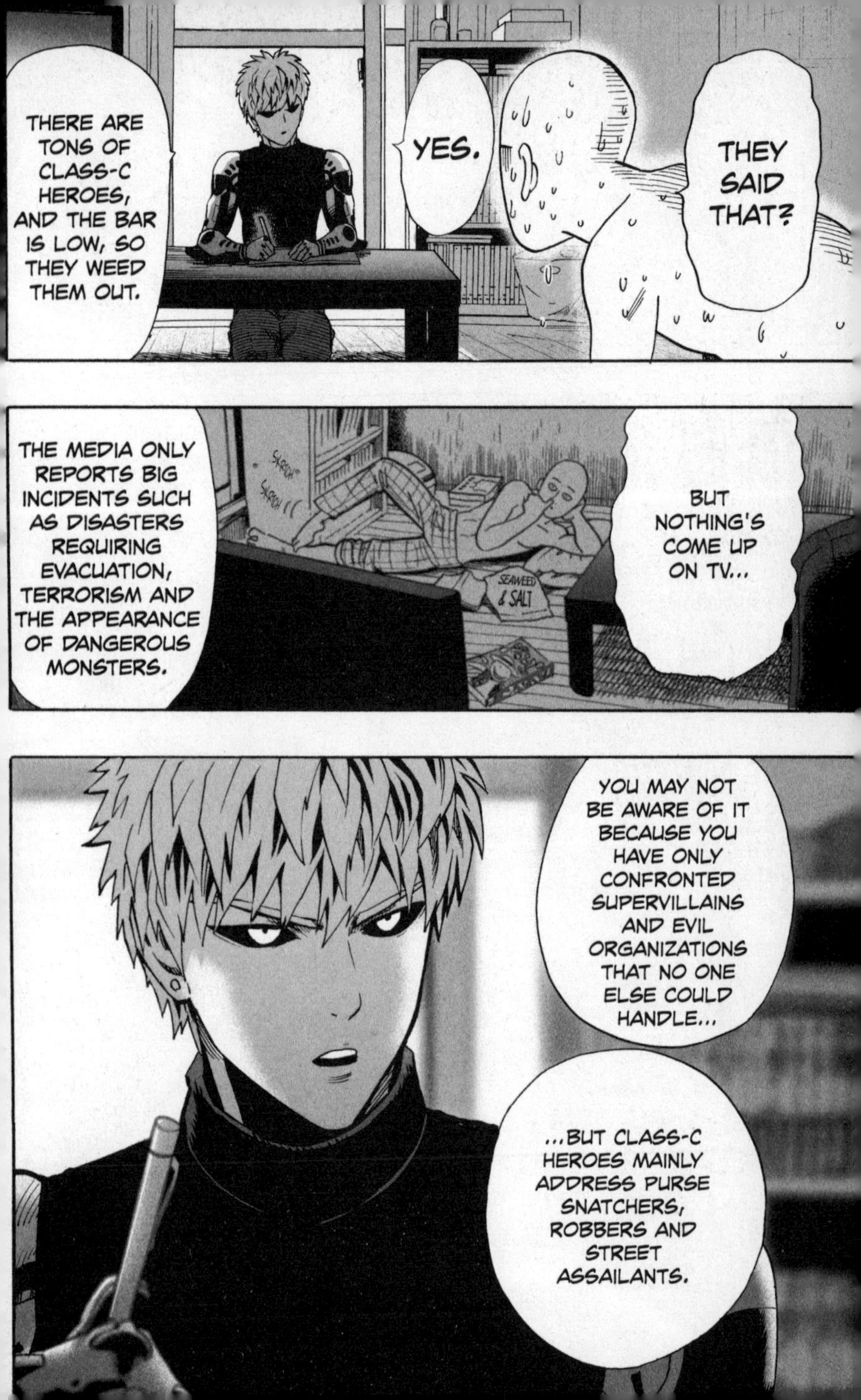
THEY SAID THAT?
YES.
THERE ARE TONS OF CLASS-C HEROES, AND THE BAR IS LOW, SO THEY WEED THEM OUT.
BUT NOTHING'S COME UP ON TV...
SEAWEED & SALT
THE MEDIA ONLY REPORTS BIG INCIDENTS SUCH AS DISASTERS REQUIRING EVACUATION, TERRORISM AND THE APPEARANCE OF DANGEROUS MONSTERS.
YOU MAY NOT BE AWARE OF IT BECAUSE YOU HAVE ONLY CONFRONTED SUPERVILLAINS AND EVIL ORGANIZATIONS THAT NO ONE ELSE COULD HANDLE...
...BUT CLASS-C HEROES MAINLY ADDRESS PURSE SNATCHERS, ROBBERS AND STREET ASSAILANTS.

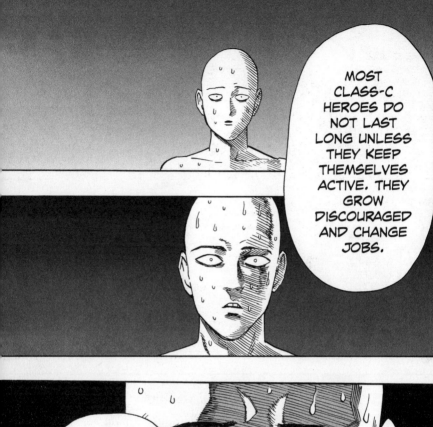

MOST CLASS-C HEROES DO NOT LAST LONG UNLESS THEY KEEP THEMSELVES ACTIVE. THEY GROW DISCOURAGED AND CHANGE JOBS.

IF THEY DO NOT POUND THE PAVEMENT AND DRUM UP RESULTS LIKE A SALARYMAN, NO ONE PAYS ANY ATTENTION TO THEM.

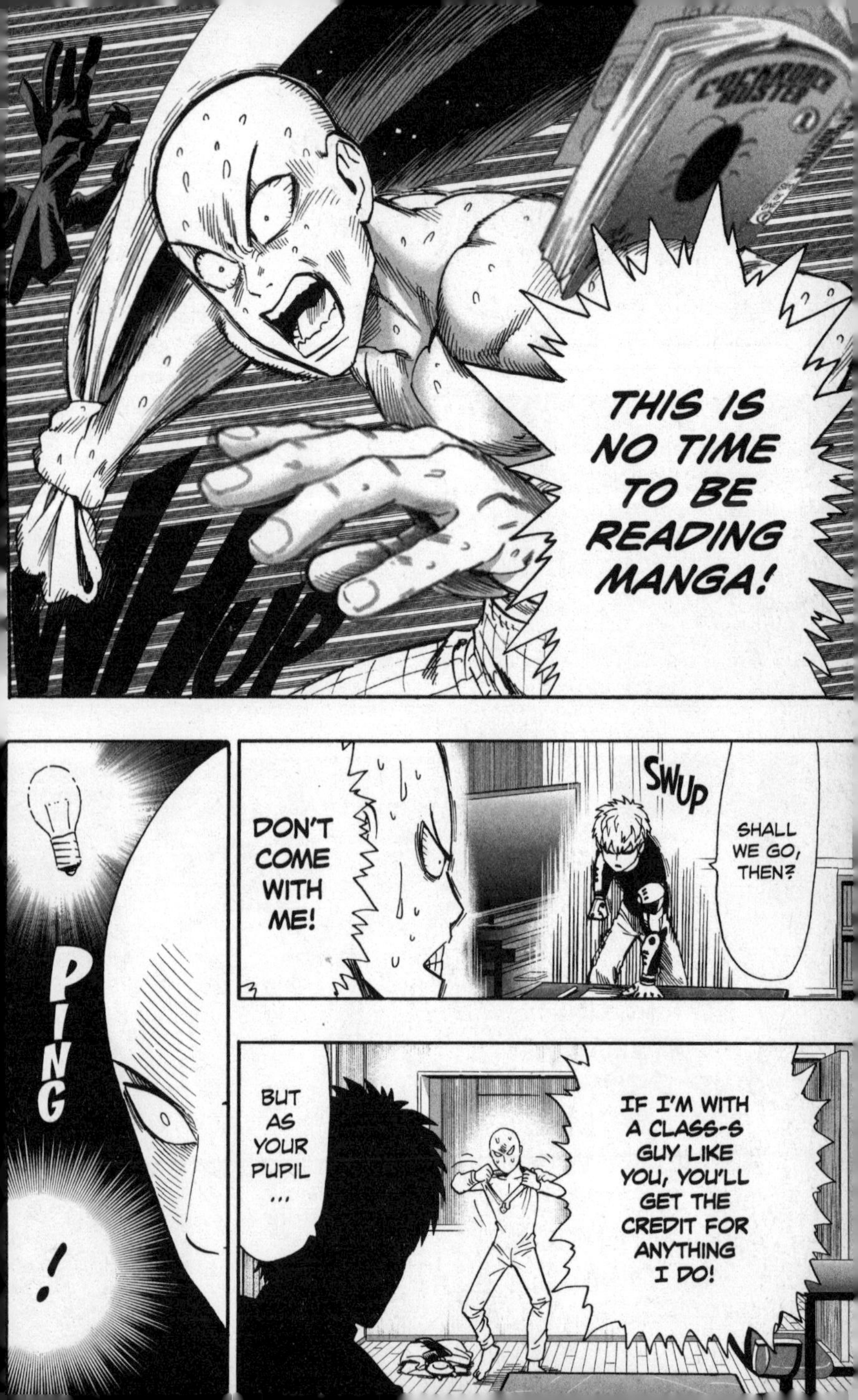
THIS IS NO TIME TO BE READING MANGA!
WHUP
SWUP
SHALL WE GO, THEN?
DON'T COME WITH ME!
IF I'M WITH A CLASS-S GUY LIKE YOU, YOU'LL GET THE CREDIT FOR ANYTHING I DO!
BUT AS YOUR PUPIL ...
PING
!

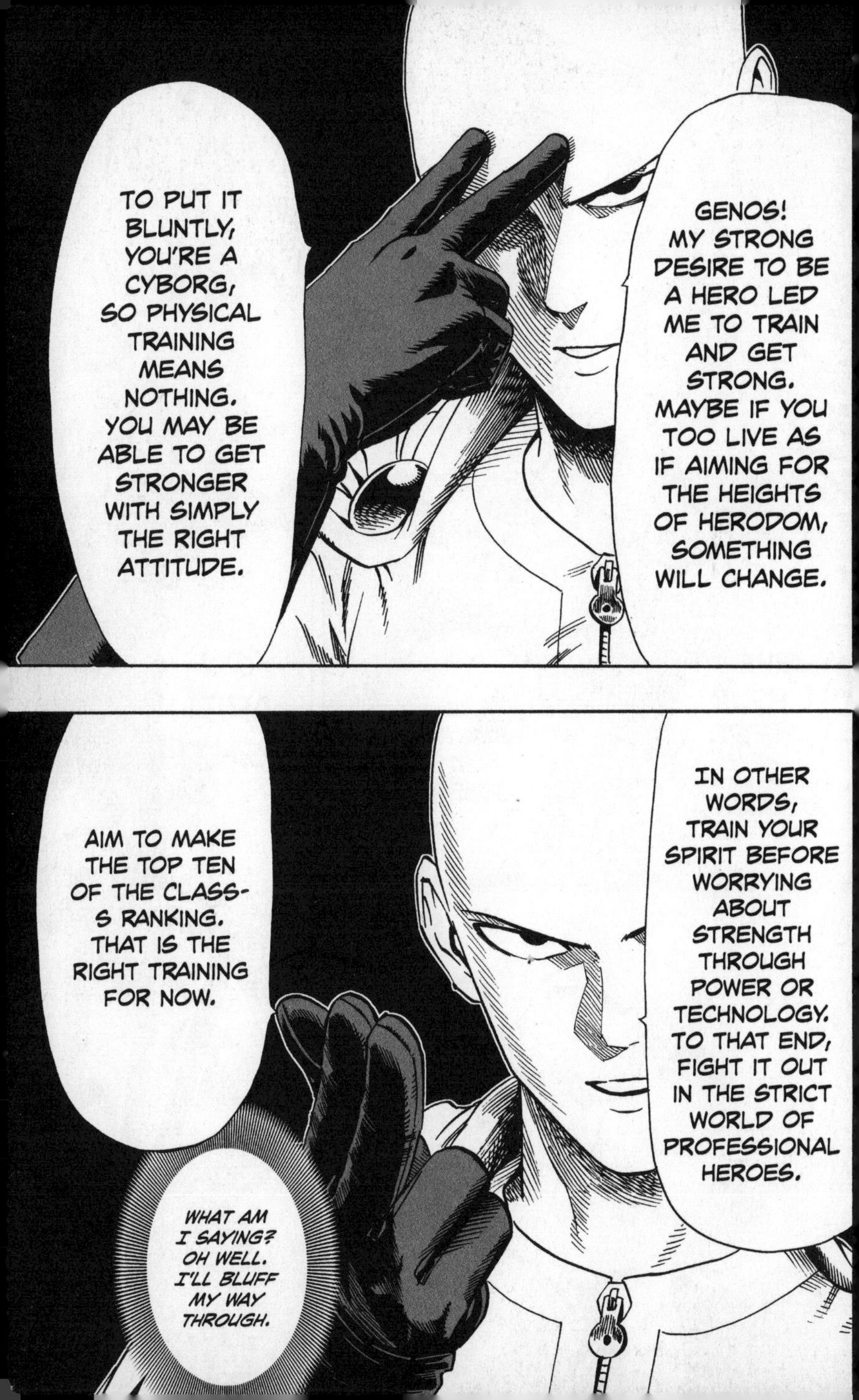
GENOS! MY STRONG DESIRE TO BE A HERO LED ME TO TRAIN AND GET STRONG. MAYBE IF YOU TOO LIVE AS IF AIMING FOR THE HEIGHTS OF HERODOM, SOMETHING WILL CHANGE.
TO PUT IT BLUNTLY, YOU'RE A CYBORG, SO PHYSICAL TRAINING MEANS NOTHING. YOU MAY BE ABLE TO GET STRONGER WITH SIMPLY THE RIGHT ATTITUDE.
IN OTHER WORDS, TRAIN YOUR SPIRIT BEFORE WORRYING ABOUT STRENGTH THROUGH POWER OR TECHNOLOGY. TO THAT END, FIGHT IT OUT IN THE STRICT WORLD OF PROFESSIONAL HEROES.
AIM TO MAKE THE TOP TEN OF THE CLASS-S RANKING. THAT IS THE RIGHT TRAINING FOR NOW.
WHAT AM I SAYING? OH WELL. I'LL BLUFF MY WAY THROUGH.

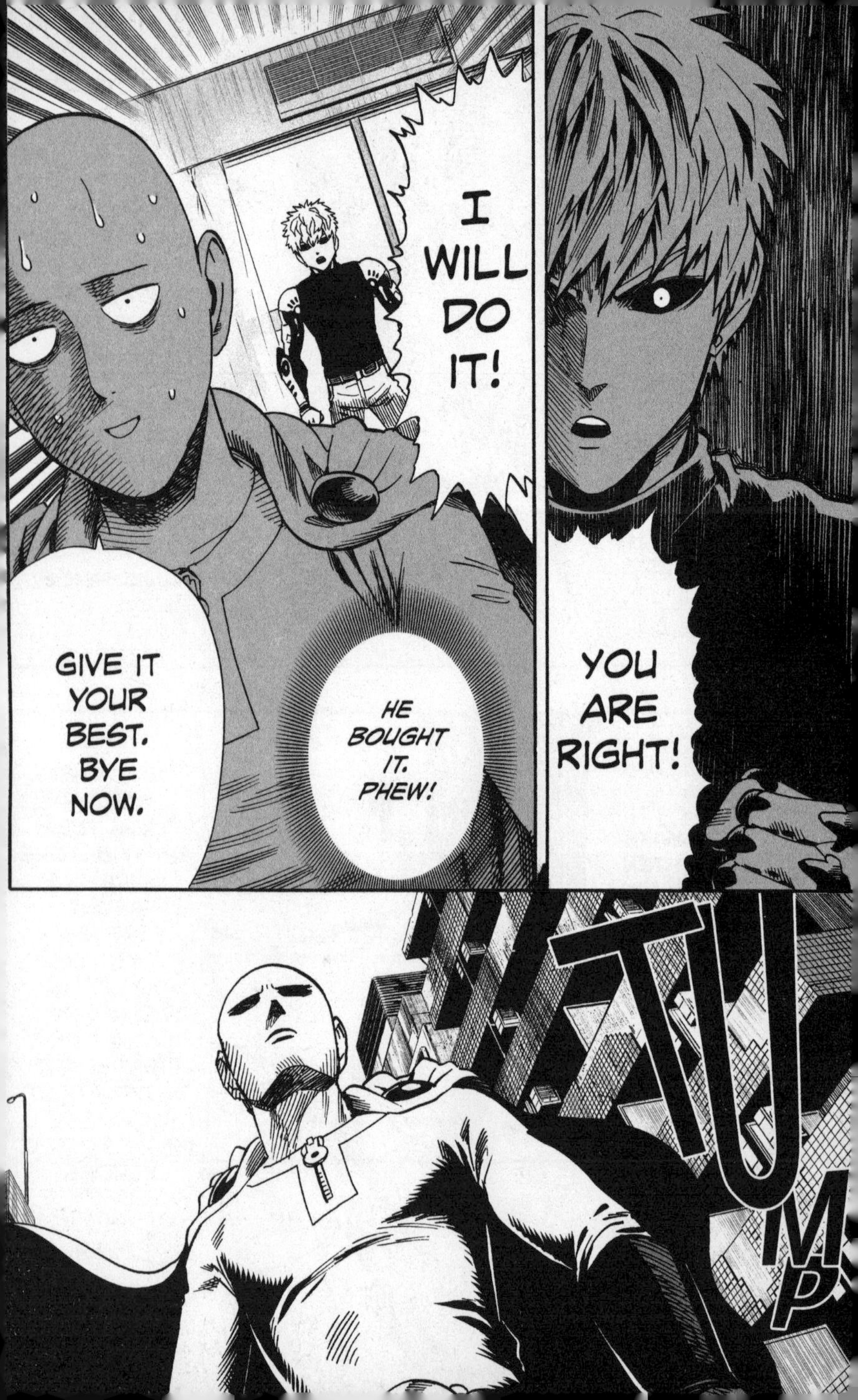
YOU ARE RIGHT!
I WILL DO IT!
GIVE IT YOUR BEST. BYE NOW.
HE BOUGHT IT. PHEW!
TUMP

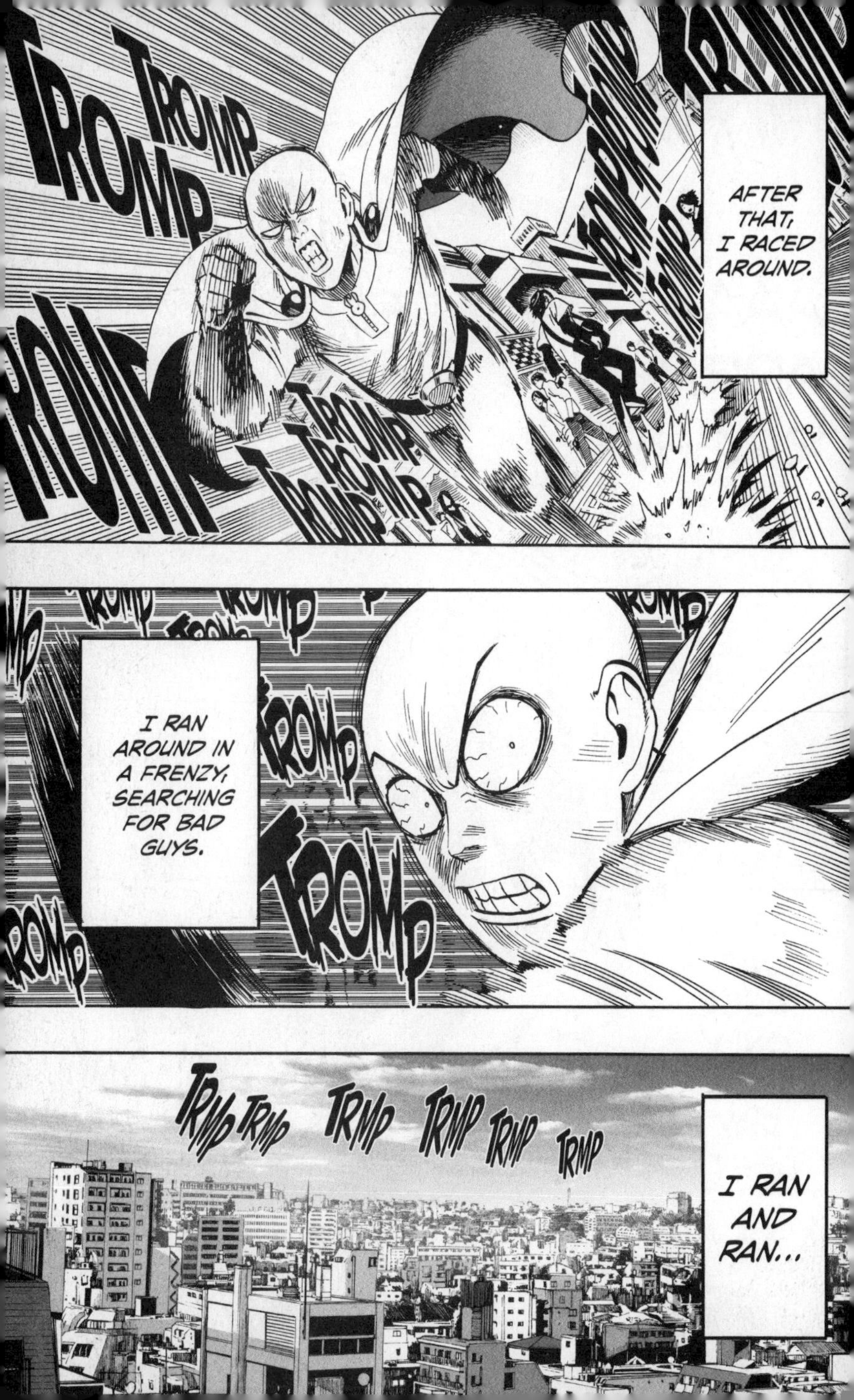
AFTER THAT, I RACED AROUND.
TROMP TROMP
TROMP TROMP TROMP
I RAN AROUND IN A FRENZY, SEARCHING FOR BAD GUYS.
TROMP
TROMP
I RAN AND RAN...
TRMP TRMP TRMP TRMP TRMP TRMP

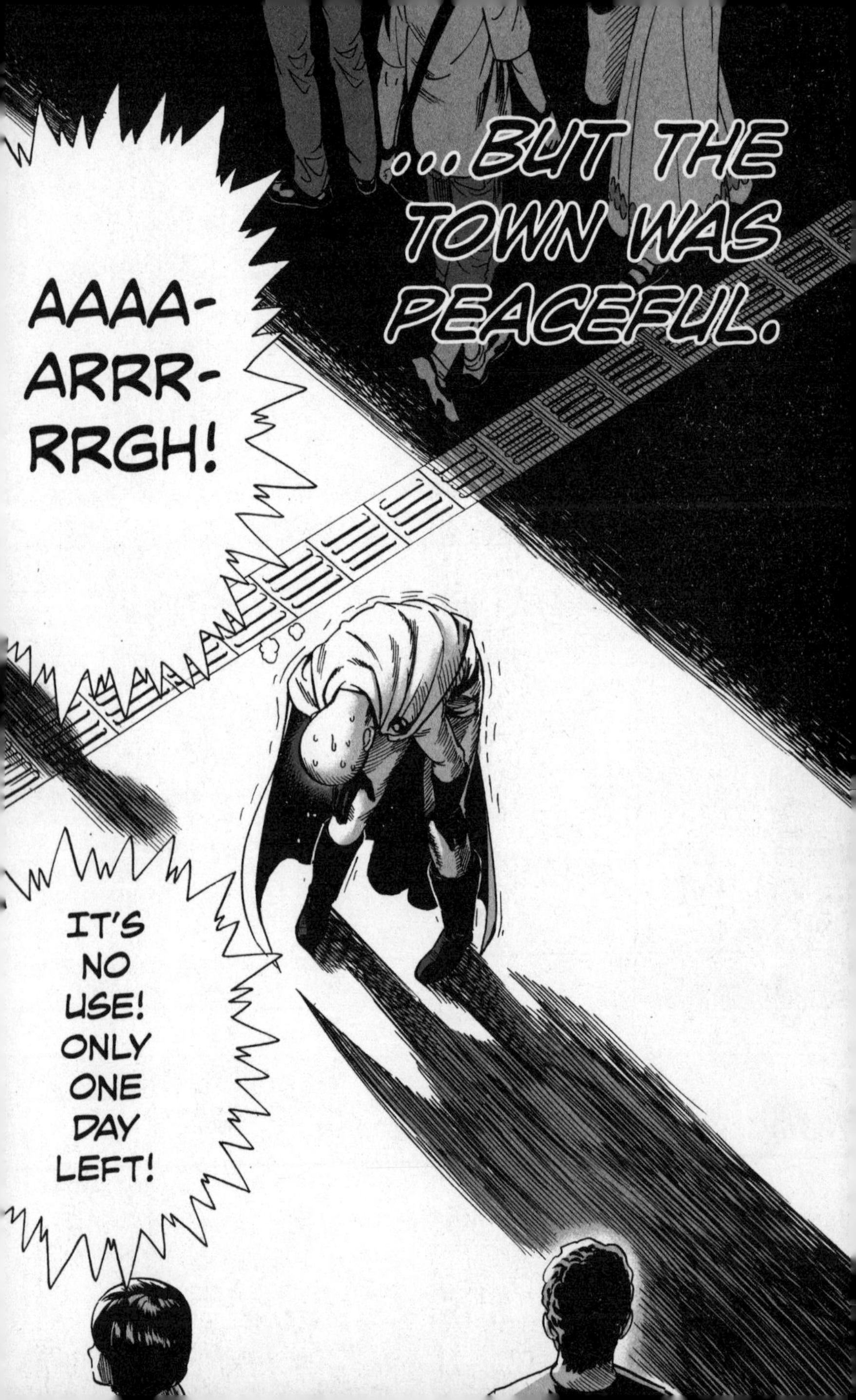
...BUT THE TOWN WAS PEACEFUL.
AAAA-ARRR-RRGH!
IT'S NO USE! ONLY ONE DAY LEFT!

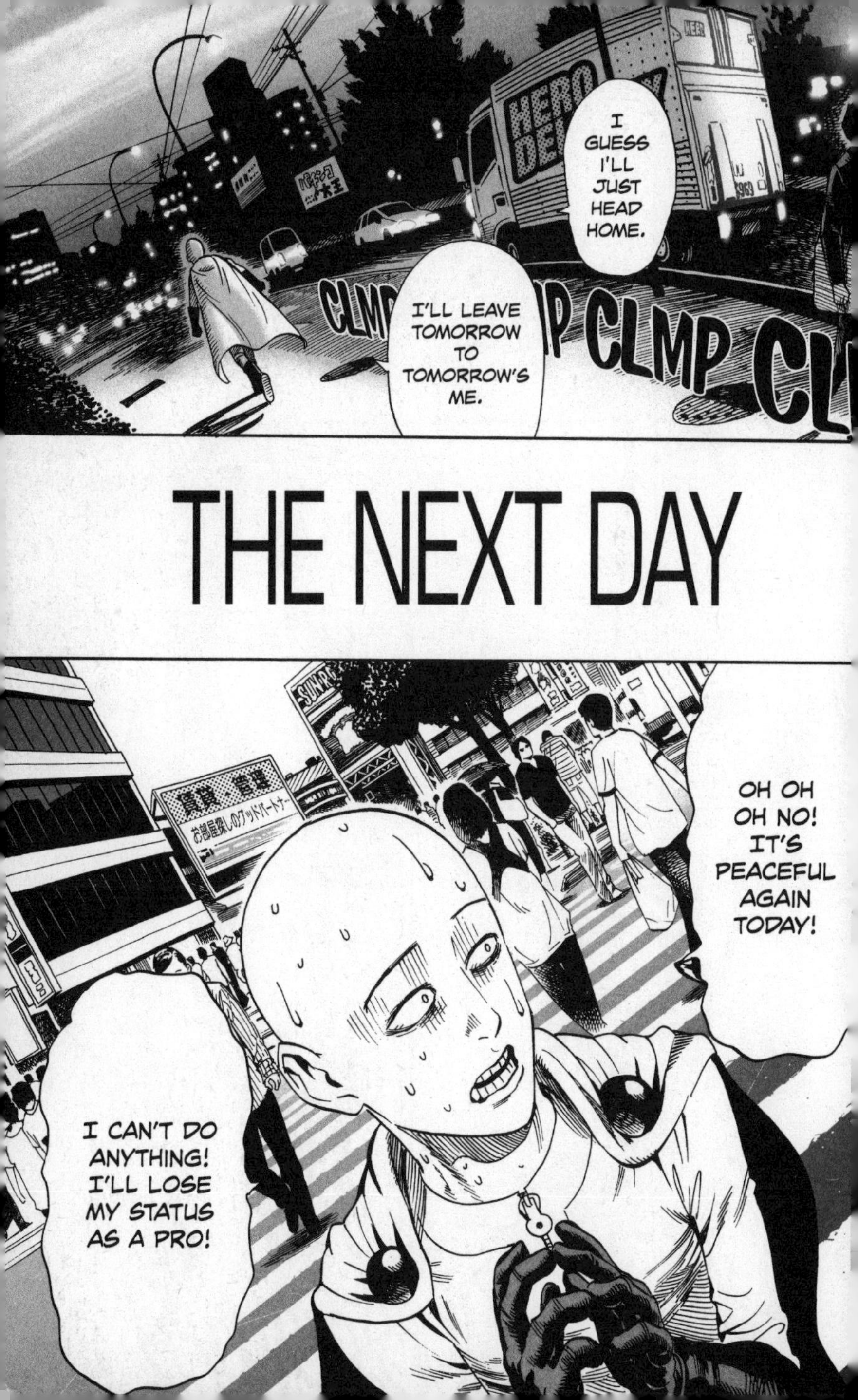
I GUESS I'LL JUST HEAD HOME.
I'LL LEAVE TOMORROW TO TOMORROW'S ME.
CLMP CLMP
THE NEXT DAY
OH OH OH NO! IT'S PEACEFUL AGAIN TODAY!
I CAN'T DO ANYTHING! I'LL LOSE MY STATUS AS A PRO!

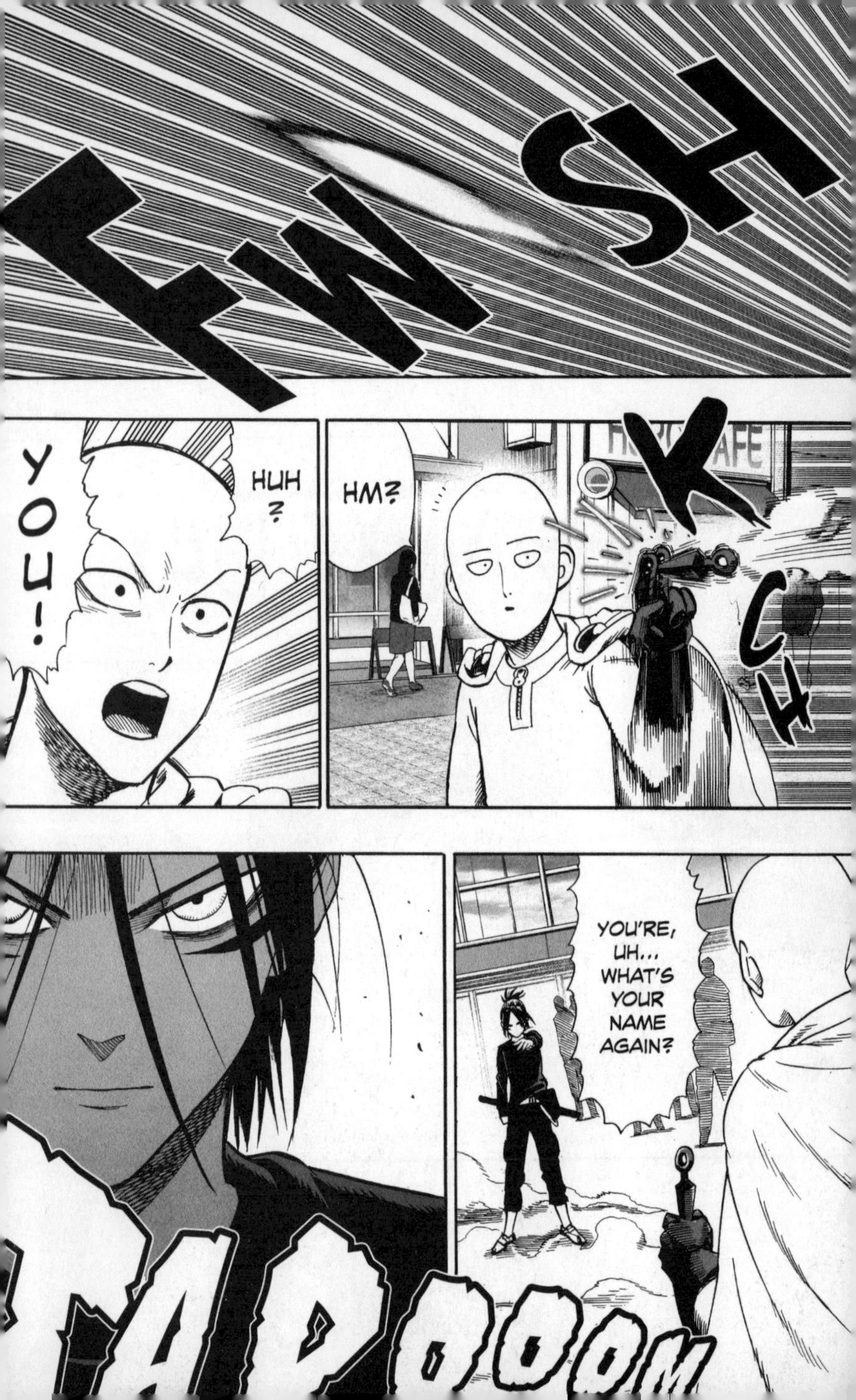
FWISH
KCH
HM?
HUH?
YOU!
YOU'RE, UH... WHAT'S YOUR NAME AGAIN?
ADOOOM

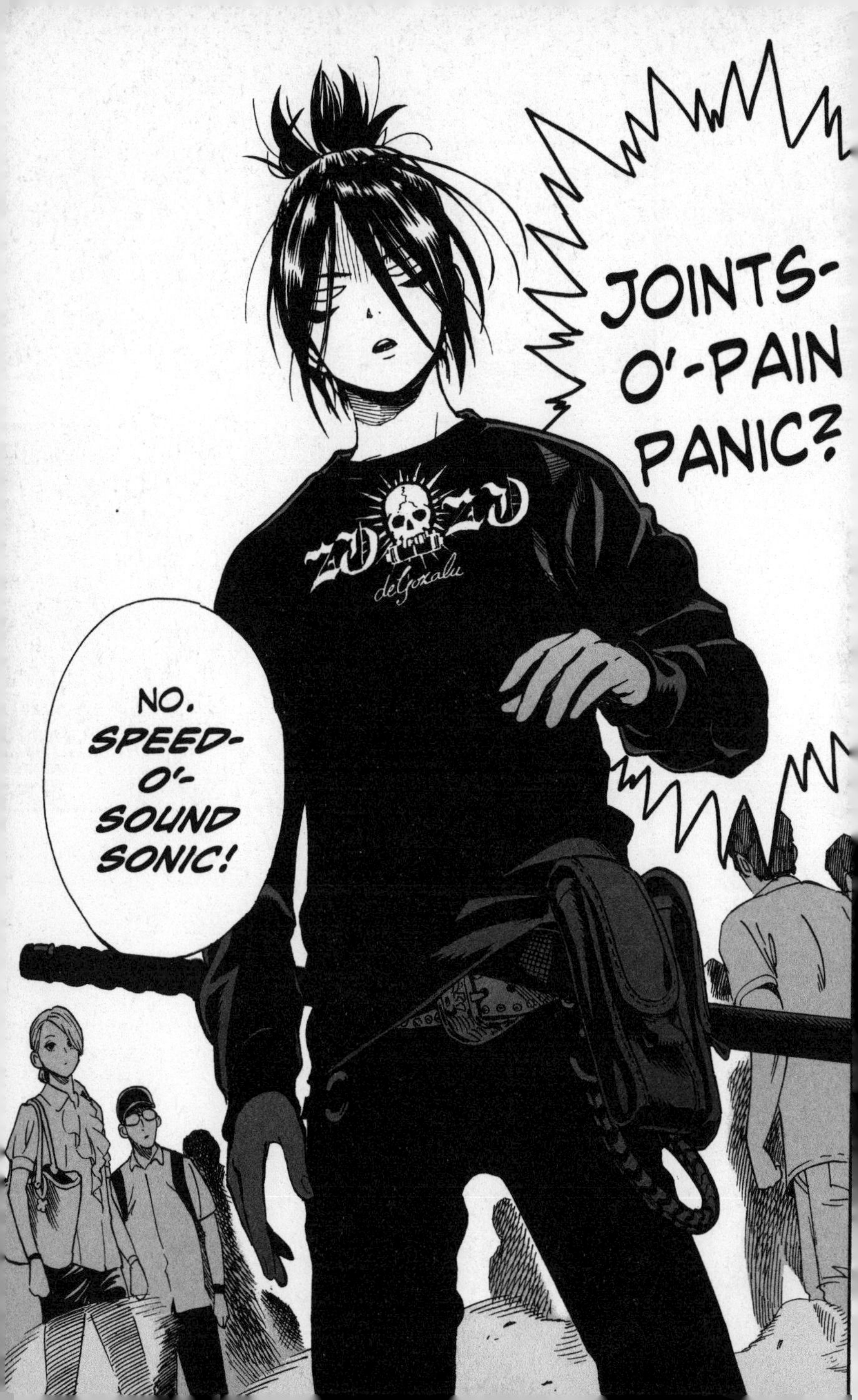
JOINTS-O'-PAIN PANIC?
NO. SPEED-O'-SOUND SONIC!

LET'S EAT

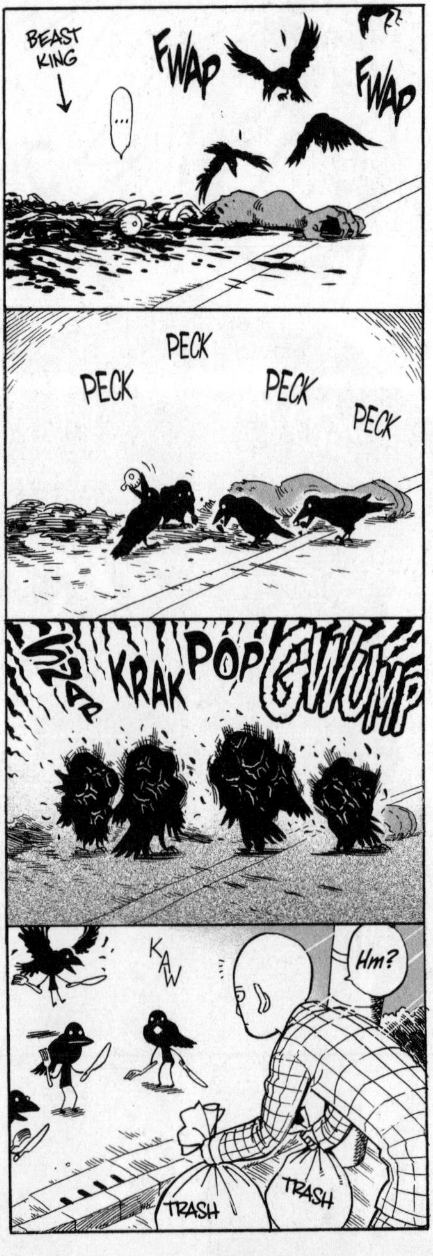
BEAST KING
FWAP
FWAP
...
PECK
PECK
PECK
PECK
SNAP
KRAK
POP
GWUMP
KAW
Hm?
TRASH
TRASH

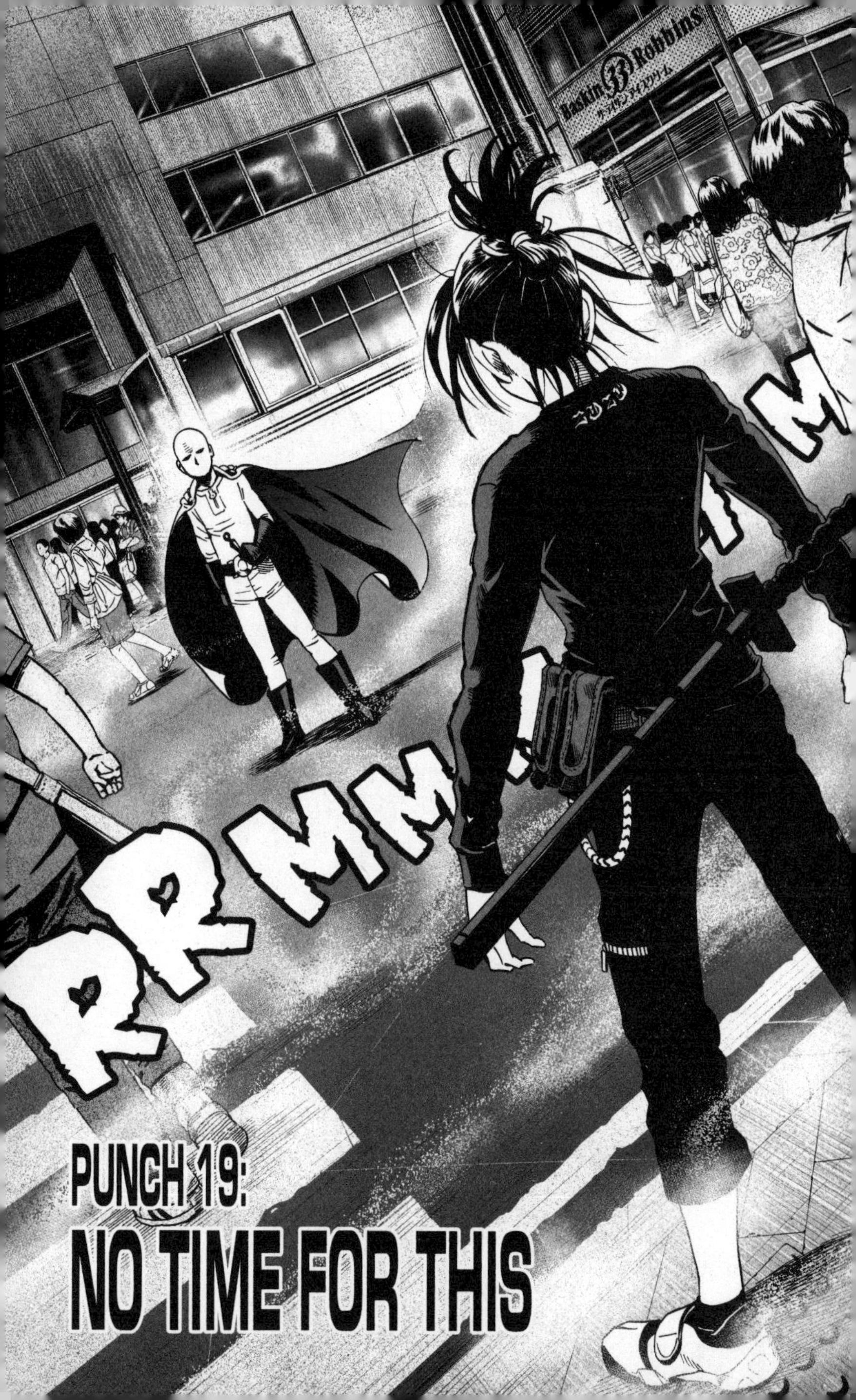
Baskin Robbins
RRMMMM

PUNCH 19: NO TIME FOR THIS

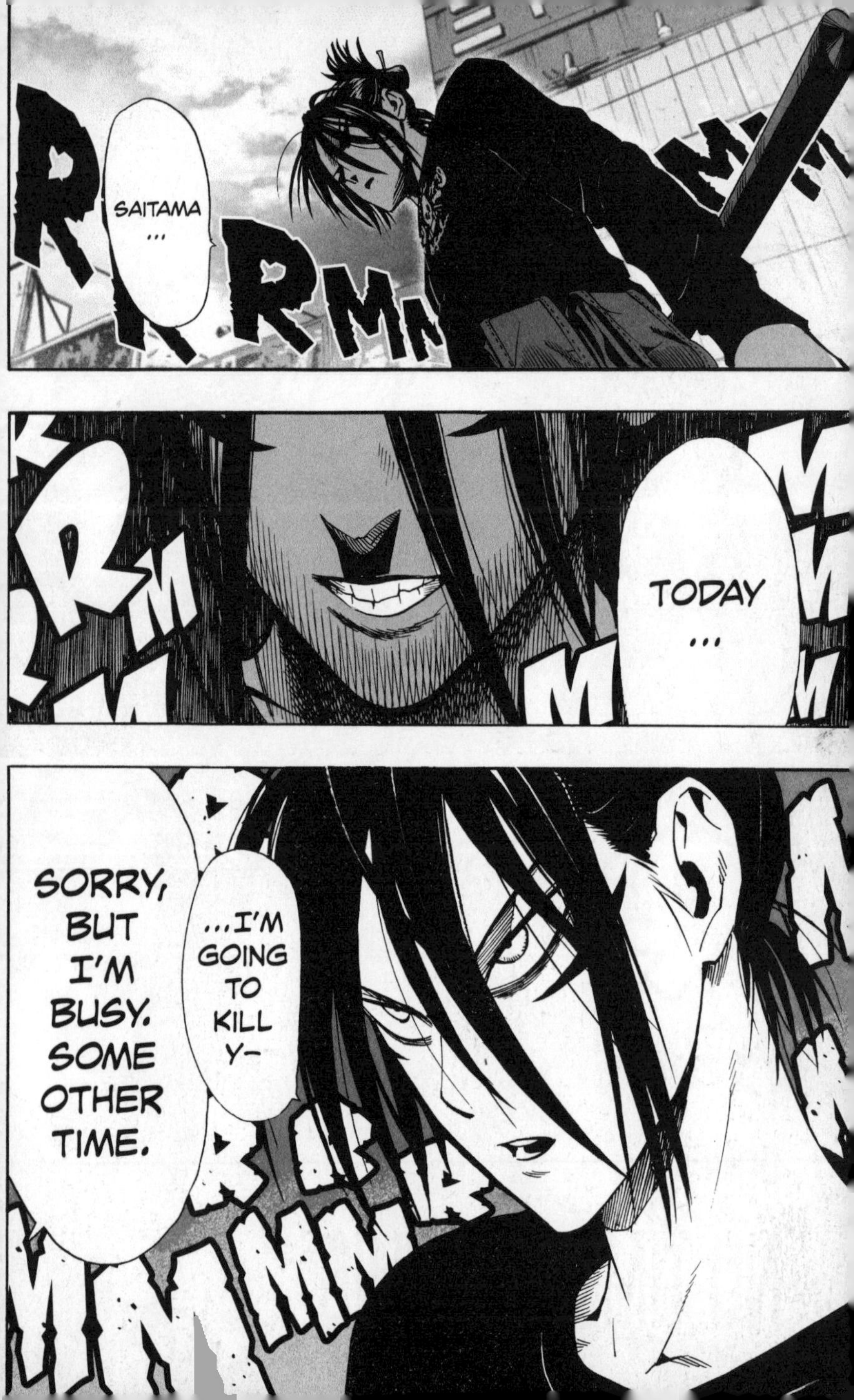
SAITAMA ...
TODAY ...
...I'M GOING TO KILL Y–
SORRY, BUT I'M BUSY. SOME OTHER TIME.

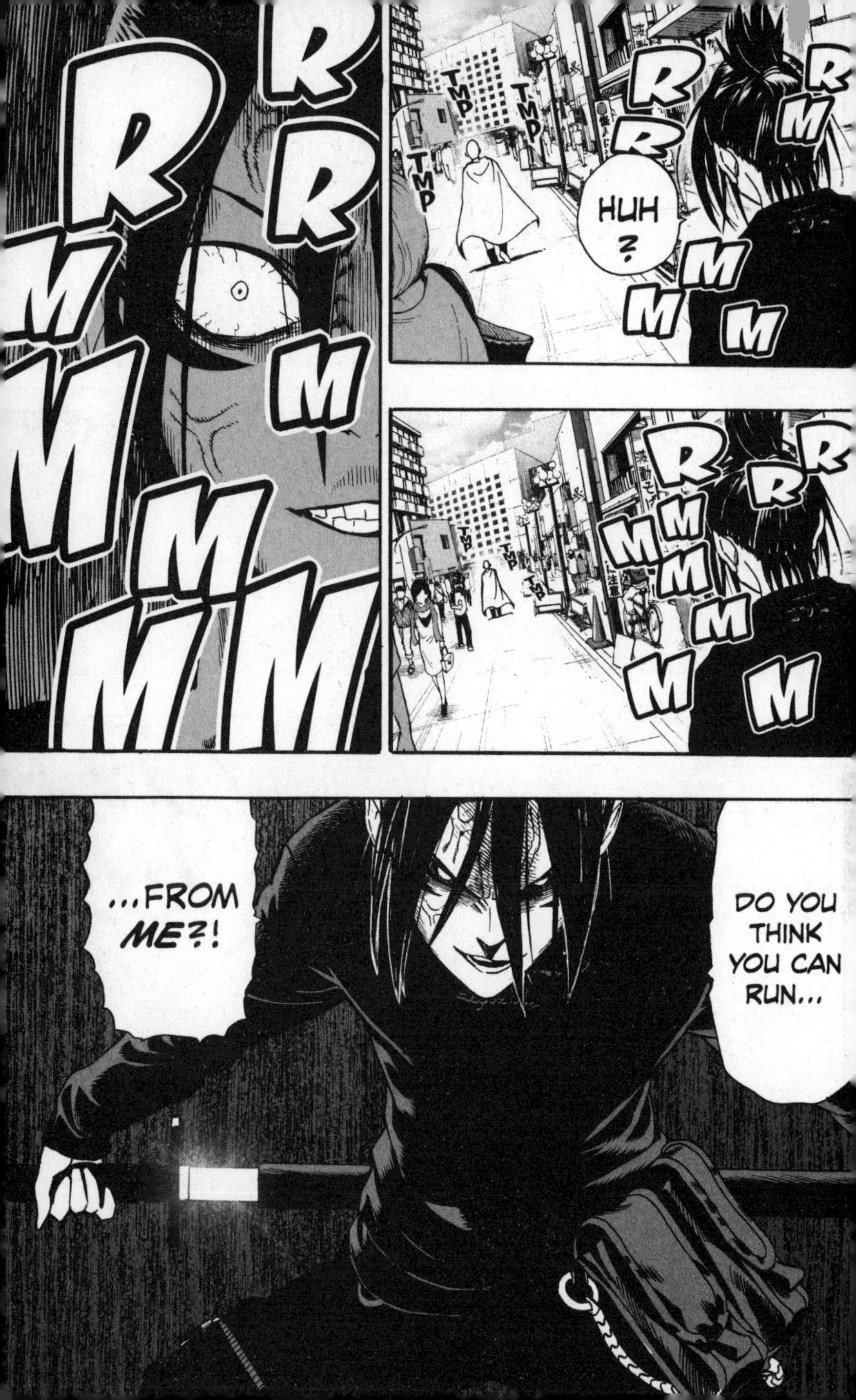
RRMMM
TMP TMP TMP TMP
HUH?
RRMMMM
RRRMMMMMMM
TMP TMP TMP
RRRMMMMMMMM
DO YOU THINK YOU CAN RUN...
...FROM *ME*?!

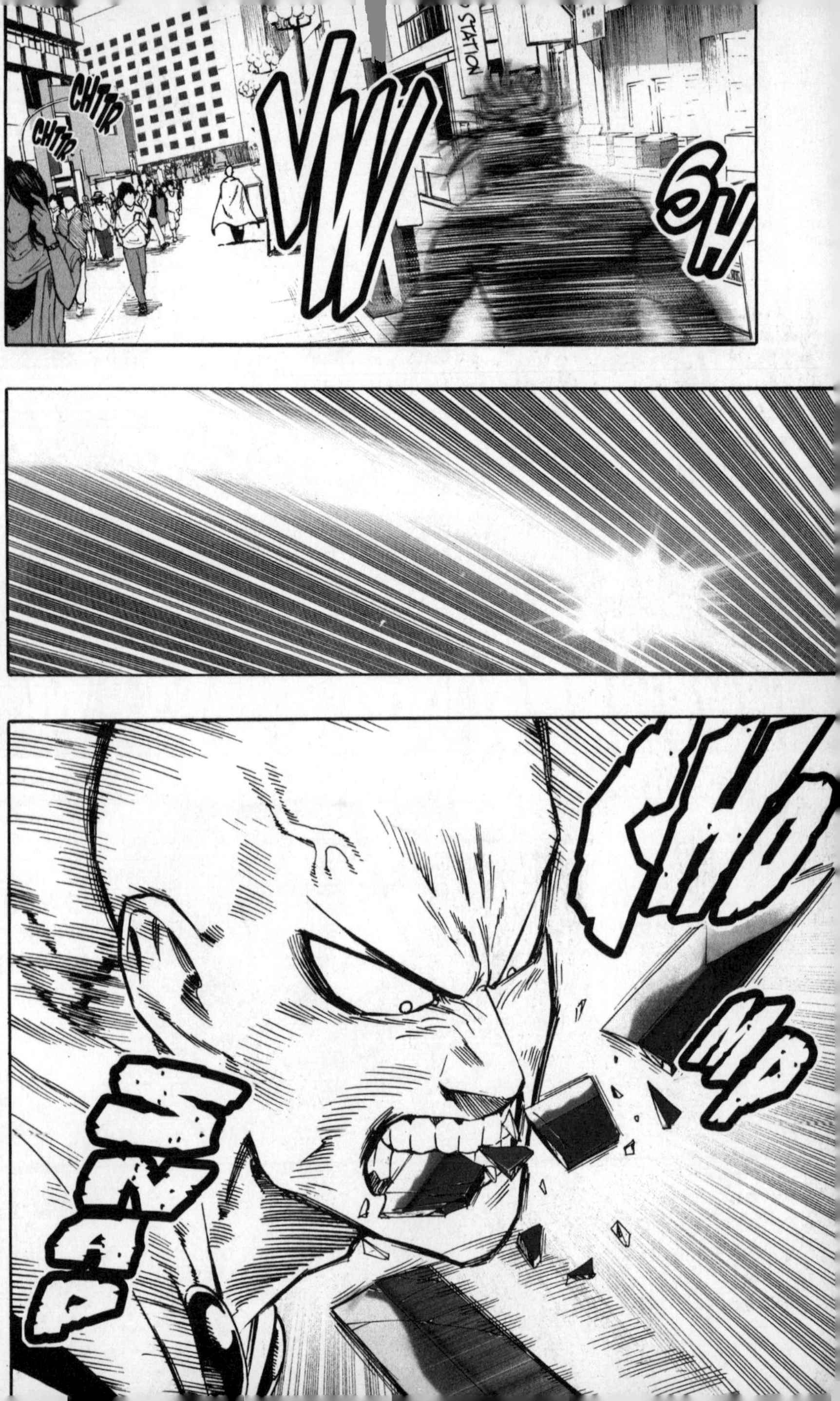
CHTTR
CHTTR
STATION
VWW
SH
CHOMP
PAKU

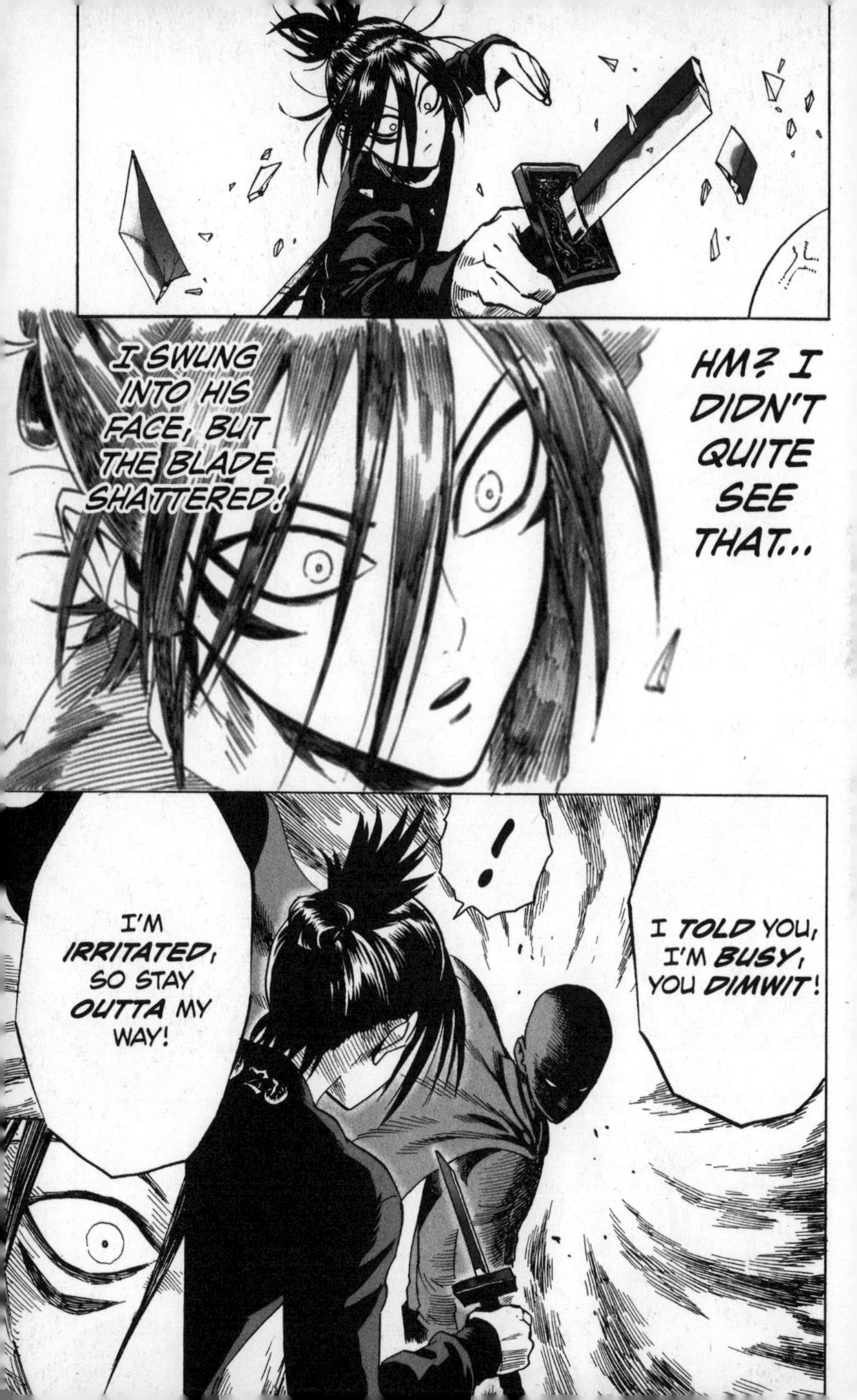
HM? I DIDN'T QUITE SEE THAT...
I SWUNG INTO HIS FACE, BUT THE BLADE SHATTERED!
I TOLD YOU, I'M BUSY, YOU DIMWIT!
I'M IRRITATED, SO STAY OUTTA MY WAY!

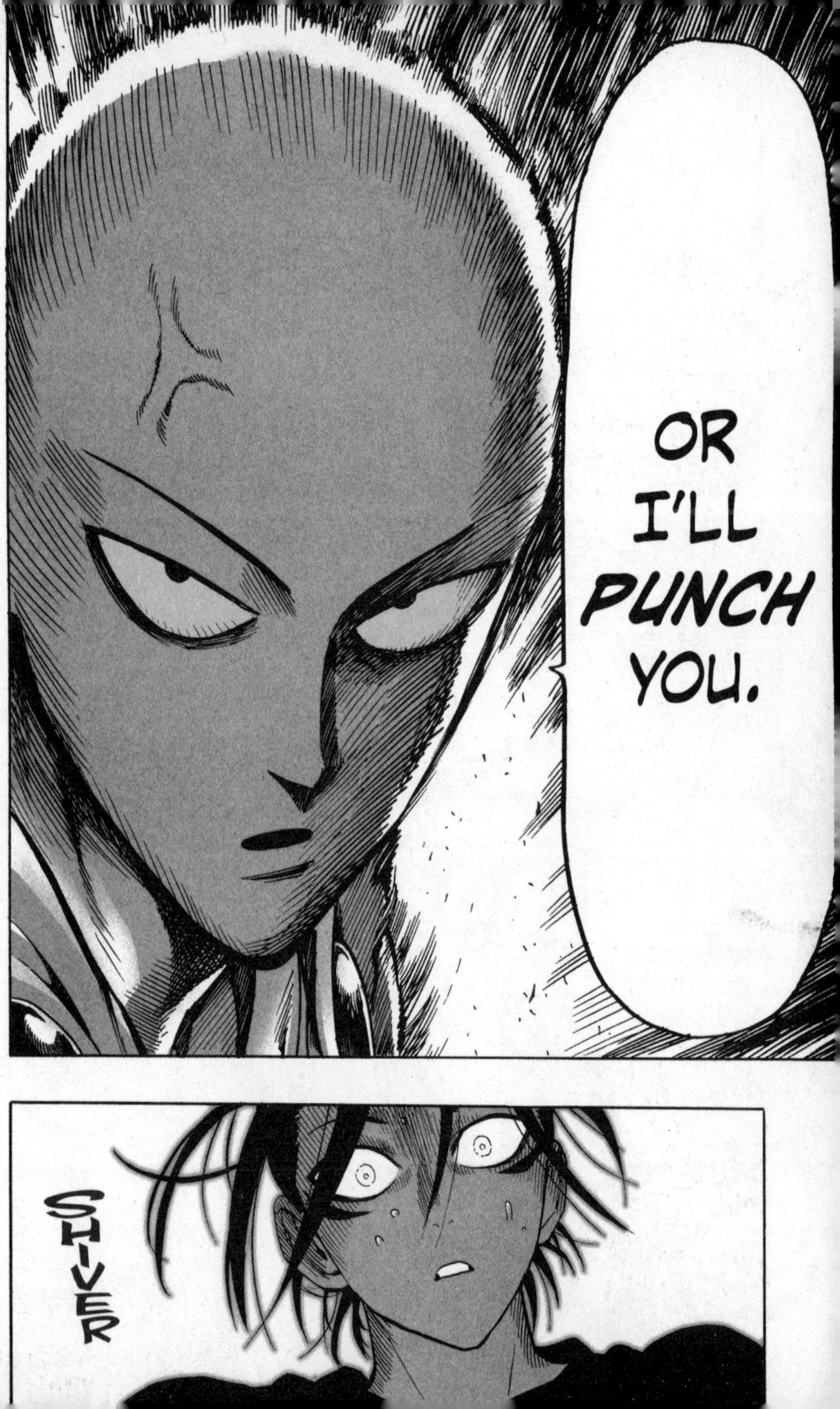
OR I'LL PUNCH YOU.
SHIVER

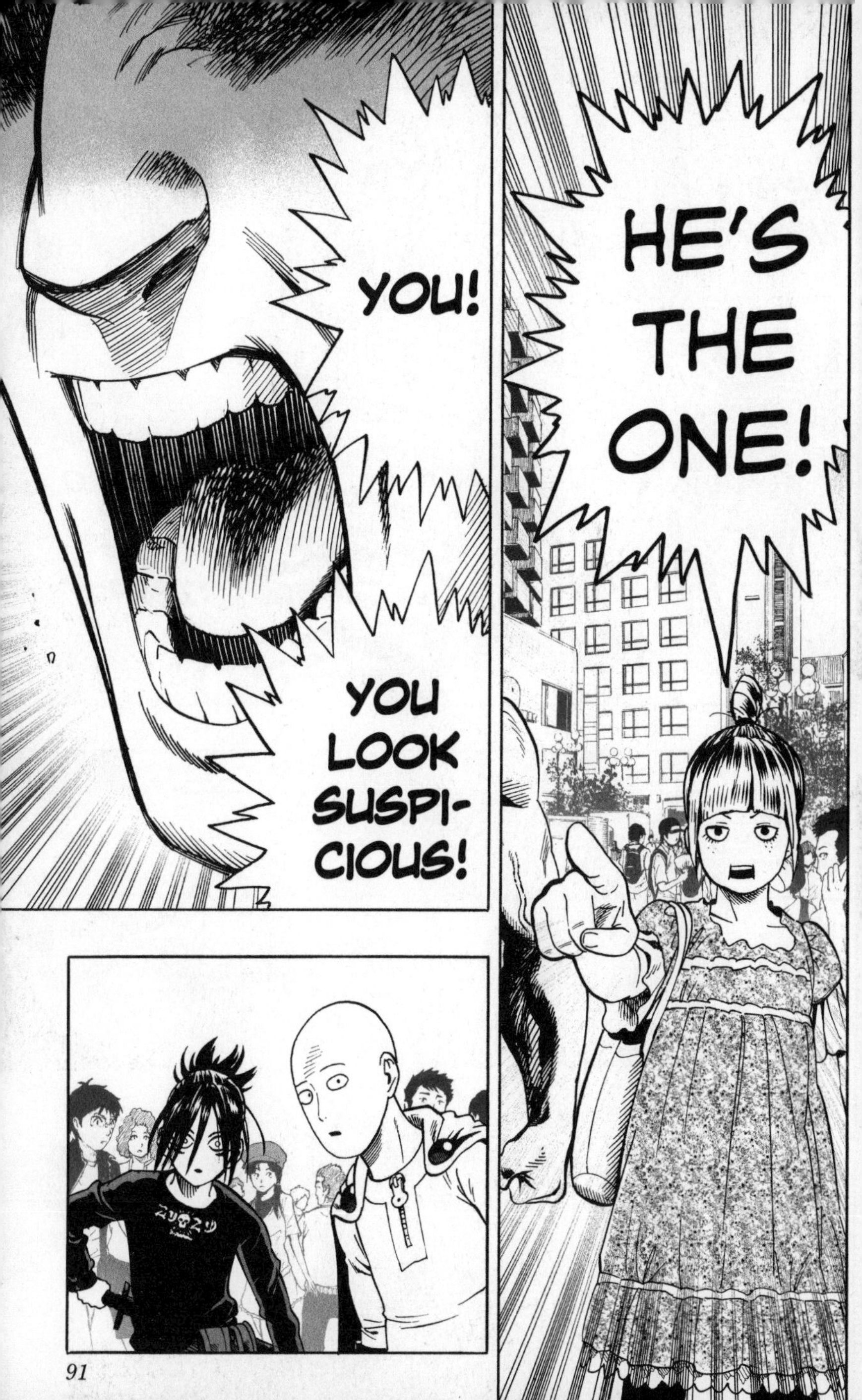
HE'S THE ONE!
YOU!
YOU LOOK SUSPI-CIOUS!

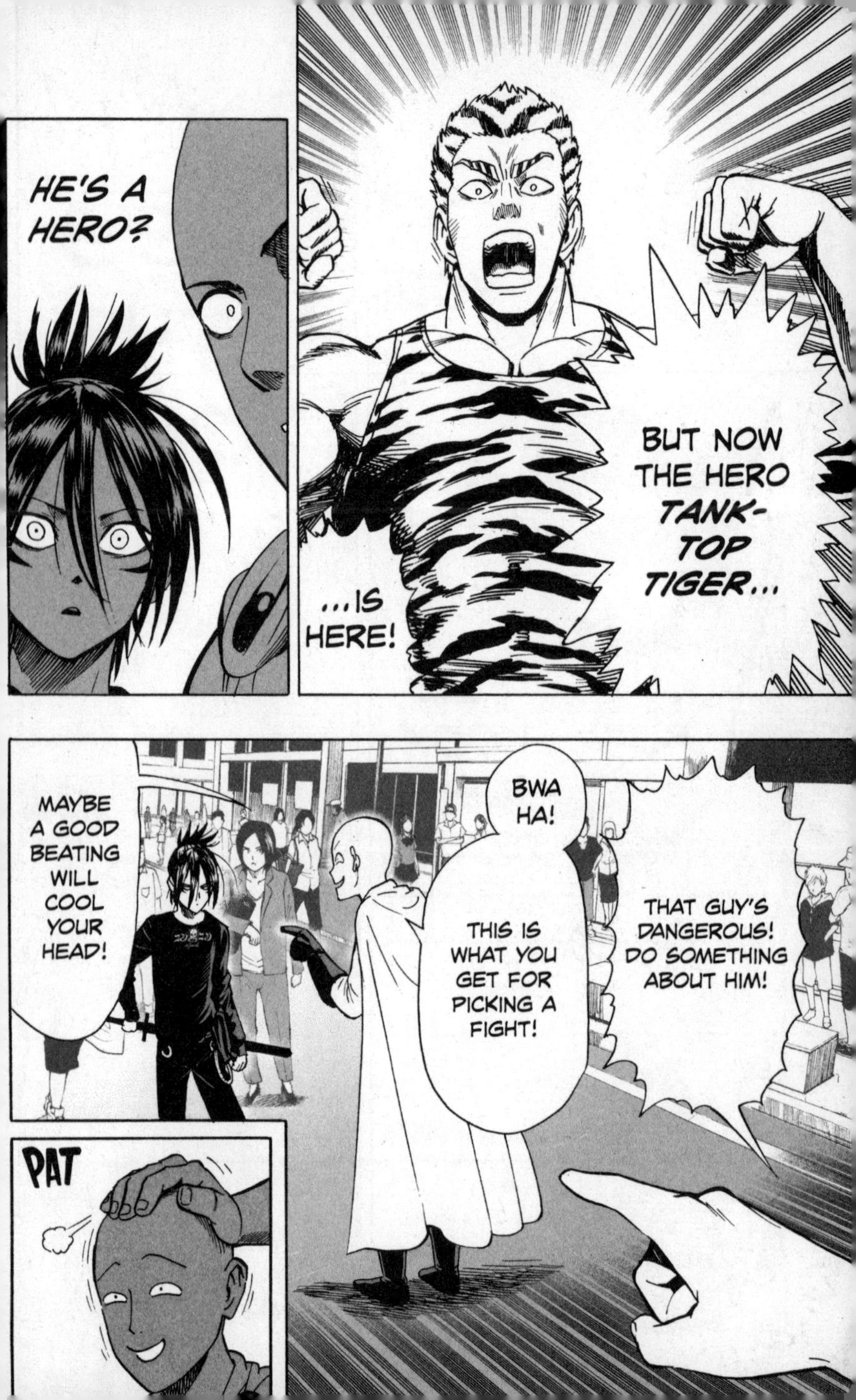
BUT NOW THE HERO TANK-TOP TIGER...
...IS HERE!
HE'S A HERO?
THAT GUY'S DANGEROUS! DO SOMETHING ABOUT HIM!
BWA HA!
THIS IS WHAT YOU GET FOR PICKING A FIGHT!
MAYBE A GOOD BEATING WILL COOL YOUR HEAD!
PAT

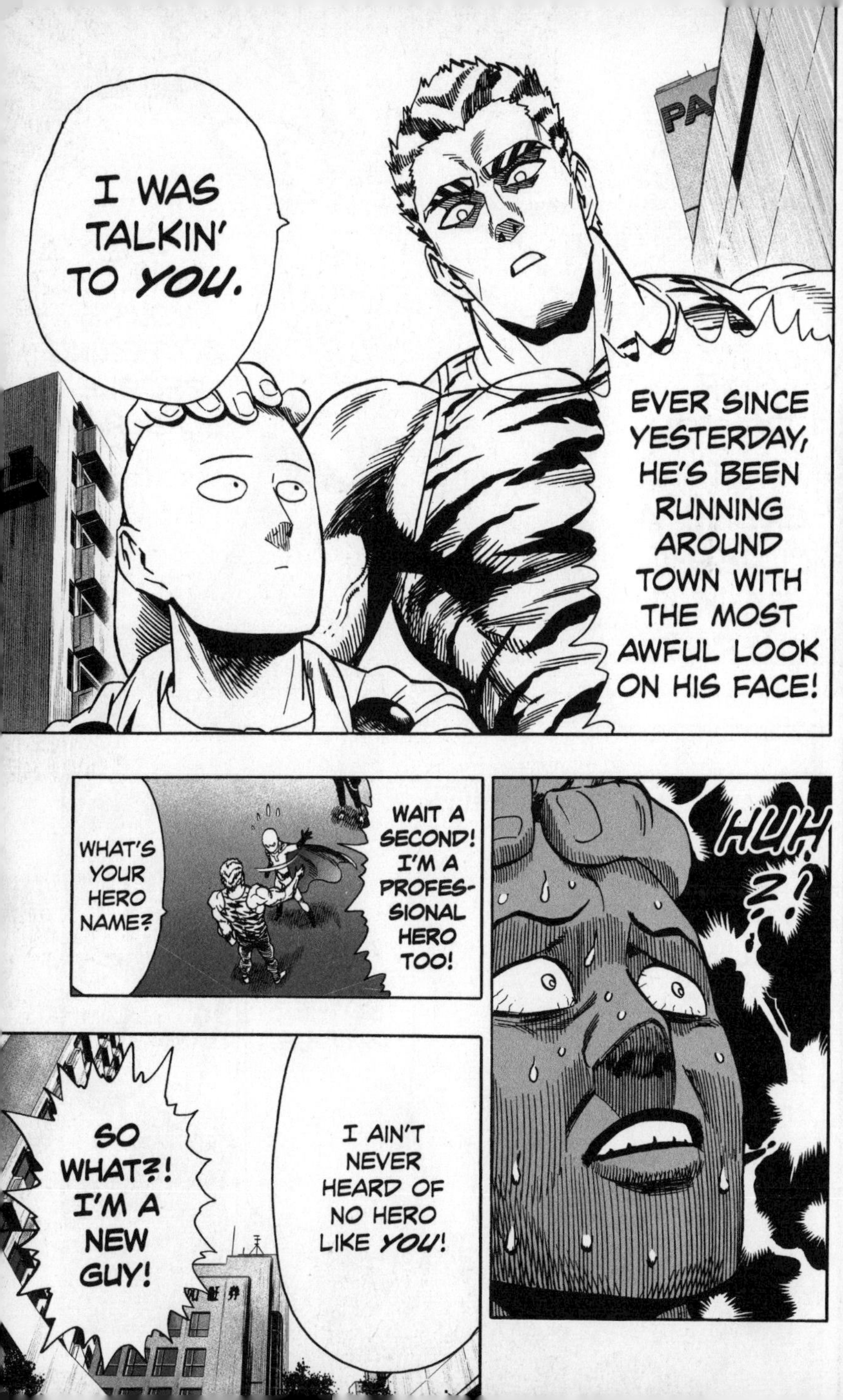
I WAS TALKIN' TO YOU.
EVER SINCE YESTERDAY, HE'S BEEN RUNNING AROUND TOWN WITH THE MOST AWFUL LOOK ON HIS FACE!
HUH?!
WAIT A SECOND! I'M A PROFES-SIONAL HERO TOO!
WHAT'S YOUR HERO NAME?
I AIN'T NEVER HEARD OF NO HERO LIKE YOU!
SO WHAT?! I'M A NEW GUY!

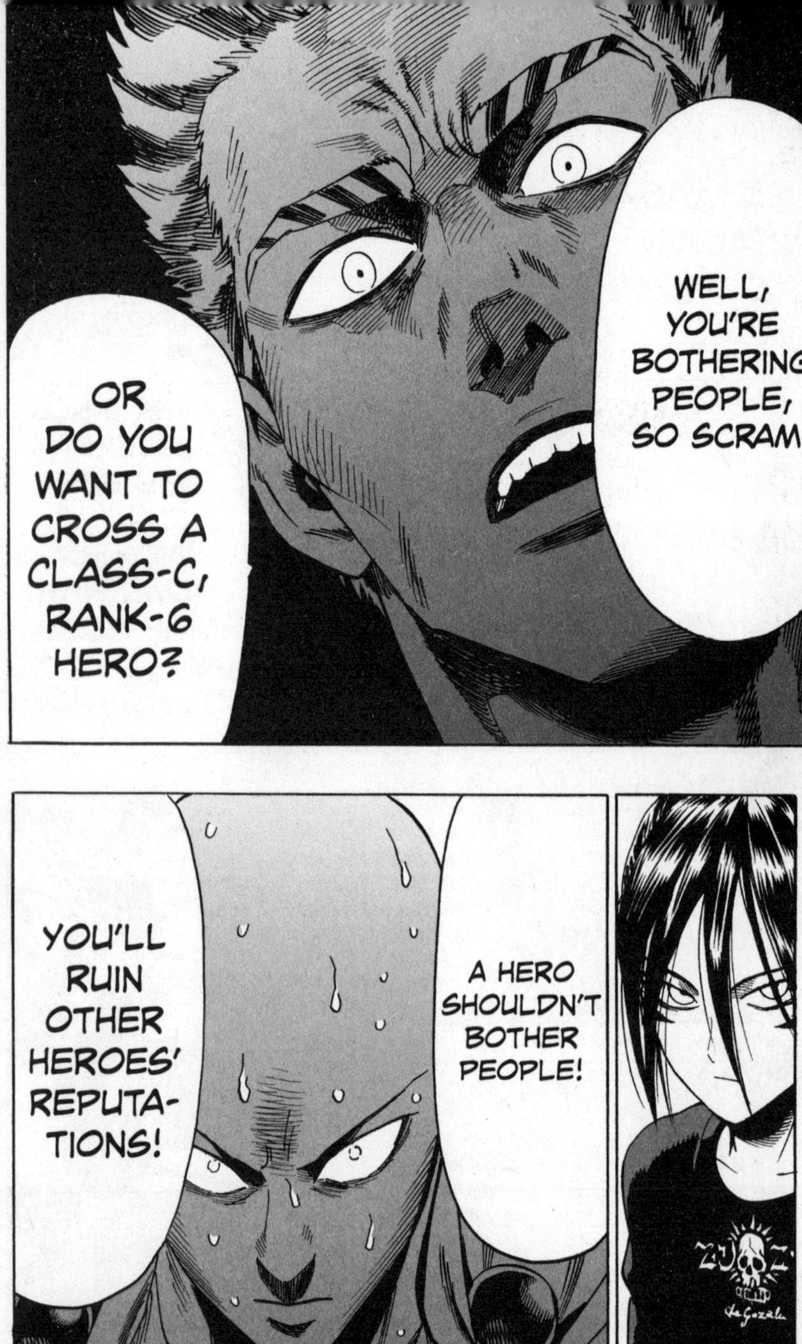
WELL, YOU'RE BOTHERING PEOPLE, SO SCRAM.
OR DO YOU WANT TO CROSS A CLASS-C, RANK-6 HERO?
A HERO SHOULDN'T BOTHER PEOPLE!
YOU'LL RUIN OTHER HEROES' REPUTA-TIONS!

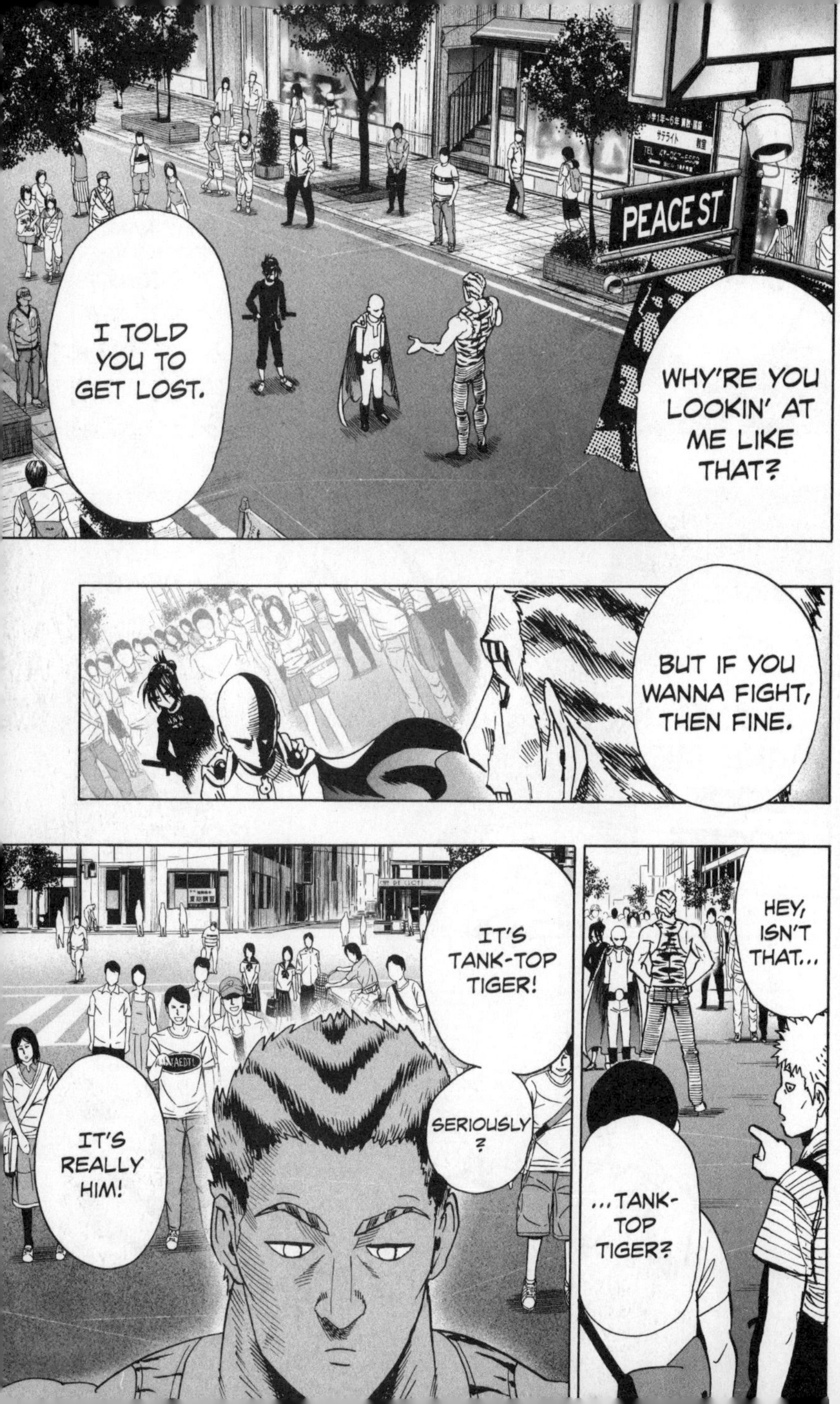
PEACE ST
WHY'RE YOU LOOKIN' AT ME LIKE THAT?
I TOLD YOU TO GET LOST.
BUT IF YOU WANNA FIGHT, THEN FINE.
HEY, ISN'T THAT...
...TANK-TOP TIGER?
IT'S TANK-TOP TIGER!
SERIOUSLY?
IT'S REALLY HIM!

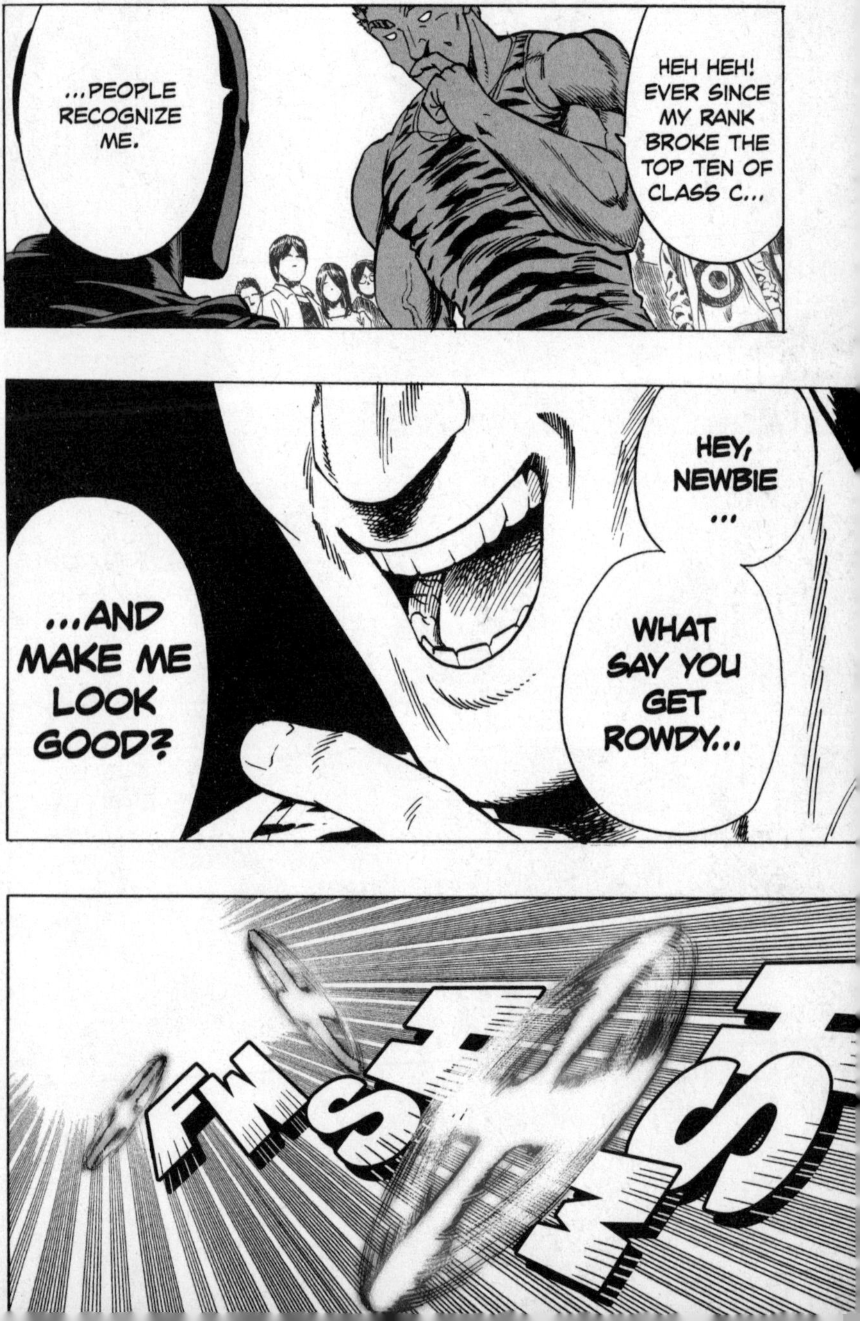
HEH HEH! EVER SINCE MY RANK BROKE THE TOP TEN OF CLASS C...
...PEOPLE RECOGNIZE ME.
HEY, NEWBIE ...
WHAT SAY YOU GET ROWDY...
...AND MAKE ME LOOK GOOD?
FWSH

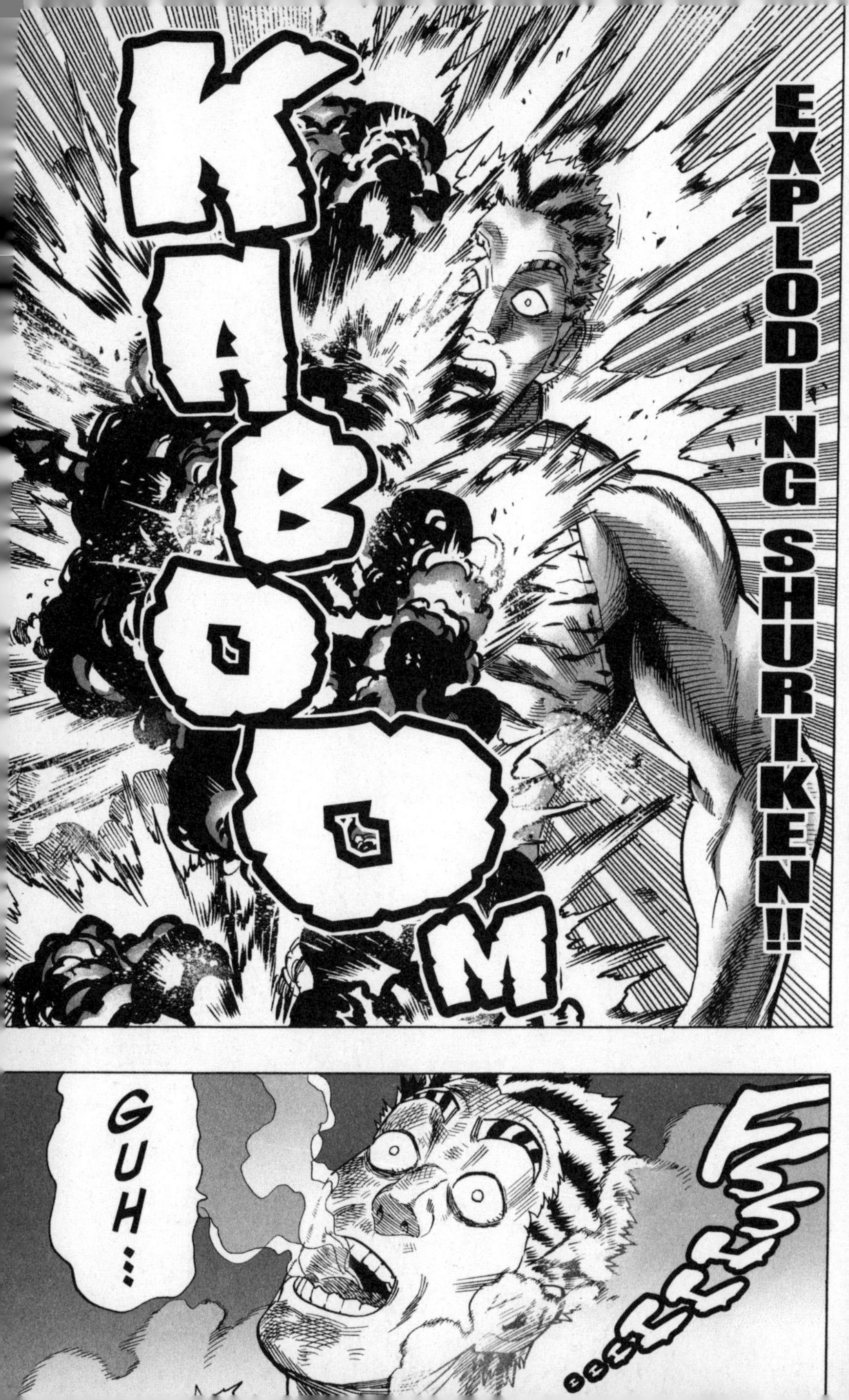
EXPLODING SHURIKEN!!
KABOOM
FSSHHH...
GUH...

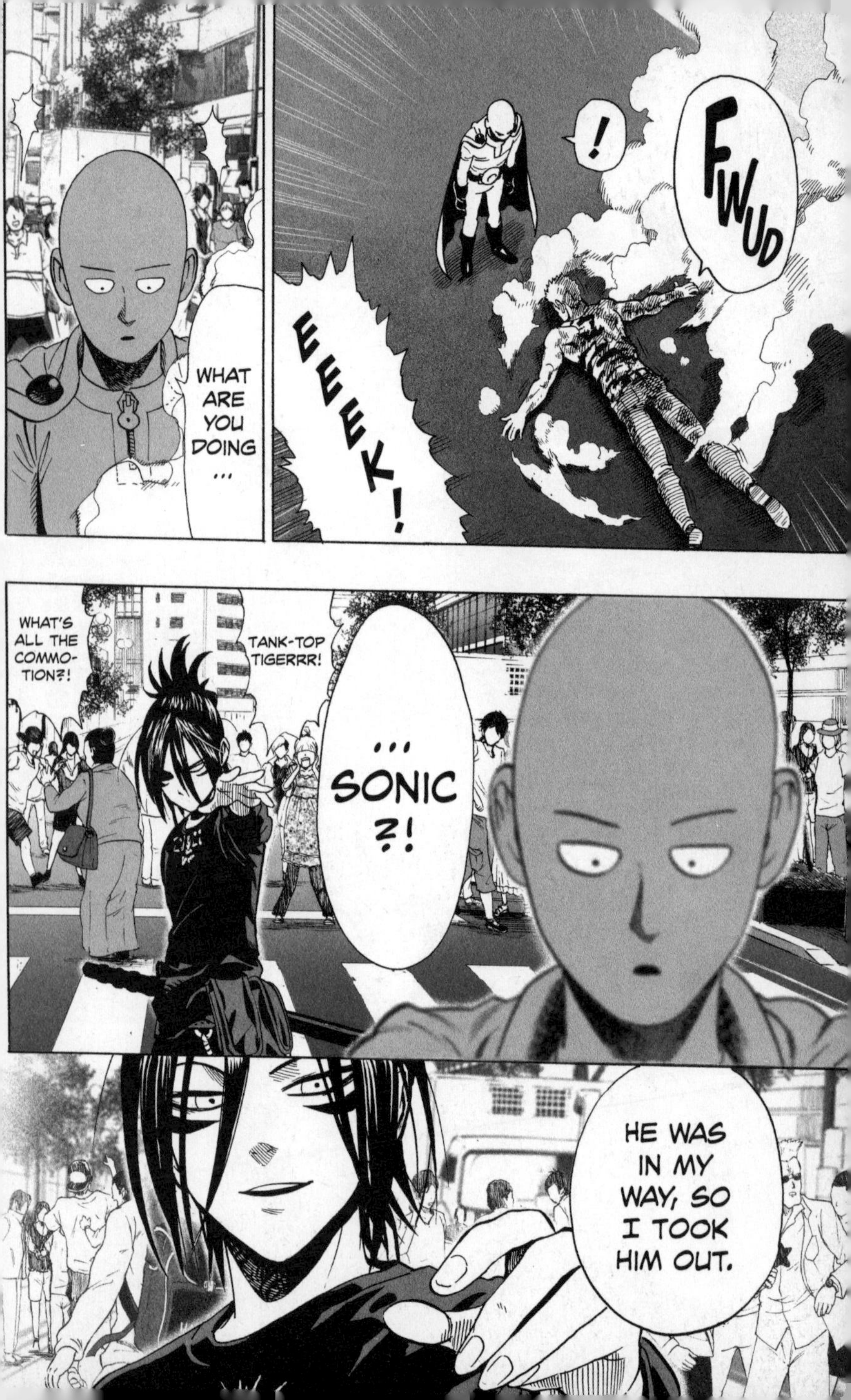
FWUD
!
EEEK!
WHAT ARE YOU DOING ...
... SONIC ?!
TANK-TOP TIGERRR!
WHAT'S ALL THE COMMOTION?!
HE WAS IN MY WAY, SO I TOOK HIM OUT.

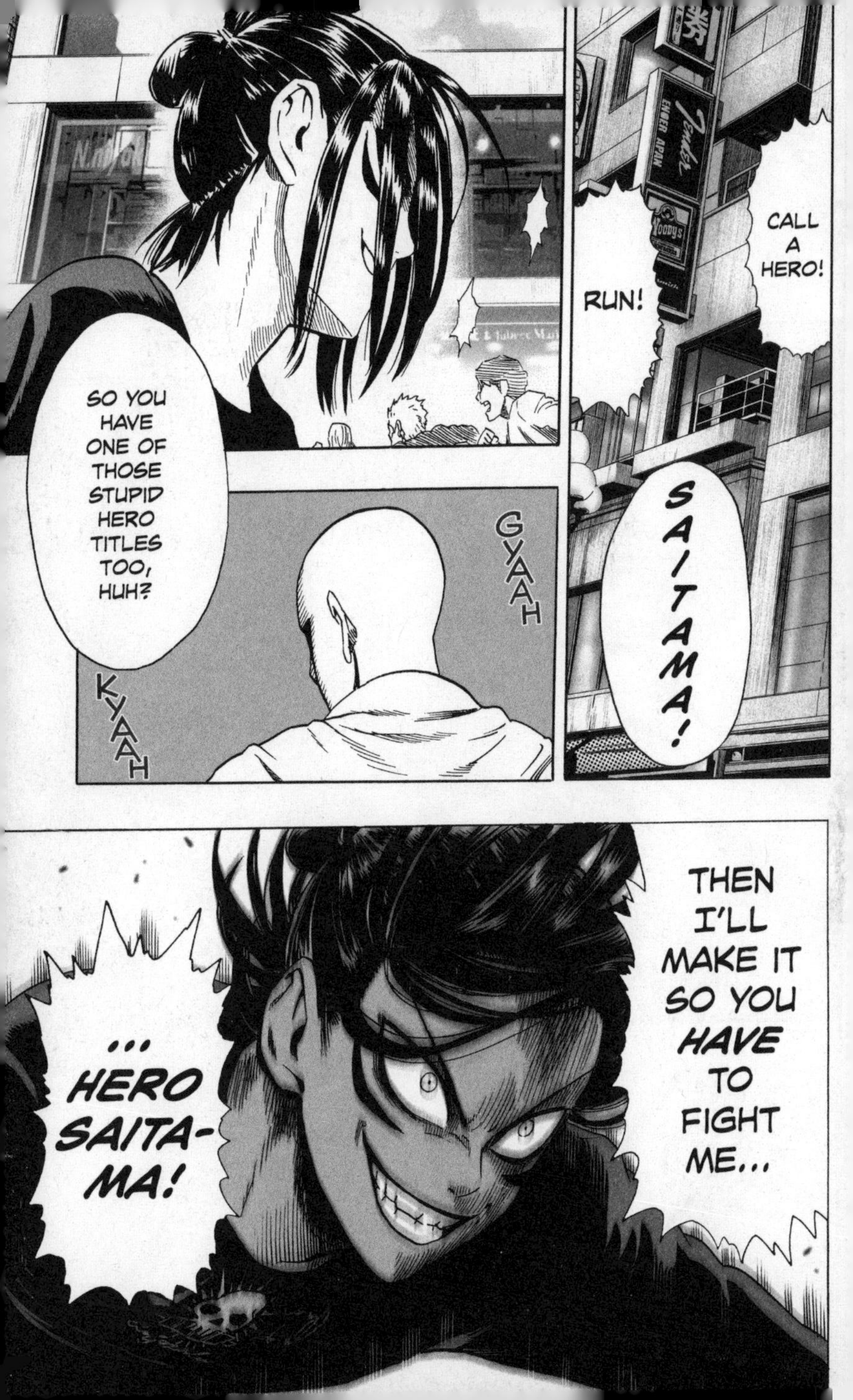
CALL A HERO!
RUN!
SAITAMA!
SO YOU HAVE ONE OF THOSE STUPID HERO TITLES TOO, HUH?
GYAAH
KYAAH
THEN I'LL MAKE IT SO YOU *HAVE* TO FIGHT ME...
...HERO SAITAMA!

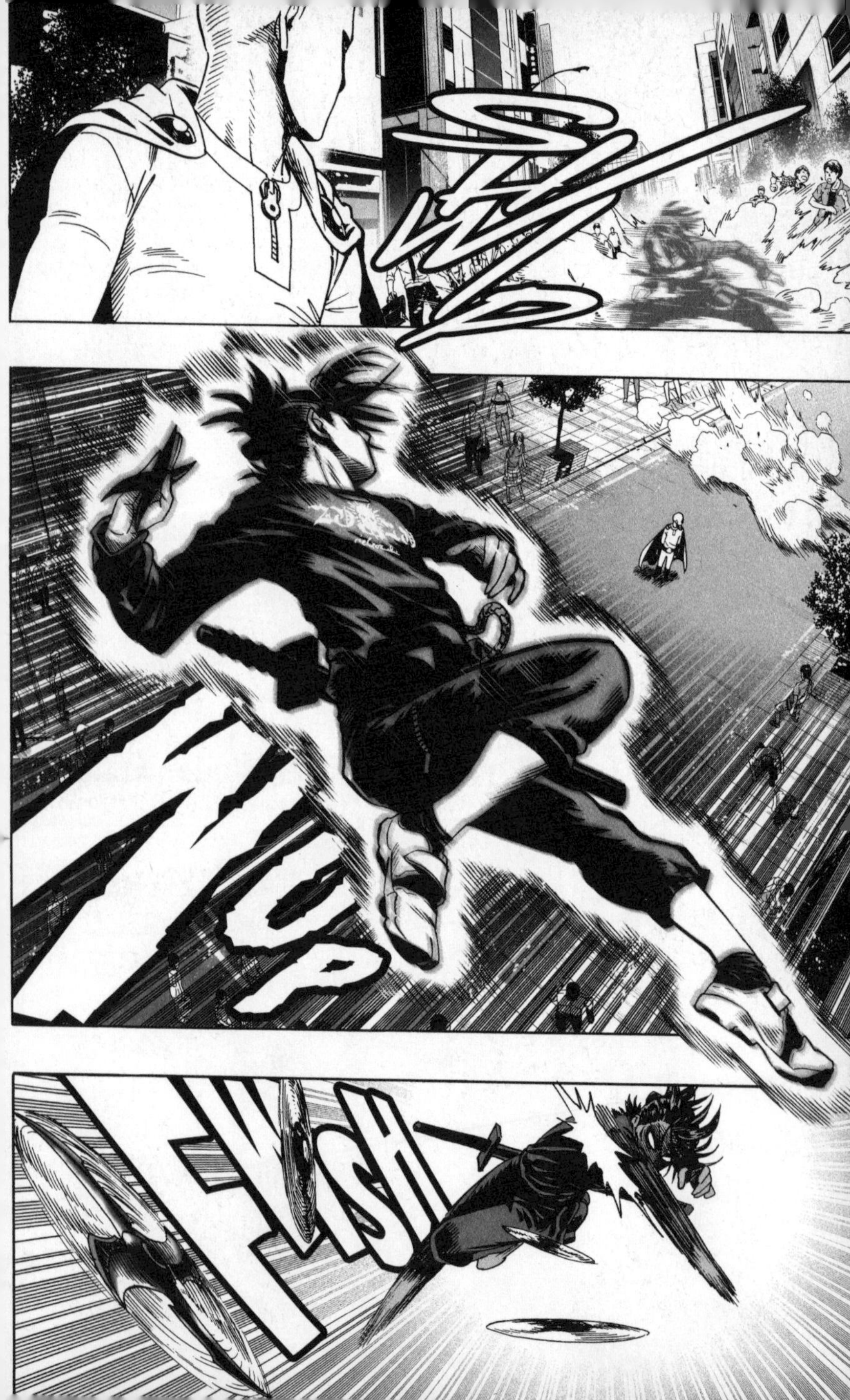
FWISH

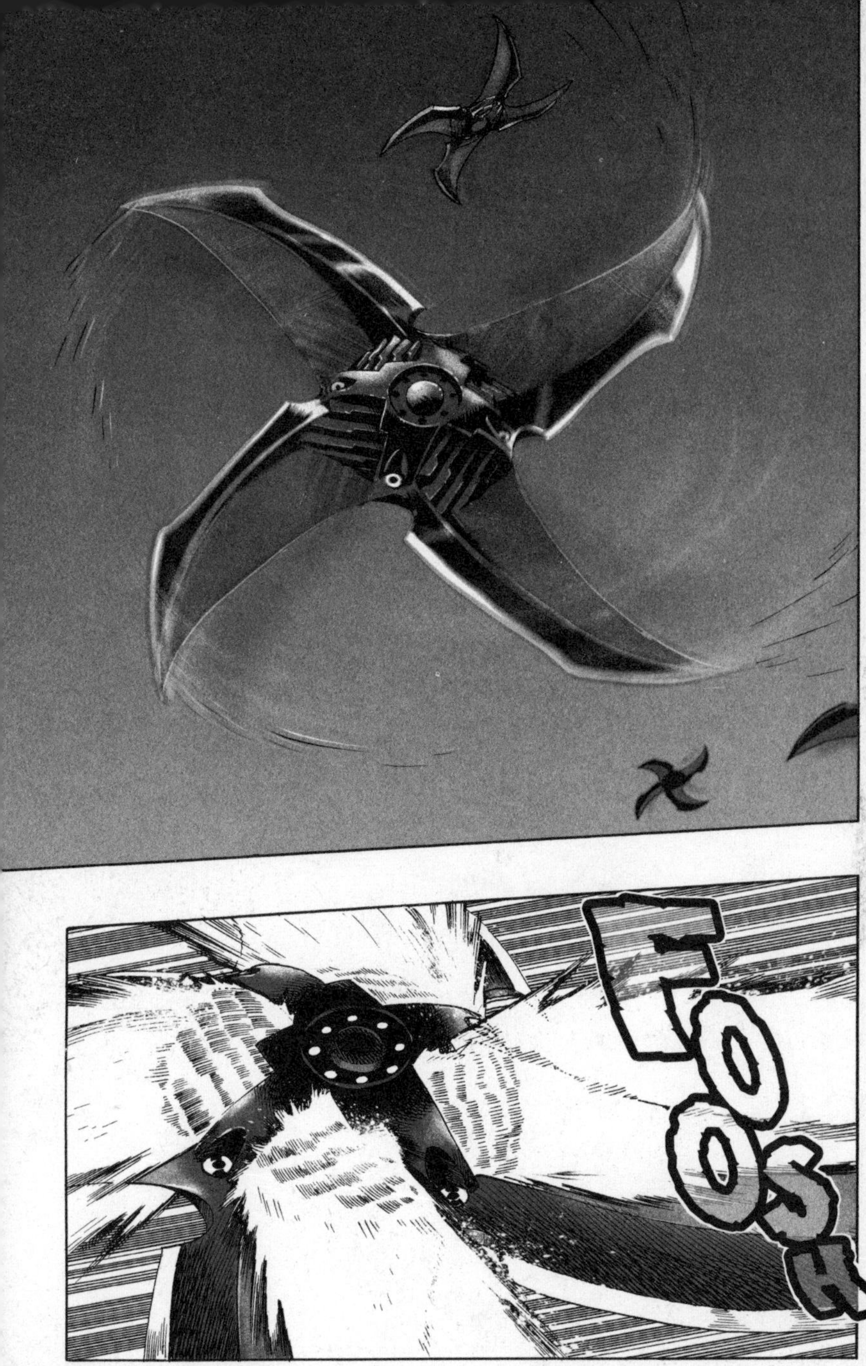
FOOSH

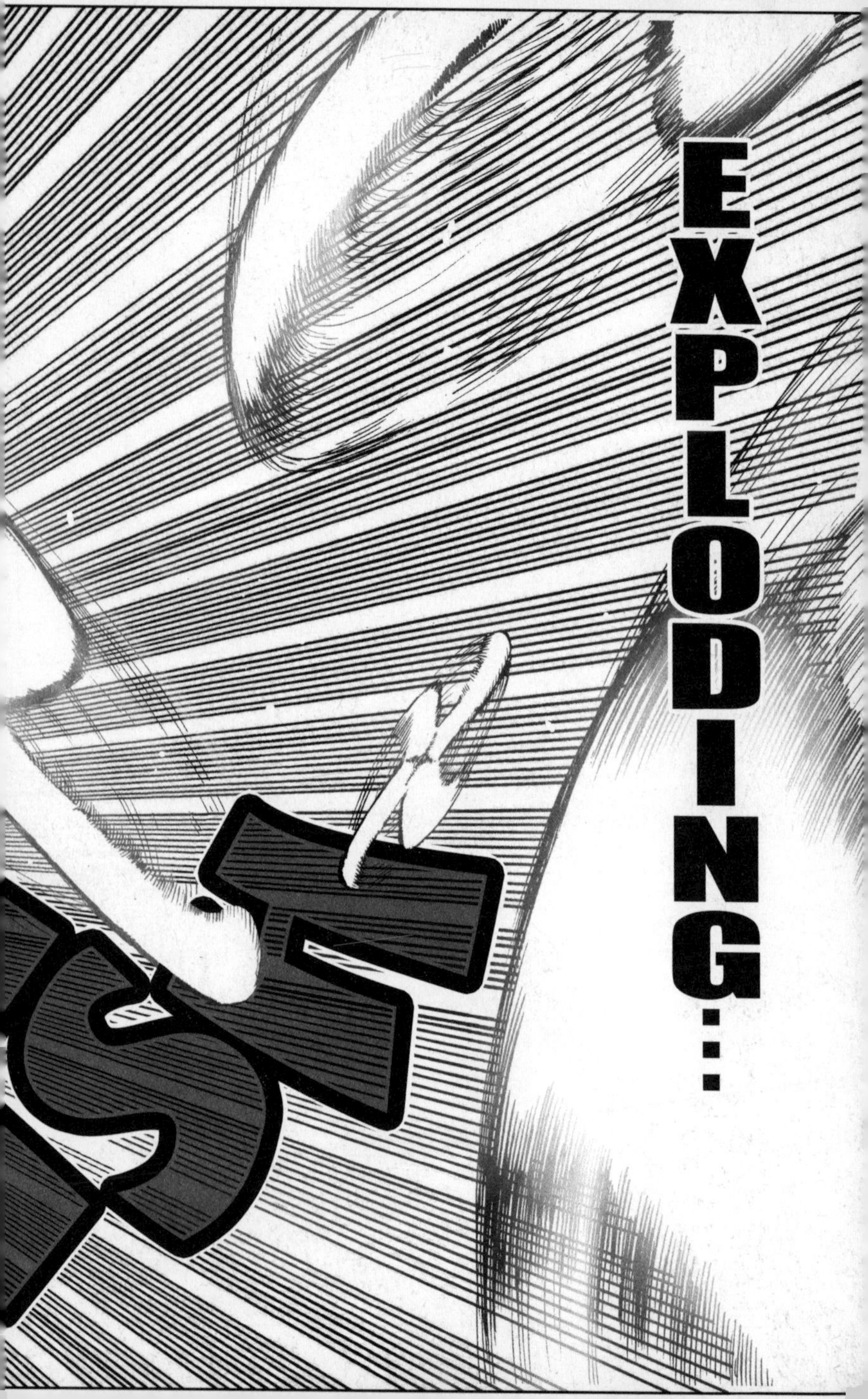
EXPLODING...

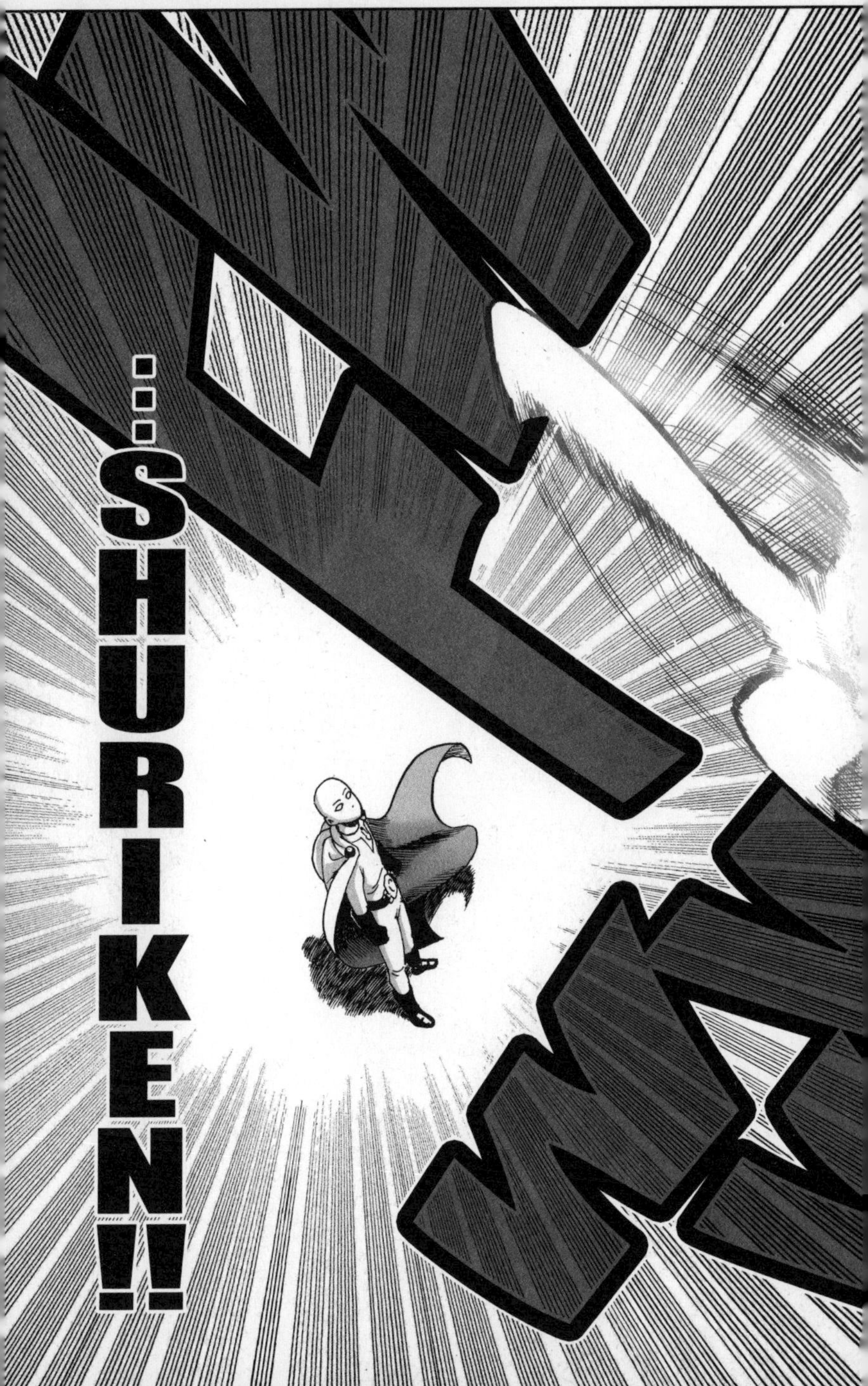

...SHURIKEN!!

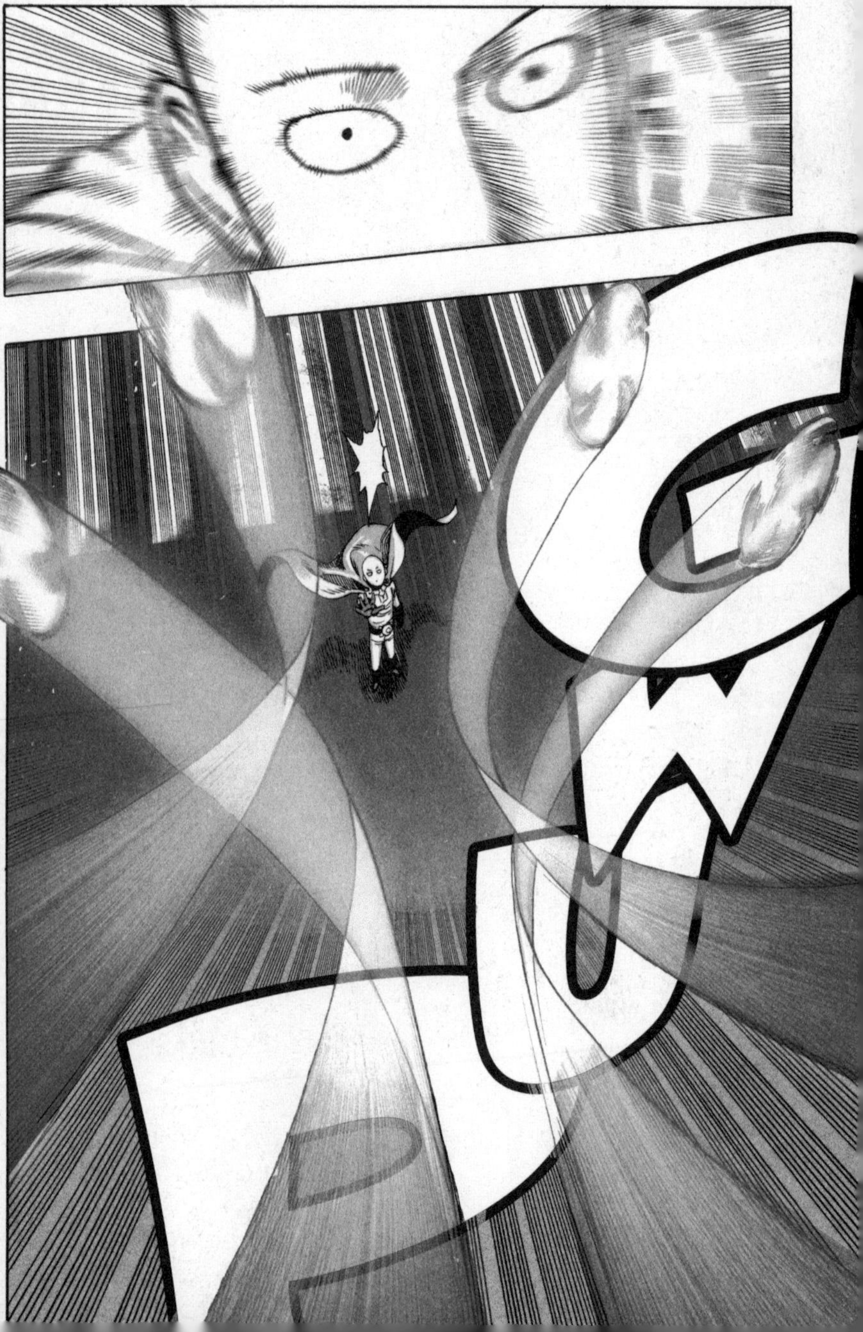

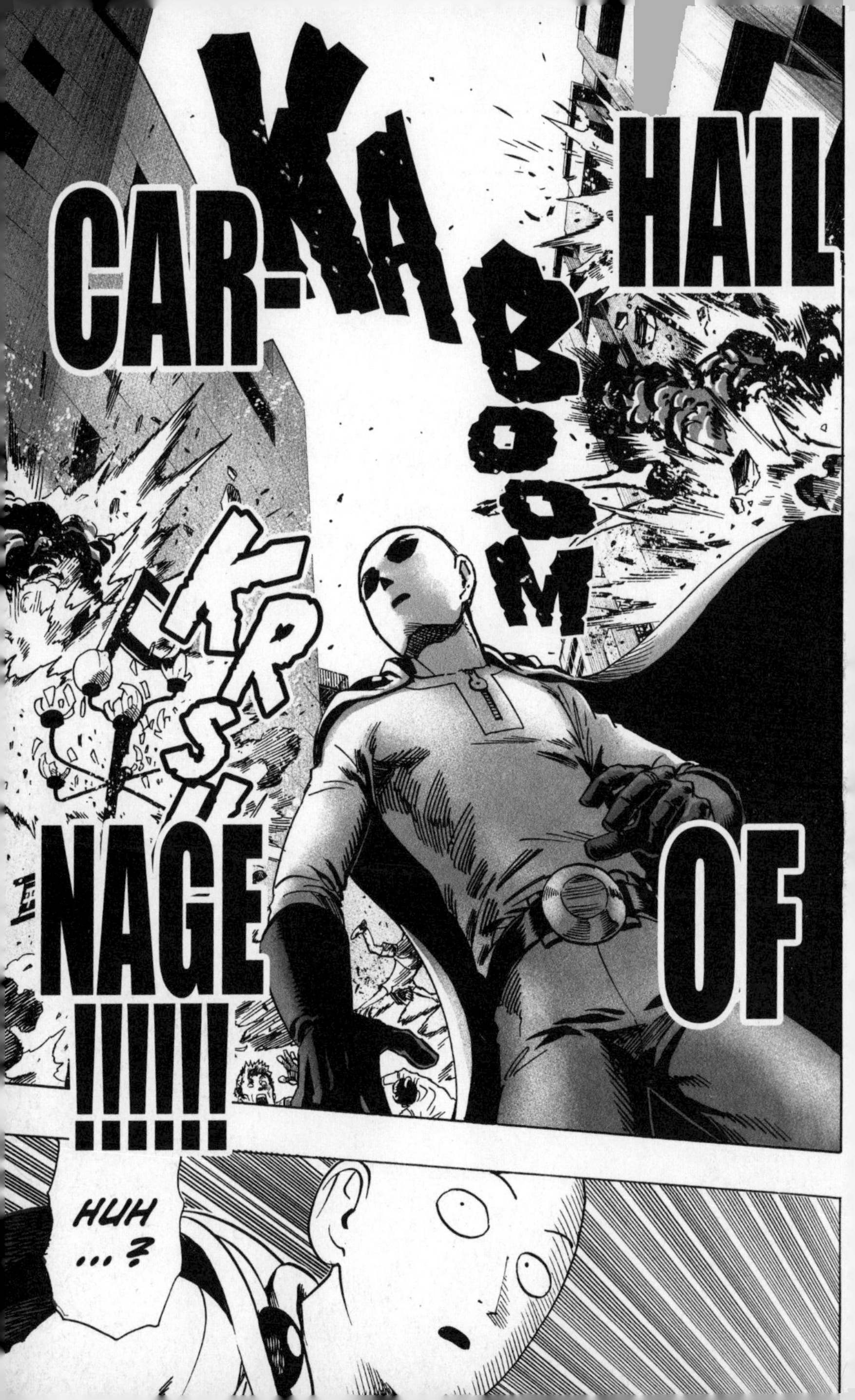
HAIL
OF
CAR-
NAGE
!!!!!!!
KABOOM
KRSH
HUH ...?

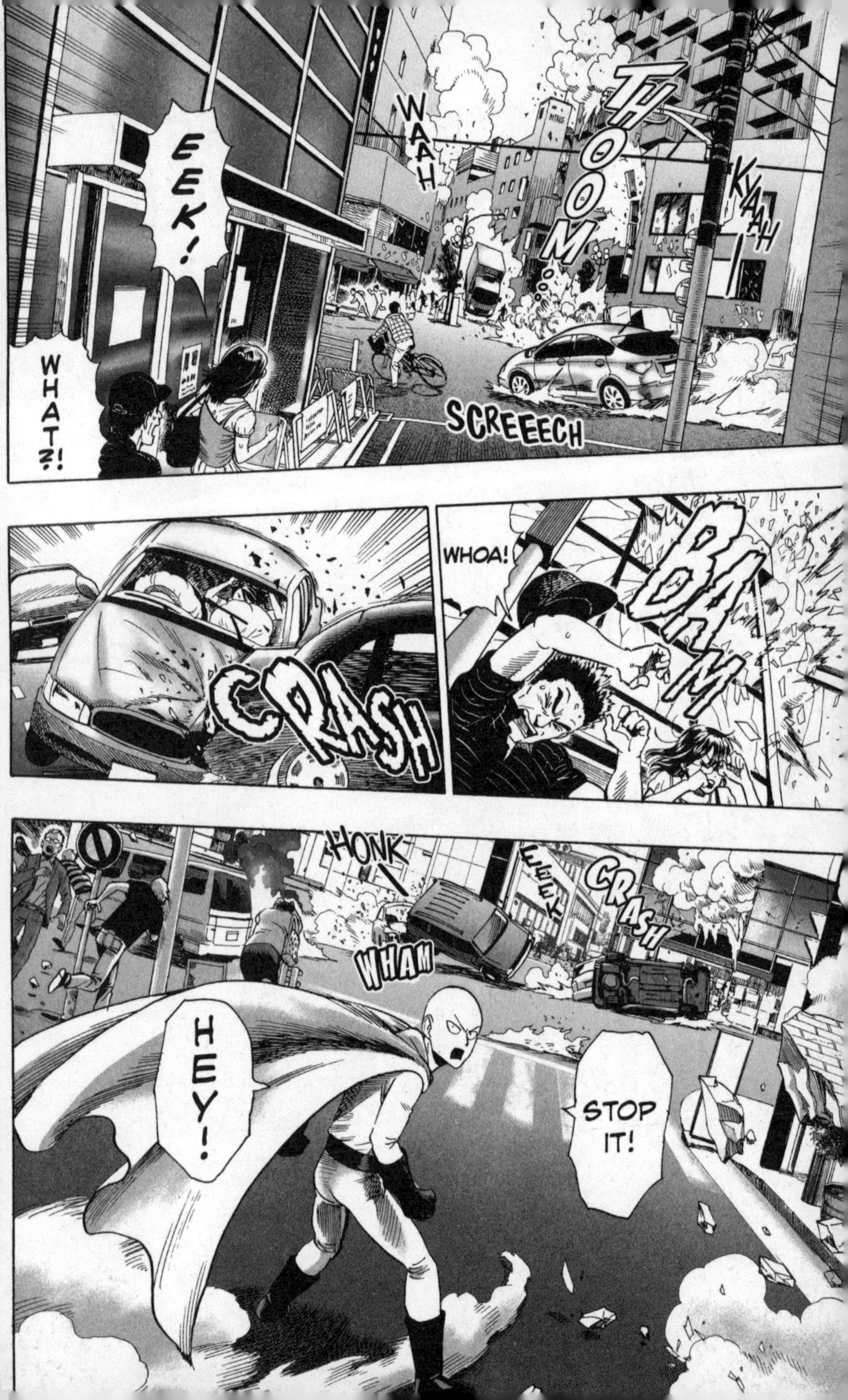

KYAAH
THOOM
WAAH
EEK!
SCREEECH
WHAT?!
WHOA!
BAM
CRASH
CRASH
EEEK
HONK
WHAM
STOP IT!
HEY!

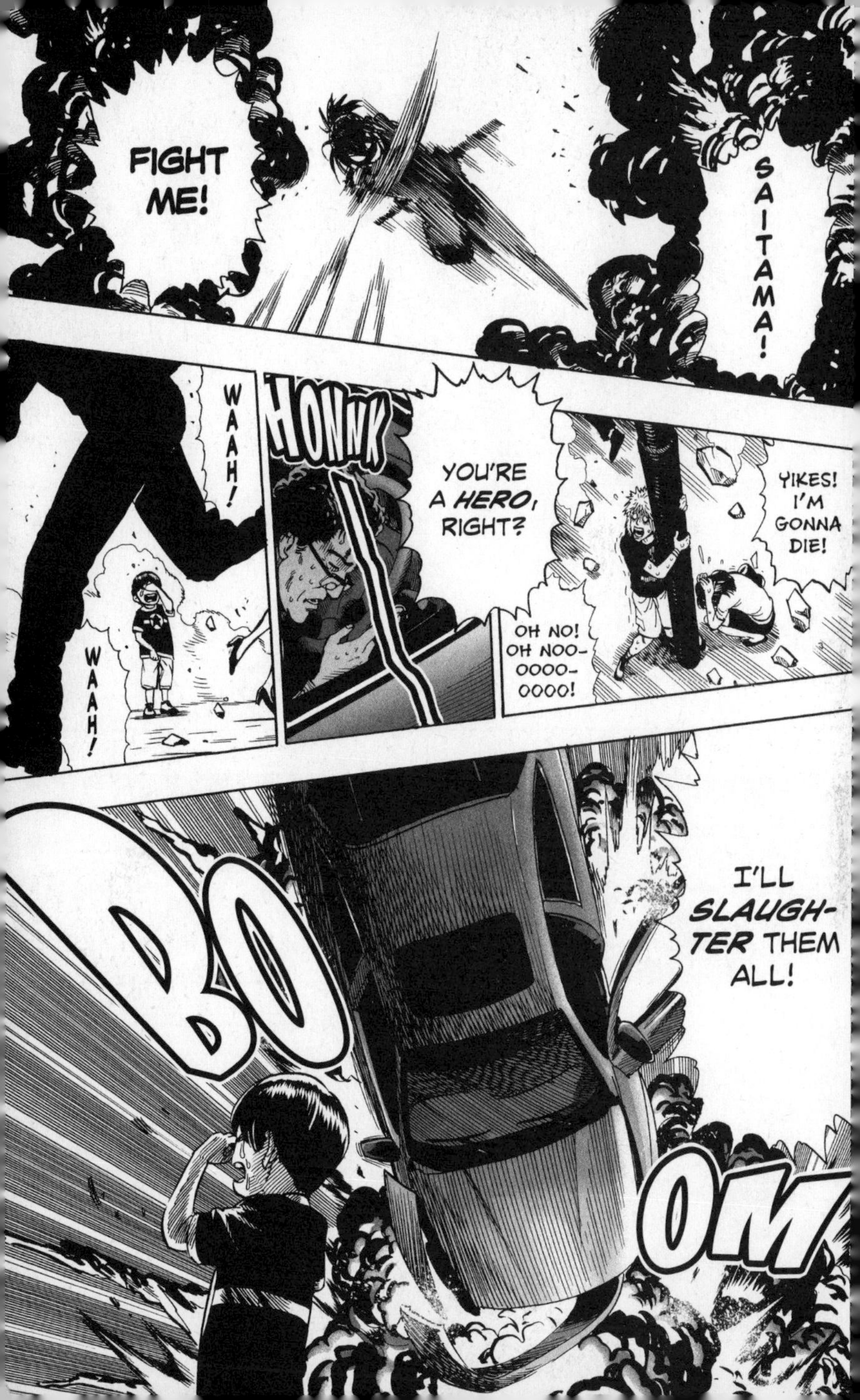
SAITAMA!
FIGHT ME!
YIKES! I'M GONNA DIE!
OH NO! OH NOO-OOOO-OOOO!
YOU'RE A *HERO*, RIGHT?
HONNK
WAAAH!
WAAAH!
I'LL *SLAUGHTER* THEM ALL!
BOOM

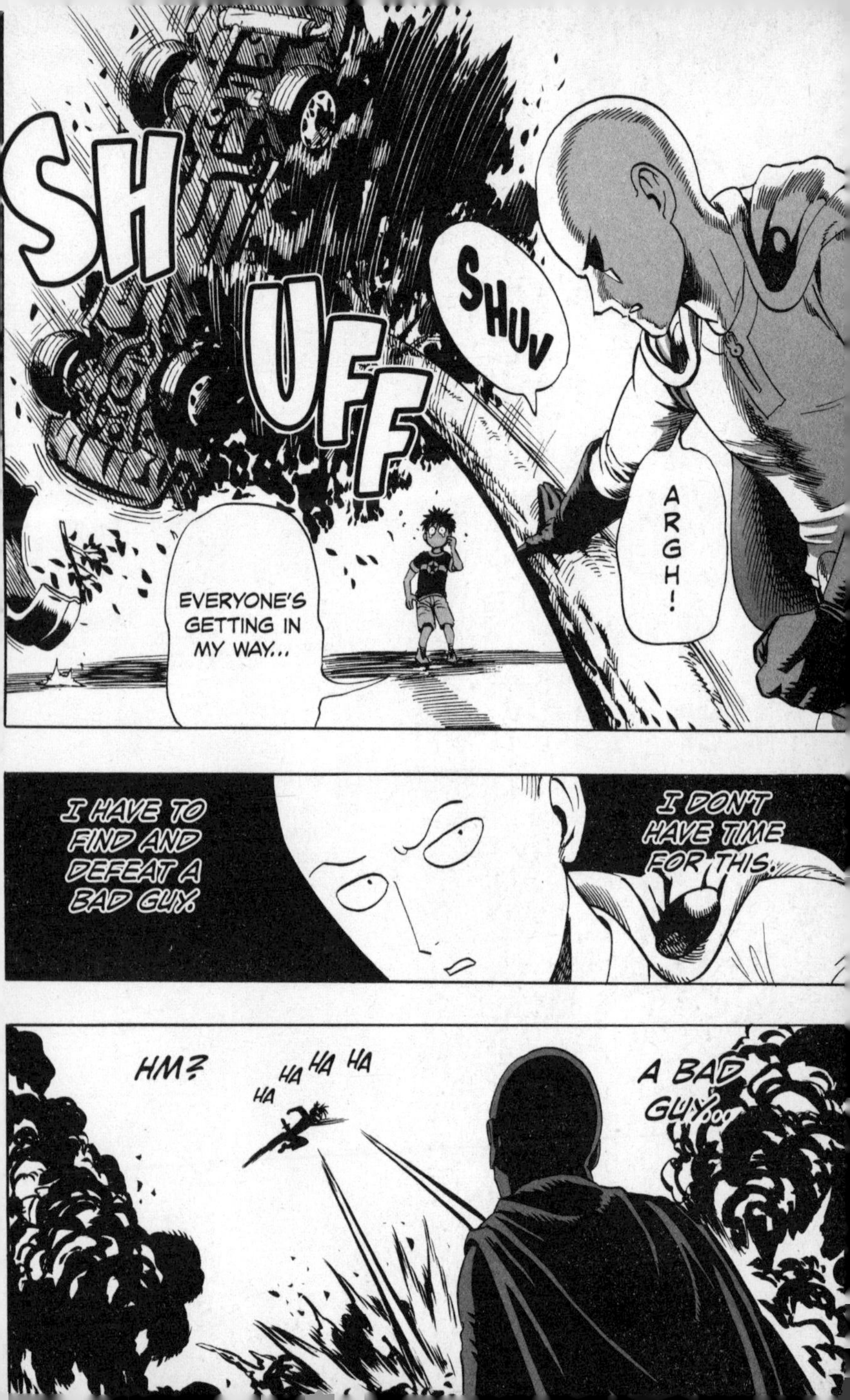
SHUFF
SHUV
ARGH!
EVERYONE'S GETTING IN MY WAY...
I DON'T HAVE TIME FOR THIS.
I HAVE TO FIND AND DEFEAT A BAD GUY.
A BAD GUY...
HM?
HA HA HA HA

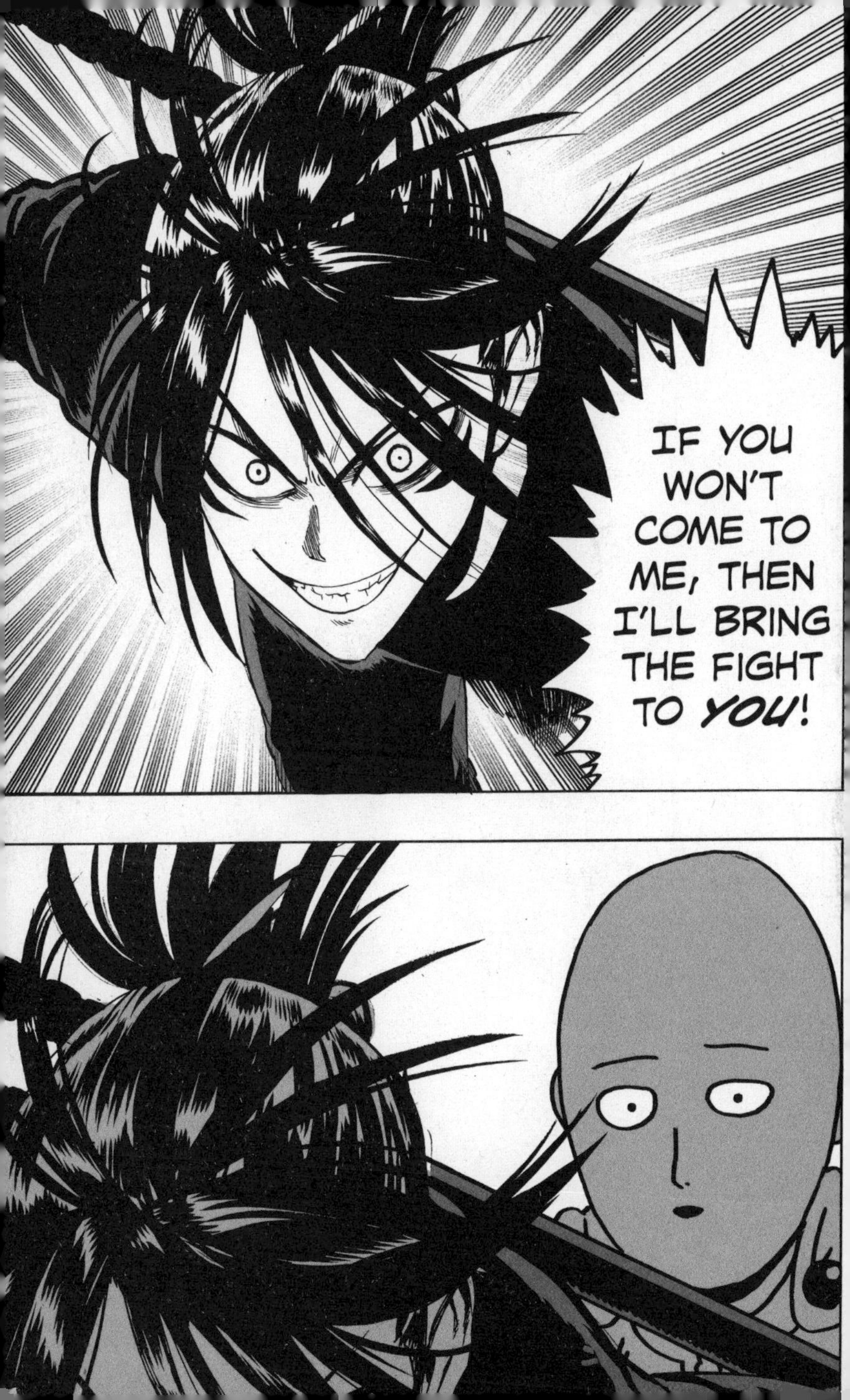
IF YOU WON'T COME TO ME, THEN I'LL BRING THE FIGHT TO *YOU*!

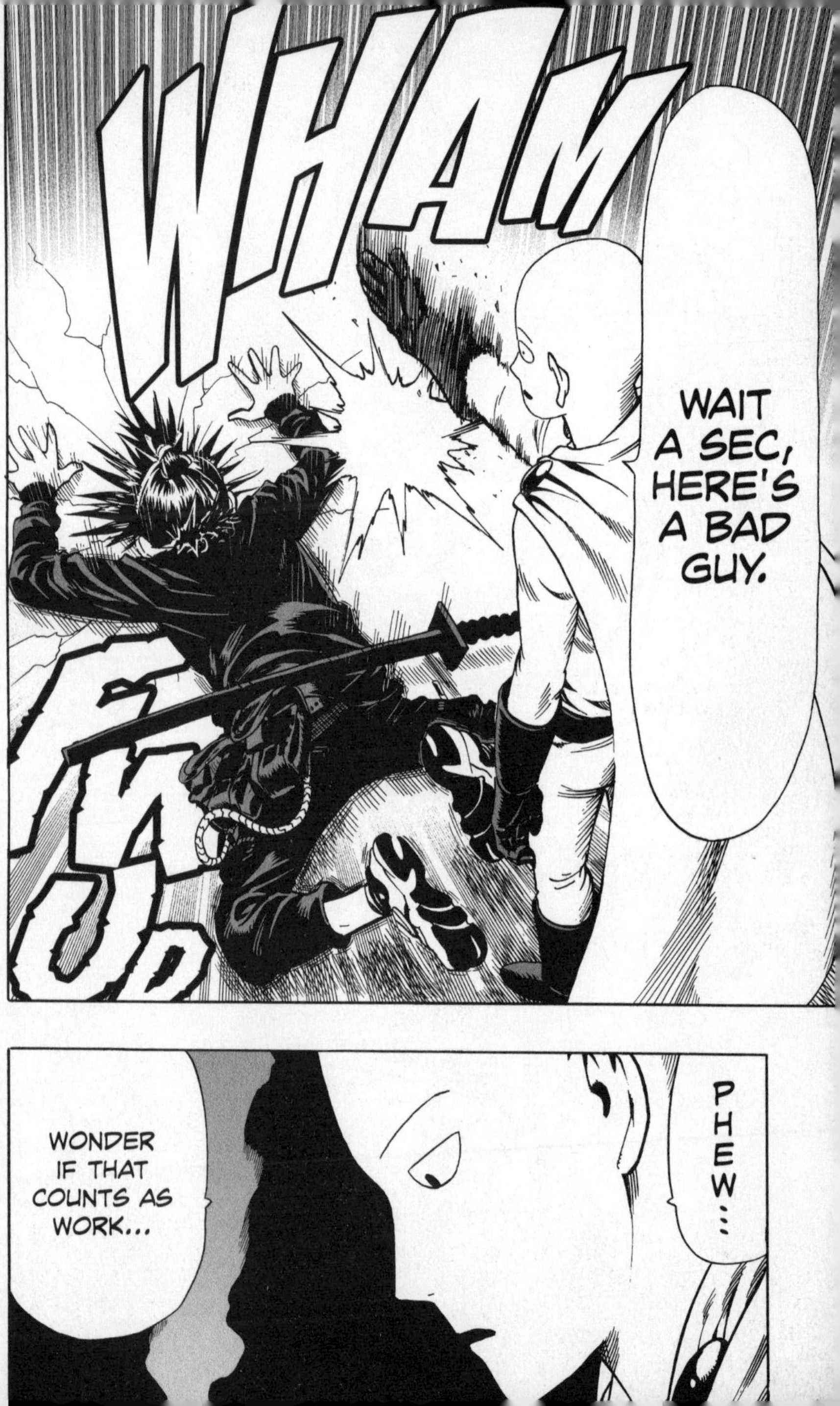
WHAM
WAIT A SEC, HERE'S A BAD GUY.
PHEW...
WONDER IF THAT COUNTS AS WORK...

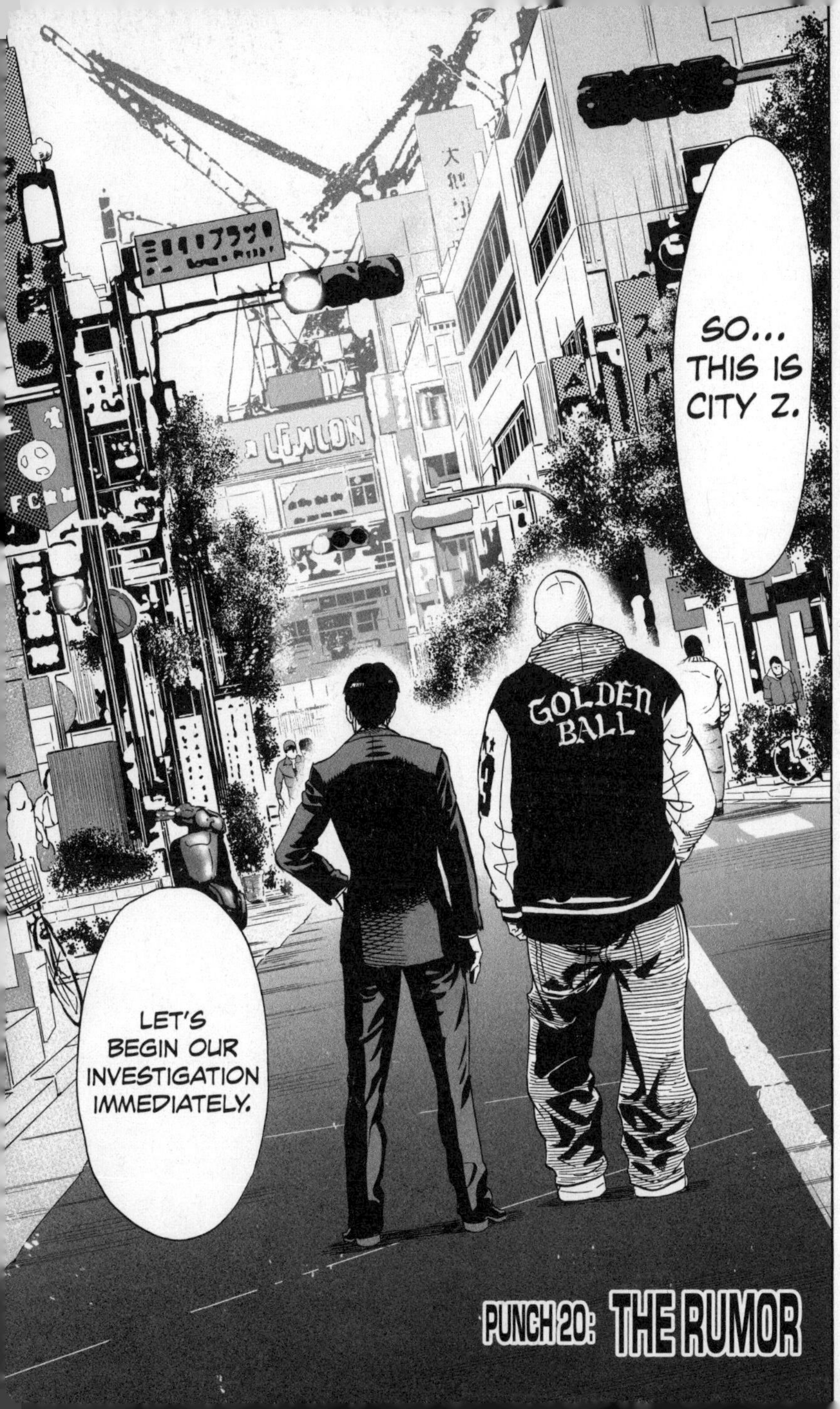
SO... THIS IS CITY Z.
GOLDEN BALL
LET'S BEGIN OUR INVESTIGATION IMMEDIATELY.
PUNCH 20: THE RUMOR

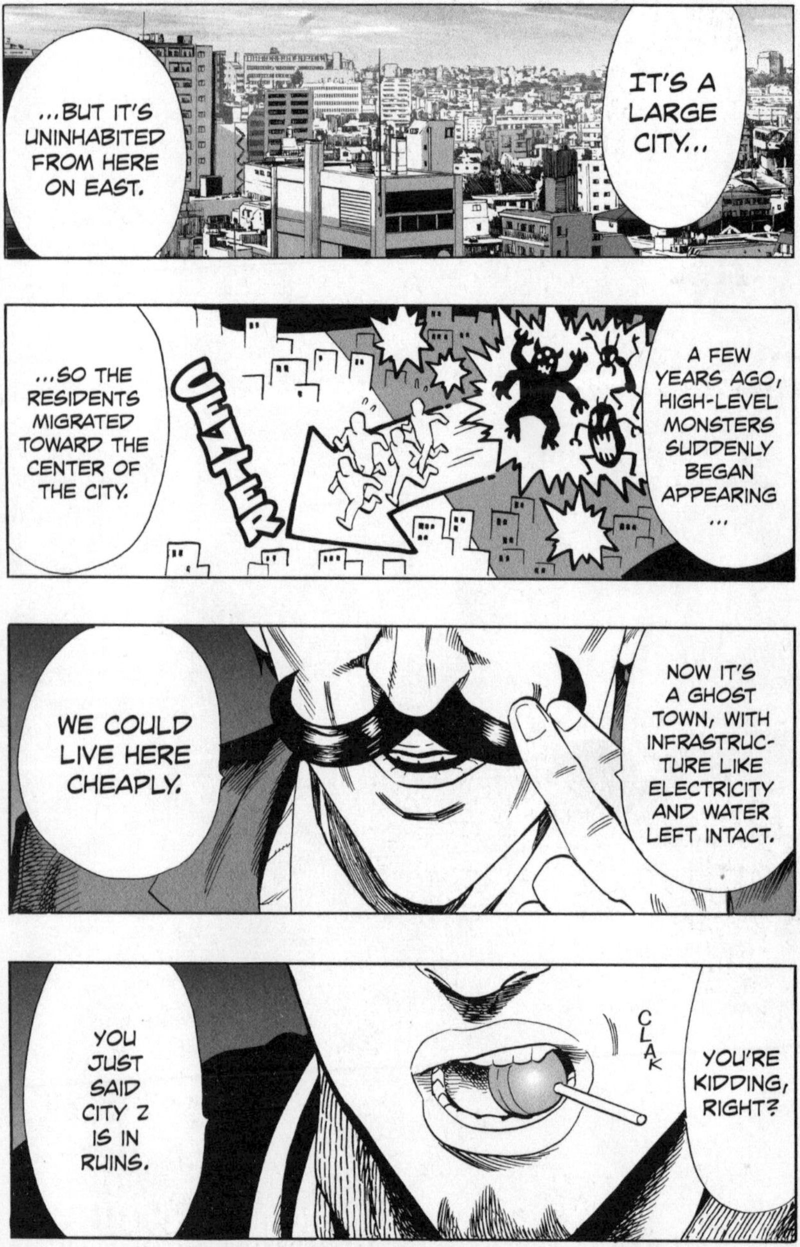
IT'S A LARGE CITY...
...BUT IT'S UNINHABITED FROM HERE ON EAST.
A FEW YEARS AGO, HIGH-LEVEL MONSTERS SUDDENLY BEGAN APPEARING...
CENTER
...SO THE RESIDENTS MIGRATED TOWARD THE CENTER OF THE CITY.
NOW IT'S A GHOST TOWN, WITH INFRASTRUCTURE LIKE ELECTRICITY AND WATER LEFT INTACT.
WE COULD LIVE HERE CHEAPLY.
YOU'RE KIDDING, RIGHT?
CLAK
YOU JUST SAID CITY Z IS IN RUINS.

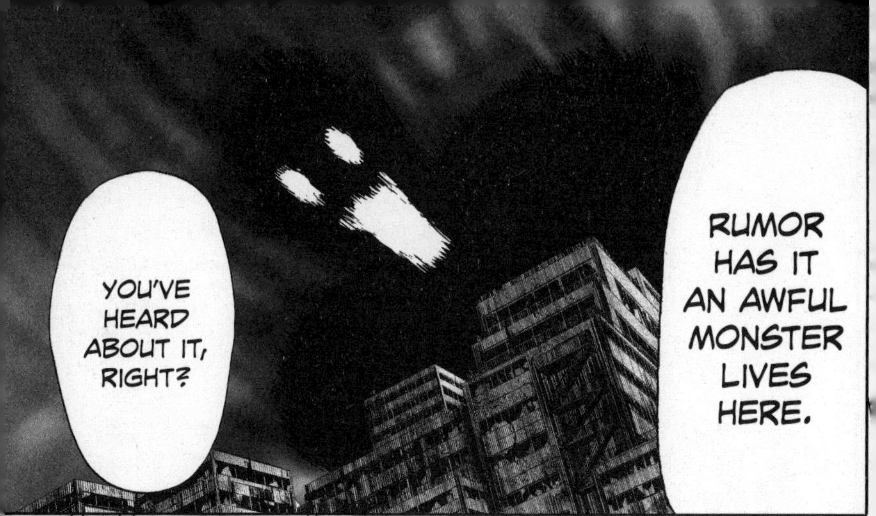
RUMOR HAS IT AN AWFUL MONSTER LIVES HERE.
YOU'VE HEARD ABOUT IT, RIGHT?

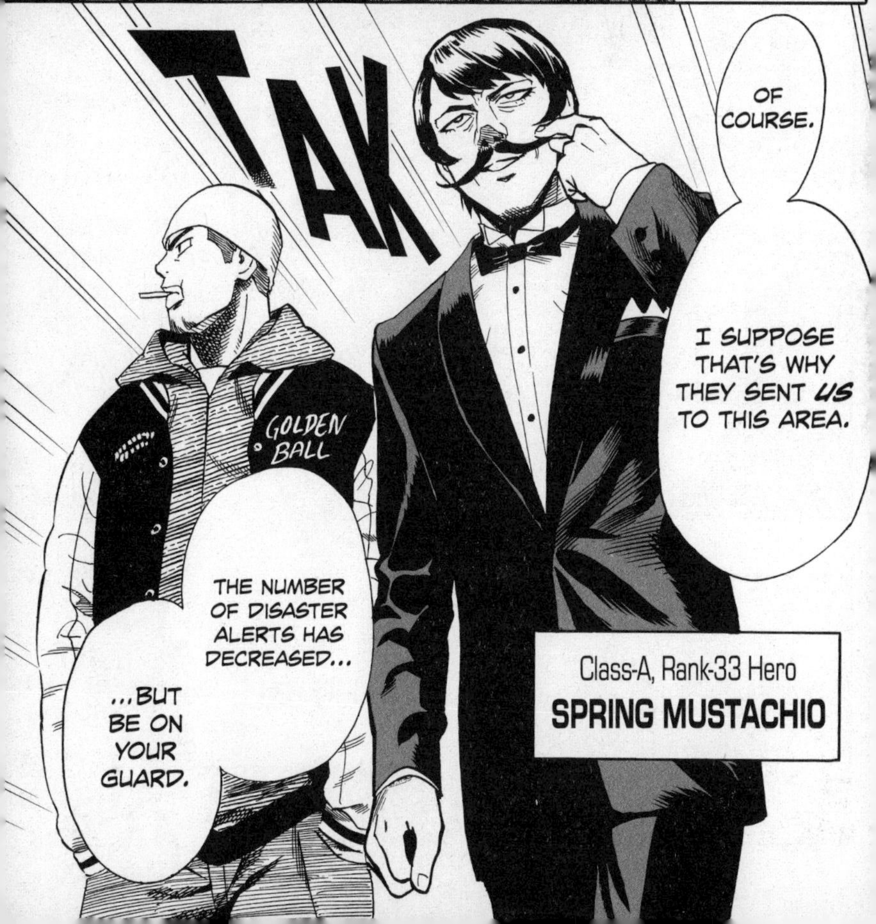
TAK
OF COURSE.
I SUPPOSE THAT'S WHY THEY SENT *US* TO THIS AREA.
Class-A, Rank-33 Hero
SPRING MUSTACHIO
GOLDEN BALL
THE NUMBER OF DISASTER ALERTS HAS DECREASED...
...BUT BE ON YOUR GUARD.

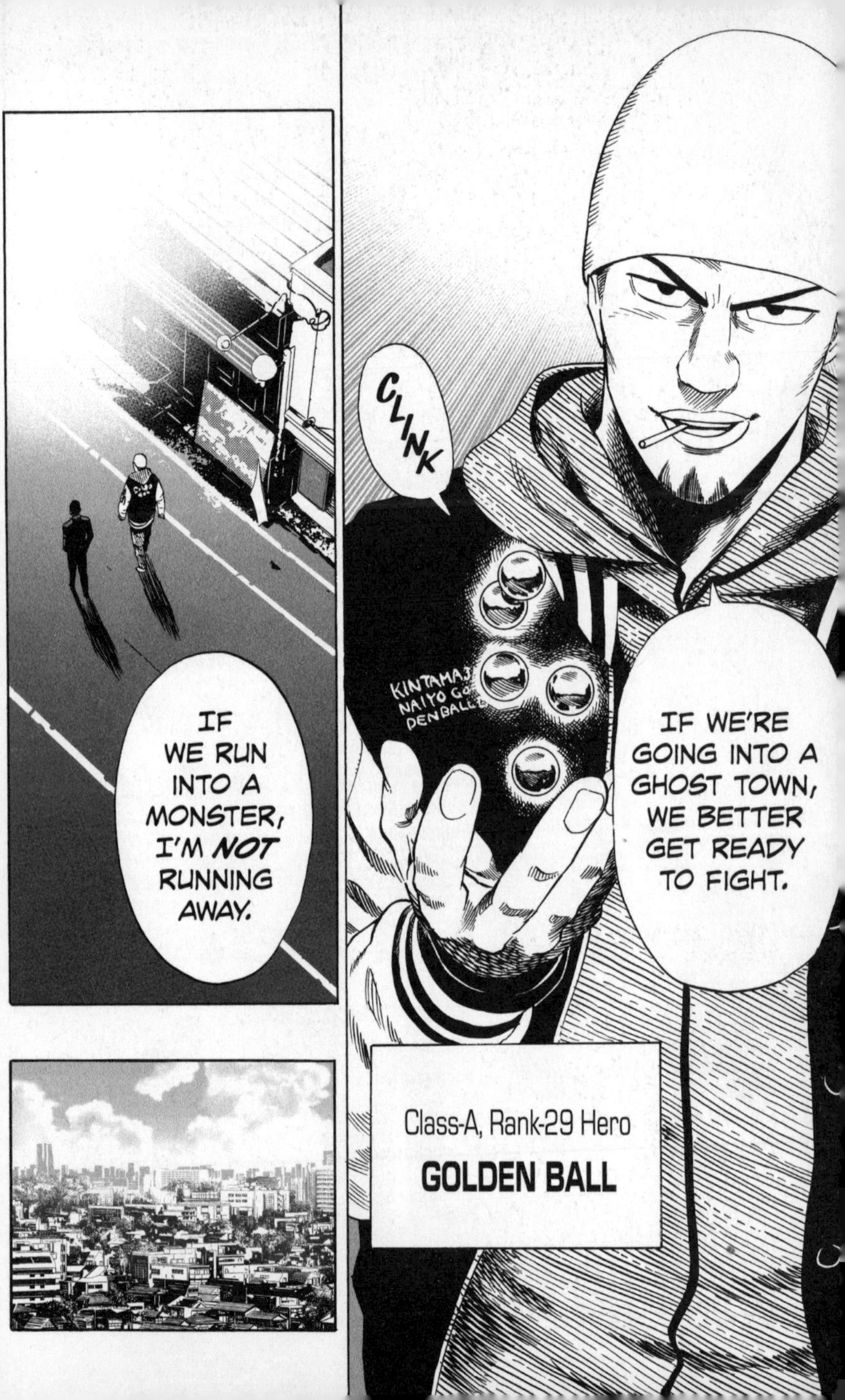
CLINK
IF WE'RE GOING INTO A GHOST TOWN, WE BETTER GET READY TO FIGHT.
Class-A, Rank-29 Hero
GOLDEN BALL
IF WE RUN INTO A MONSTER, I'M *NOT* RUNNING AWAY.

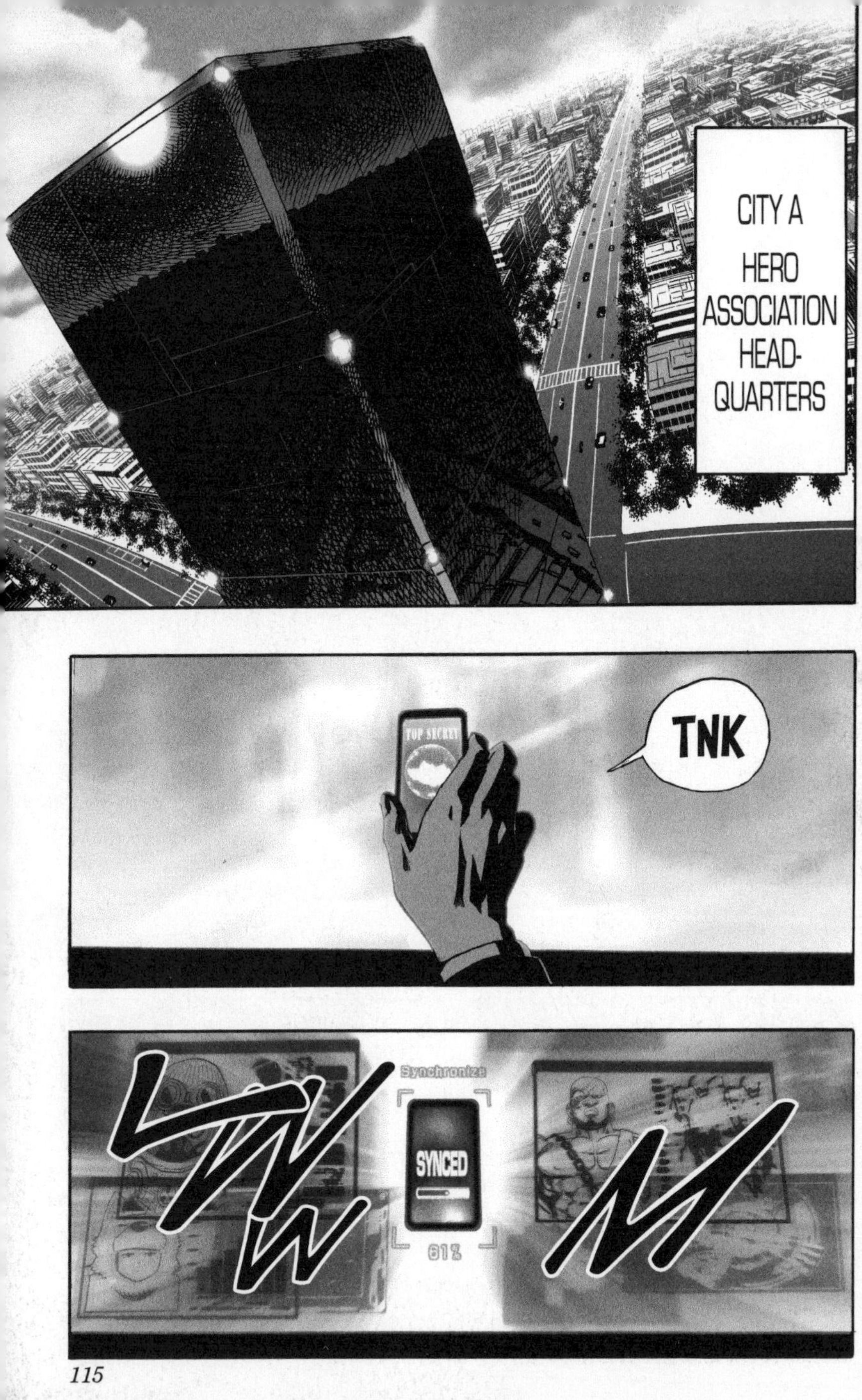
CITY A
HERO ASSOCIATION HEAD-QUARTERS
TOP SECRET
TNK
Synchronize
SYNCED
61%
VWWM

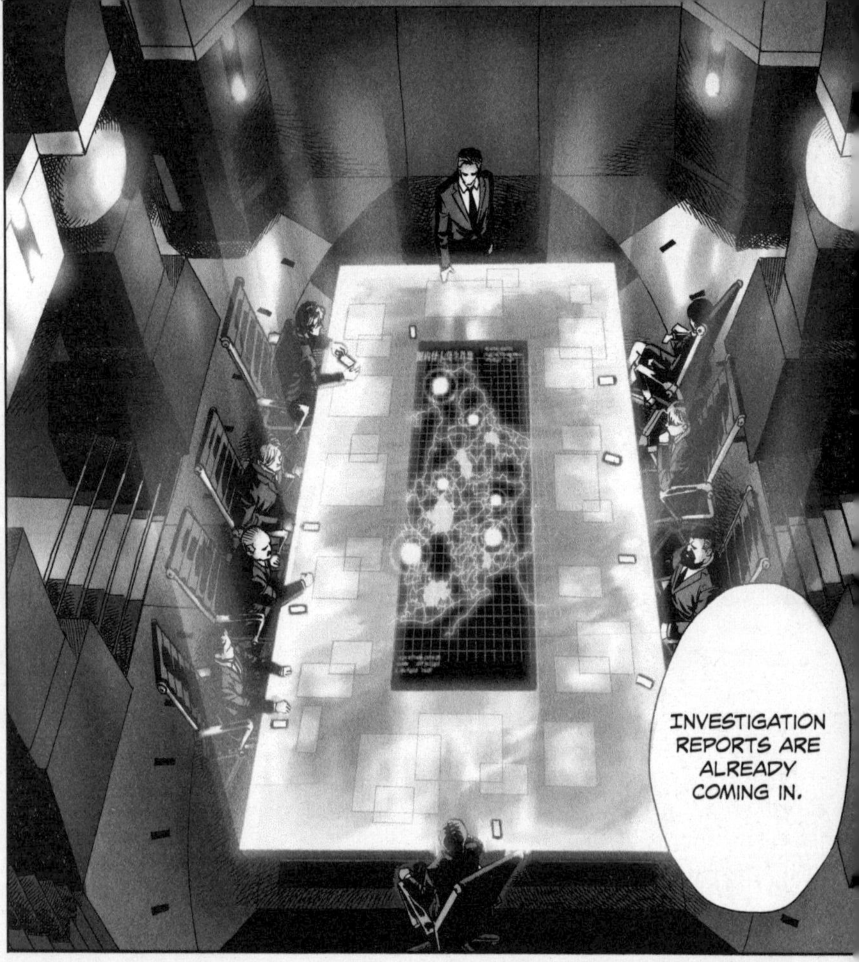
INVESTIGATION REPORTS ARE ALREADY COMING IN.

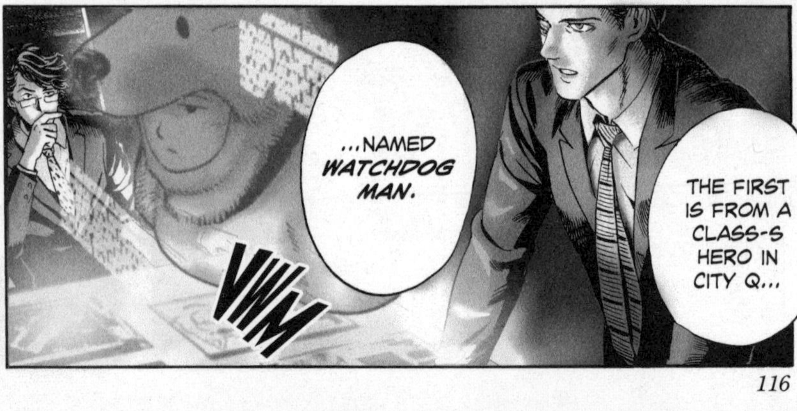
THE FIRST IS FROM A CLASS-S HERO IN CITY Q...
...NAMED *WATCHDOG MAN.*
VWM

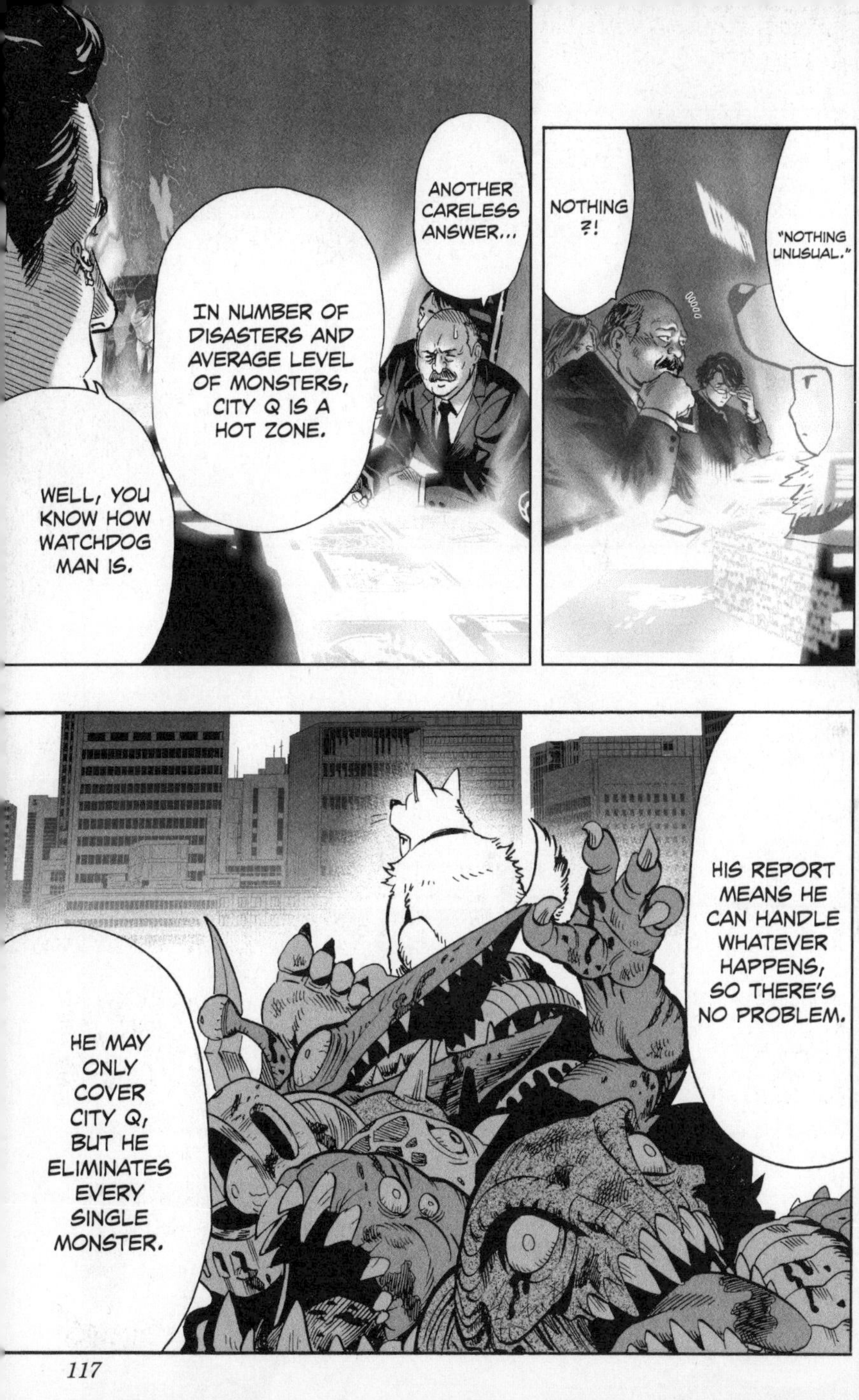
"NOTHING UNUSUAL."
NOTHING ?!
ANOTHER CARELESS ANSWER...
IN NUMBER OF DISASTERS AND AVERAGE LEVEL OF MONSTERS, CITY Q IS A HOT ZONE.
WELL, YOU KNOW HOW WATCHDOG MAN IS.
HIS REPORT MEANS HE CAN HANDLE WHATEVER HAPPENS, SO THERE'S NO PROBLEM.
HE MAY ONLY COVER CITY Q, BUT HE ELIMINATES EVERY SINGLE MONSTER.

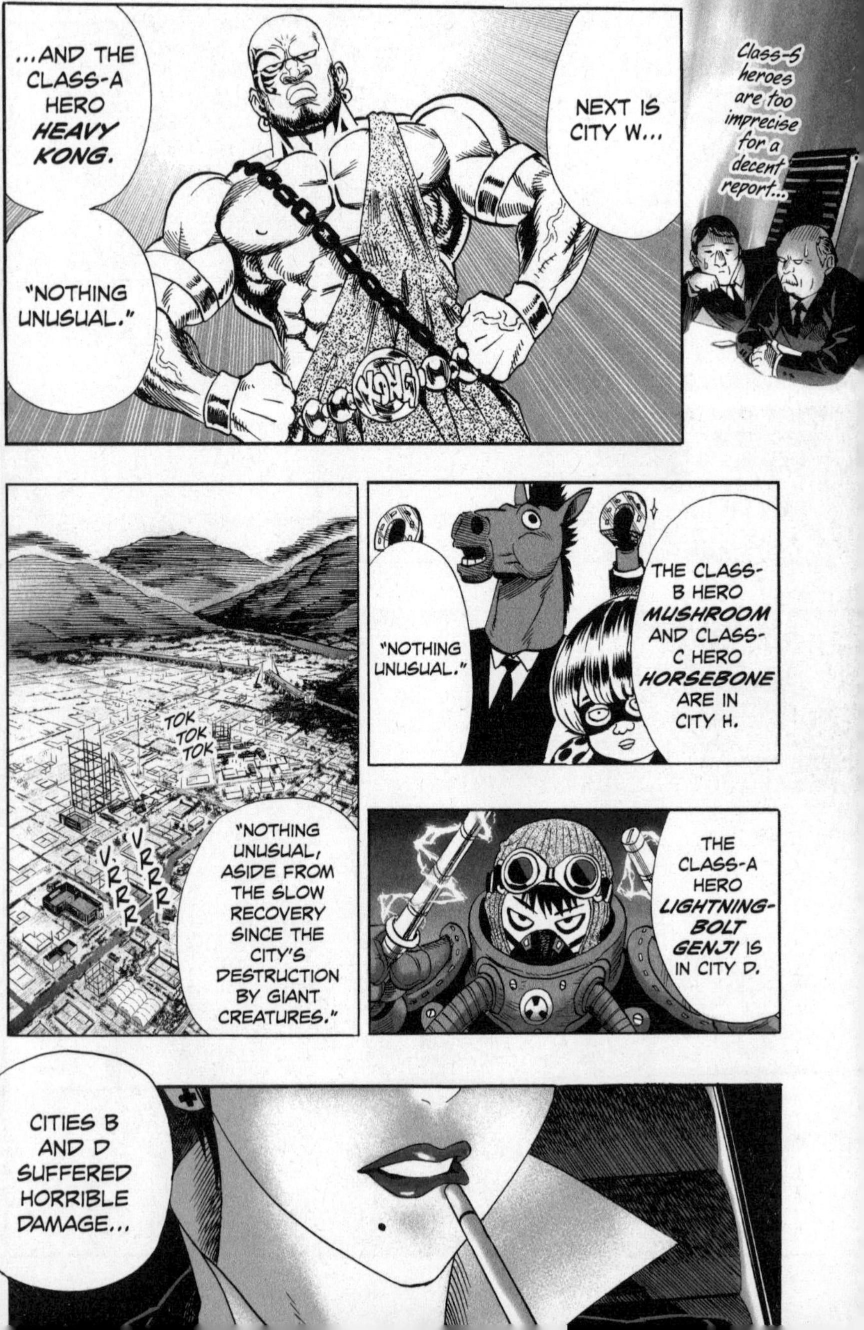
Class-S heroes are too imprecise for a decent report...
NEXT IS CITY W...
...AND THE CLASS-A HERO HEAVY KONG.
"NOTHING UNUSUAL."
THE CLASS-B HERO MUSHROOM AND CLASS-C HERO HORSEBONE ARE IN CITY H.
"NOTHING UNUSUAL."
THE CLASS-A HERO LIGHTNING-BOLT GENJI IS IN CITY D.
"NOTHING UNUSUAL, ASIDE FROM THE SLOW RECOVERY SINCE THE CITY'S DESTRUCTION BY GIANT CREATURES."
TOK TOK TOK
VRRR VRRR
CITIES B AND D SUFFERED HORRIBLE DAMAGE...

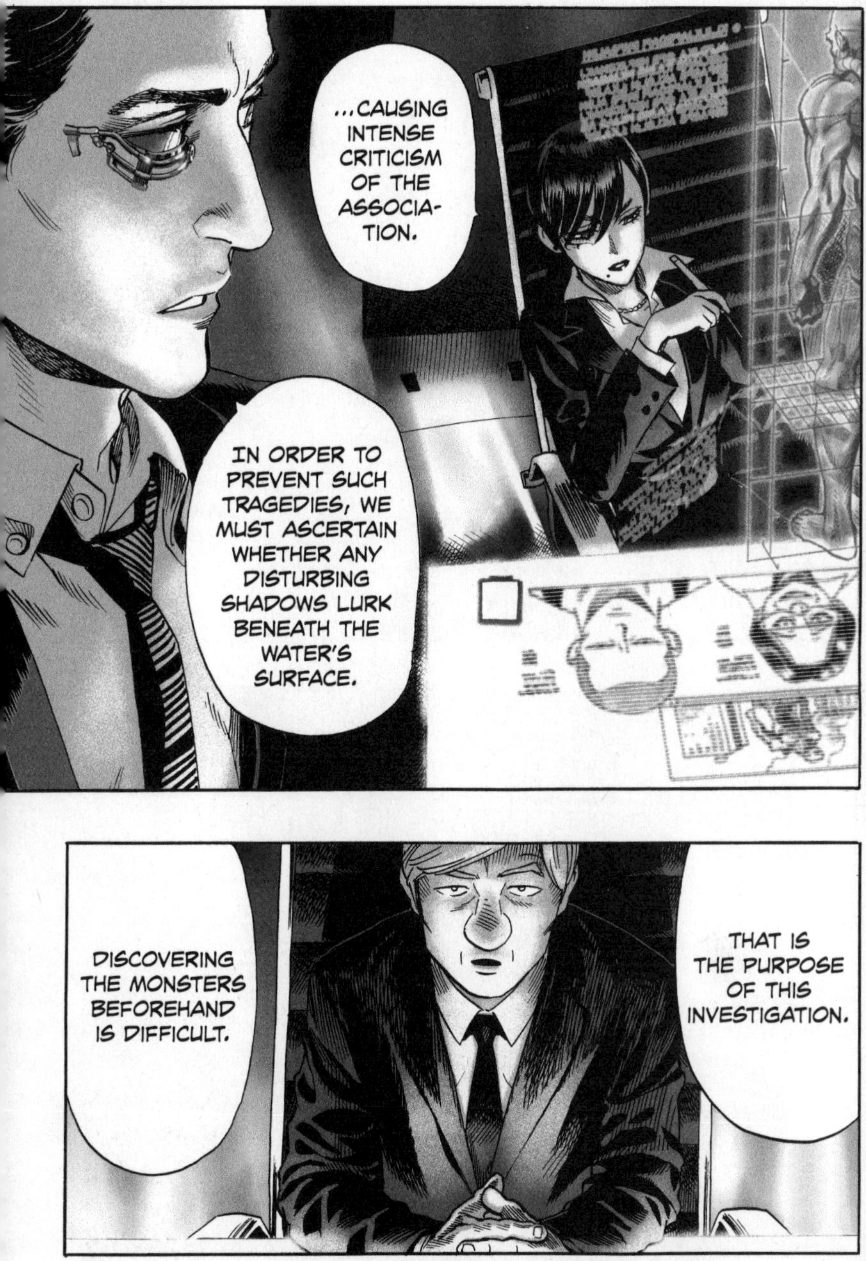
...CAUSING INTENSE CRITICISM OF THE ASSOCIA- TION.
IN ORDER TO PREVENT SUCH TRAGEDIES, WE MUST ASCERTAIN WHETHER ANY DISTURBING SHADOWS LURK BENEATH THE WATER'S SURFACE.
THAT IS THE PURPOSE OF THIS INVESTIGATION.
DISCOVERING THE MONSTERS BEFOREHAND IS DIFFICULT.

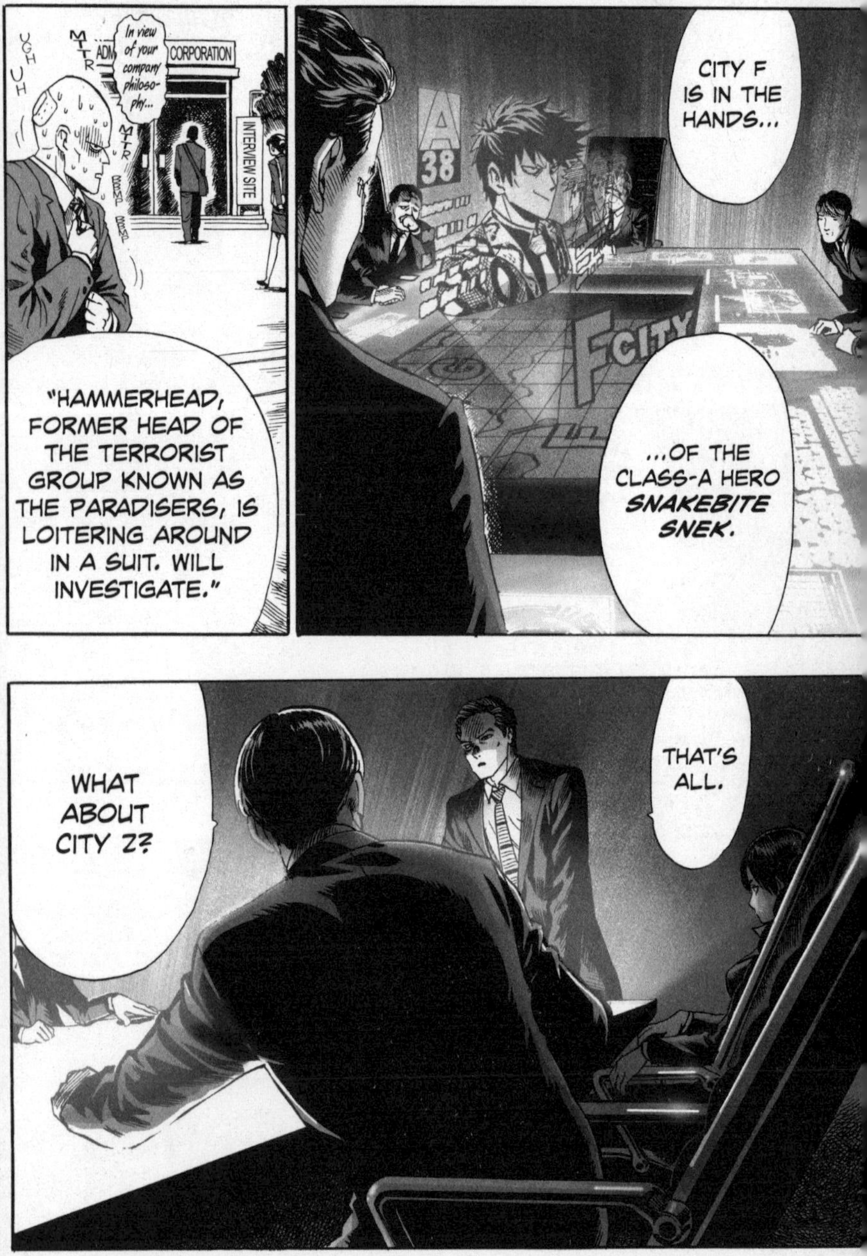
CITY F IS IN THE HANDS...
...OF THE CLASS-A HERO *SNAKEBITE SNEK.*
UGH UH
MTTR
In view of your company philoso-phy...
ADM
CORPORATION
INTERVIEW SITE
"HAMMERHEAD, FORMER HEAD OF THE TERRORIST GROUP KNOWN AS THE PARADISERS, IS LOITERING AROUND IN A SUIT. WILL INVESTIGATE."
THAT'S ALL.
WHAT ABOUT CITY Z?

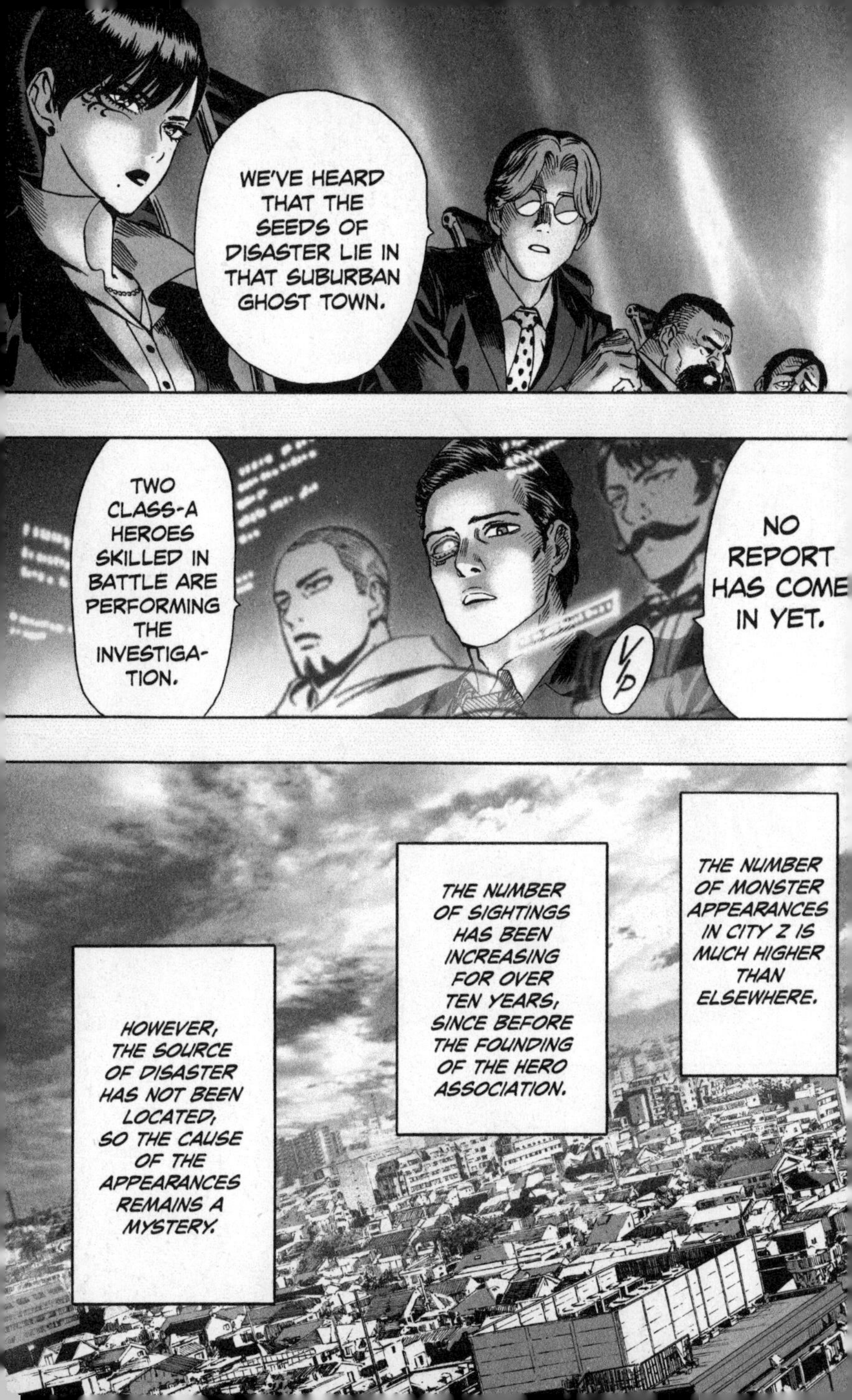
WE'VE HEARD THAT THE SEEDS OF DISASTER LIE IN THAT SUBURBAN GHOST TOWN.
NO REPORT HAS COME IN YET.
TWO CLASS-A HEROES SKILLED IN BATTLE ARE PERFORMING THE INVESTIGA-TION.
THE NUMBER OF MONSTER APPEARANCES IN CITY Z IS MUCH HIGHER THAN ELSEWHERE.
THE NUMBER OF SIGHTINGS HAS BEEN INCREASING FOR OVER TEN YEARS, SINCE BEFORE THE FOUNDING OF THE HERO ASSOCIATION.
HOWEVER, THE SOURCE OF DISASTER HAS NOT BEEN LOCATED, SO THE CAUSE OF THE APPEARANCES REMAINS A MYSTERY.

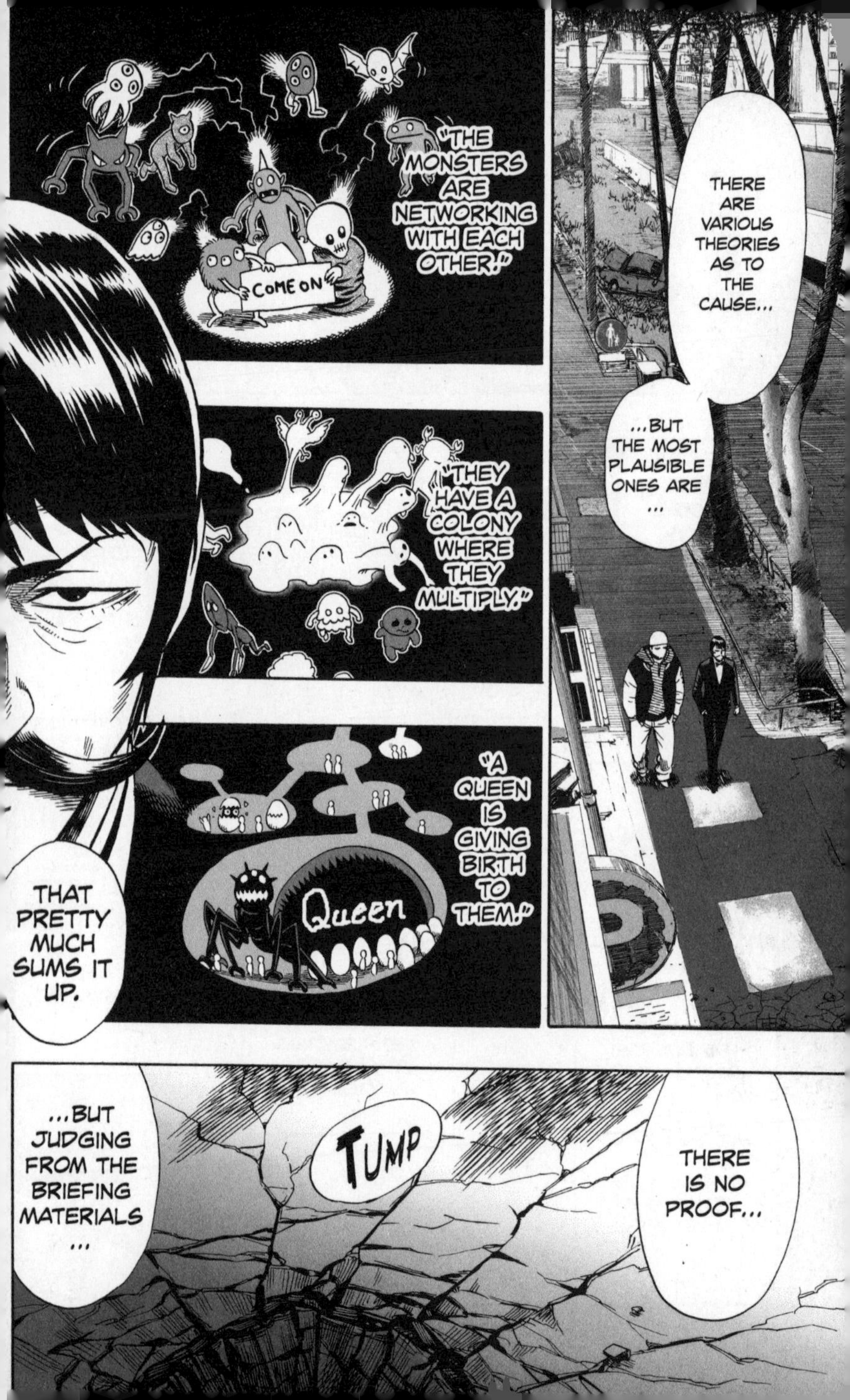

THERE ARE VARIOUS THEORIES AS TO THE CAUSE...
...BUT THE MOST PLAUSIBLE ONES ARE...
"THE MONSTERS ARE NETWORKING WITH EACH OTHER!"
COME ON
"THEY HAVE A COLONY WHERE THEY MULTIPLY."
"A QUEEN IS GIVING BIRTH TO THEM."
Queen
THAT PRETTY MUCH SUMS IT UP.
THERE IS NO PROOF...
TUMP
...BUT JUDGING FROM THE BRIEFING MATERIALS...

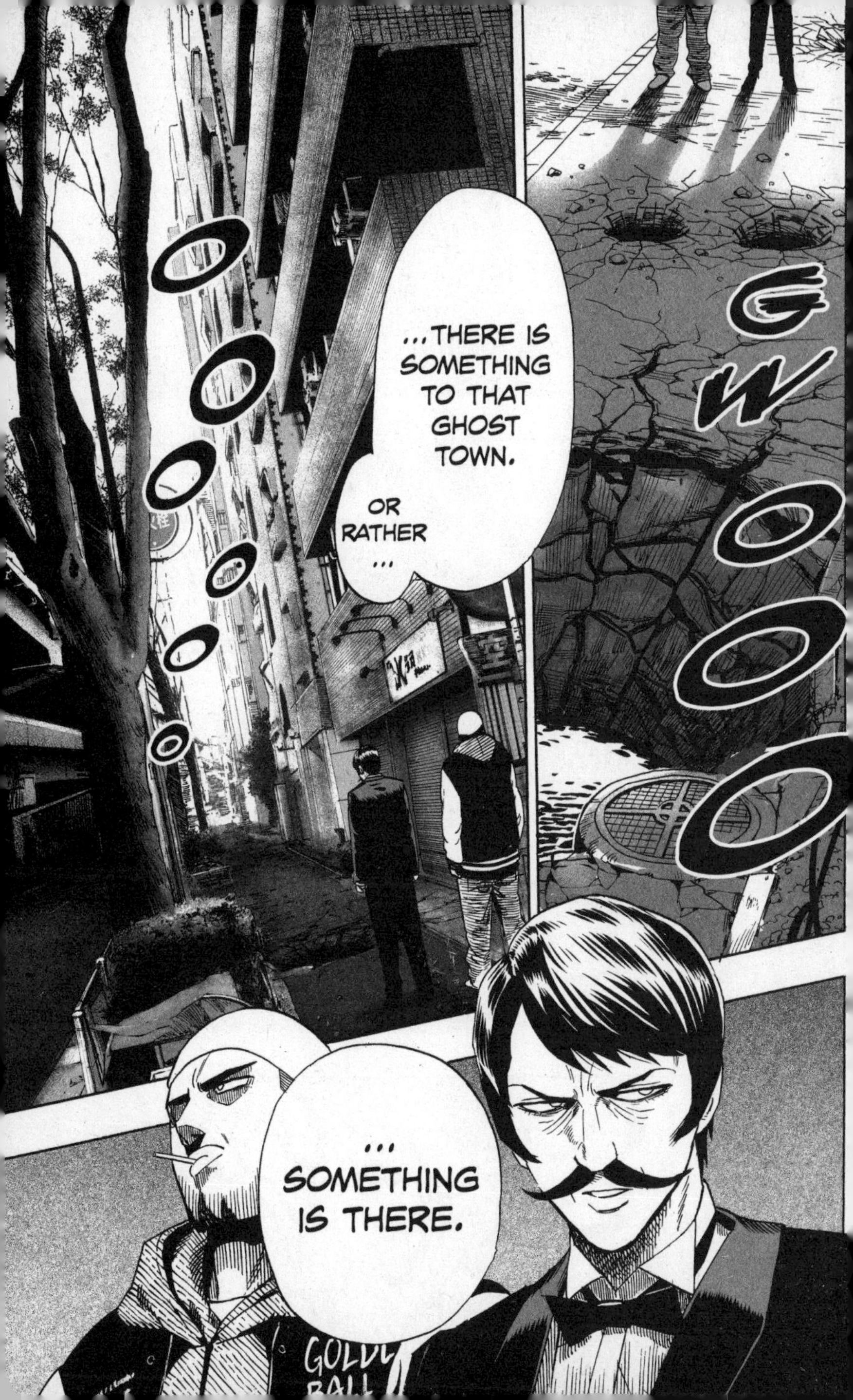
GWOOOO
...THERE IS SOMETHING TO THAT GHOST TOWN.
OR RATHER ...
... SOMETHING IS THERE.

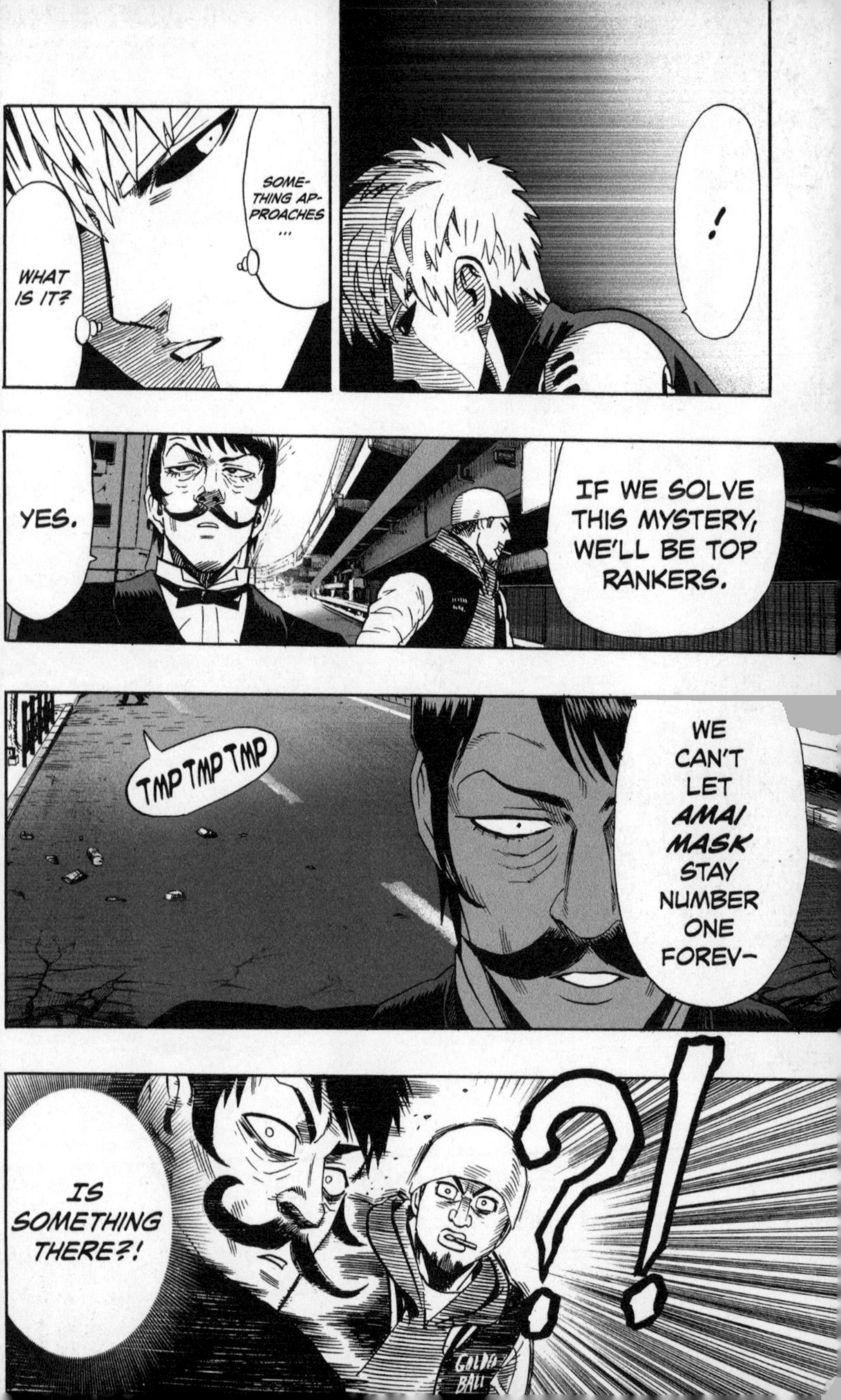
!
SOME-THING AP-PROACHES ...
WHAT IS IT?
IF WE SOLVE THIS MYSTERY, WE'LL BE TOP RANKERS.
YES.
WE CAN'T LET AMAI MASK STAY NUMBER ONE FOREV-
TMP TMP TMP
?!
IS SOMETHING THERE?!

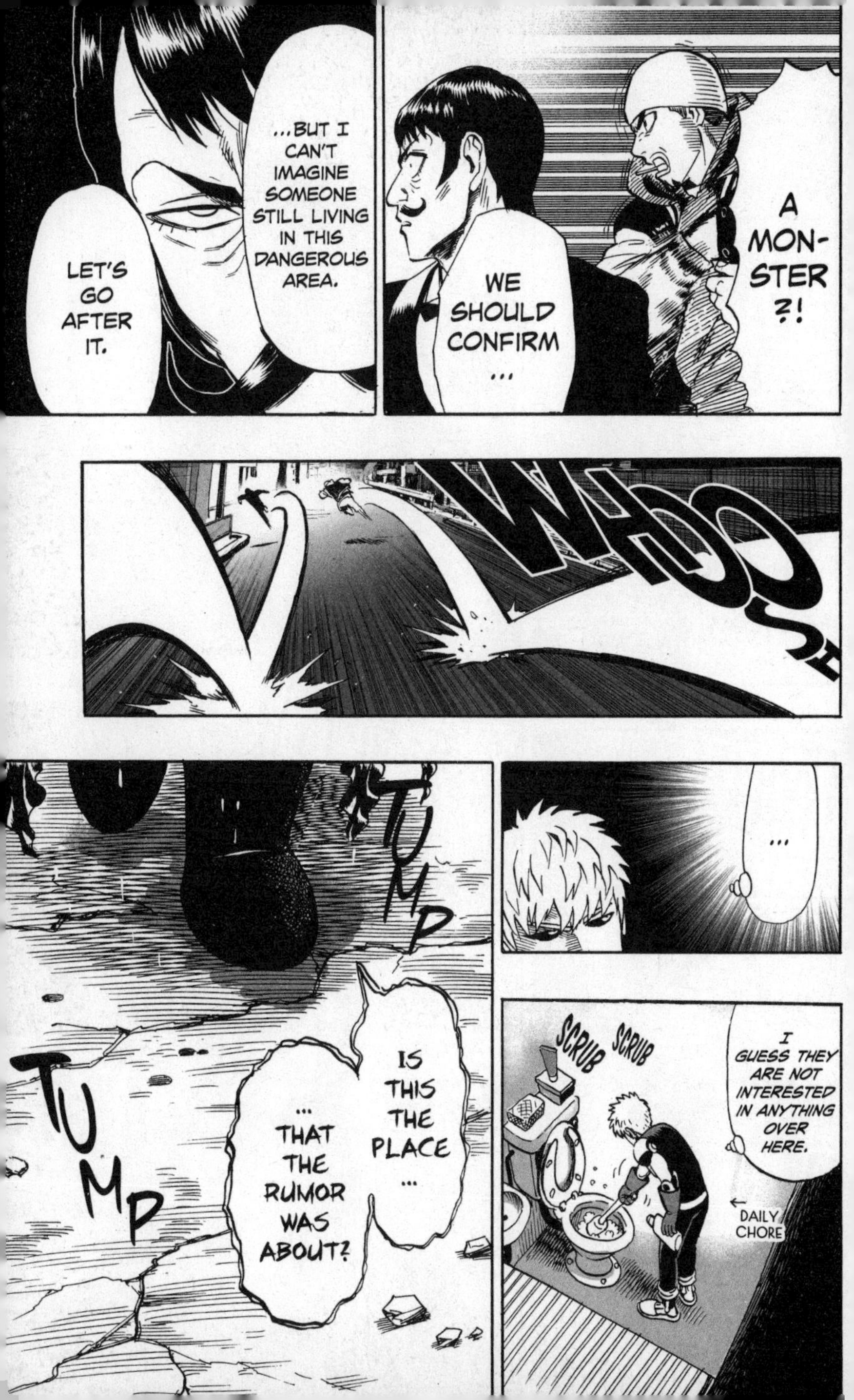
A MONSTER?!
WE SHOULD CONFIRM...
...BUT I CAN'T IMAGINE SOMEONE STILL LIVING IN THIS DANGEROUS AREA.
LET'S GO AFTER IT.
WHOOSH
...
SCRUB SCRUB
I GUESS THEY ARE NOT INTERESTED IN ANYTHING OVER HERE.
← DAILY CHORE
TUMP
TUMP
IS THIS THE PLACE...
...THAT THE RUMOR WAS ABOUT?

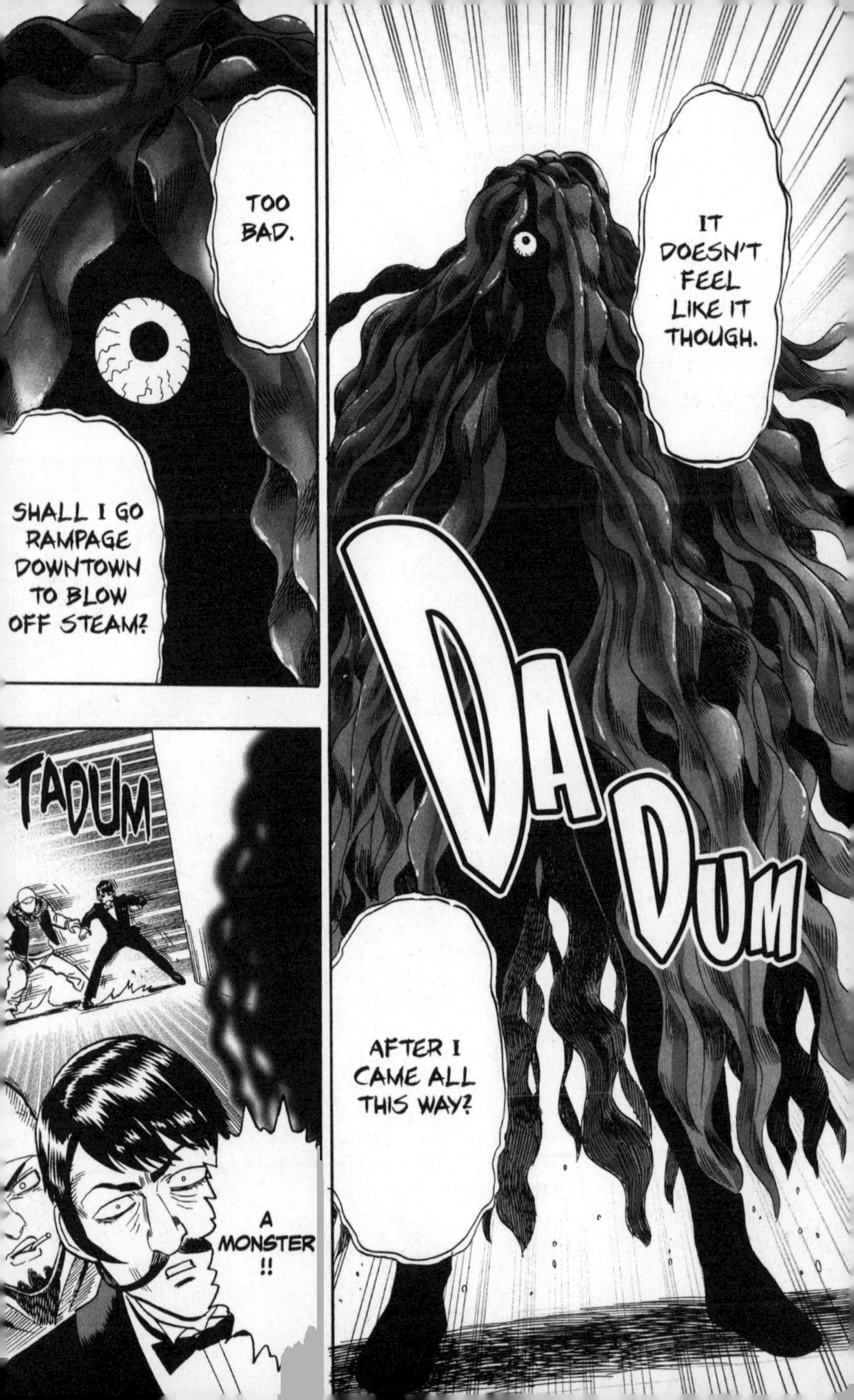
IT DOESN'T FEEL LIKE IT THOUGH.
DA DUM
AFTER I CAME ALL THIS WAY?
TOO BAD.
SHALL I GO RAMPAGE DOWNTOWN TO BLOW OFF STEAM?
TADUM
A MONSTER !!

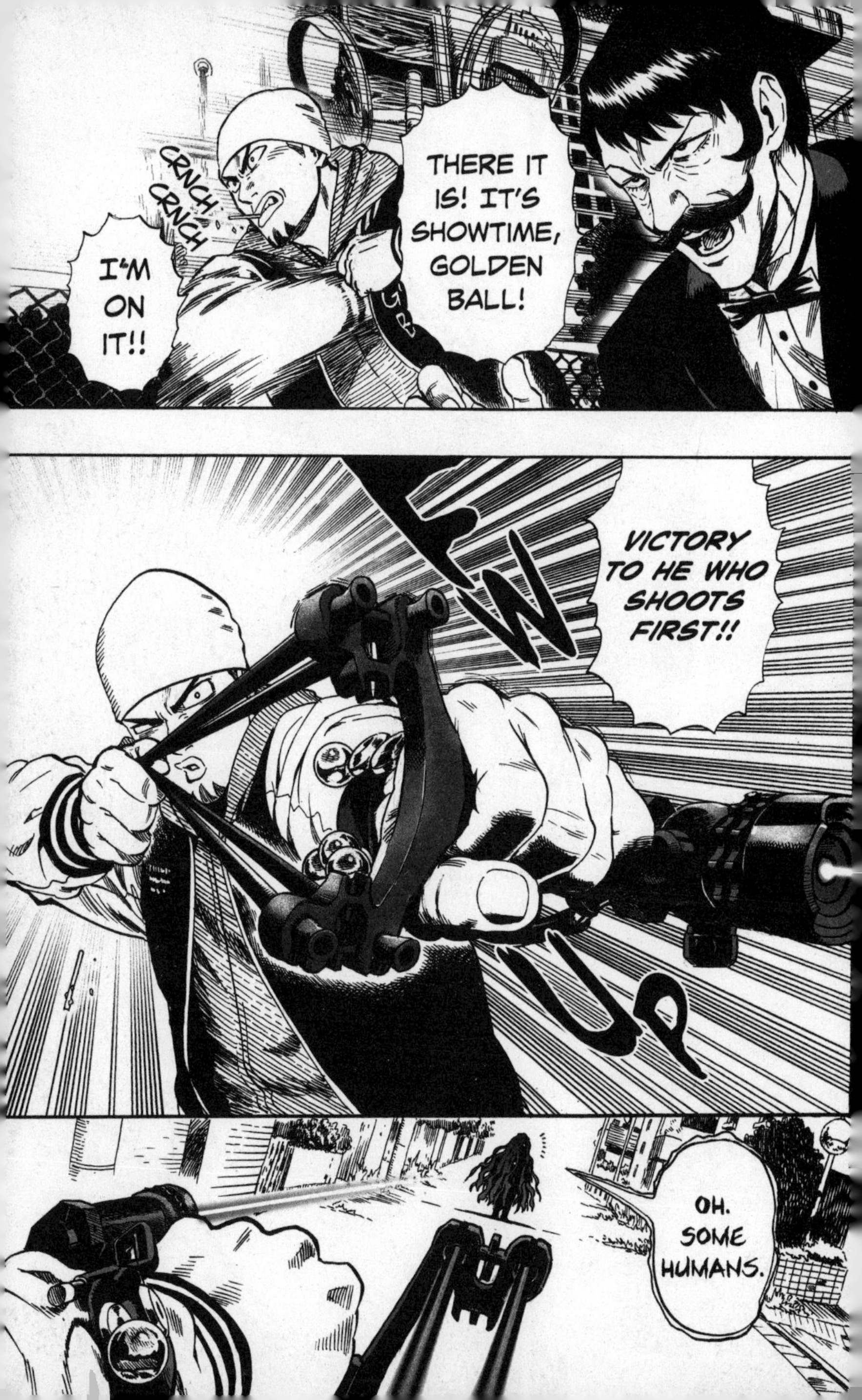
THERE IT IS! IT'S SHOWTIME, GOLDEN BALL!
CRNCH CRNCH
I'M ON IT!!
VICTORY TO HE WHO SHOOTS FIRST!!
FWUP
OH. SOME HUMANS.

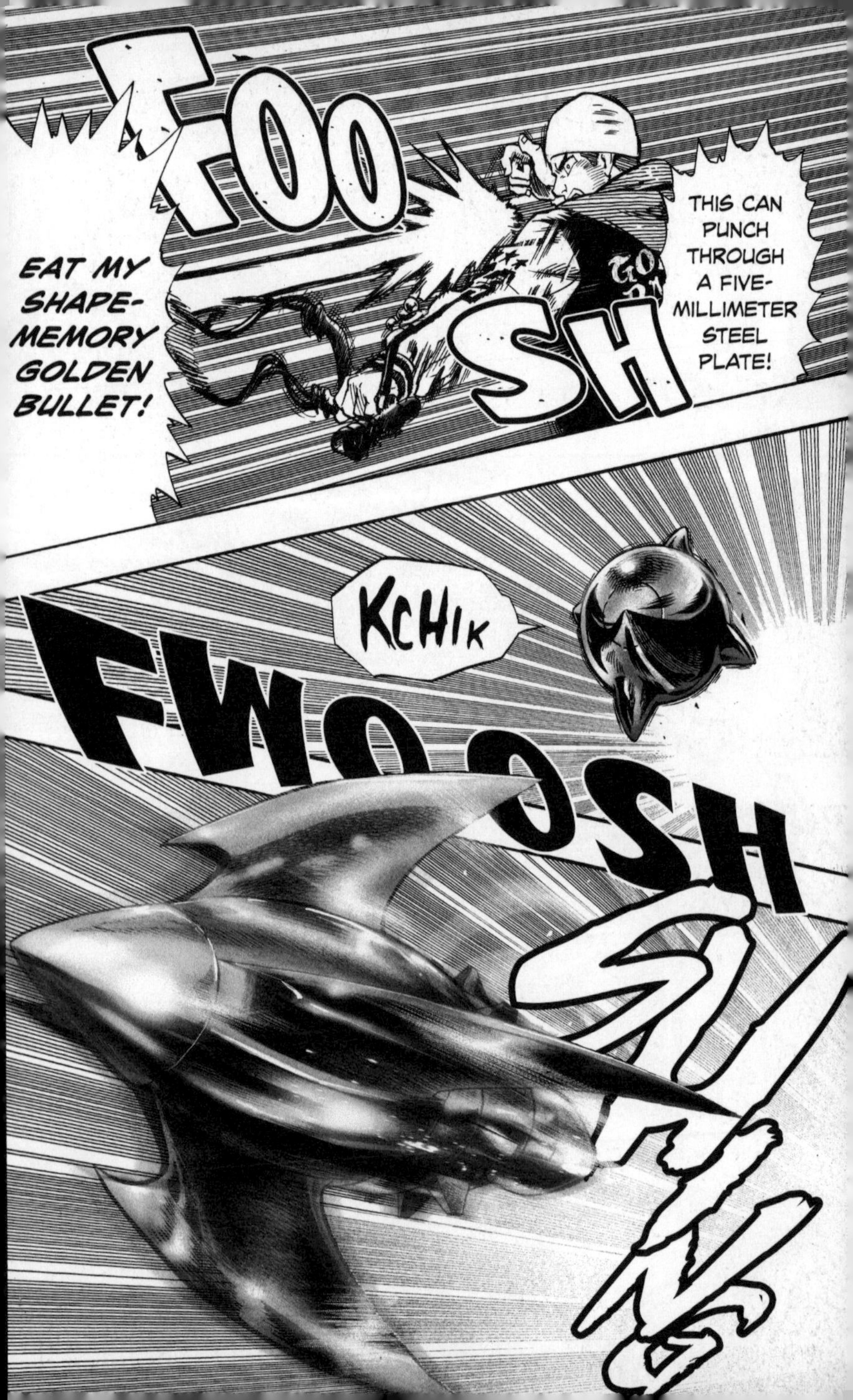
FOOSH
THIS CAN PUNCH THROUGH A FIVE-MILLIMETER STEEL PLATE!
EAT MY SHAPE-MEMORY GOLDEN BULLET!
KCHIK
FWOOSH
SHUNK

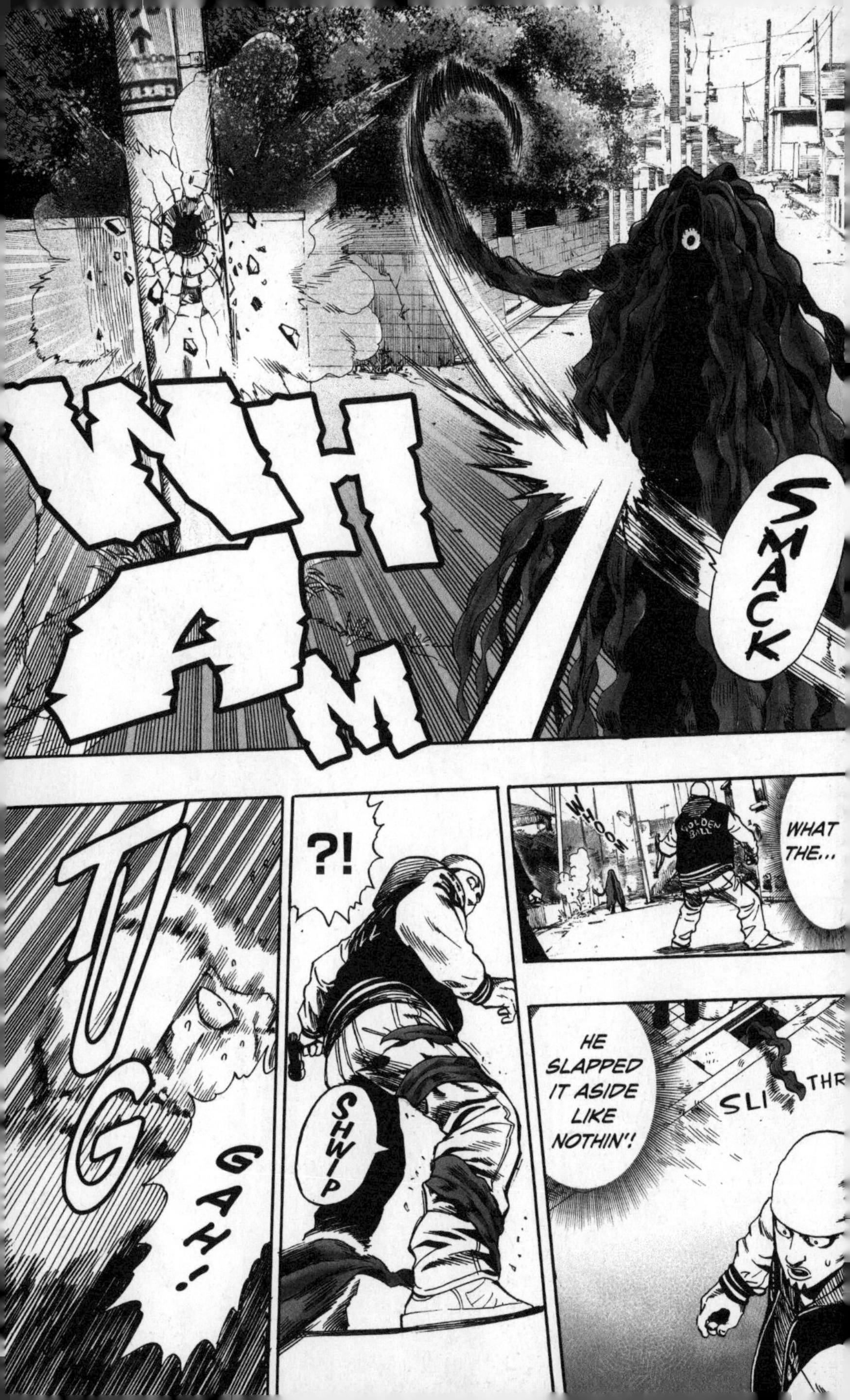
SMACK
WHAM
WHAT THE...
GOLDEN BALL
WHOOSH
HE SLAPPED IT ASIDE LIKE NOTHIN'!
SLI THR
?!
SHWIP
TUG
GAH!

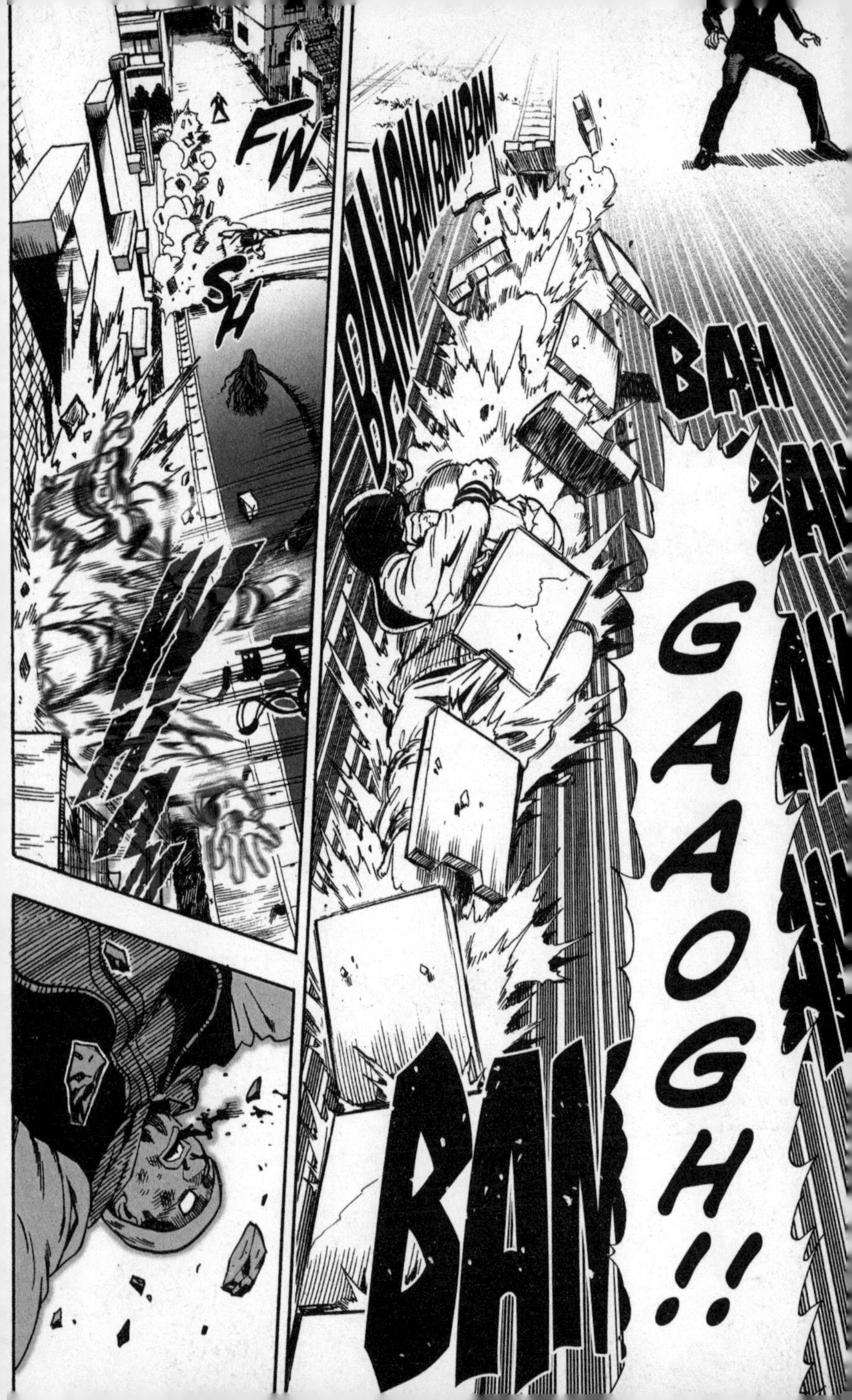

BAM
GAAOGH!!
BAM
BAM BAM BAM BAM BAM
FW
SH

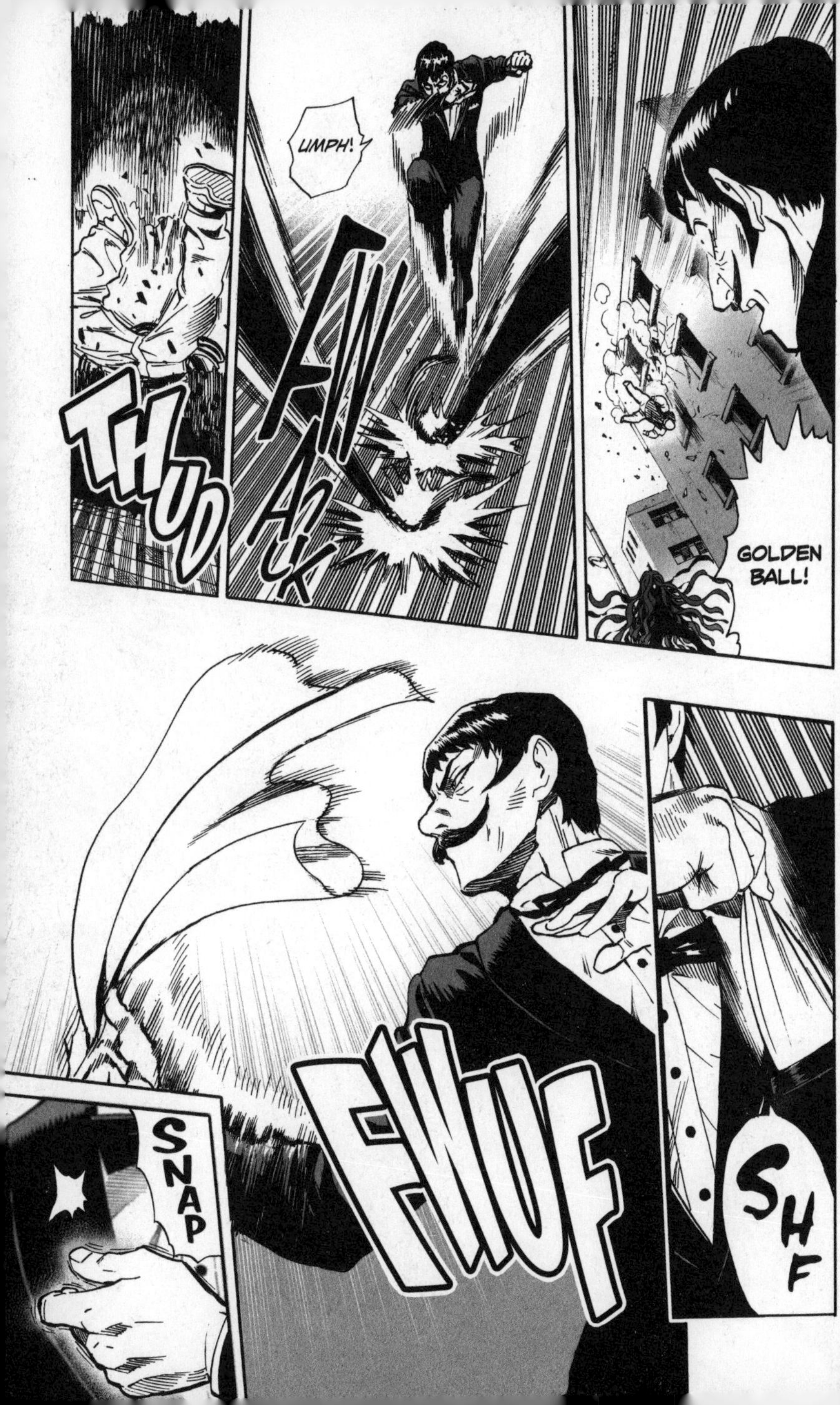

GOLDEN BALL!
UMPH!
THUD
SHF
FWUF
SNAP

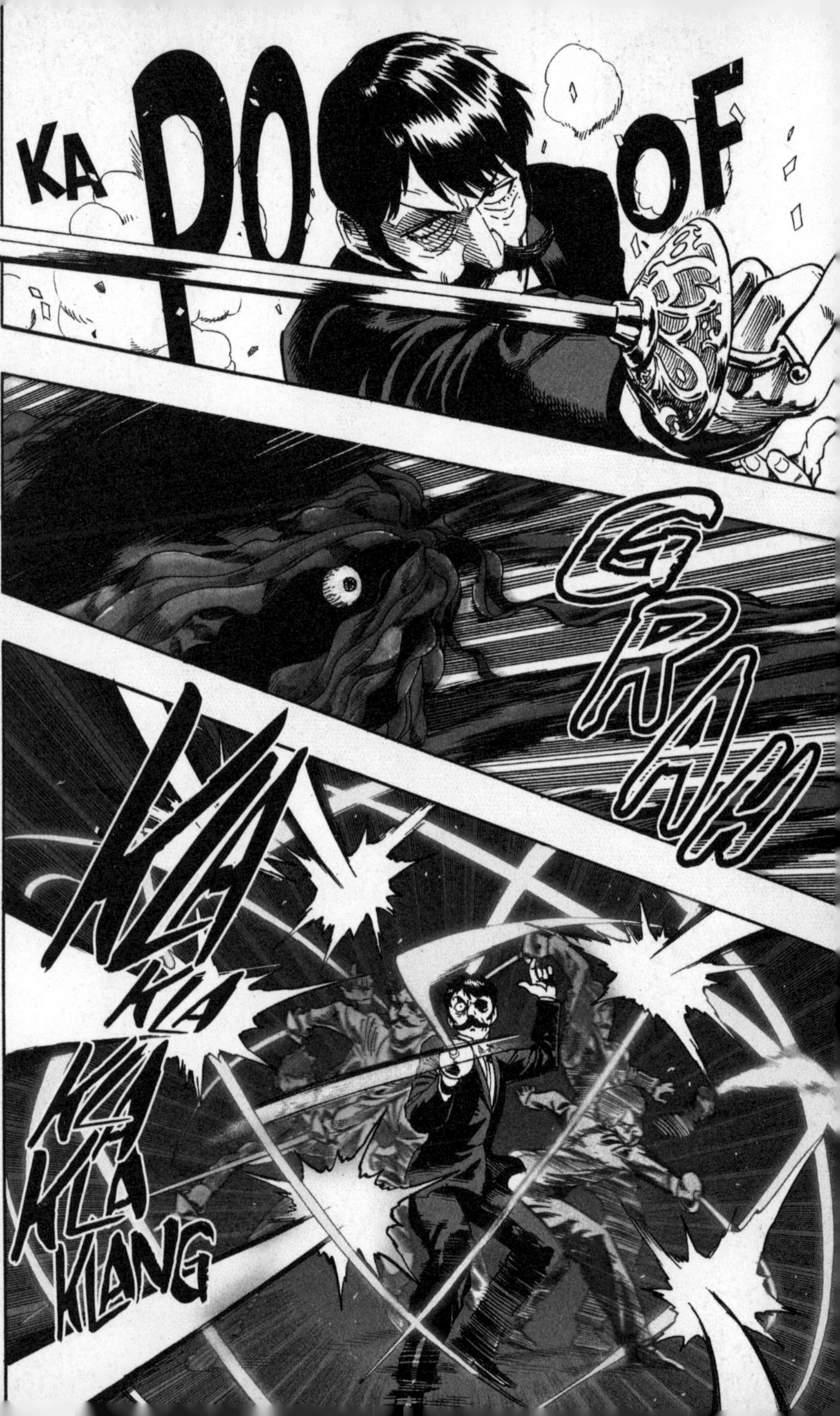
KA POOOF
GRAH
KLA
KLA
KLA
KLA
KLANG

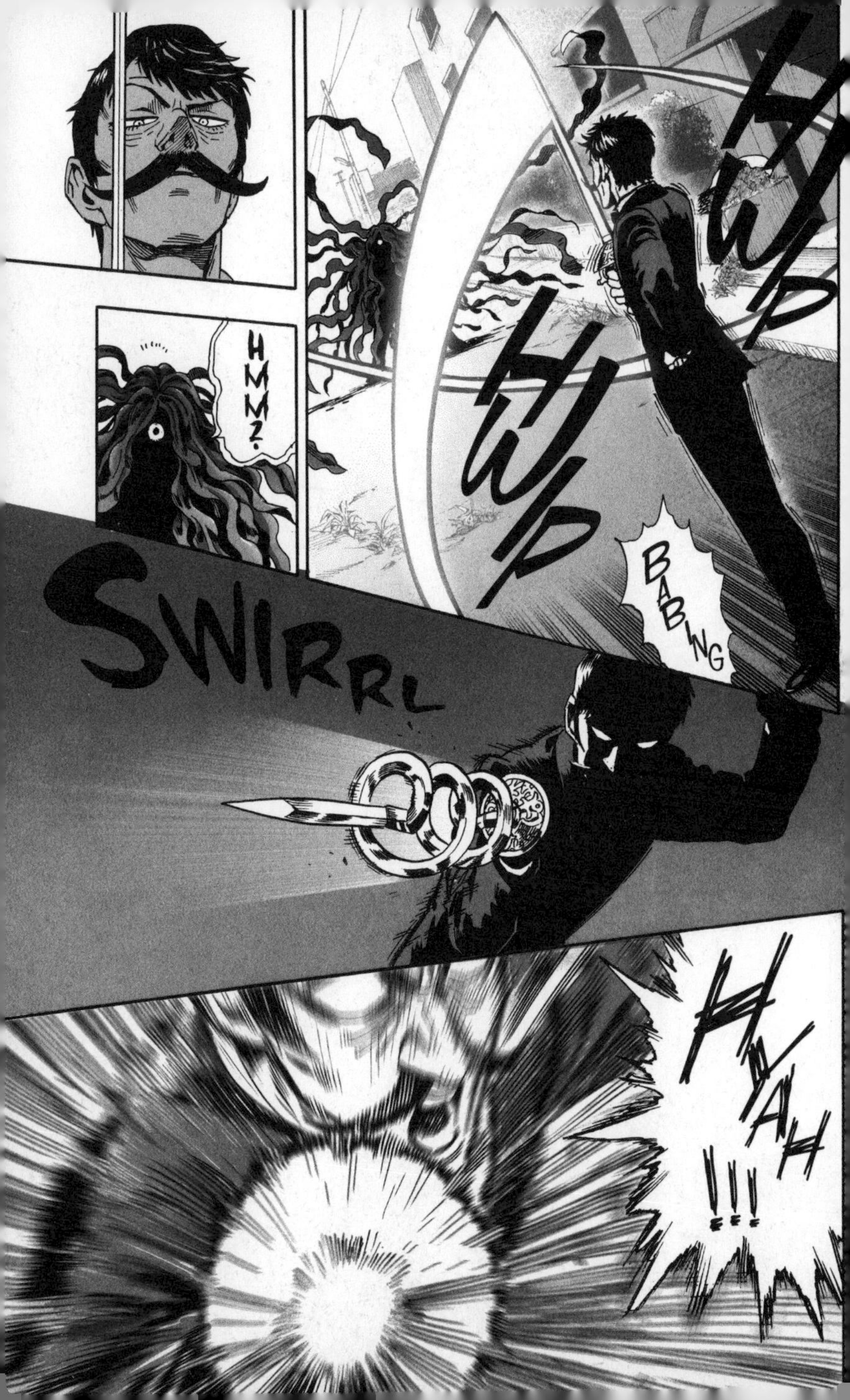

HWIP
HWIP
HMMZ?
SWIRRL
BABING
HYAH!!!

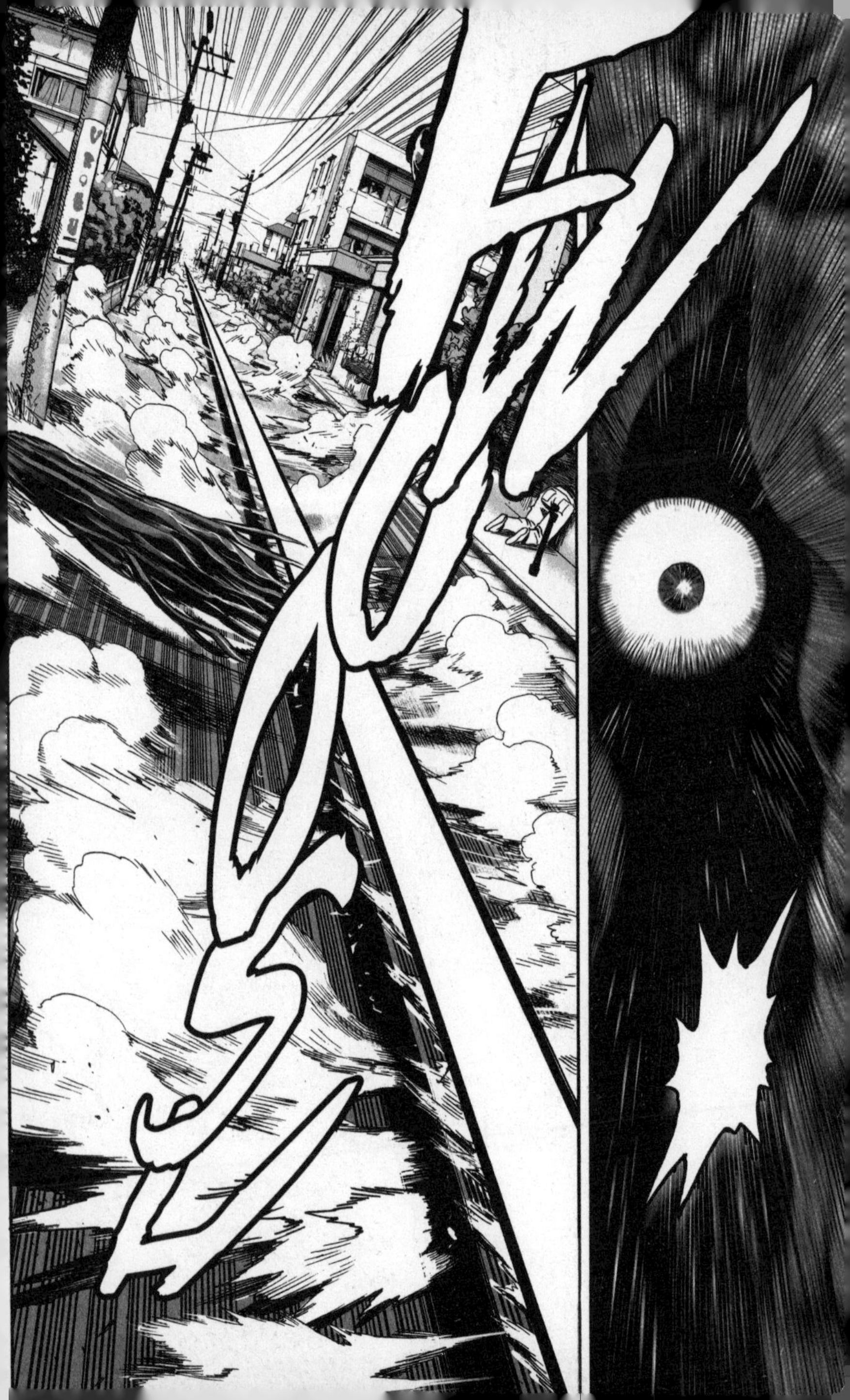

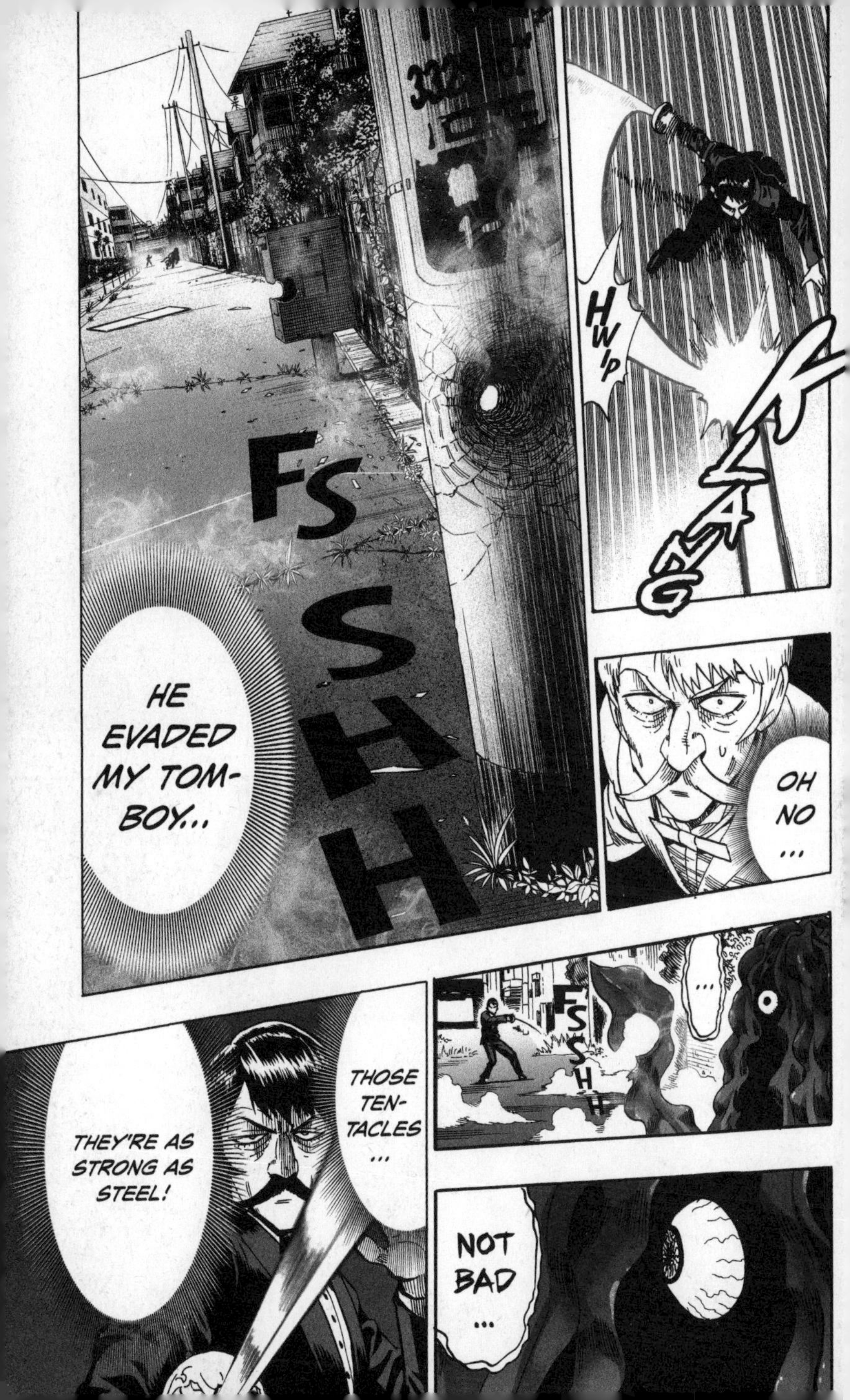

HWIP
KLANG
OH NO ...
FSSHH
HE EVADED MY TOM-BOY...
FSSHH
...
NOT BAD ...
THOSE TEN-TACLES ...
THEY'RE AS STRONG AS STEEL!

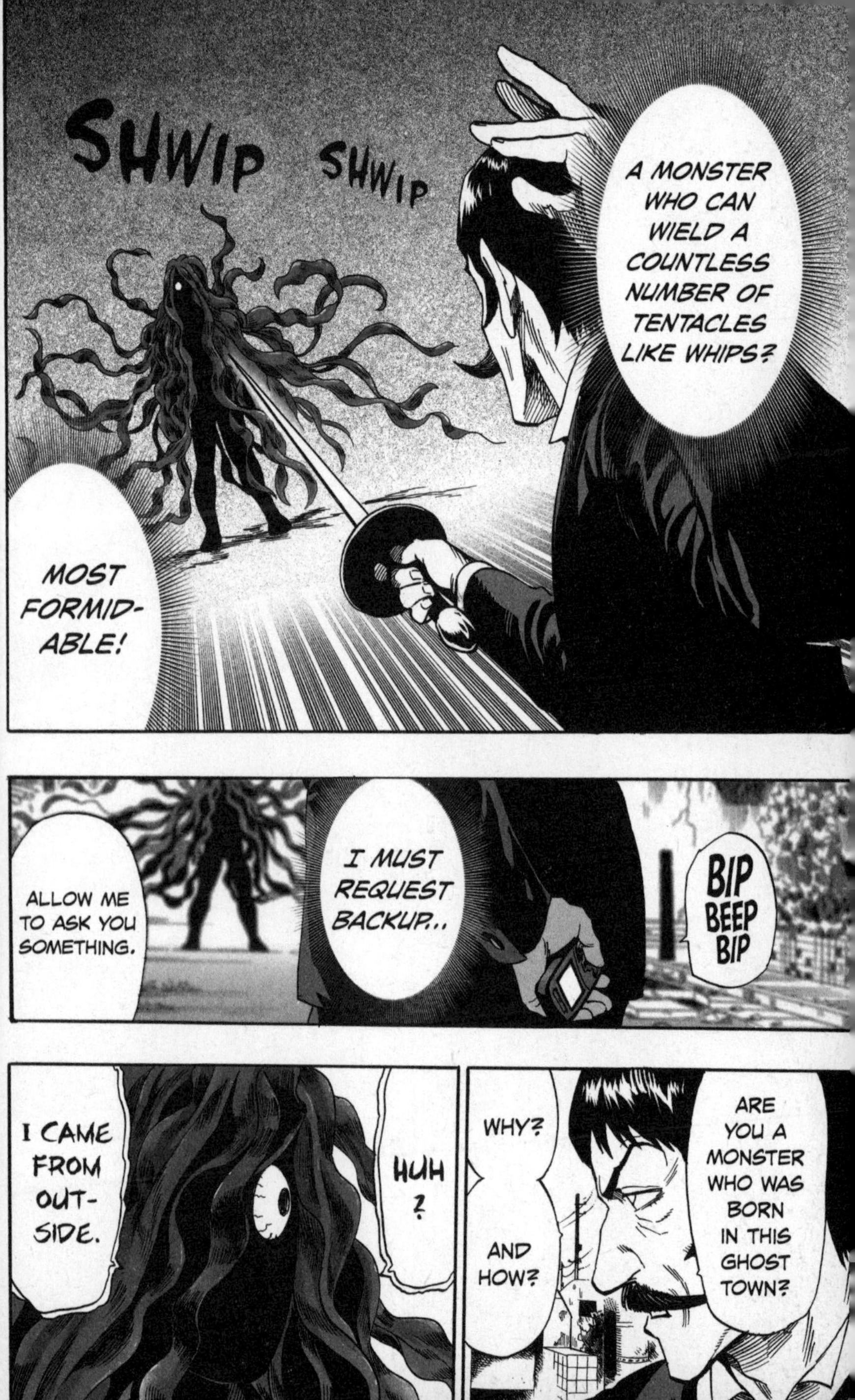
SHWIP
SHWIP
A MONSTER WHO CAN WIELD A COUNTLESS NUMBER OF TENTACLES LIKE WHIPS?
MOST FORMID-ABLE!
BIP BEEP BIP
I MUST REQUEST BACKUP...
ALLOW ME TO ASK YOU SOMETHING.
ARE YOU A MONSTER WHO WAS BORN IN THIS GHOST TOWN?
WHY?
AND HOW?
HUH?
I CAME FROM OUT-SIDE.

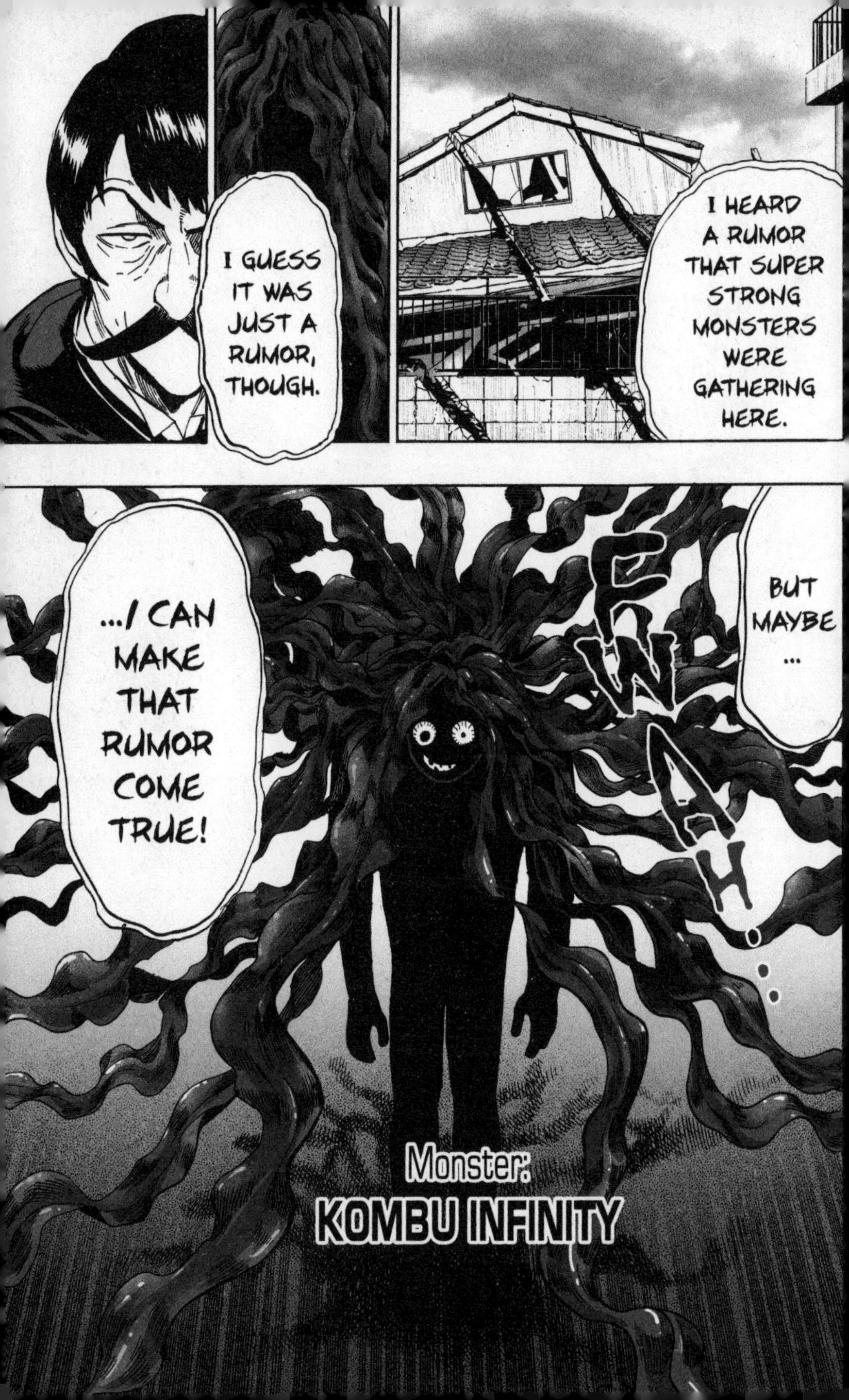
I HEARD A RUMOR THAT SUPER STRONG MONSTERS WERE GATHERING HERE.
I GUESS IT WAS JUST A RUMOR, THOUGH.
BUT MAYBE ...
...I CAN MAKE THAT RUMOR COME TRUE!
FWAAH...
Monster:
KOMBU INFINITY

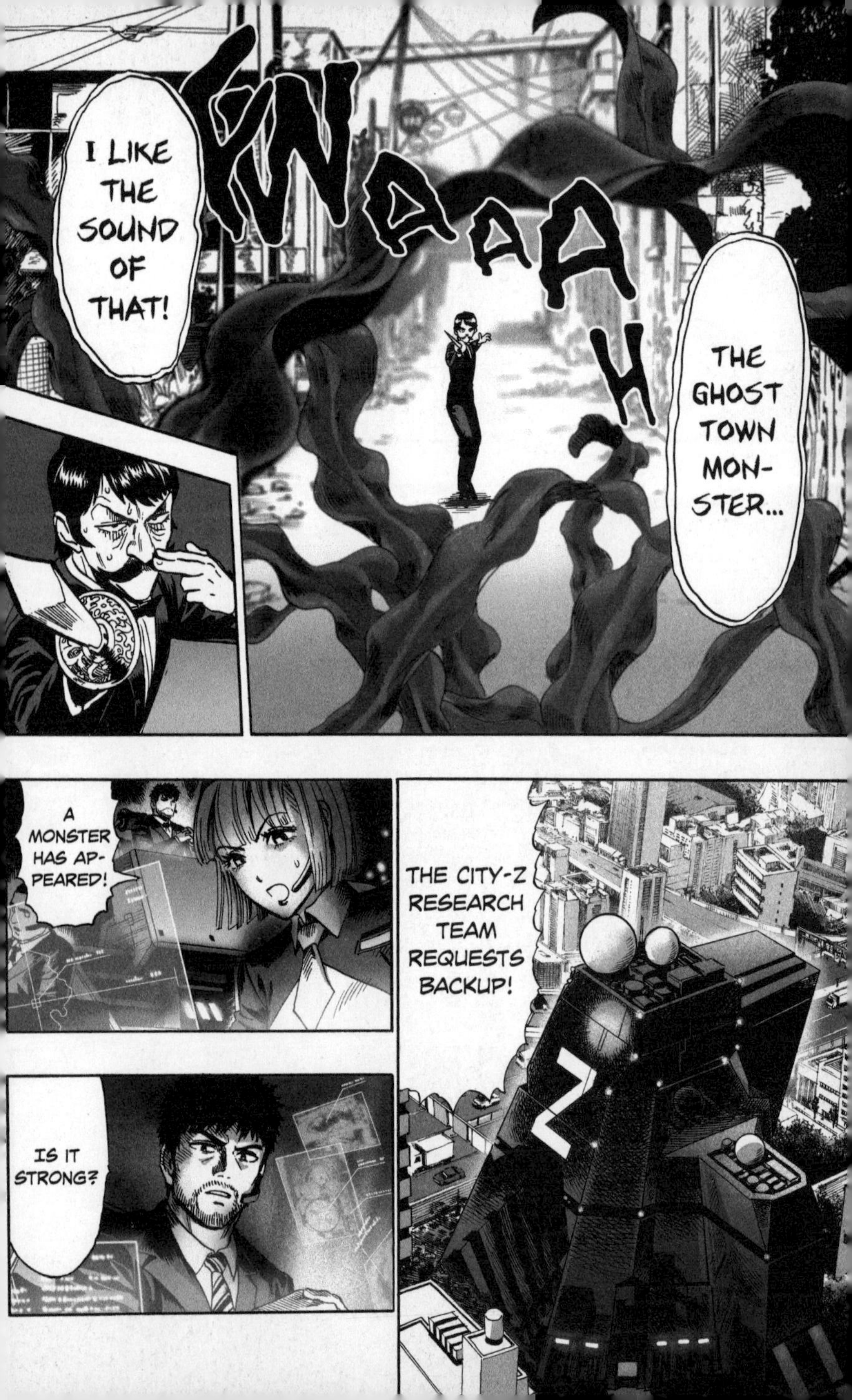
THE GHOST TOWN MON-STER...
KWAAAH
I LIKE THE SOUND OF THAT!
THE CITY-Z RESEARCH TEAM REQUESTS BACKUP!
A MONSTER HAS AP-PEARED!
IS IT STRONG?

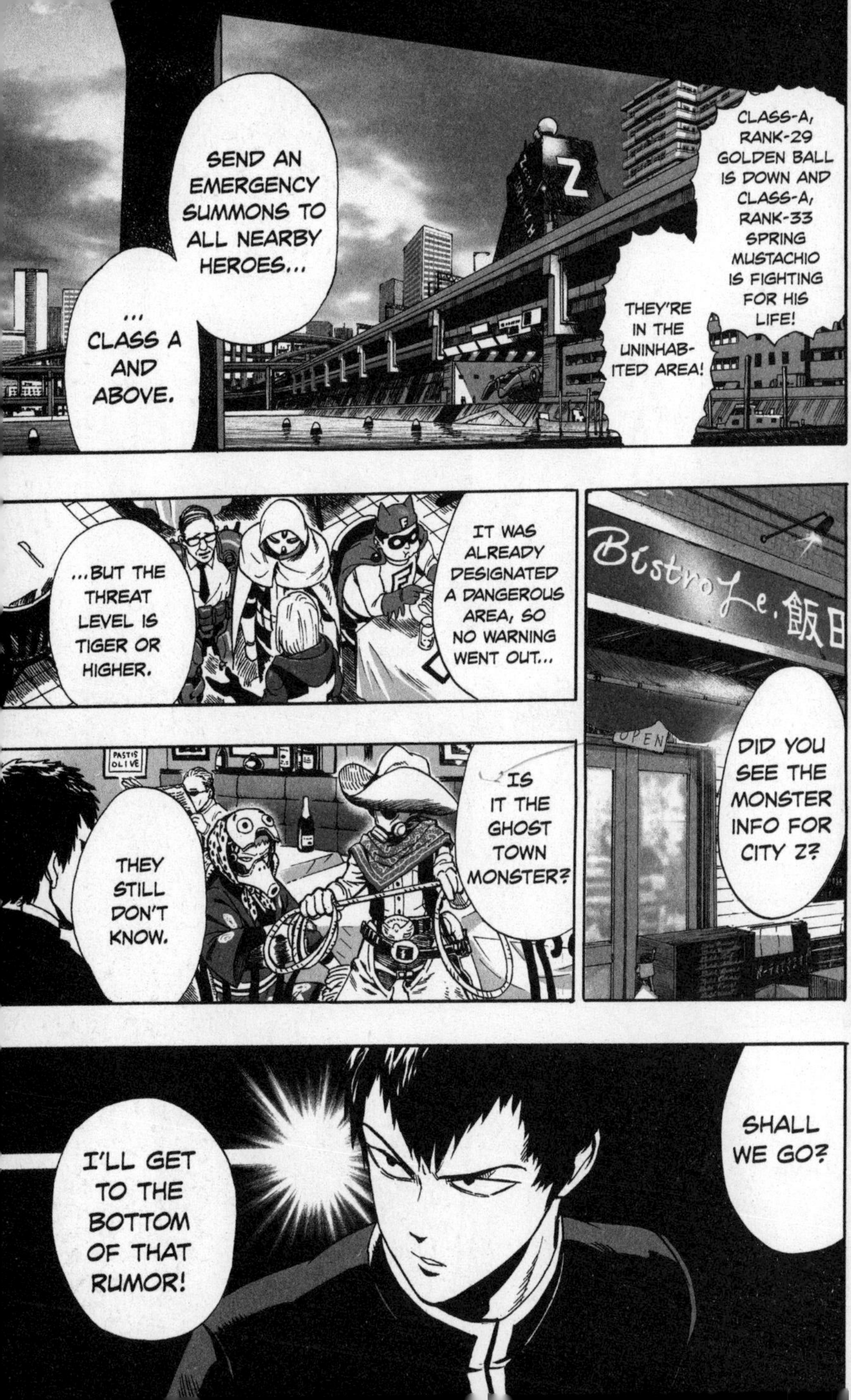
CLASS-A, RANK-29 GOLDEN BALL IS DOWN AND CLASS-A, RANK-33 SPRING MUSTACHIO IS FIGHTING FOR HIS LIFE!
THEY'RE IN THE UNINHAB-ITED AREA!
SEND AN EMERGENCY SUMMONS TO ALL NEARBY HEROES...
... CLASS A AND ABOVE.
Bistro Le. 飯
OPEN
DID YOU SEE THE MONSTER INFO FOR CITY Z?
IT WAS ALREADY DESIGNATED A DANGEROUS AREA, SO NO WARNING WENT OUT...
...BUT THE THREAT LEVEL IS TIGER OR HIGHER.
PASTIS OLIVE
IS IT THE GHOST TOWN MONSTER?
THEY STILL DON'T KNOW.
SHALL WE GO?
I'LL GET TO THE BOTTOM OF THAT RUMOR!

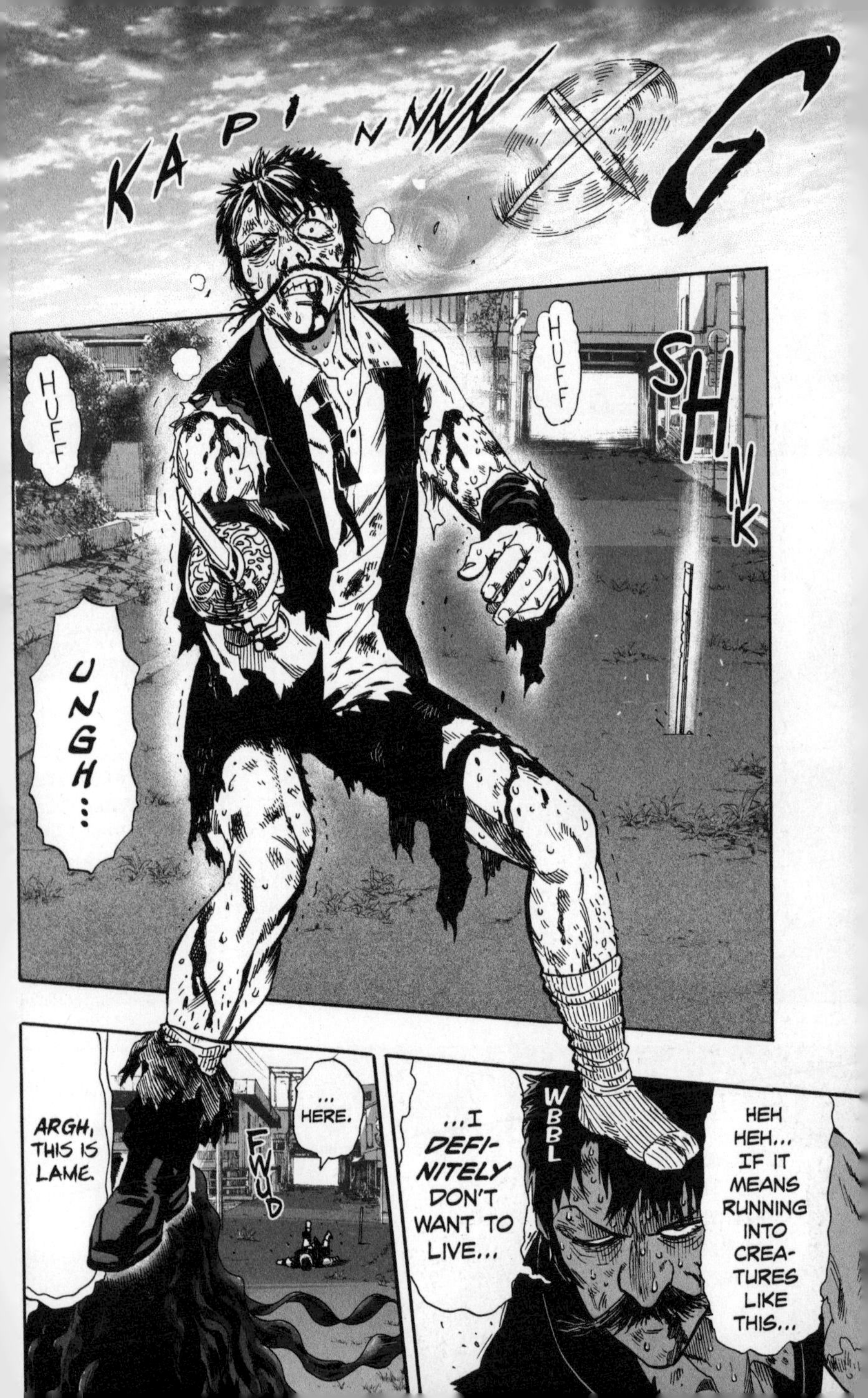
KAPINNNNG
HUFF
HUFF
SHNK
UNGH...
HEH HEH... IF IT MEANS RUNNING INTO CREATURES LIKE THIS...
WBBL
...I DEFINITELY DON'T WANT TO LIVE...
...HERE.
FWUD
ARGH, THIS IS LAME.

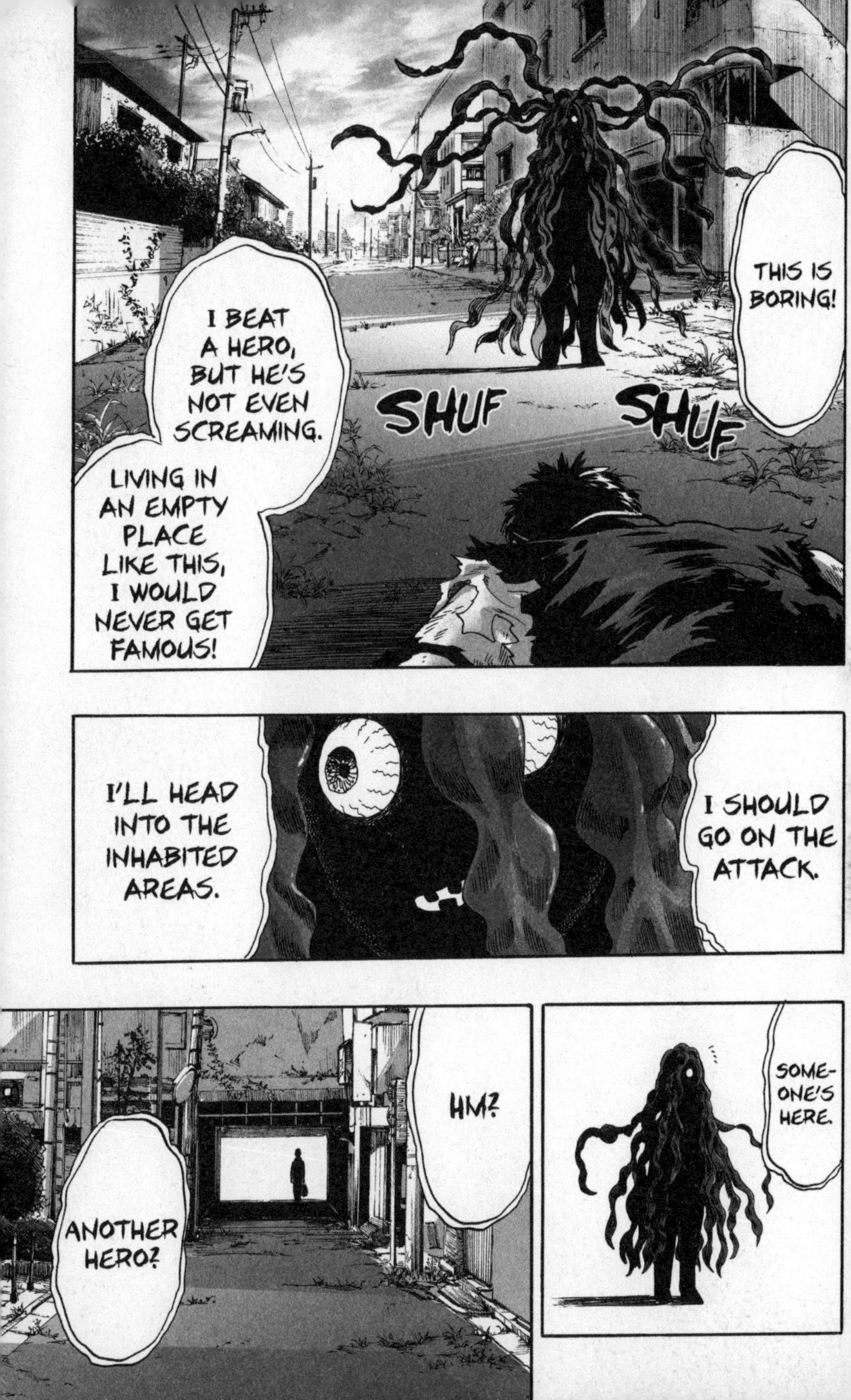
THIS IS BORING!
I BEAT A HERO, BUT HE'S NOT EVEN SCREAMING.
LIVING IN AN EMPTY PLACE LIKE THIS, I WOULD NEVER GET FAMOUS!
SHUF
SHUF
I SHOULD GO ON THE ATTACK.
I'LL HEAD INTO THE INHABITED AREAS.
SOME-ONE'S HERE.
HM?
ANOTHER HERO?

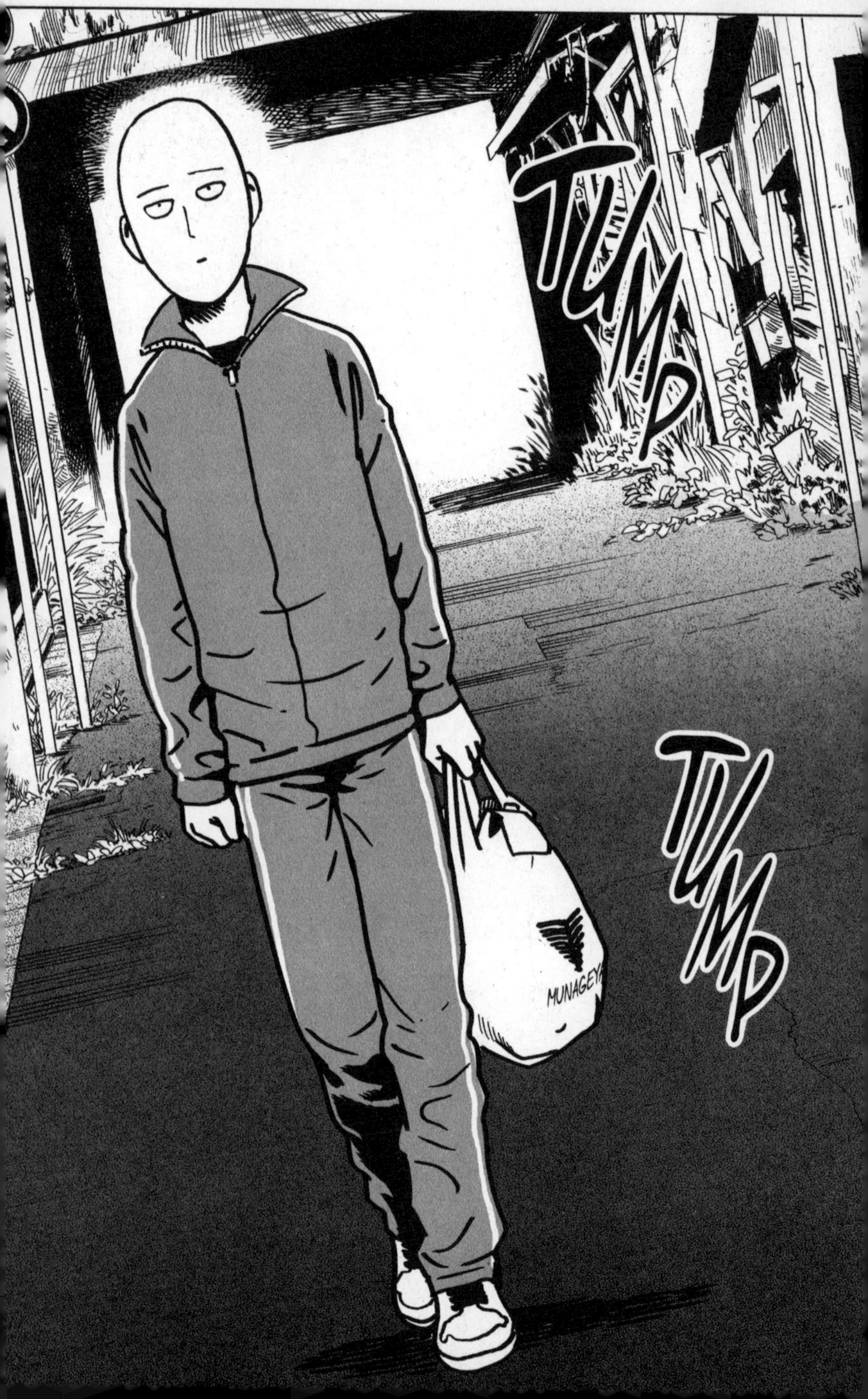
THUMP
THUMP
MUNAGEYA

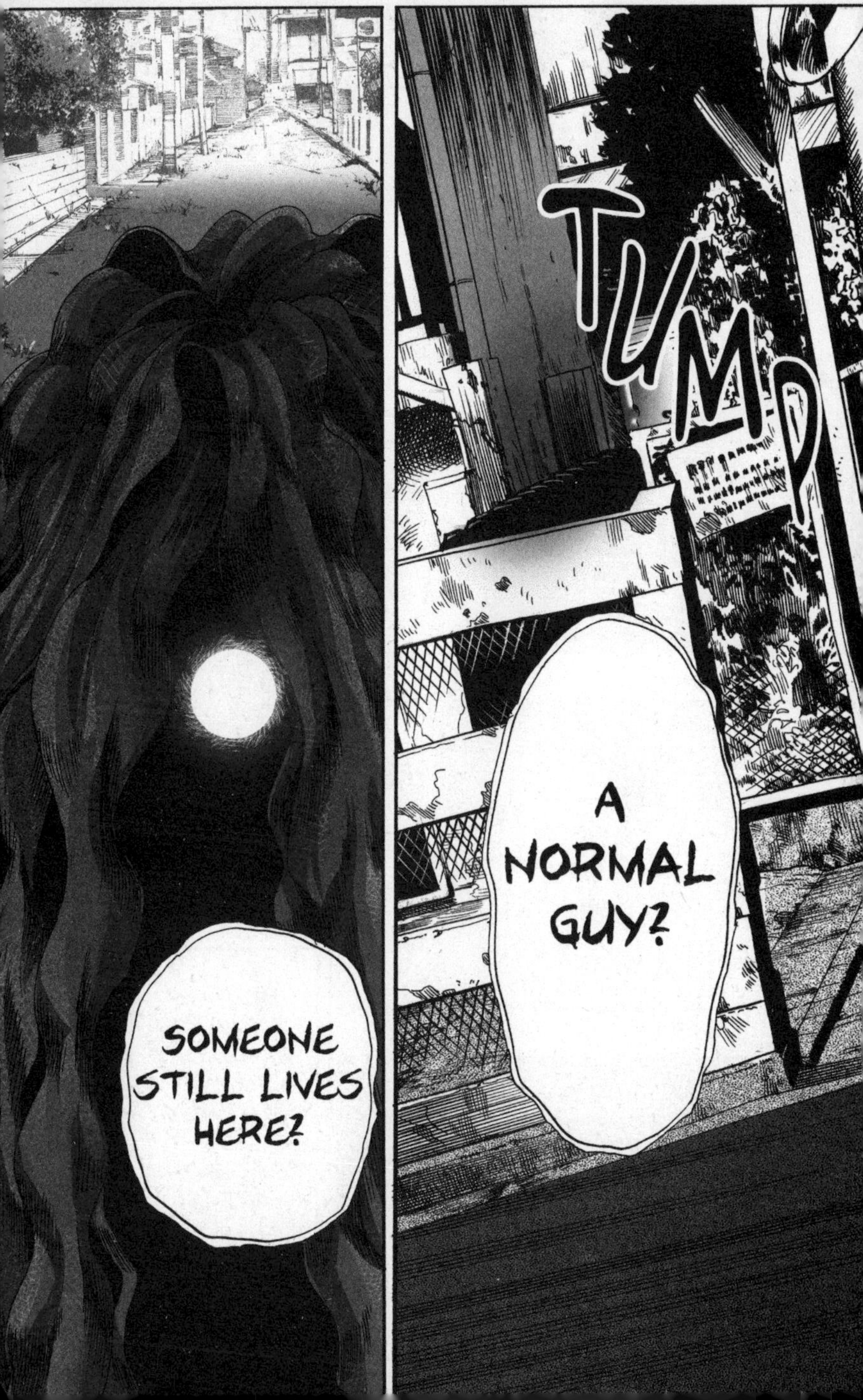
TUMP
A NORMAL GUY?
SOMEONE STILL LIVES HERE?

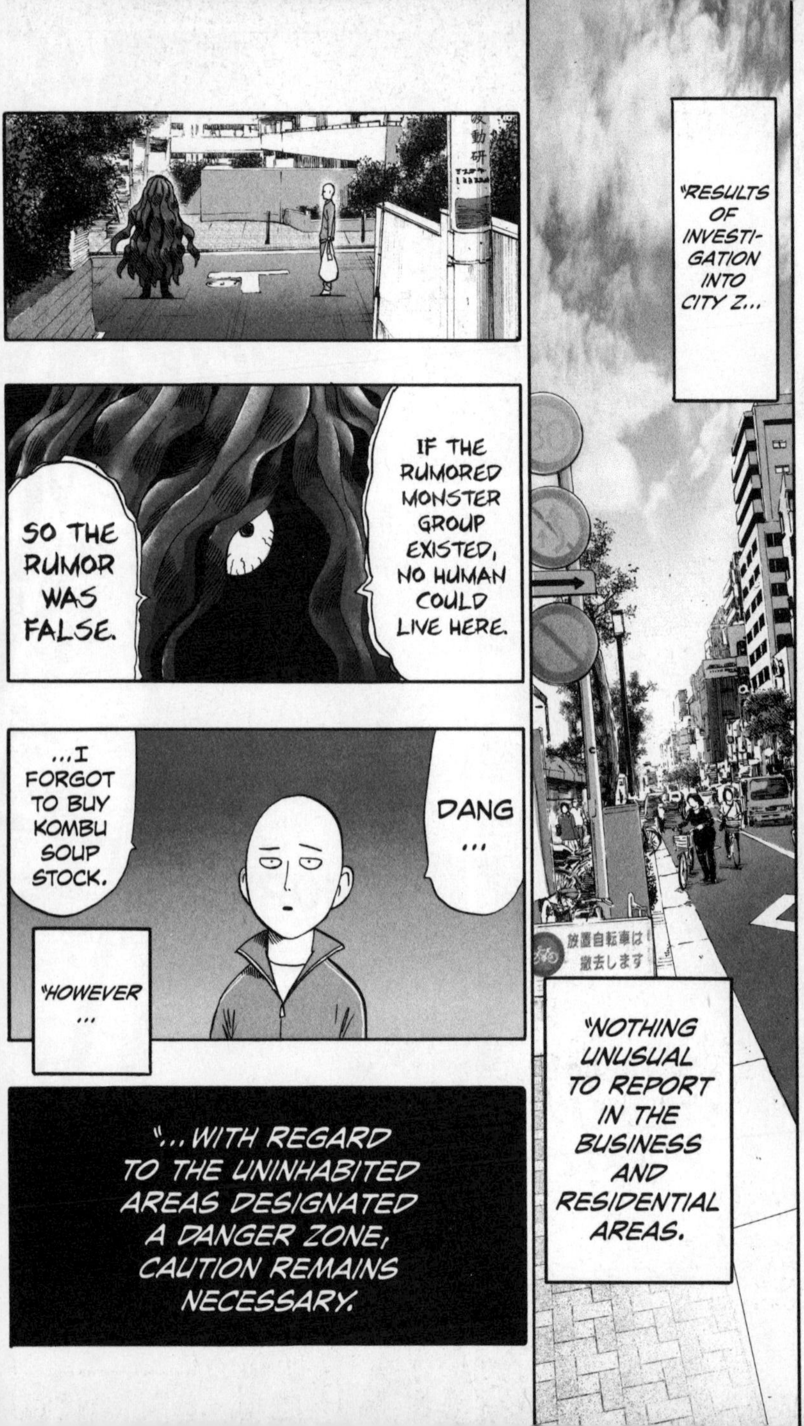
"RESULTS OF INVESTIGATION INTO CITY Z...
放置自転車は 撤去します
"NOTHING UNUSUAL TO REPORT IN THE BUSINESS AND RESIDENTIAL AREAS.
IF THE RUMORED MONSTER GROUP EXISTED, NO HUMAN COULD LIVE HERE.
SO THE RUMOR WAS FALSE.
DANG...
...I FORGOT TO BUY KOMBU SOUP STOCK.
"HOWEVER...
"...WITH REGARD TO THE UNINHABITED AREAS DESIGNATED A DANGER ZONE, CAUTION REMAINS NECESSARY.

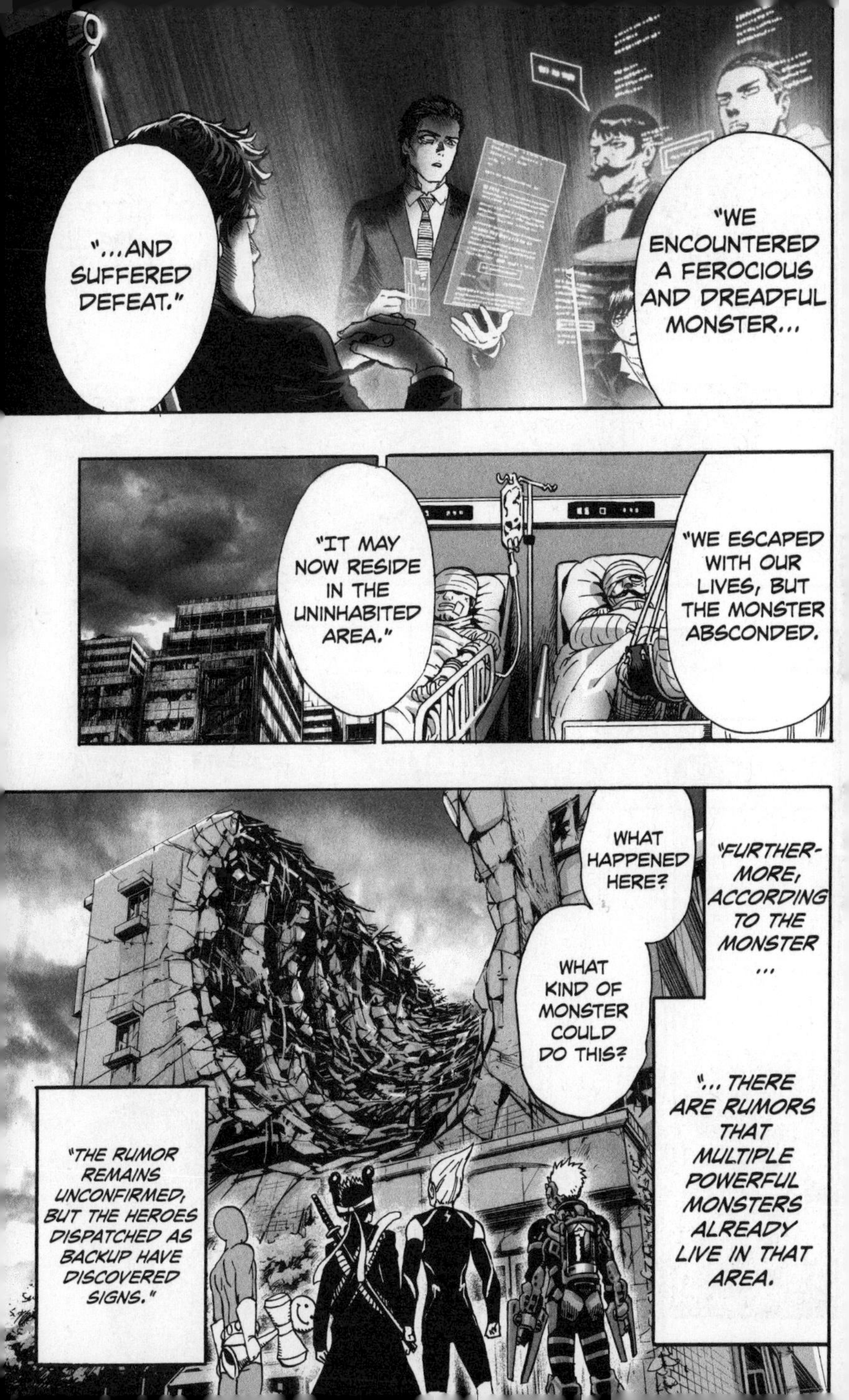
"WE ENCOUNTERED A FEROCIOUS AND DREADFUL MONSTER...
"...AND SUFFERED DEFEAT."
"WE ESCAPED WITH OUR LIVES, BUT THE MONSTER ABSCONDED.
"IT MAY NOW RESIDE IN THE UNINHABITED AREA."
"FURTHER-MORE, ACCORDING TO THE MONSTER ...
WHAT HAPPENED HERE?
WHAT KIND OF MONSTER COULD DO THIS?
"... THERE ARE RUMORS THAT MULTIPLE POWERFUL MONSTERS ALREADY LIVE IN THAT AREA.
"THE RUMOR REMAINS UNCONFIRMED, BUT THE HEROES DISPATCHED AS BACKUP HAVE DISCOVERED SIGNS."

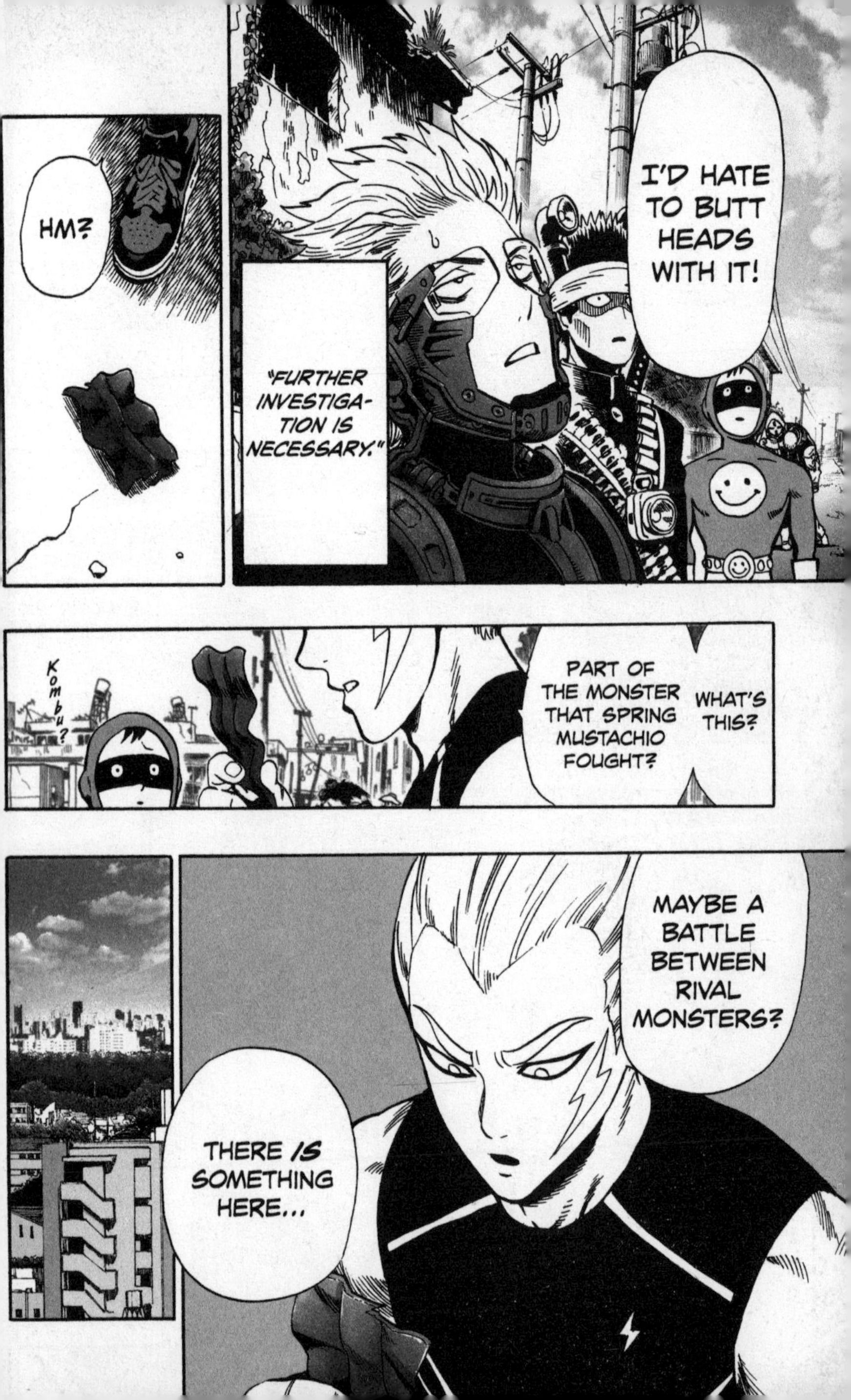
I'D HATE TO BUTT HEADS WITH IT!
"FURTHER INVESTIGATION IS NECESSARY."
HM?
WHAT'S THIS?
PART OF THE MONSTER THAT SPRING MUSTACHIO FOUGHT?
Kombu?
MAYBE A BATTLE BETWEEN RIVAL MONSTERS?
THERE IS SOMETHING HERE...

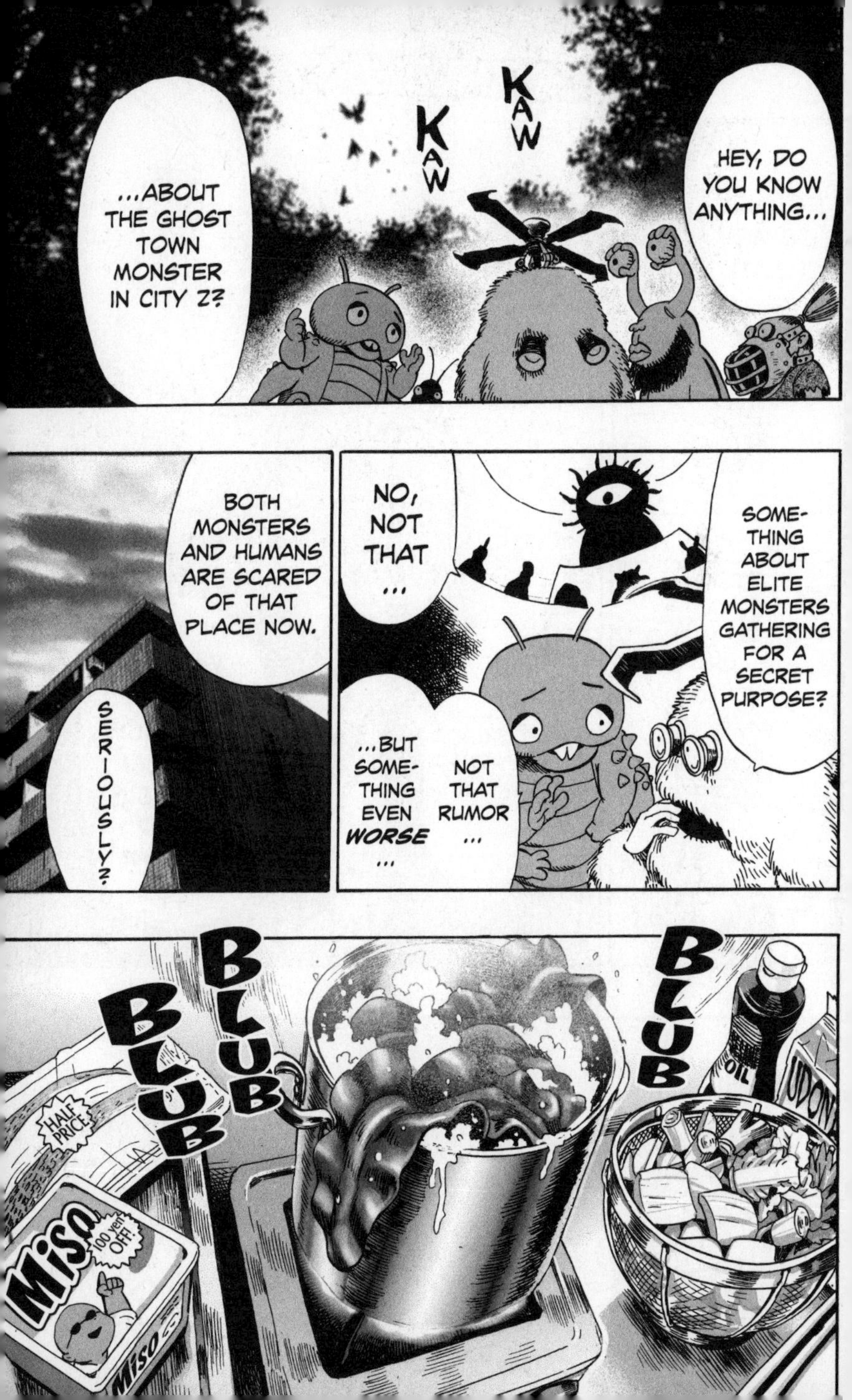
HEY, DO YOU KNOW ANYTHING...
KAW
KAW
...ABOUT THE GHOST TOWN MONSTER IN CITY Z?
SOME-THING ABOUT ELITE MONSTERS GATHERING FOR A SECRET PURPOSE?
NO, NOT THAT ...
NOT THAT RUMOR ...
...BUT SOME-THING EVEN WORSE ...
BOTH MONSTERS AND HUMANS ARE SCARED OF THAT PLACE NOW.
SERIOUSLY?
BLUB
BLUB
BLUB
BLUB
OIL
UDON
HALF PRICE
Miso
100 yen OFF!
MISO

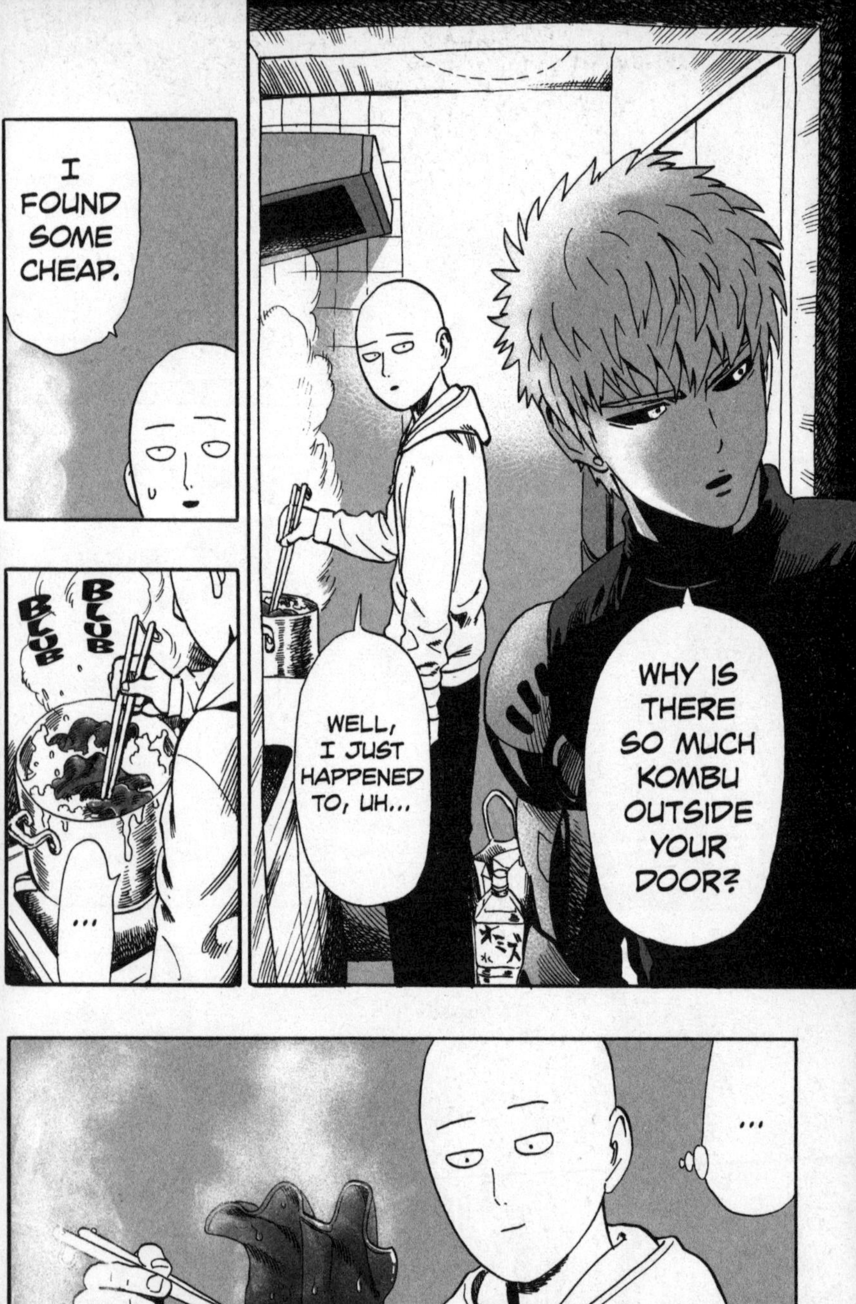
WHY IS THERE SO MUCH KOMBU OUTSIDE YOUR DOOR?
WELL, I JUST HAPPENED TO, UH...
オミズ
I FOUND SOME CHEAP.
BLUB BLUB
...
...

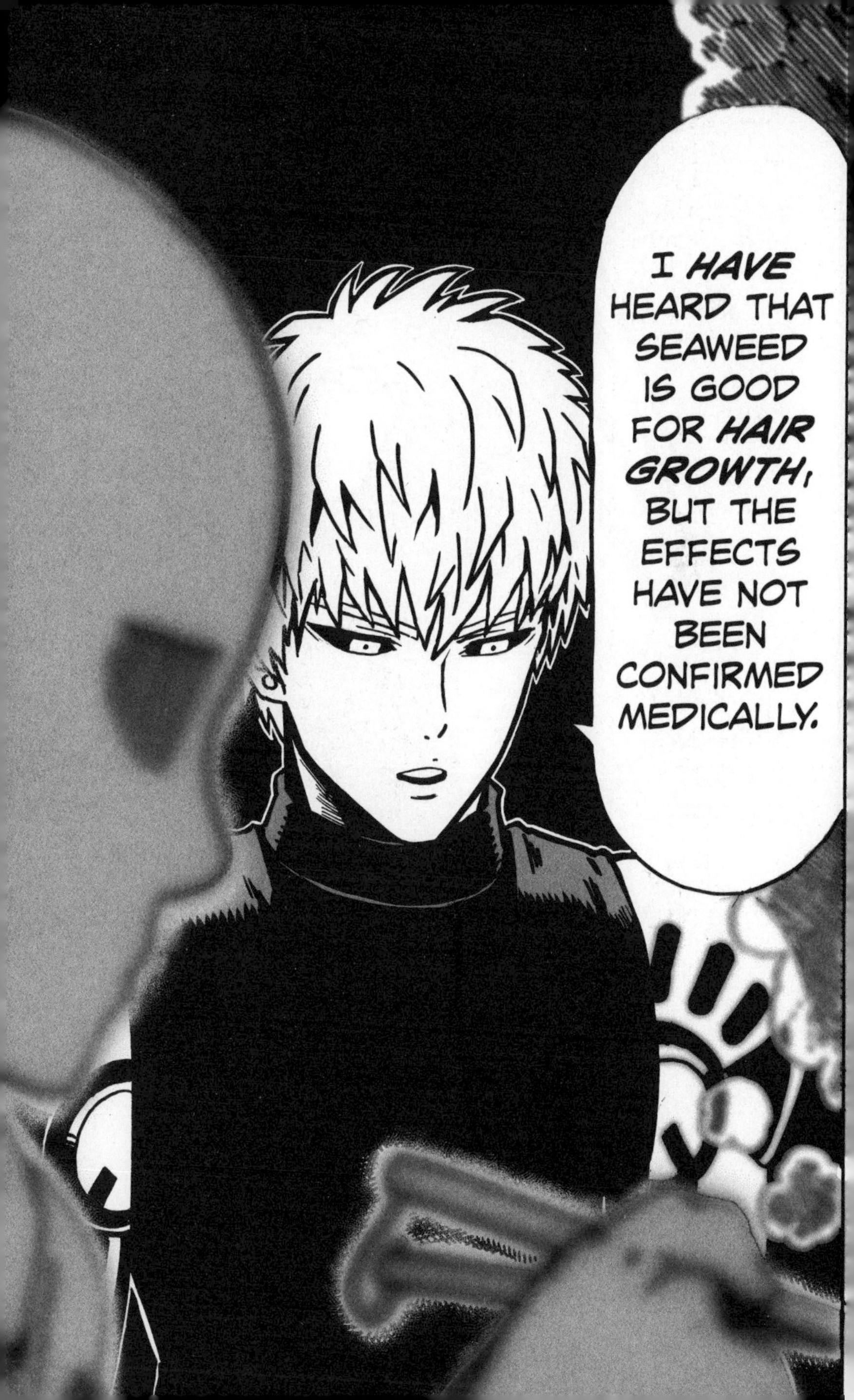
I *HAVE* HEARD THAT SEAWEED IS GOOD FOR *HAIR GROWTH*, BUT THE EFFECTS HAVE NOT BEEN CONFIRMED MEDICALLY.

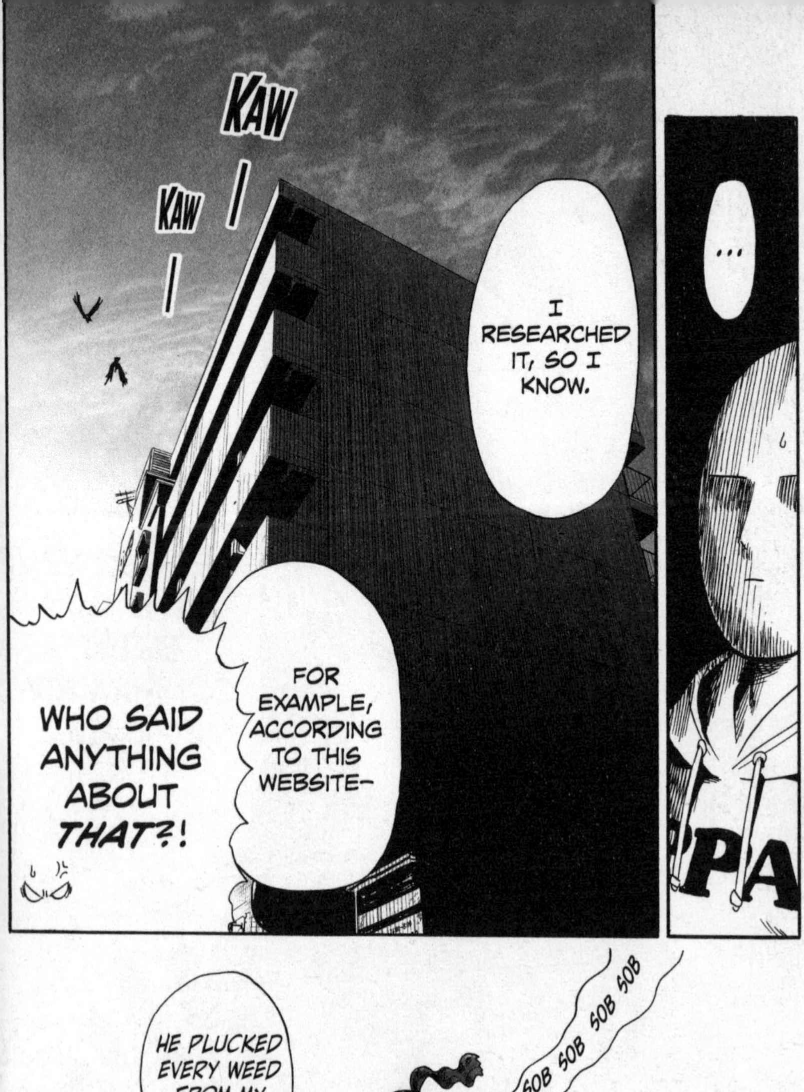
...
PA
KAW
KAW
I RESEARCHED IT, SO I KNOW.
FOR EXAMPLE, ACCORDING TO THIS WEBSITE–
WHO SAID ANYTHING ABOUT THAT?!
SOB SOB SOB SOB
HE PLUCKED EVERY WEED FROM MY BODY...

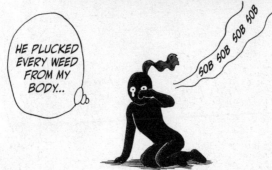

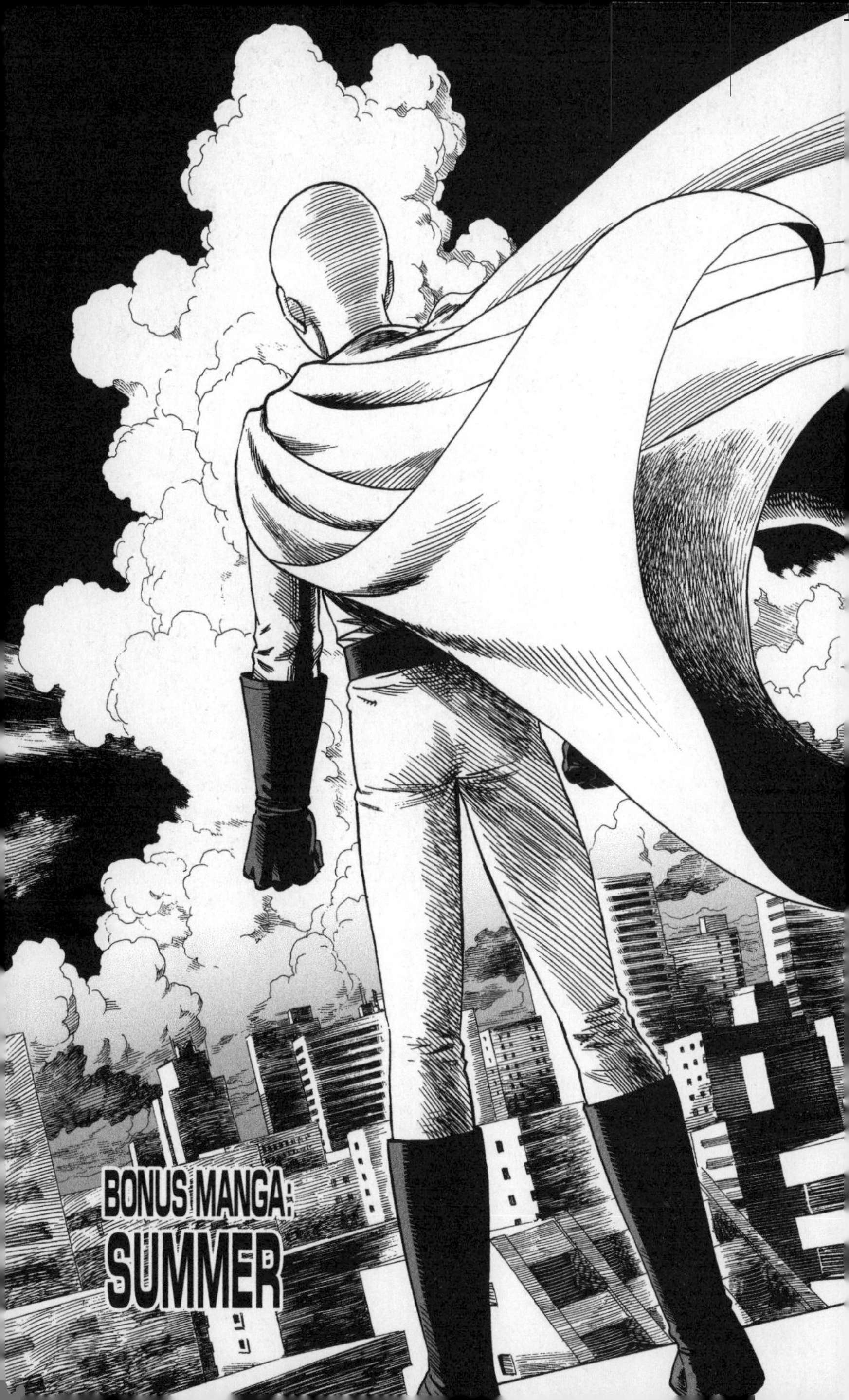
BONUS MANGA:
SUMMER

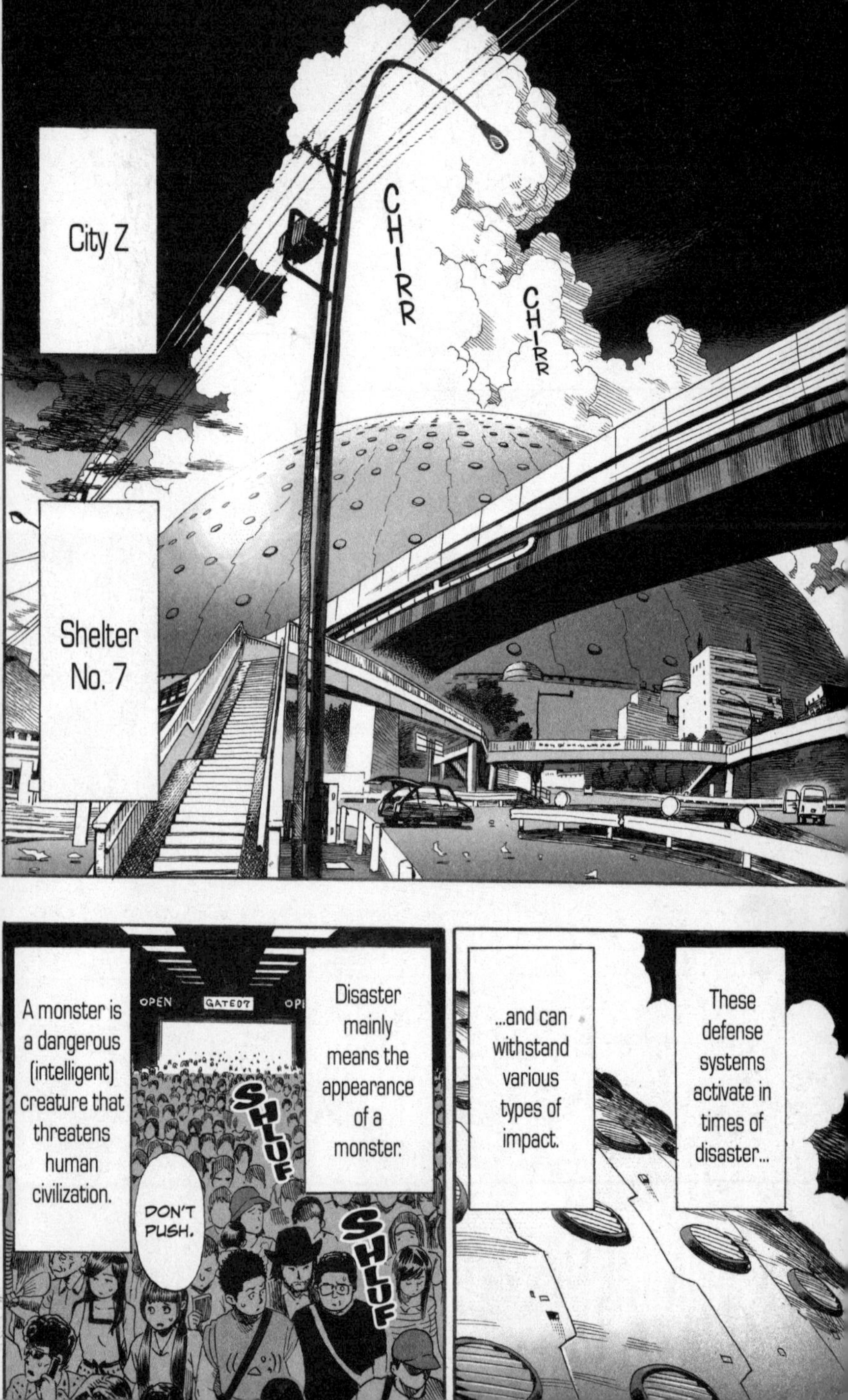
City Z
CHIRR
CHIRR
Shelter No. 7
These defense systems activate in times of disaster...
...and can withstand various types of impact.
OPEN
GATE07
Disaster mainly means the appearance of a monster.
SHLUF
SHLUF
A monster is a dangerous (intelligent) creature that threatens human civilization.
DON'T PUSH.

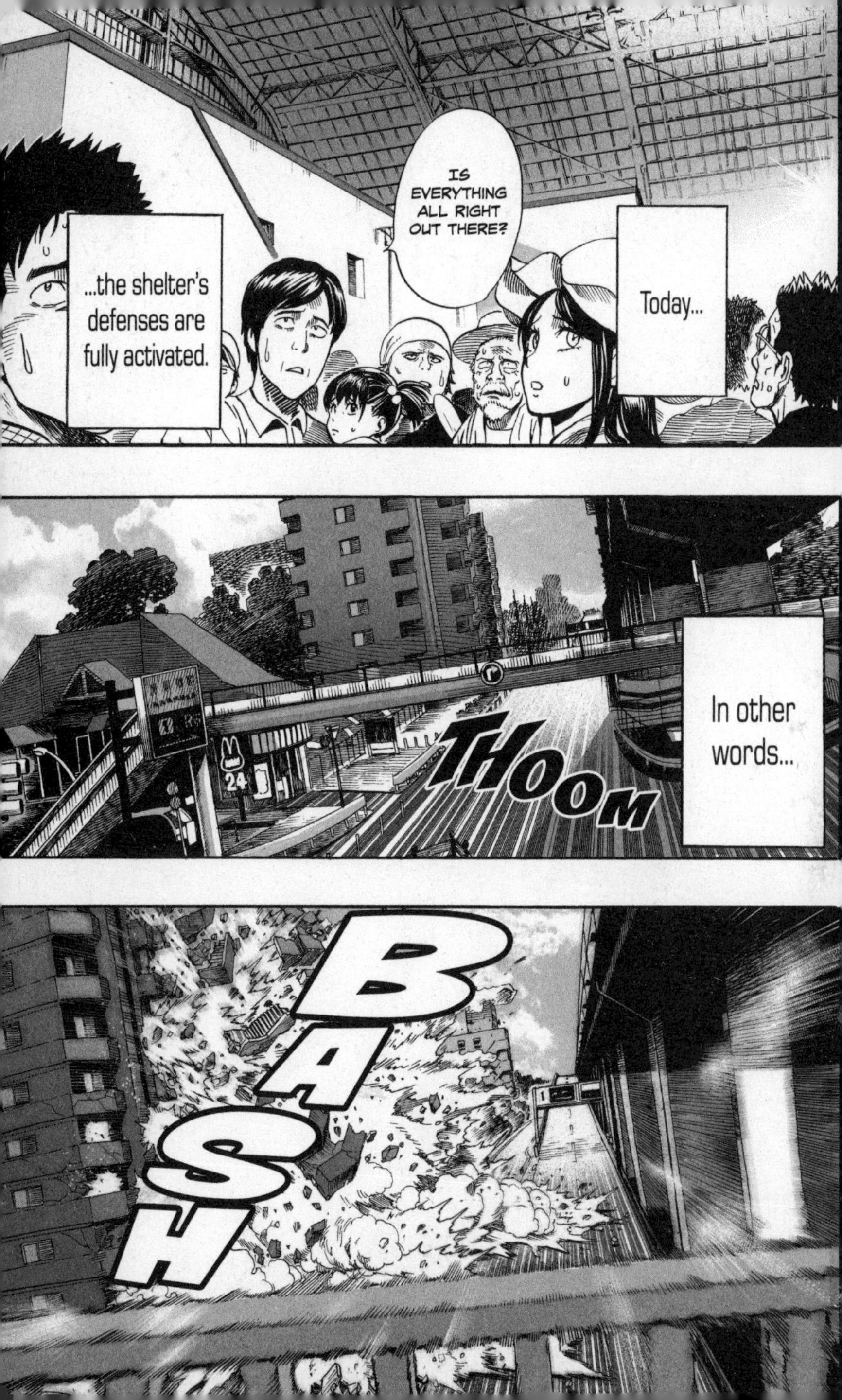
Today...
IS EVERYTHING ALL RIGHT OUT THERE?
...the shelter's defenses are fully activated.
In other words...
THOOM
BASH

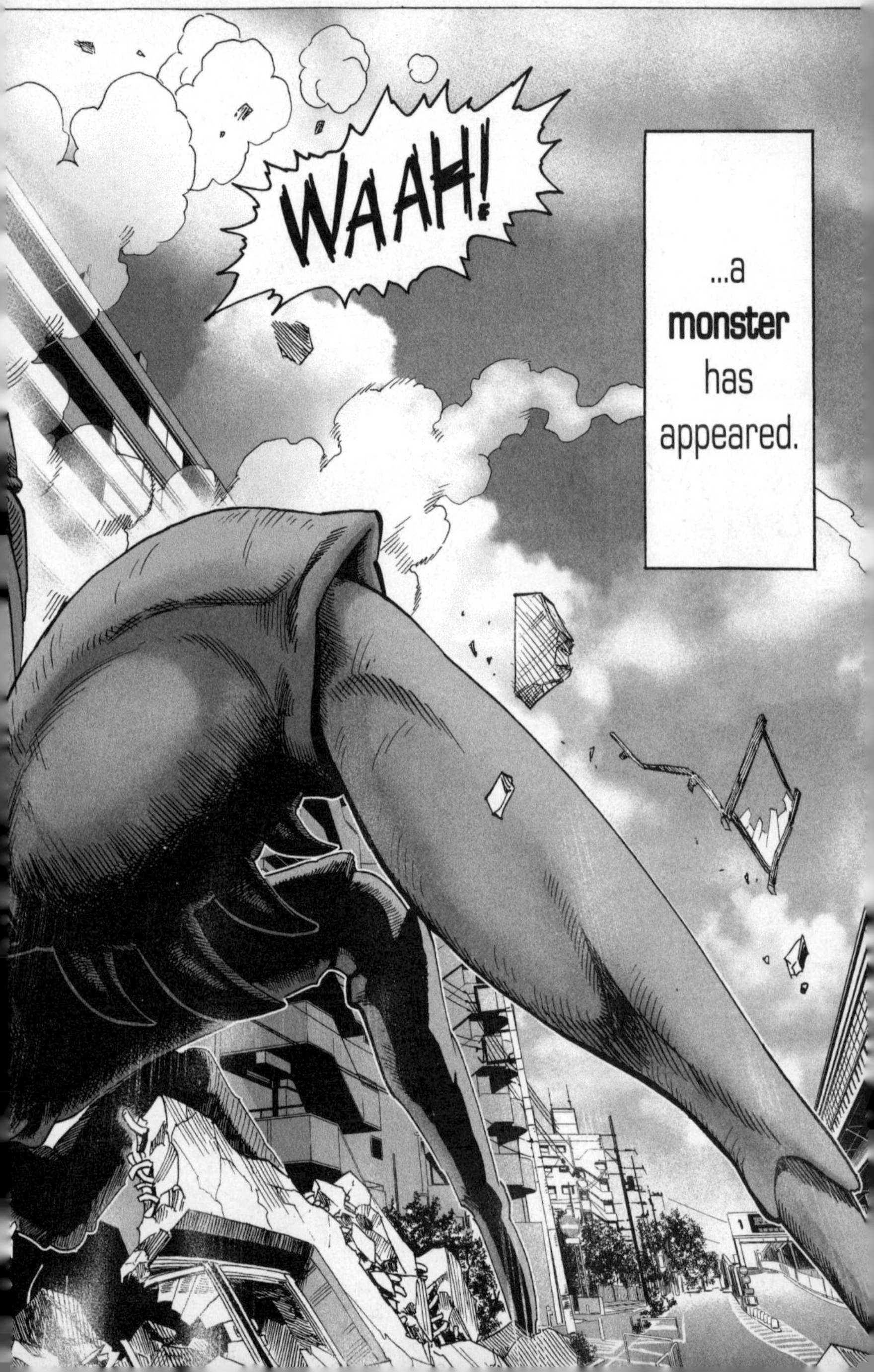

WAAH!
...a monster has appeared.

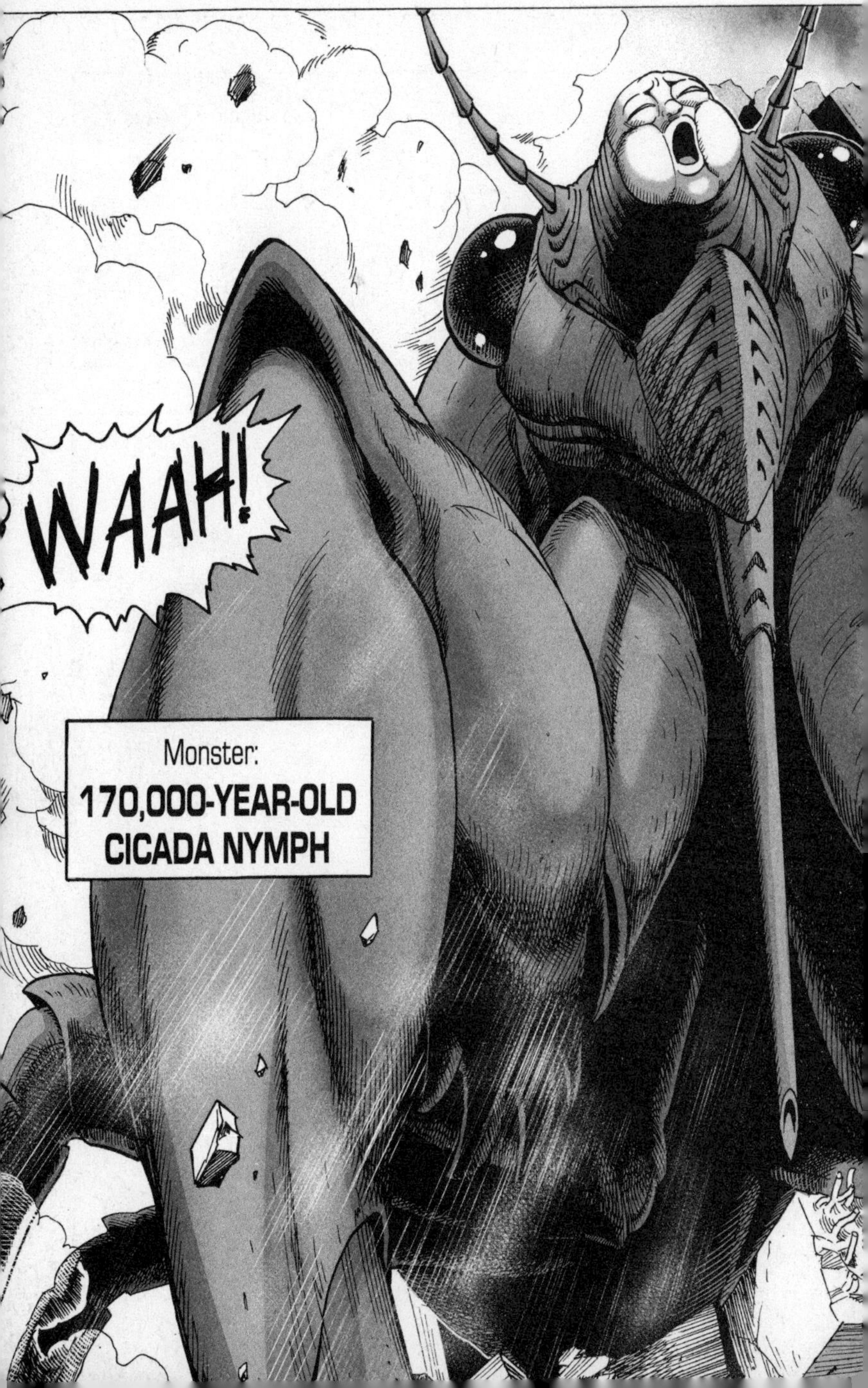
WAAH!
Monster:
170,000-YEAR-OLD
CICADA NYMPH

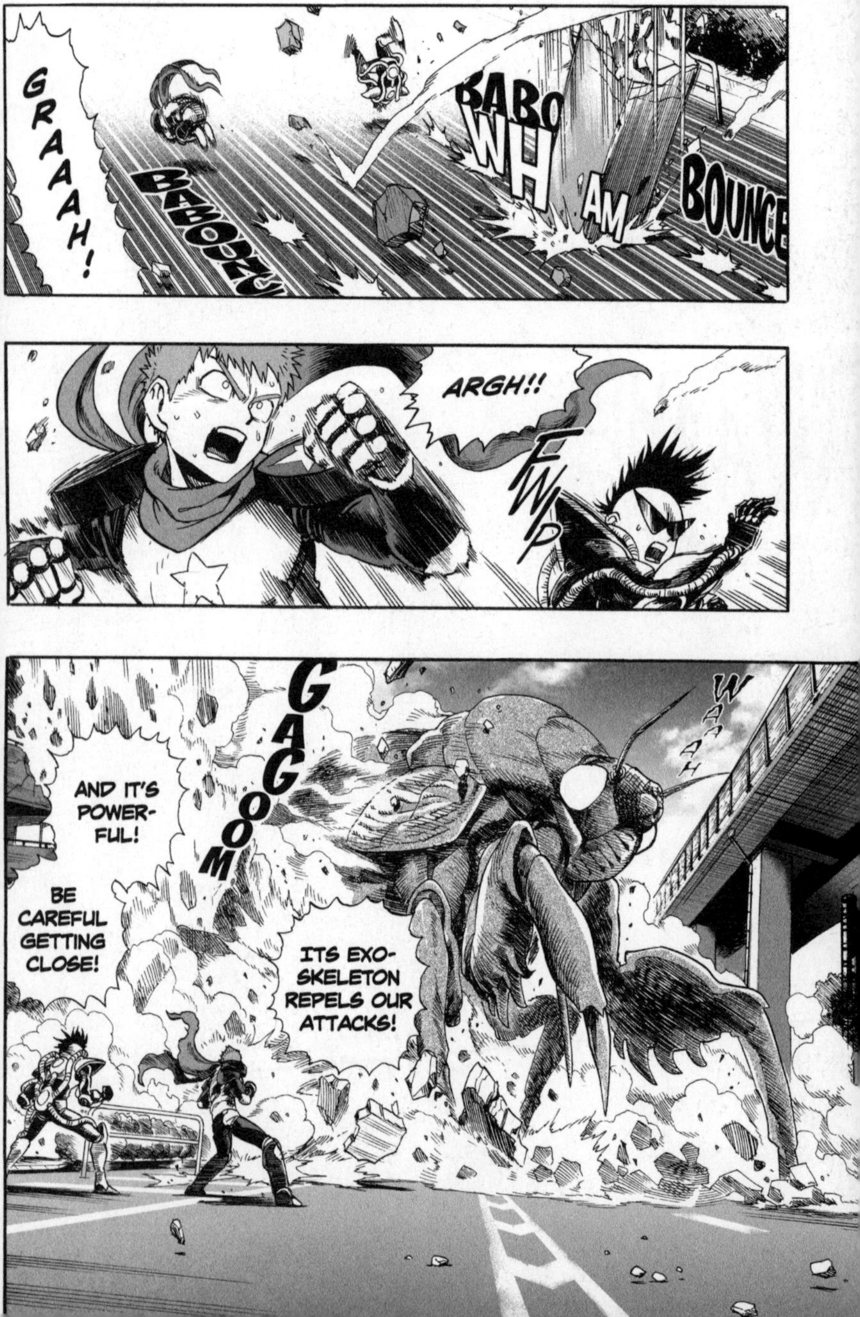
BOUNCE
WHAM
BABO
BABOUNCE
GRAAAH!
ARGH!!
FWIP
WAAAAH
GAGOOOM
ITS EXO-SKELETON REPELS OUR ATTACKS!
AND IT'S POWER-FUL!
BE CAREFUL GETTING CLOSE!

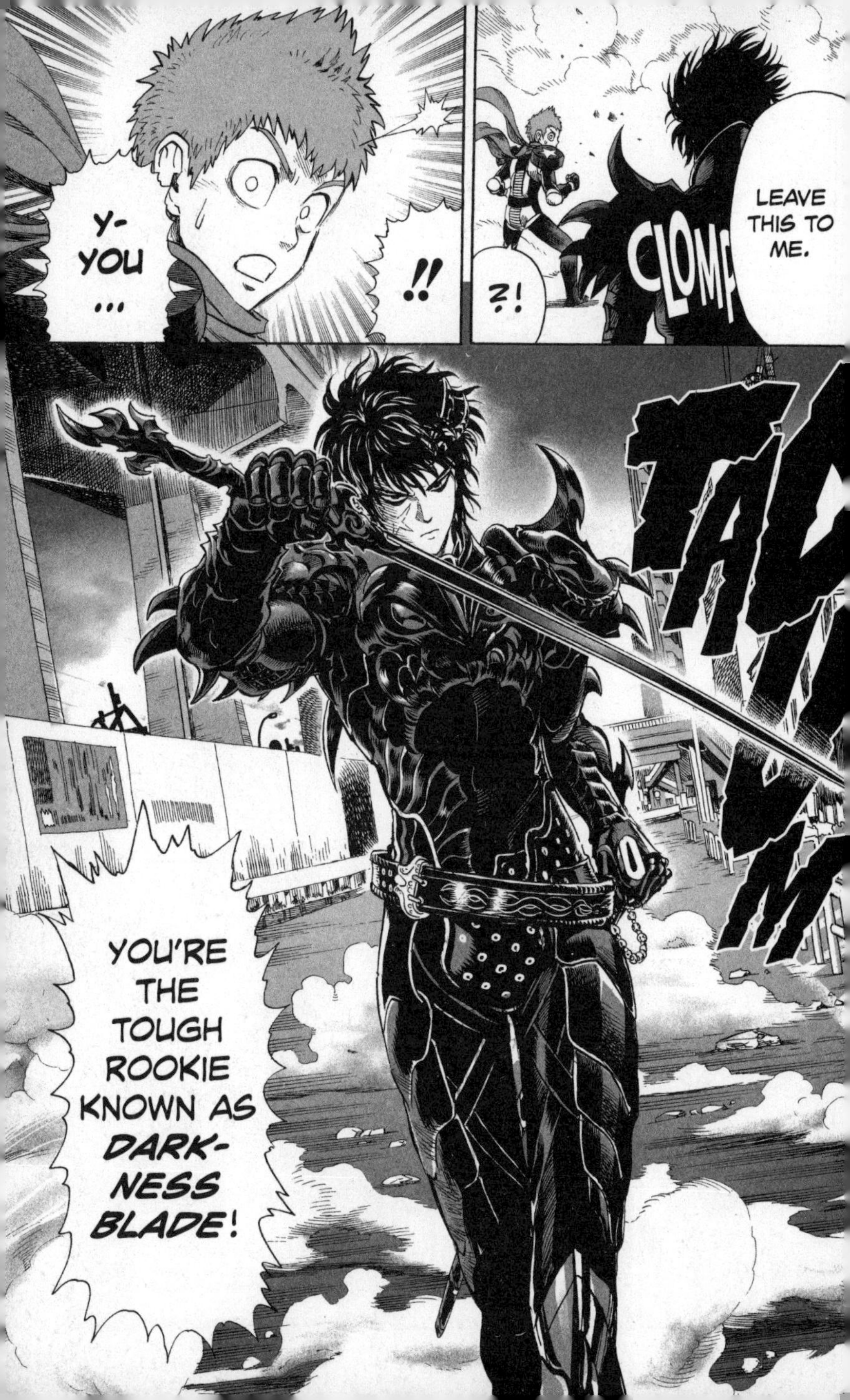
LEAVE THIS TO ME.
CLOMP
?!
!!
Y-YOU ...
YOU'RE THE TOUGH ROOKIE KNOWN AS *DARK-NESS BLADE*!

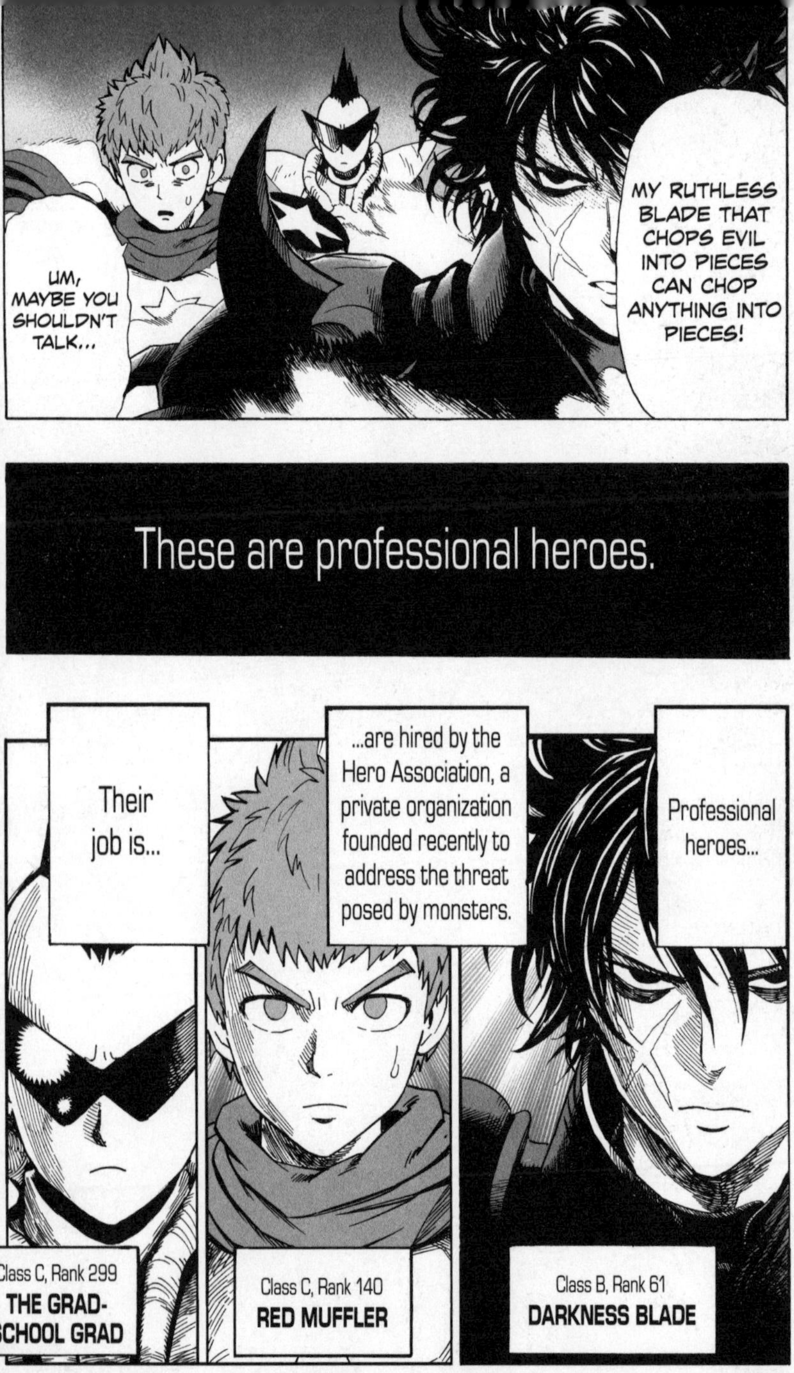
MY RUTHLESS BLADE THAT CHOPS EVIL INTO PIECES CAN CHOP ANYTHING INTO PIECES!
UM, MAYBE YOU SHOULDN'T TALK...
These are professional heroes.
Professional heroes...
...are hired by the Hero Association, a private organization founded recently to address the threat posed by monsters.
Their job is...
Class B, Rank 61
DARKNESS BLADE
Class C, Rank 140
RED MUFFLER
Class C, Rank 299
THE GRAD-SCHOOL GRAD

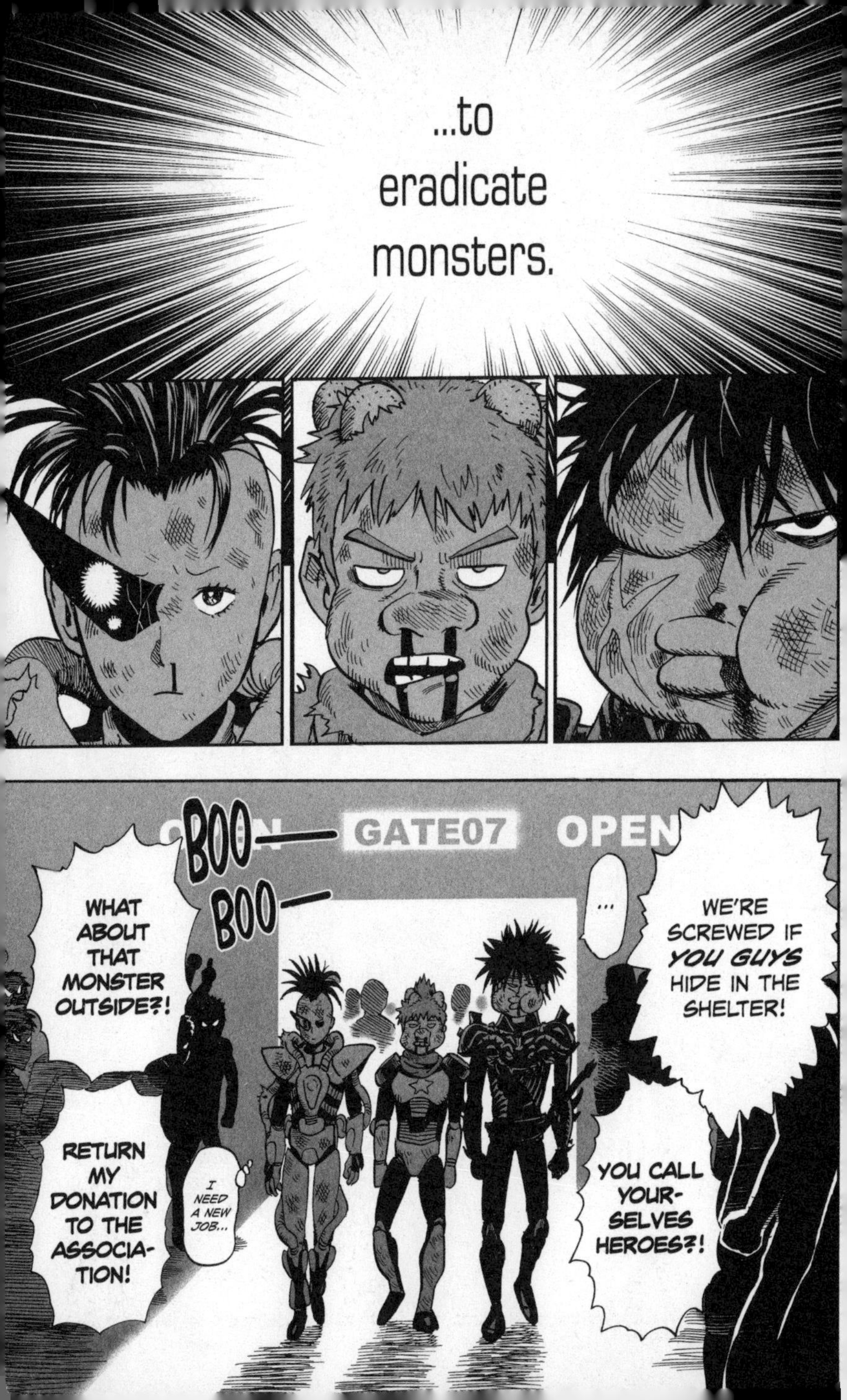
...to eradicate monsters.
WE'RE SCREWED IF YOU GUYS HIDE IN THE SHELTER!
...
GATE07
OPEN
BOO—
BOO—
WHAT ABOUT THAT MONSTER OUTSIDE?!
YOU CALL YOURSELVES HEROES?!
I NEED A NEW JOB...
RETURN MY DONATION TO THE ASSOCIATION!

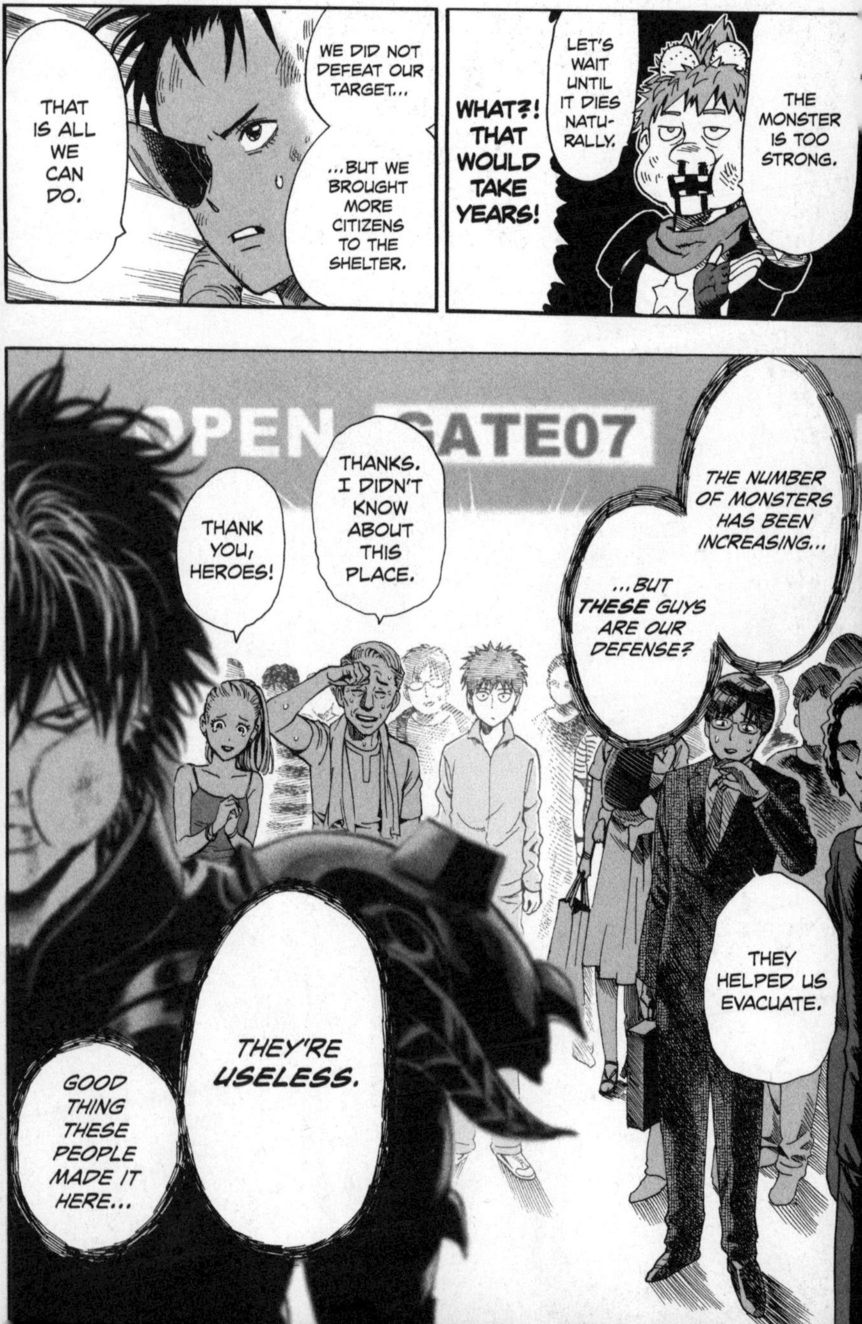
THE MONSTER IS TOO STRONG.
LET'S WAIT UNTIL IT DIES NATU-RALLY.
WHAT?! THAT WOULD TAKE YEARS!
WE DID NOT DEFEAT OUR TARGET...
...BUT WE BROUGHT MORE CITIZENS TO THE SHELTER.
THAT IS ALL WE CAN DO.
OPEN GATE07
THE NUMBER OF MONSTERS HAS BEEN INCREASING...
...BUT THESE GUYS ARE OUR DEFENSE?
THANKS. I DIDN'T KNOW ABOUT THIS PLACE.
THANK YOU, HEROES!
THEY HELPED US EVACUATE.
THEY'RE USELESS.
GOOD THING THESE PEOPLE MADE IT HERE...

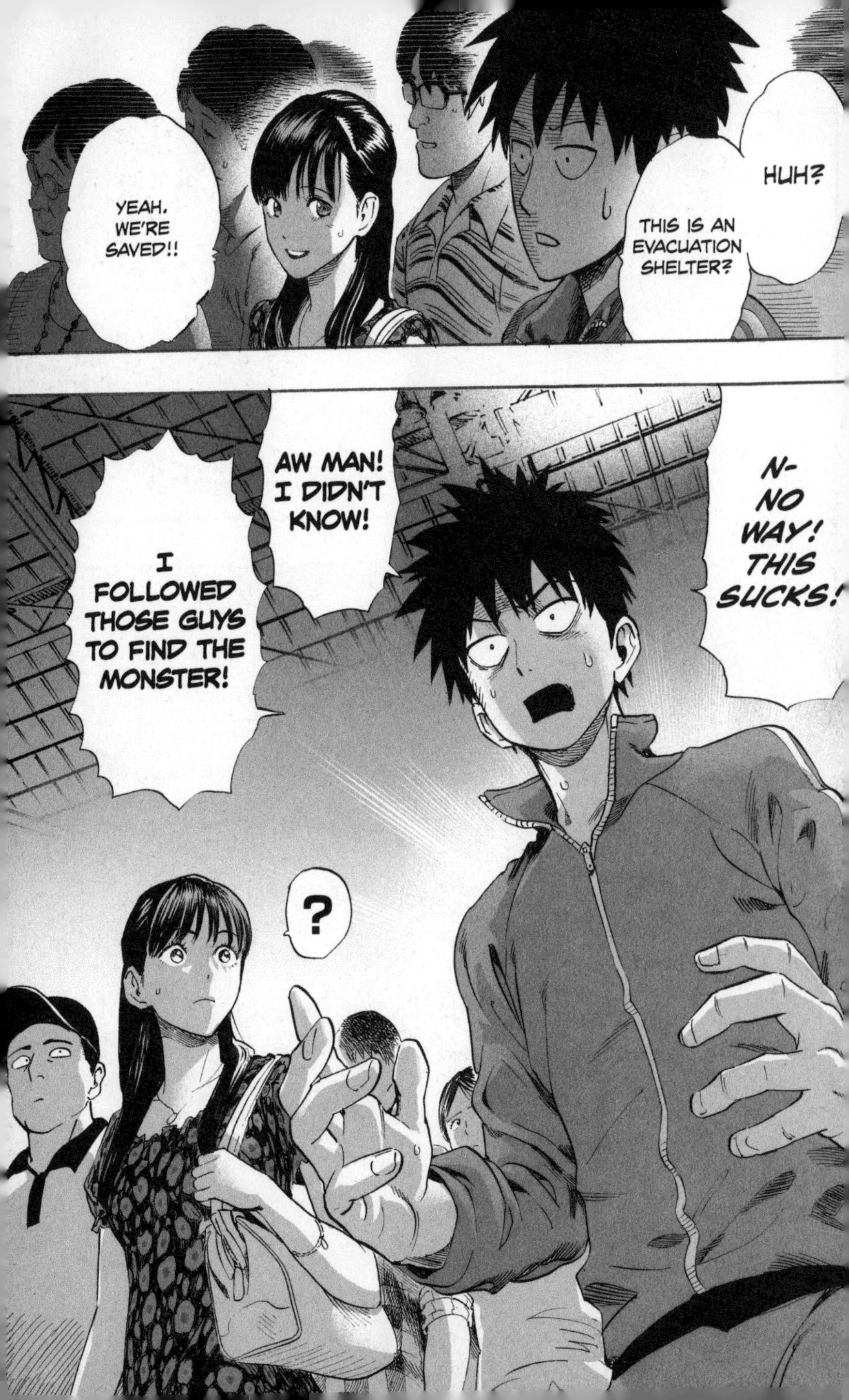

HUH?
THIS IS AN EVACUATION SHELTER?
YEAH. WE'RE SAVED!!
N-NO WAY! THIS SUCKS!
AW MAN! I DIDN'T KNOW!
I FOLLOWED THOSE GUYS TO FIND THE MONSTER!
?

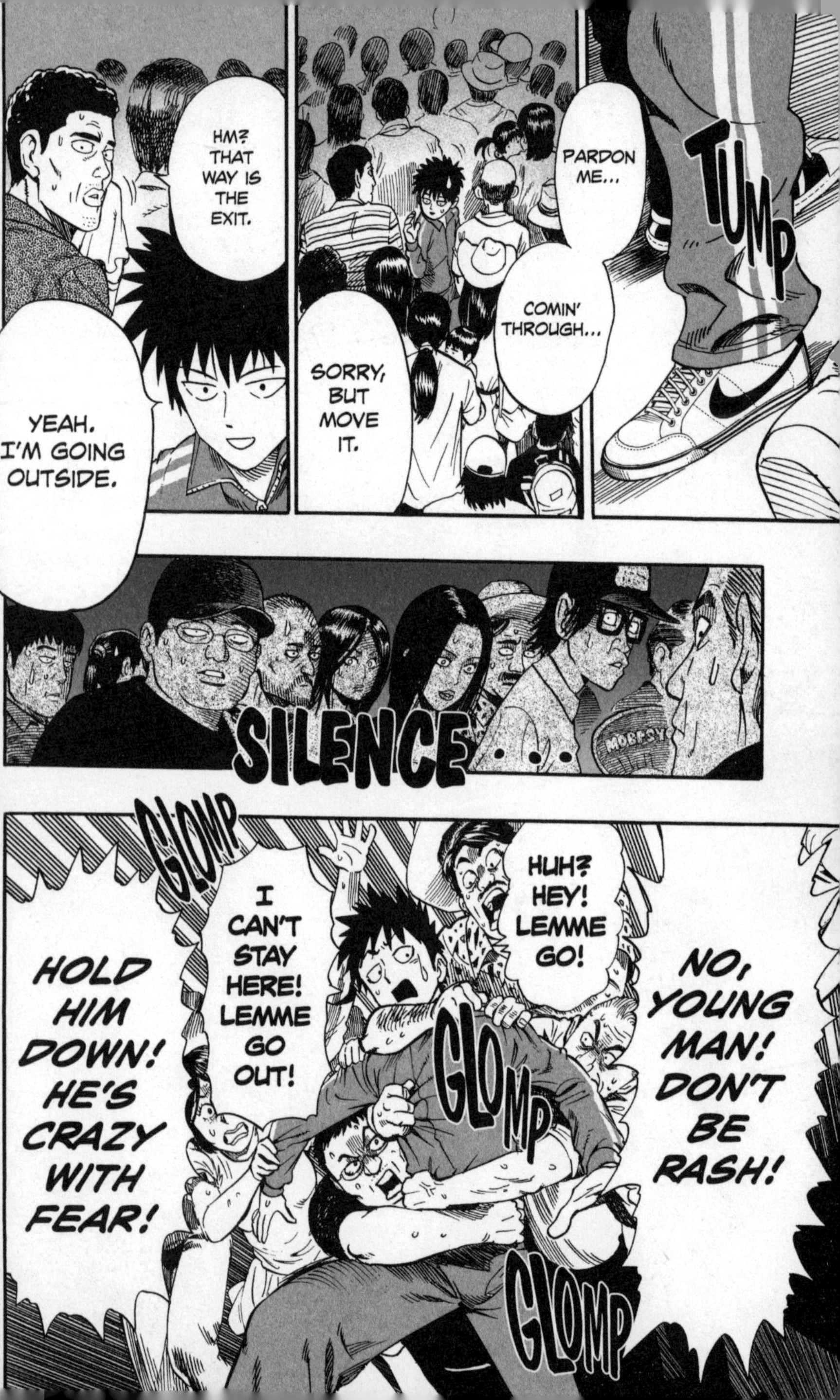
PARDON ME...
TUMP
COMIN' THROUGH...
SORRY, BUT MOVE IT.
HM? THAT WAY IS THE EXIT.
YEAH. I'M GOING OUTSIDE.
SILENCE
...
GLOMP
NO, YOUNG MAN! DON'T BE RASH!
HUH? HEY! LEMME GO!
I CAN'T STAY HERE! LEMME GO OUT!
HOLD HIM DOWN! HE'S CRAZY WITH FEAR!
GLOMP
GLOMP

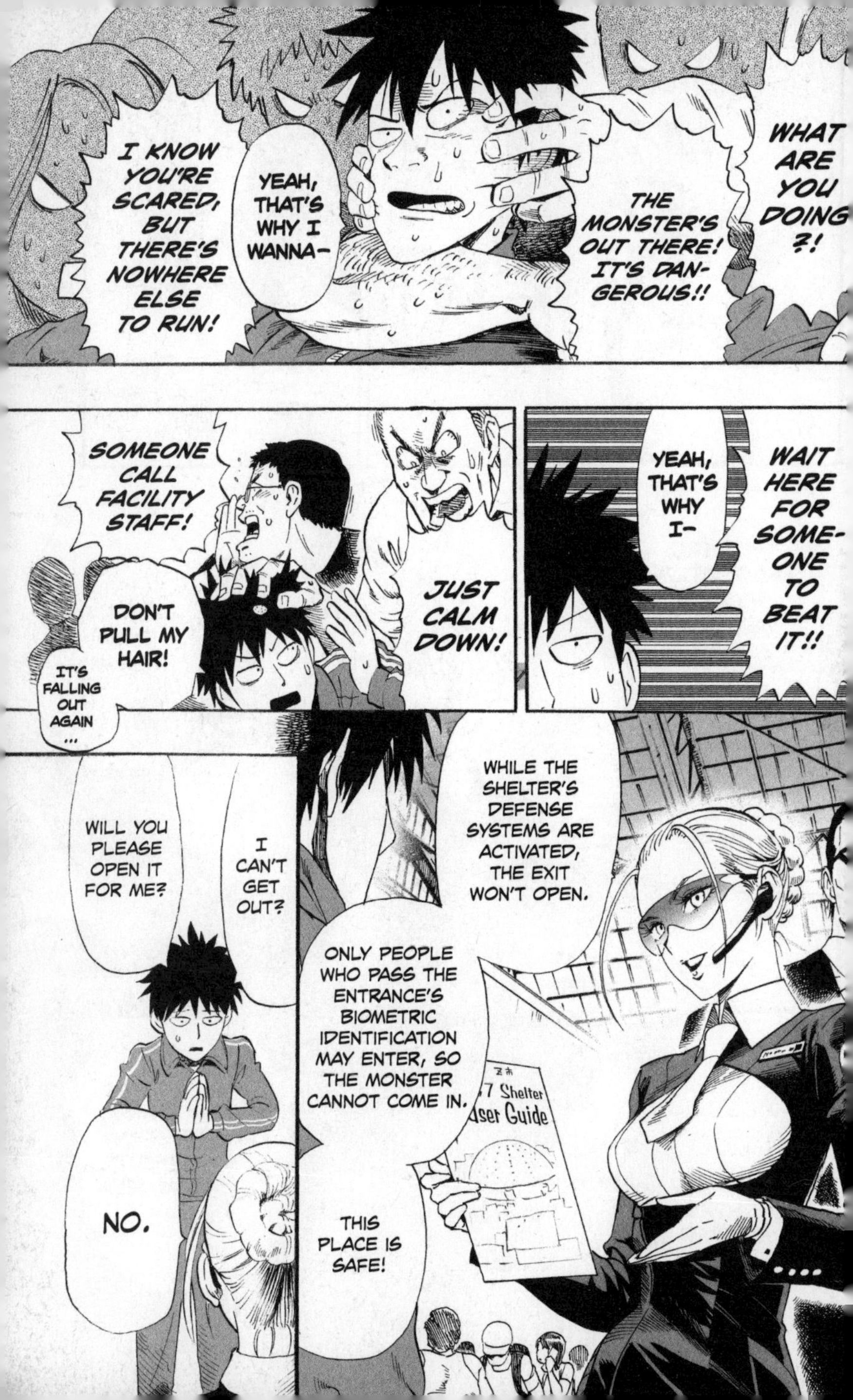
WHAT ARE YOU DOING?!
THE MONSTER'S OUT THERE! IT'S DANGEROUS!!
YEAH, THAT'S WHY I WANNA-
I KNOW YOU'RE SCARED, BUT THERE'S NOWHERE ELSE TO RUN!
WAIT HERE FOR SOMEONE TO BEAT IT!!
YEAH, THAT'S WHY I-
JUST CALM DOWN!
SOMEONE CALL FACILITY STAFF!
DON'T PULL MY HAIR!
IT'S FALLING OUT AGAIN ...
....
WHILE THE SHELTER'S DEFENSE SYSTEMS ARE ACTIVATED, THE EXIT WON'T OPEN.
ONLY PEOPLE WHO PASS THE ENTRANCE'S BIOMETRIC IDENTIFICATION MAY ENTER, SO THE MONSTER CANNOT COME IN.
THIS PLACE IS SAFE!
I CAN'T GET OUT?
WILL YOU PLEASE OPEN IT FOR ME?
NO.

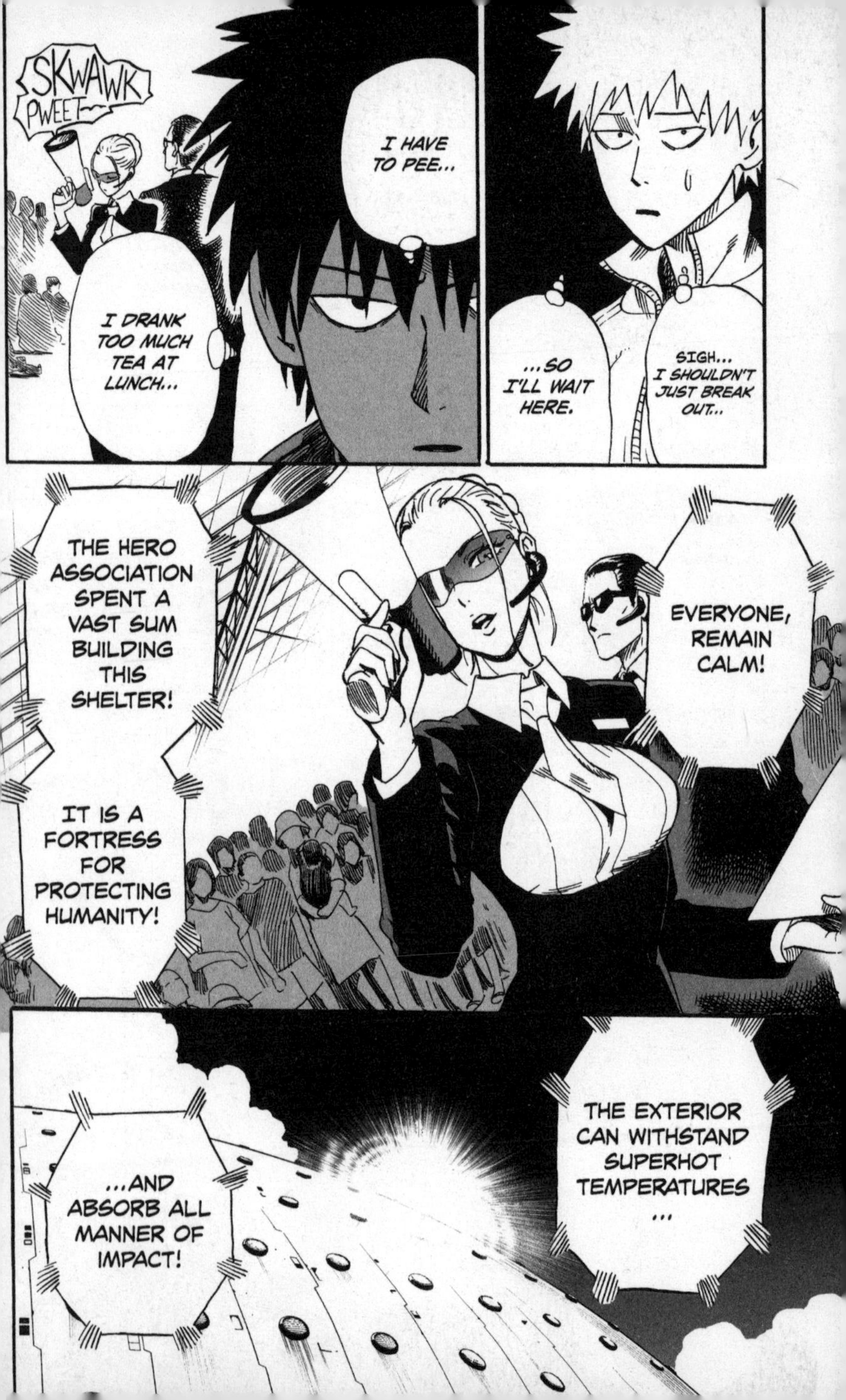
SIGH... I SHOULDN'T JUST BREAK OUT...
...SO I'LL WAIT HERE.
I HAVE TO PEE...
I DRANK TOO MUCH TEA AT LUNCH...
SKWAWK PWEET
EVERYONE, REMAIN CALM!
THE HERO ASSOCIATION SPENT A VAST SUM BUILDING THIS SHELTER!
IT IS A FORTRESS FOR PROTECTING HUMANITY!
THE EXTERIOR CAN WITHSTAND SUPERHOT TEMPERATURES...
...AND ABSORB ALL MANNER OF IMPACT!

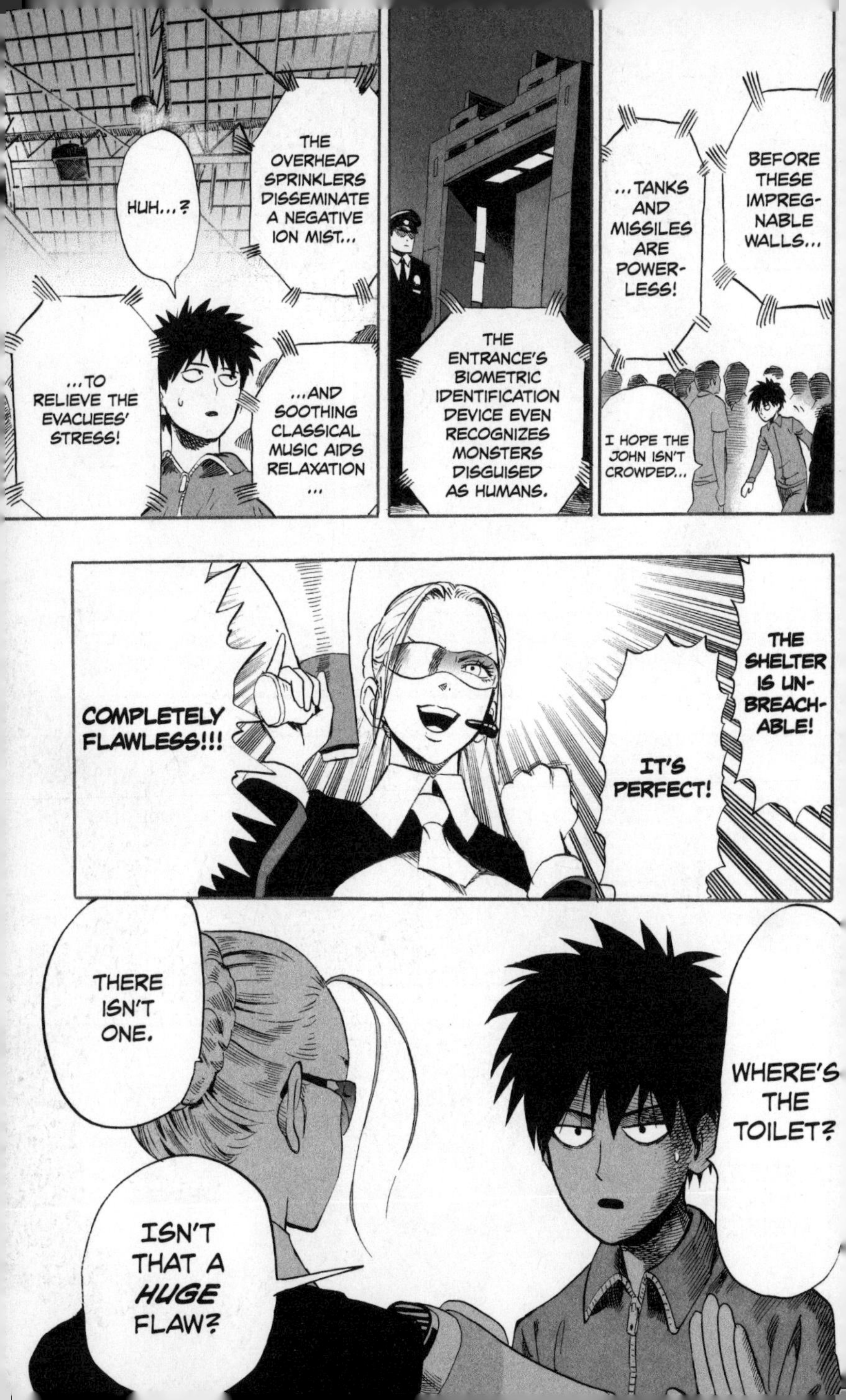
BEFORE THESE IMPREGNABLE WALLS...
...TANKS AND MISSILES ARE POWERLESS!
I HOPE THE JOHN ISN'T CROWDED...
THE ENTRANCE'S BIOMETRIC IDENTIFICATION DEVICE EVEN RECOGNIZES MONSTERS DISGUISED AS HUMANS.
THE OVERHEAD SPRINKLERS DISSEMINATE A NEGATIVE ION MIST...
HUH...?
...AND SOOTHING CLASSICAL MUSIC AIDS RELAXATION...
...TO RELIEVE THE EVACUEES' STRESS!
THE SHELTER IS UNBREACHABLE!
IT'S PERFECT!
COMPLETELY FLAWLESS!!!
WHERE'S THE TOILET?
THERE ISN'T ONE.
ISN'T THAT A *HUGE* FLAW?

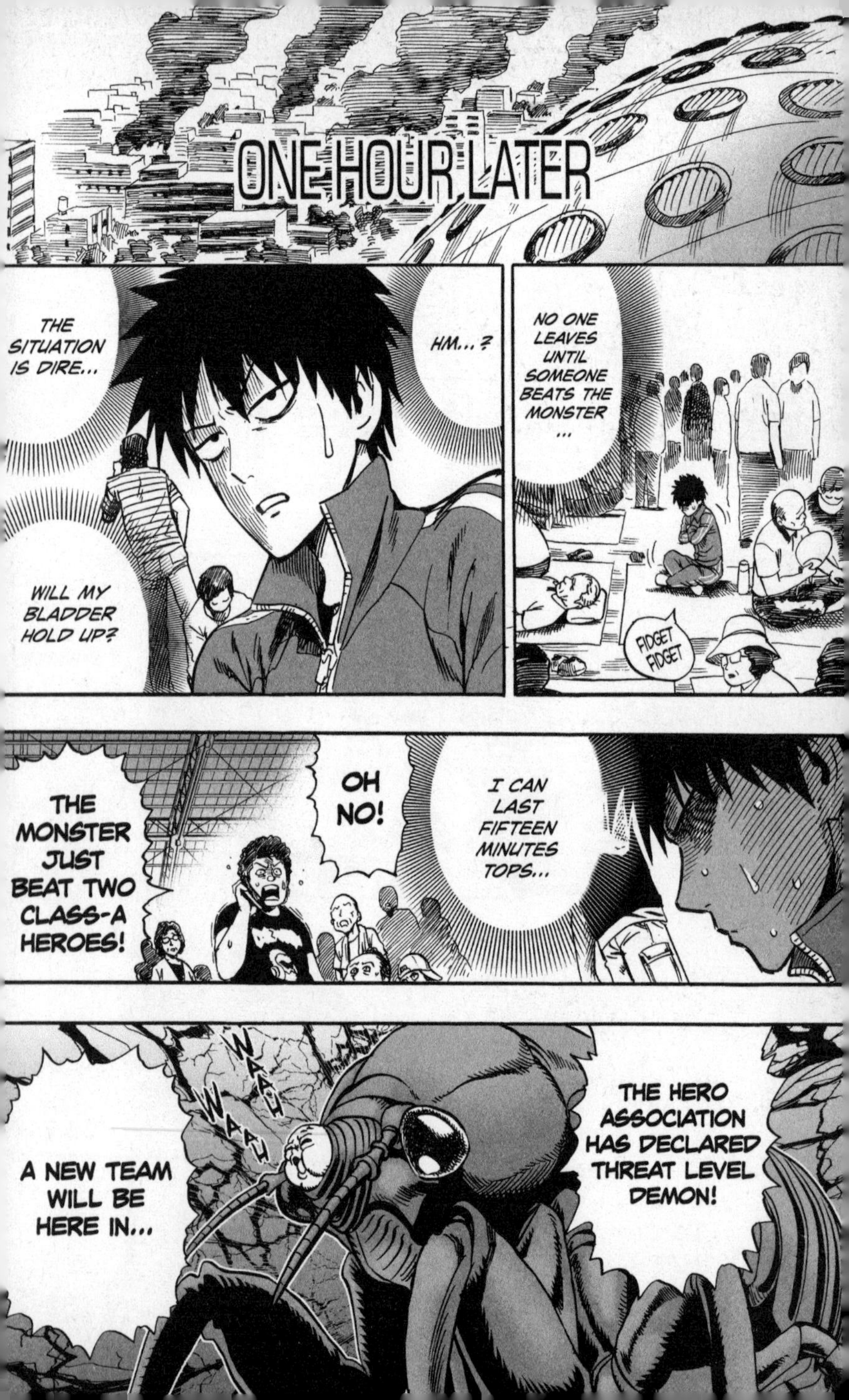
ONE HOUR LATER
NO ONE LEAVES UNTIL SOMEONE BEATS THE MONSTER...
FIDGET FIDGET
HM...?
THE SITUATION IS DIRE...
WILL MY BLADDER HOLD UP?
I CAN LAST FIFTEEN MINUTES TOPS...
OH NO!
THE MONSTER JUST BEAT TWO CLASS-A HEROES!
THE HERO ASSOCIATION HAS DECLARED THREAT LEVEL DEMON!
WAAH
WAAH
A NEW TEAM WILL BE HERE IN...

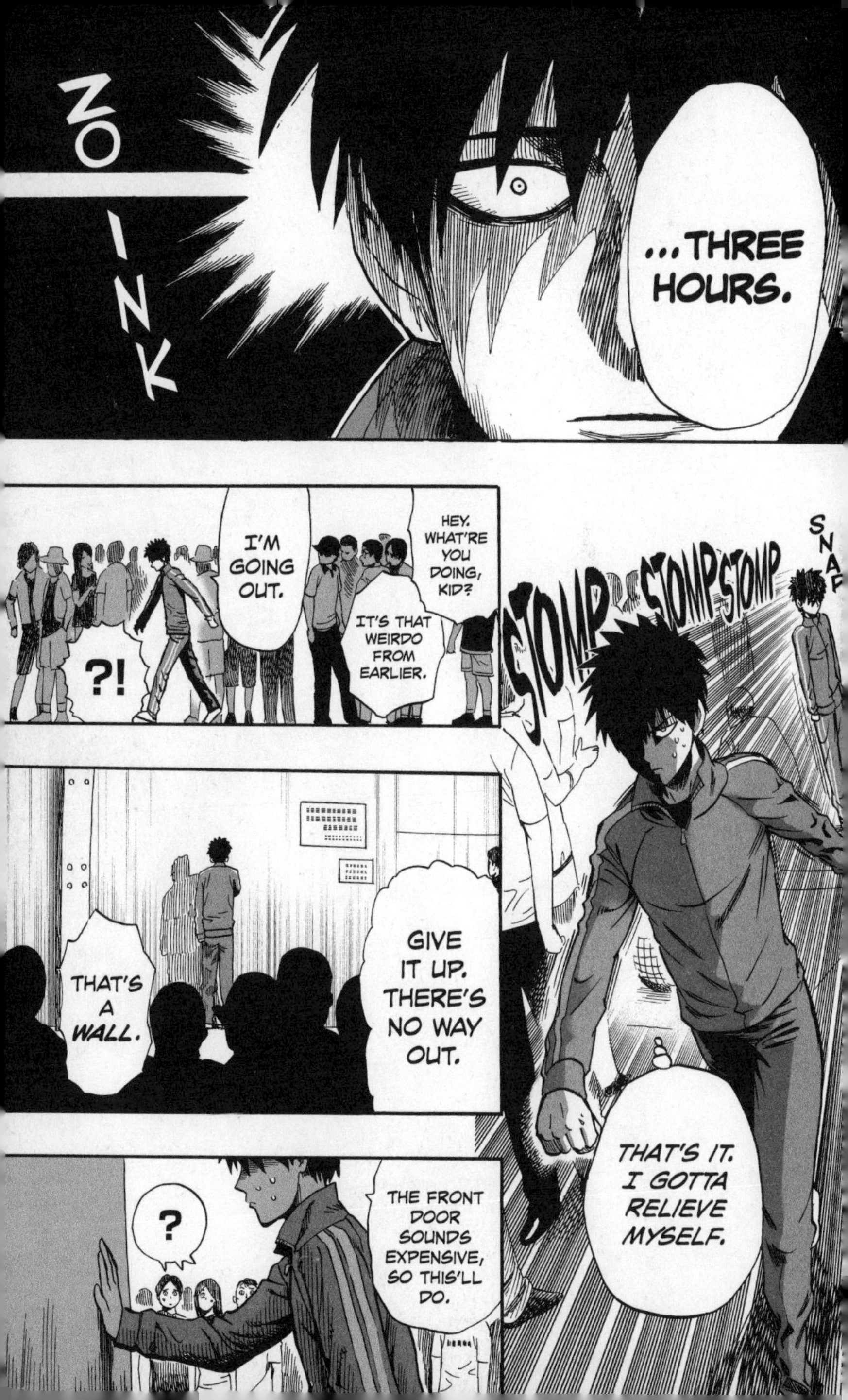
...THREE HOURS.
ZOINK
HEY. WHAT'RE YOU DOING, KID?
IT'S THAT WEIRDO FROM EARLIER.
I'M GOING OUT.
?!
SNAP
STOMP STOMP STOMP
GIVE IT UP. THERE'S NO WAY OUT.
THAT'S A WALL.
THAT'S IT. I GOTTA RELIEVE MYSELF.
THE FRONT DOOR SOUNDS EXPENSIVE, SO THIS'LL DO.
?

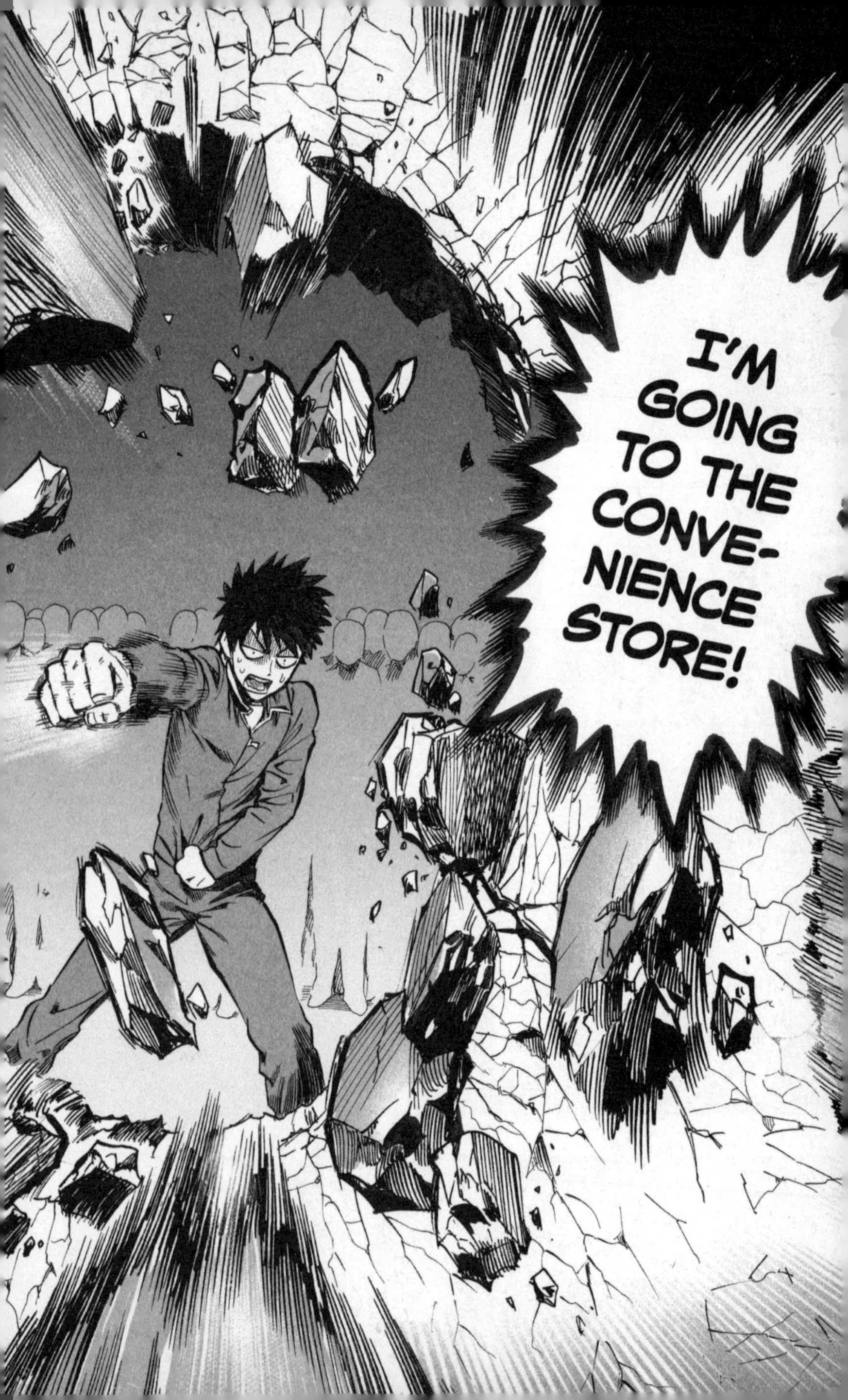
I'M GOING TO THE CONVE-NIENCE STORE!

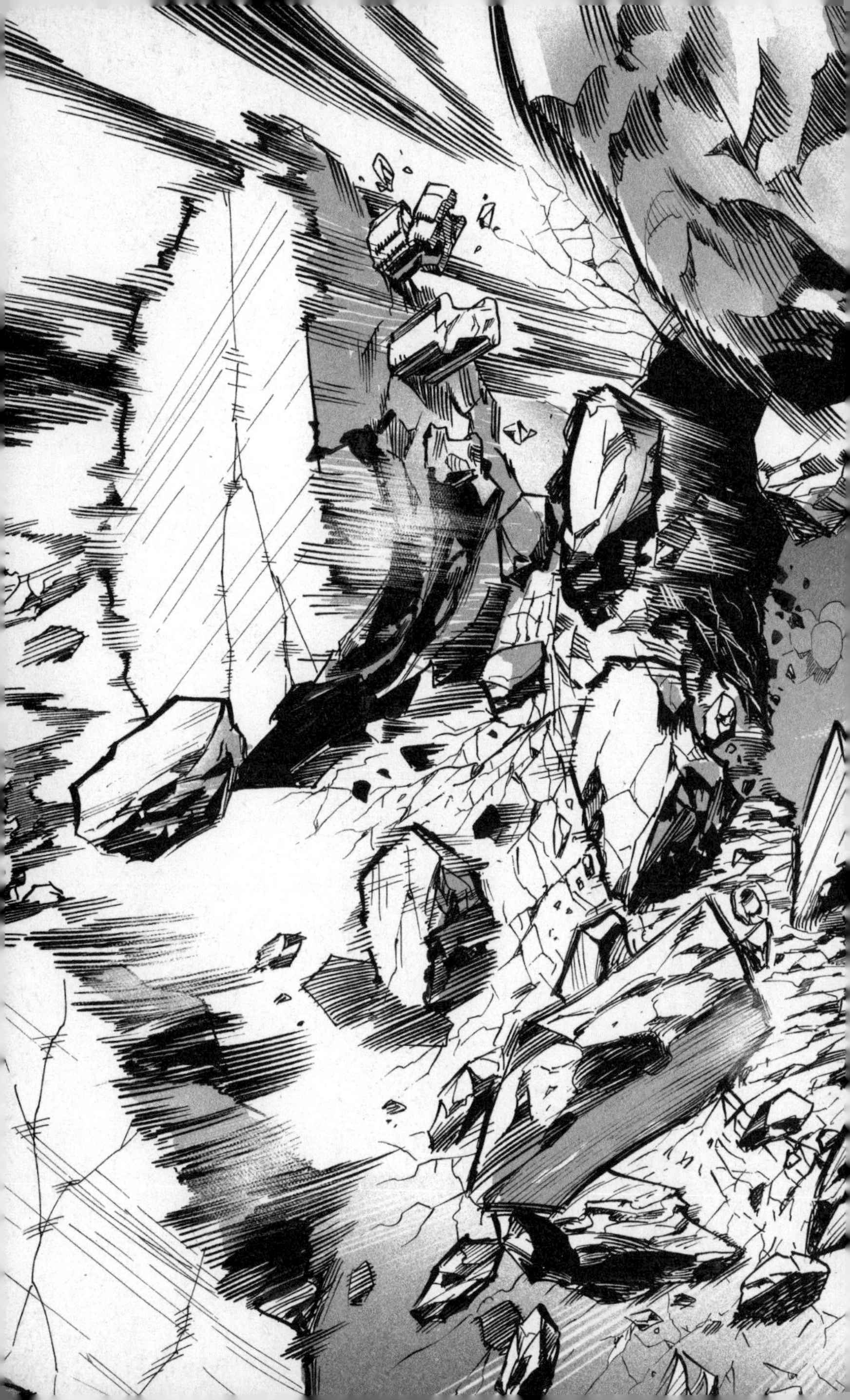

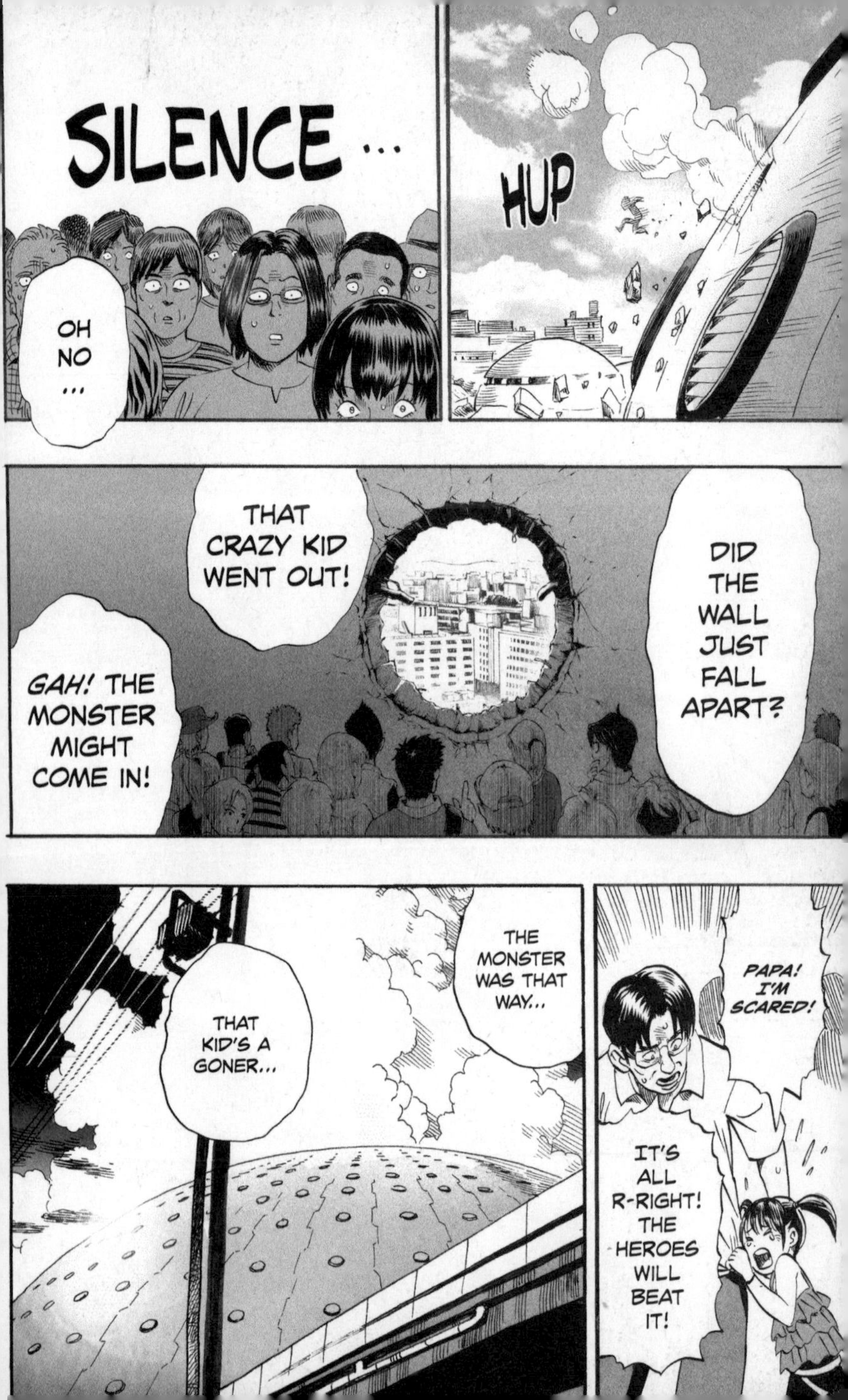
SILENCE...
OH NO...
HUP
THAT CRAZY KID WENT OUT!
GAH! THE MONSTER MIGHT COME IN!
DID THE WALL JUST FALL APART?
THE MONSTER WAS THAT WAY...
THAT KID'S A GONER...
PAPA! I'M SCARED!
IT'S ALL R-RIGHT! THE HEROES WILL BEAT IT!

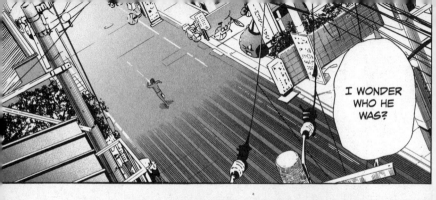

I WONDER WHO HE WAS?

His name is Saitama.

SL AM

A CONVENIENCE STORE!

THERE'S ONE!

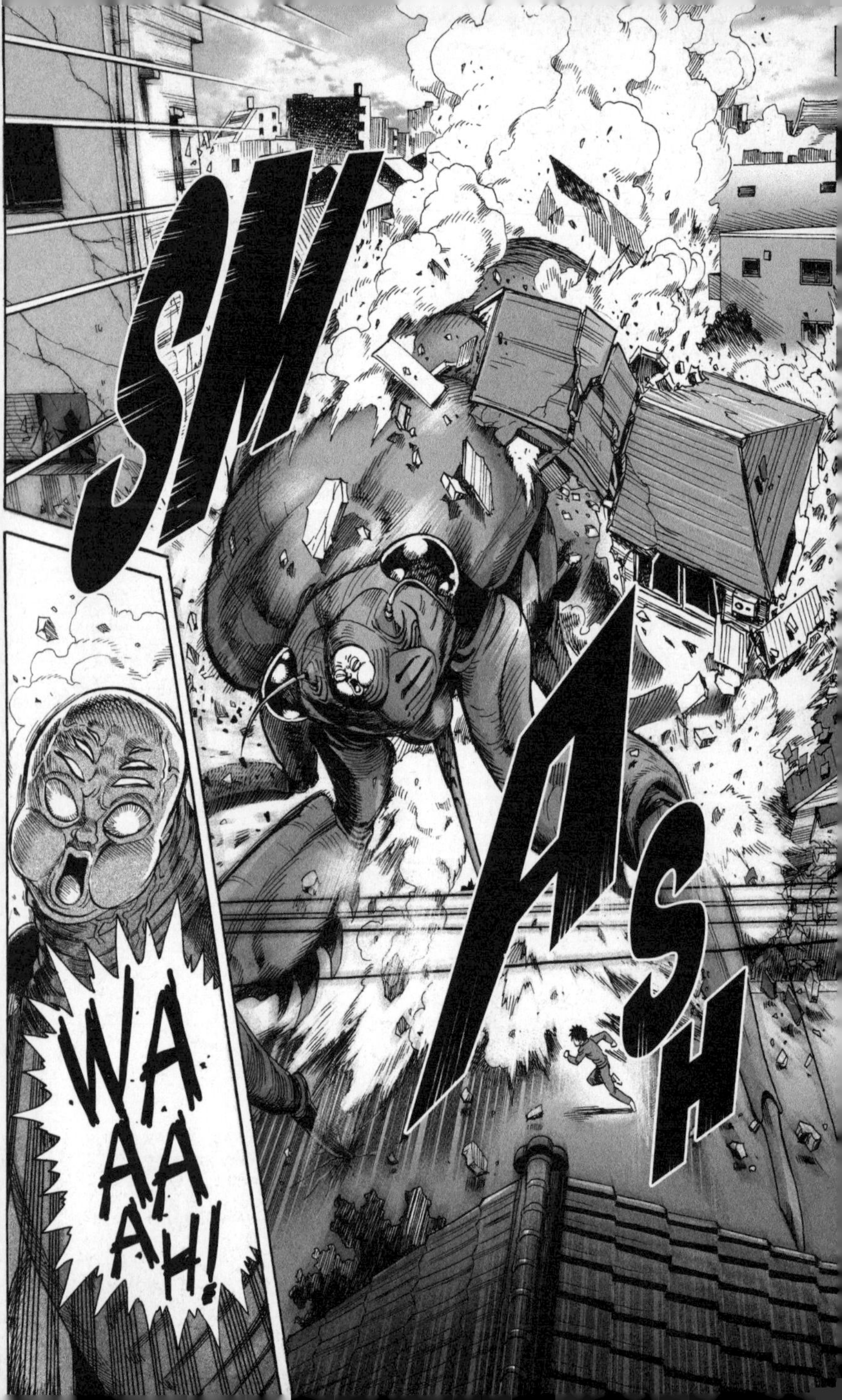
SMASH
WAAAAH!

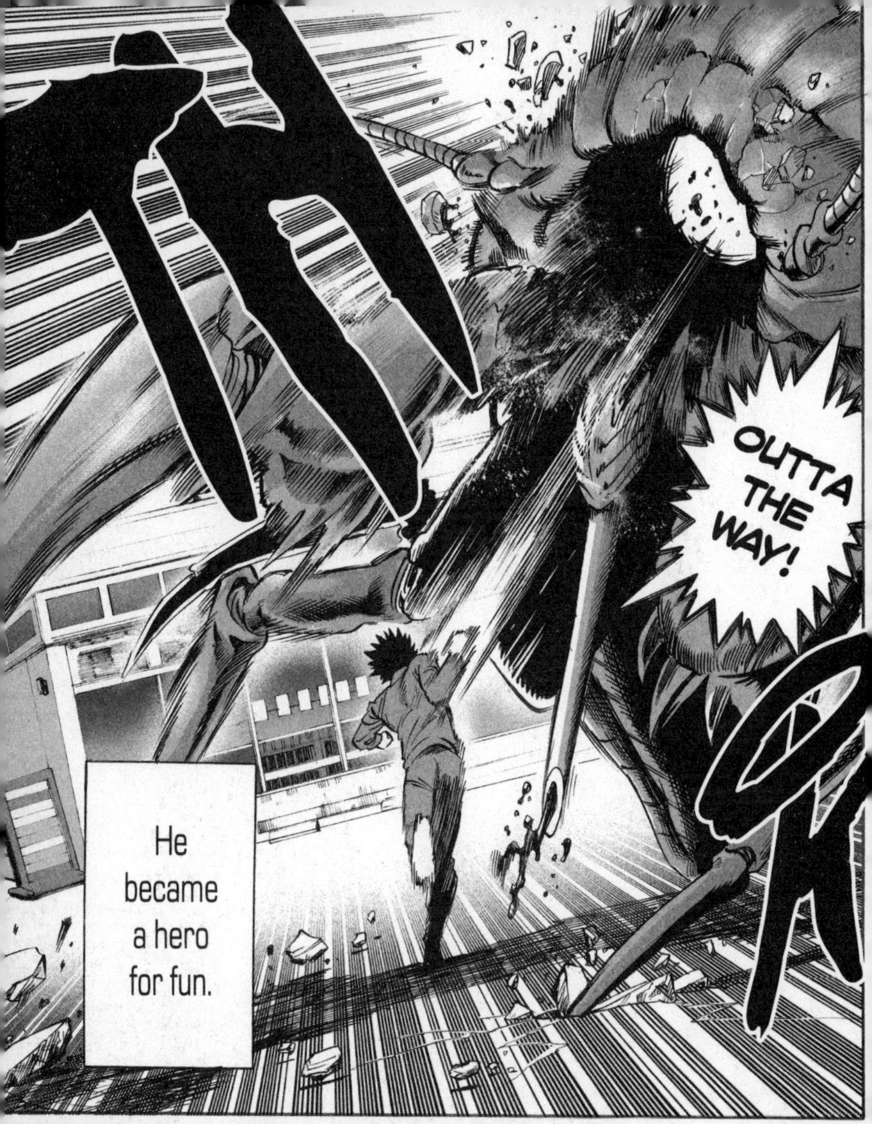
OUTTA THE WAY!
He became a hero for fun.

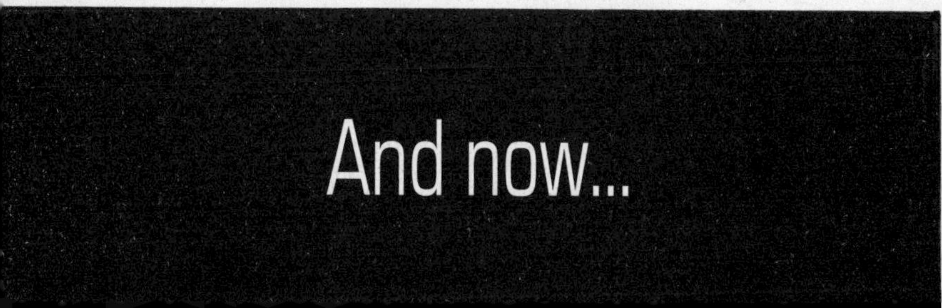
And now...

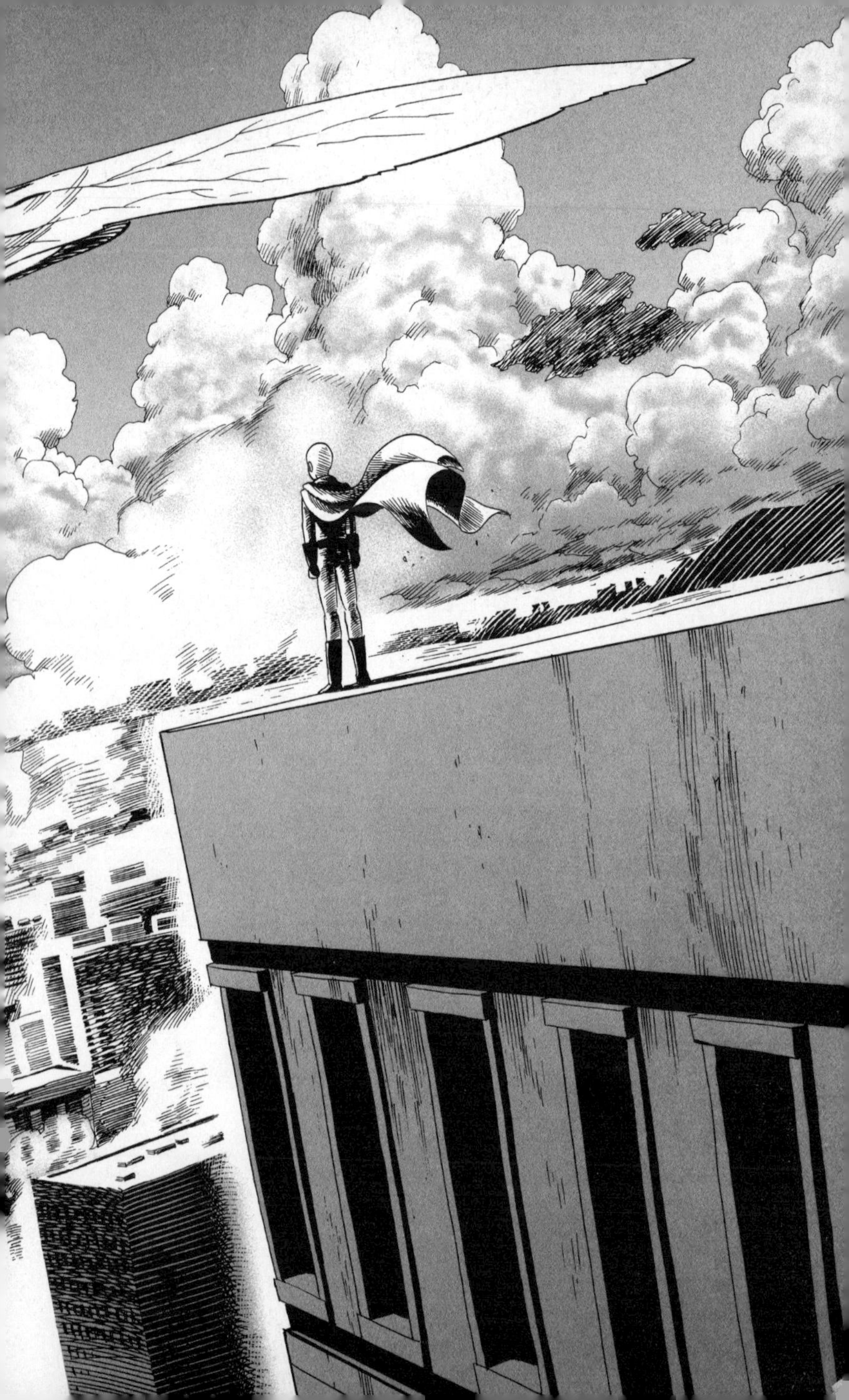

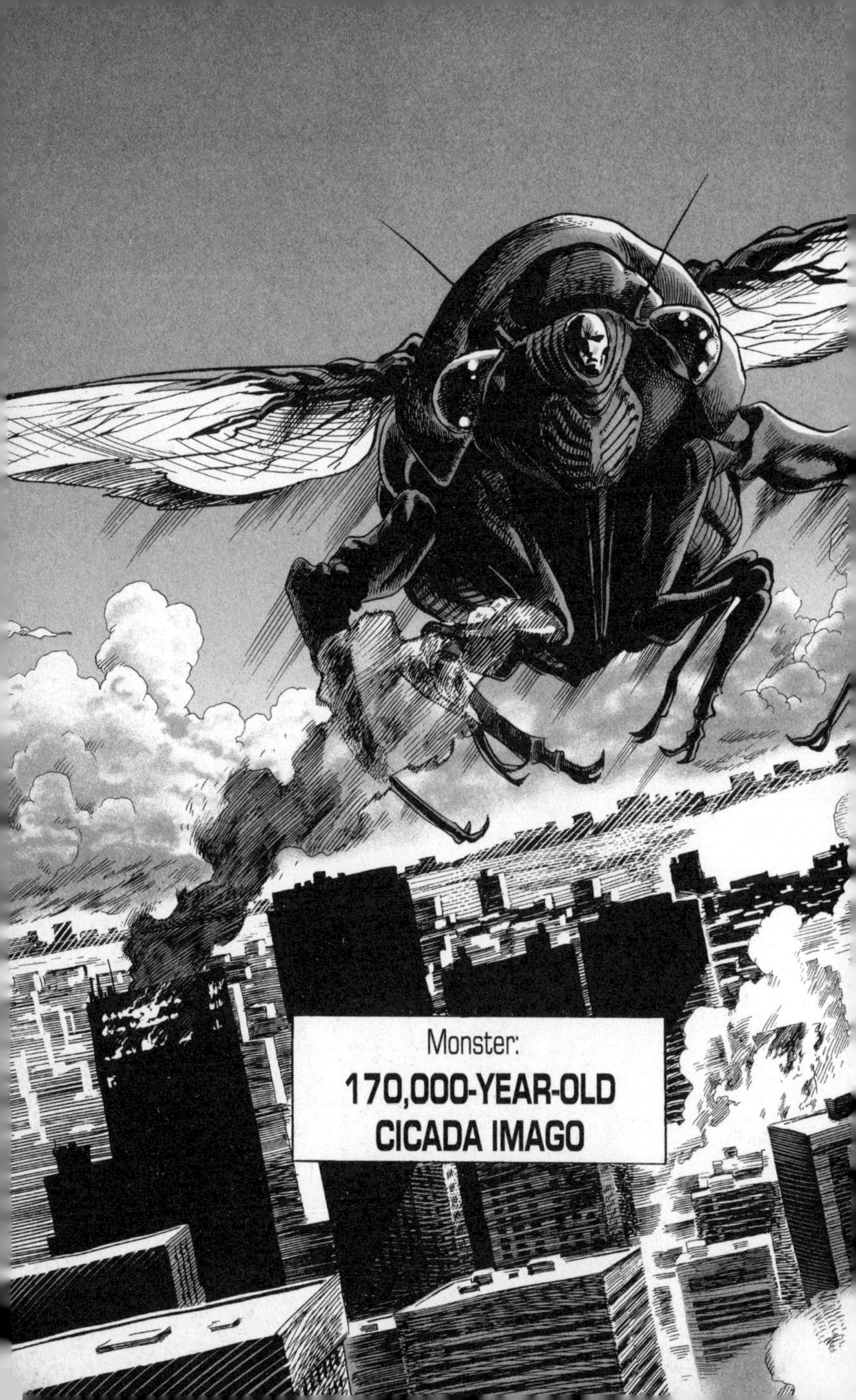
Monster:
170,000-YEAR-OLD
CICADA IMAGO

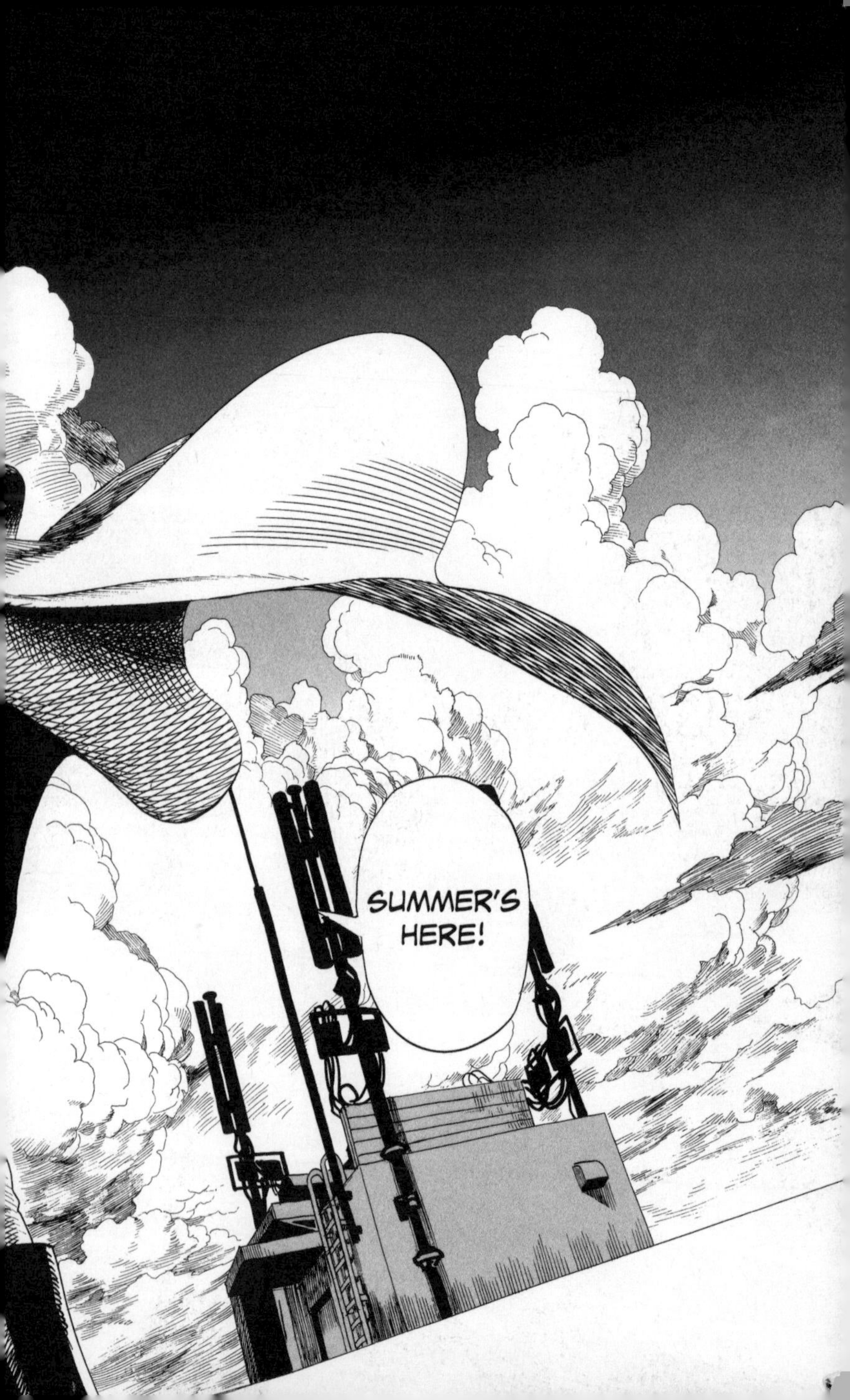
SUMMER'S HERE!

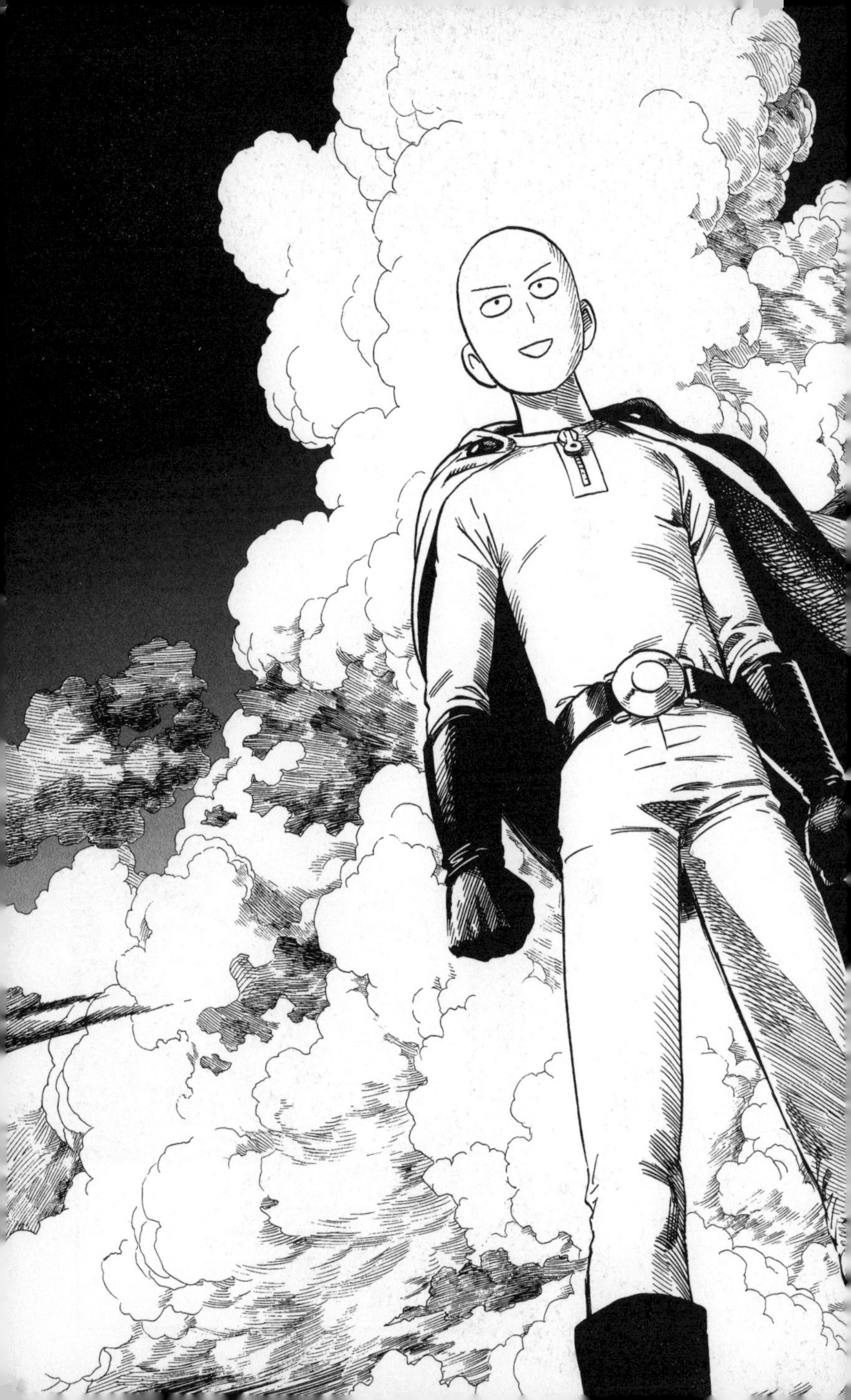

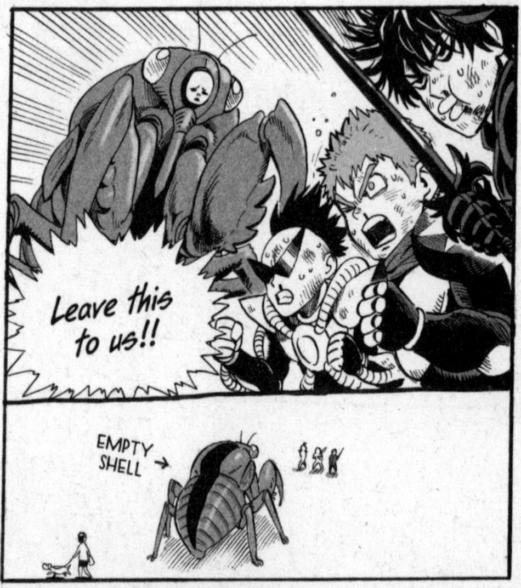
Leave this to us!!
EMPTY SHELL

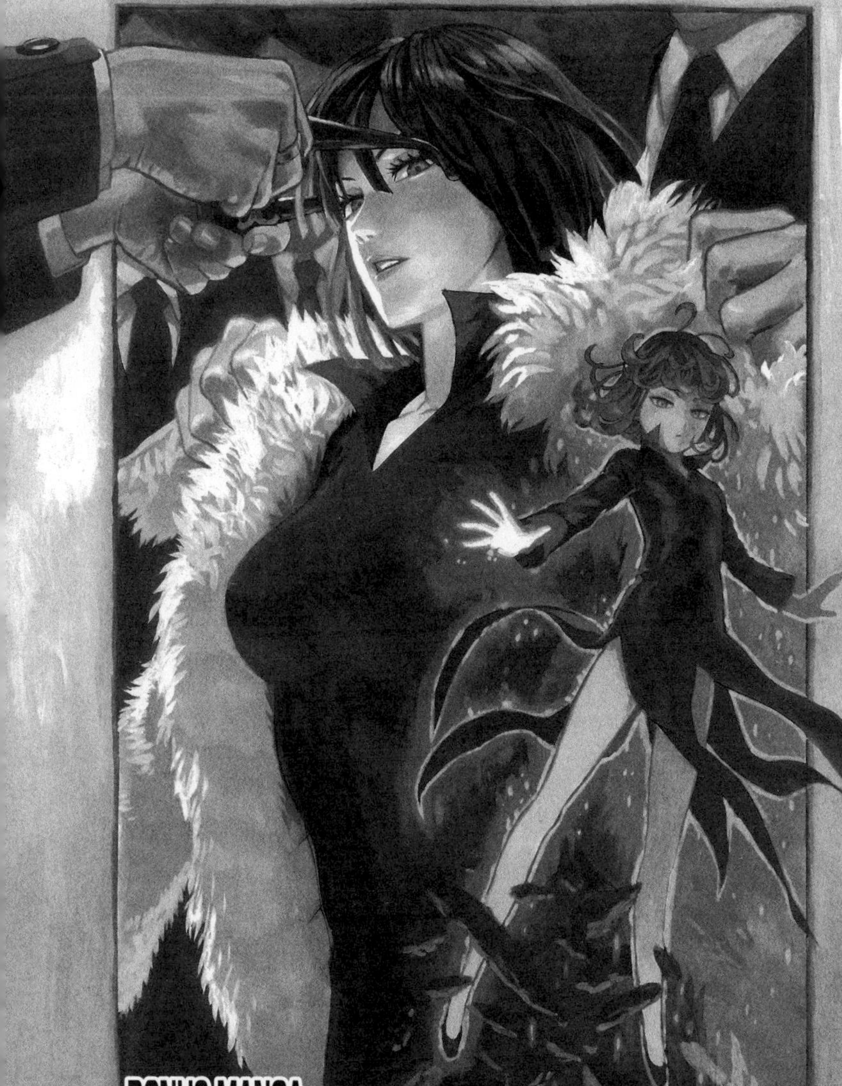

BONUS MANGA:

A NEW WIND BLOWS

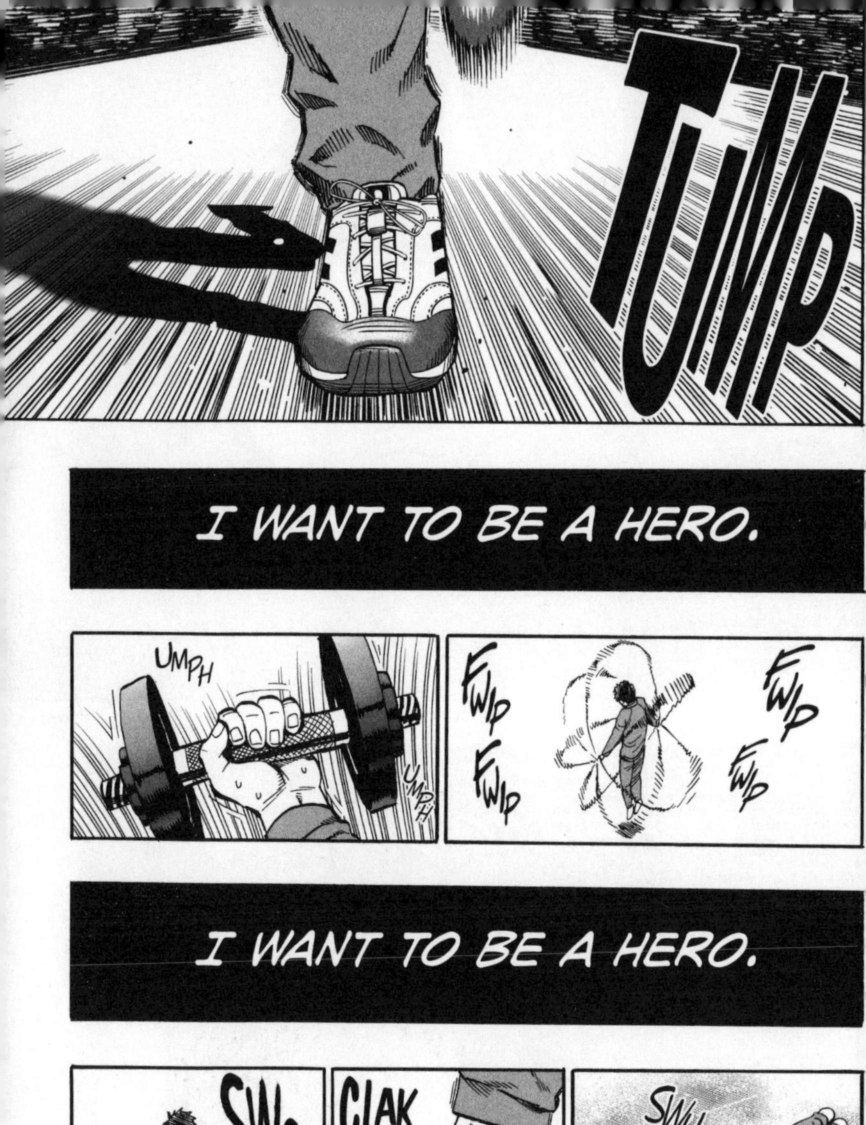
TUMP
I WANT TO BE A HERO.
FWIP
FWIP
FWIP
FWIP
UMPH
UMPH
I WANT TO BE A HERO.
SWUP
SWUP
SWUP
CLAK
CLAK
SWSH

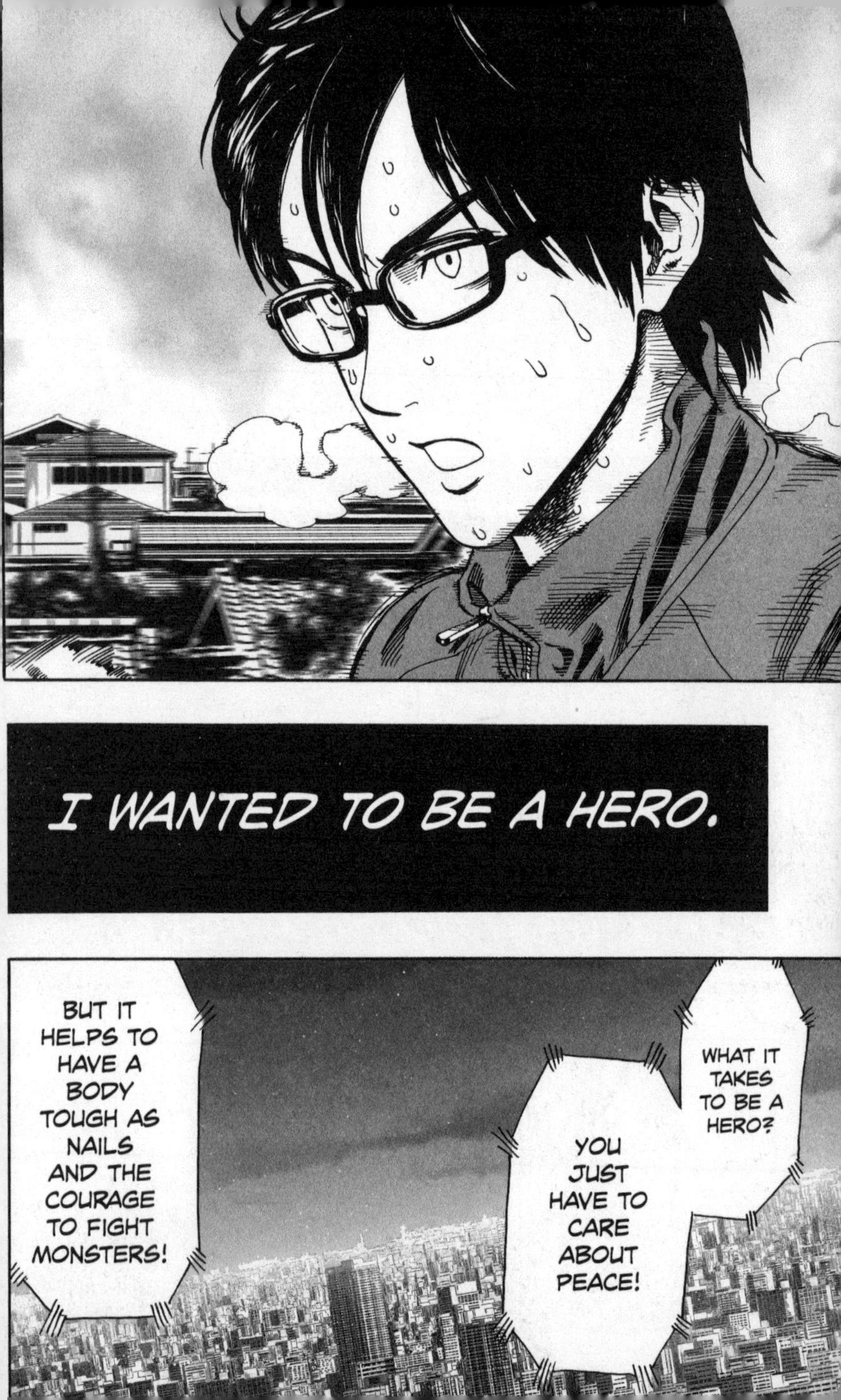
I WANTED TO BE A HERO.
WHAT IT TAKES TO BE A HERO?
YOU JUST HAVE TO CARE ABOUT PEACE!
BUT IT HELPS TO HAVE A BODY TOUGH AS NAILS AND THE COURAGE TO FIGHT MONSTERS!

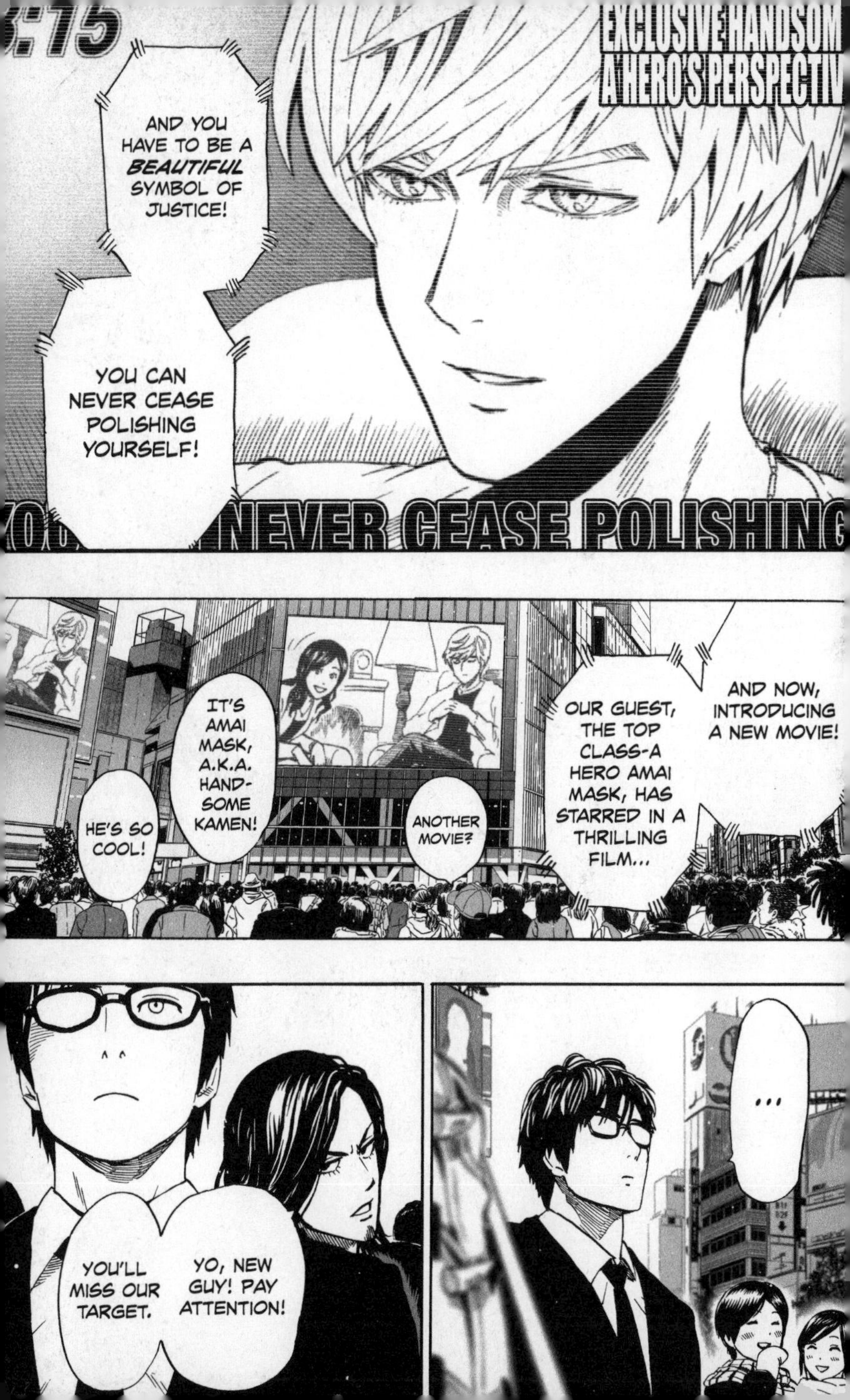
3:15
EXCLUSIVE HANDSOM
A HERO'S PERSPECTIV
AND YOU HAVE TO BE A *BEAUTIFUL* SYMBOL OF JUSTICE!
YOU CAN NEVER CEASE POLISHING YOURSELF!
NEVER CEASE POLISHING
AND NOW, INTRODUCING A NEW MOVIE!
OUR GUEST, THE TOP CLASS-A HERO AMAI MASK, HAS STARRED IN A THRILLING FILM...
ANOTHER MOVIE?
IT'S AMAI MASK, A.K.A. HANDSOME KAMEN!
HE'S SO COOL!
...
YO, NEW GUY! PAY ATTENTION!
YOU'LL MISS OUR TARGET.

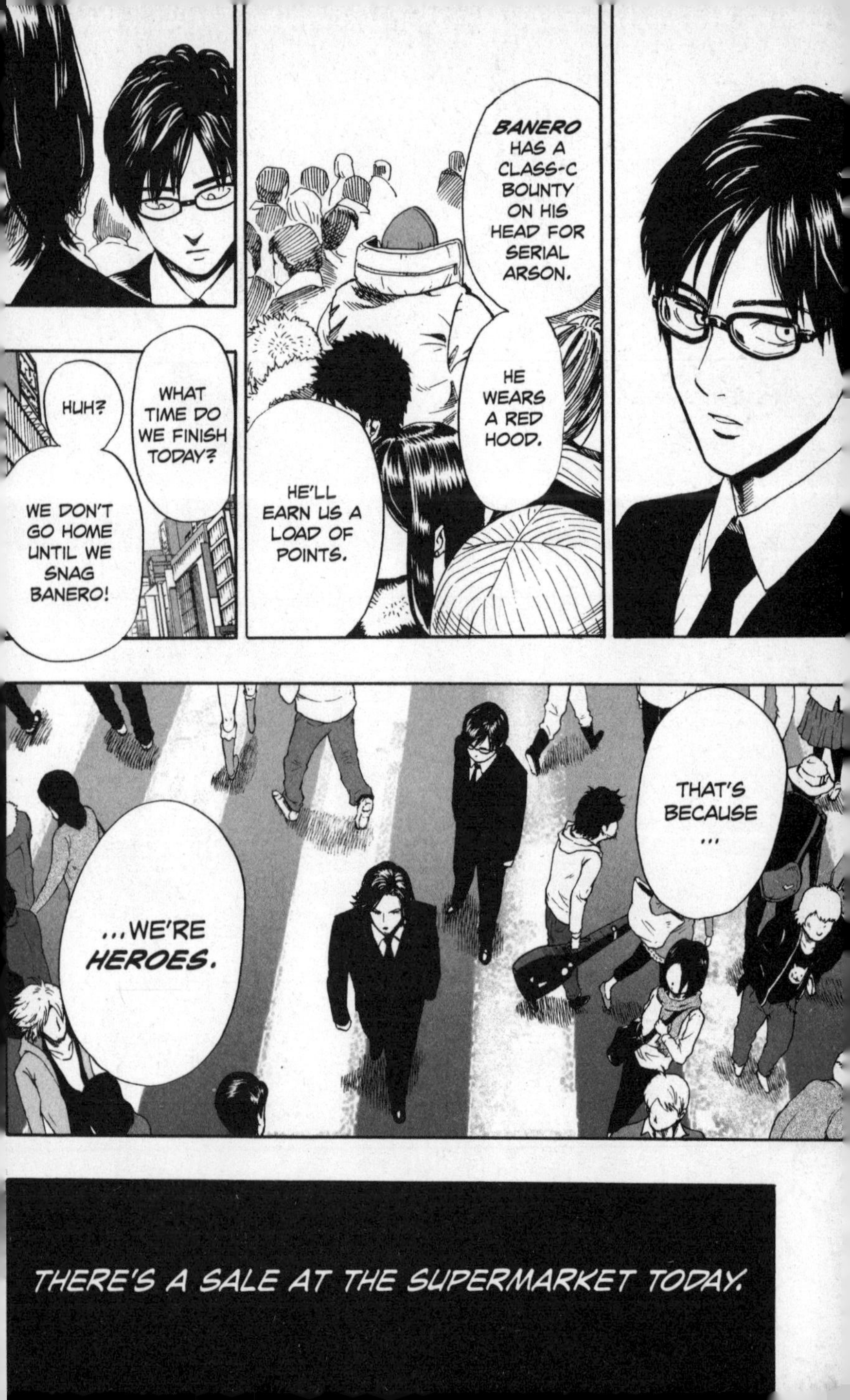
BANERO HAS A CLASS-C BOUNTY ON HIS HEAD FOR SERIAL ARSON.
HE WEARS A RED HOOD.
HE'LL EARN US A LOAD OF POINTS.
WHAT TIME DO WE FINISH TODAY?
HUH?
WE DON'T GO HOME UNTIL WE SNAG BANERO!
THAT'S BECAUSE ...
...WE'RE HEROES.
THERE'S A SALE AT THE SUPERMARKET TODAY.

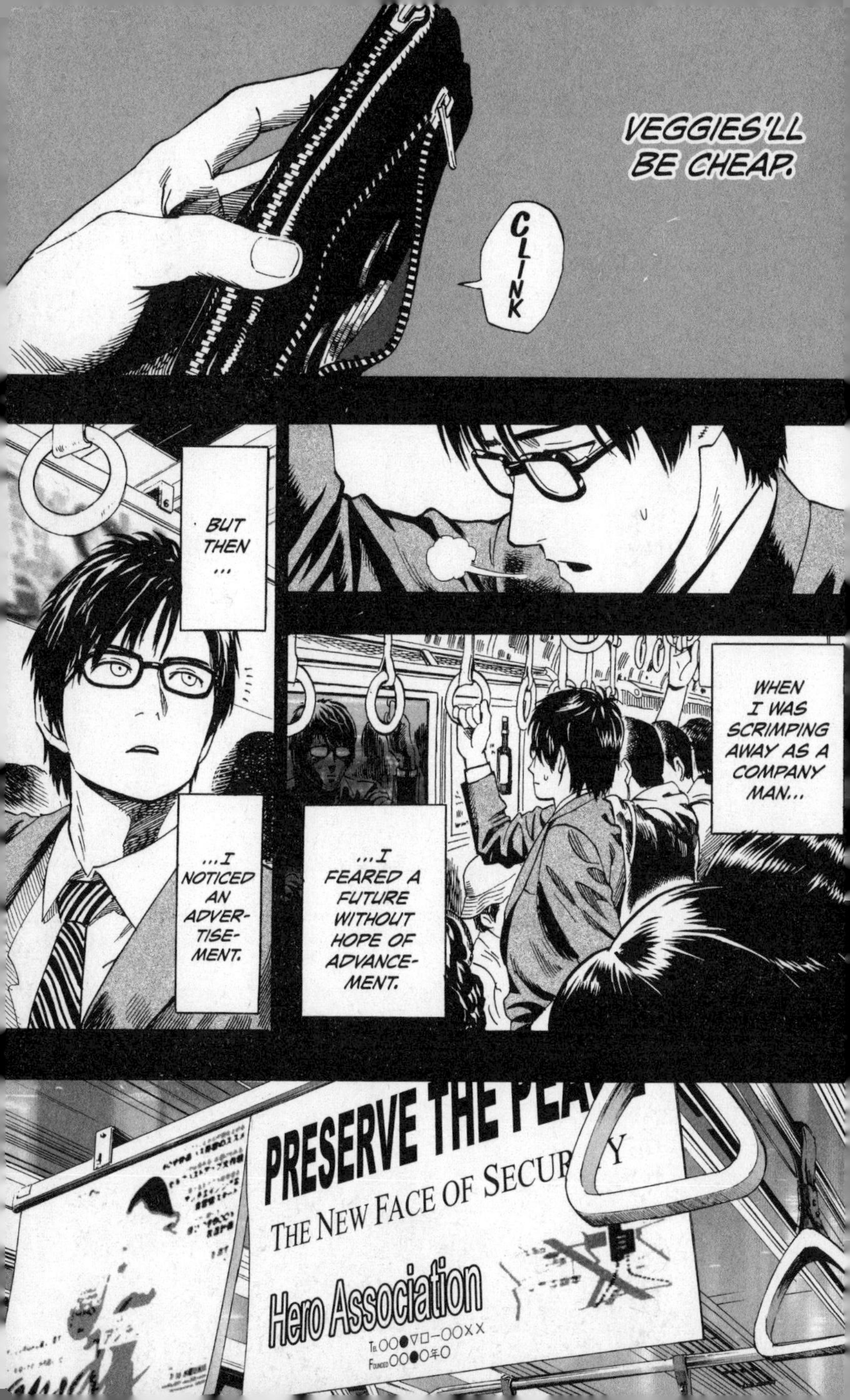
VEGGIES'LL BE CHEAP.
CLINK
WHEN I WAS SCRIMPING AWAY AS A COMPANY MAN...
...I FEARED A FUTURE WITHOUT HOPE OF ADVANCE-MENT.
BUT THEN...
...I NOTICED AN ADVER-TISE-MENT.
PRESERVE THE
THE NEW FACE OF
Hero Association

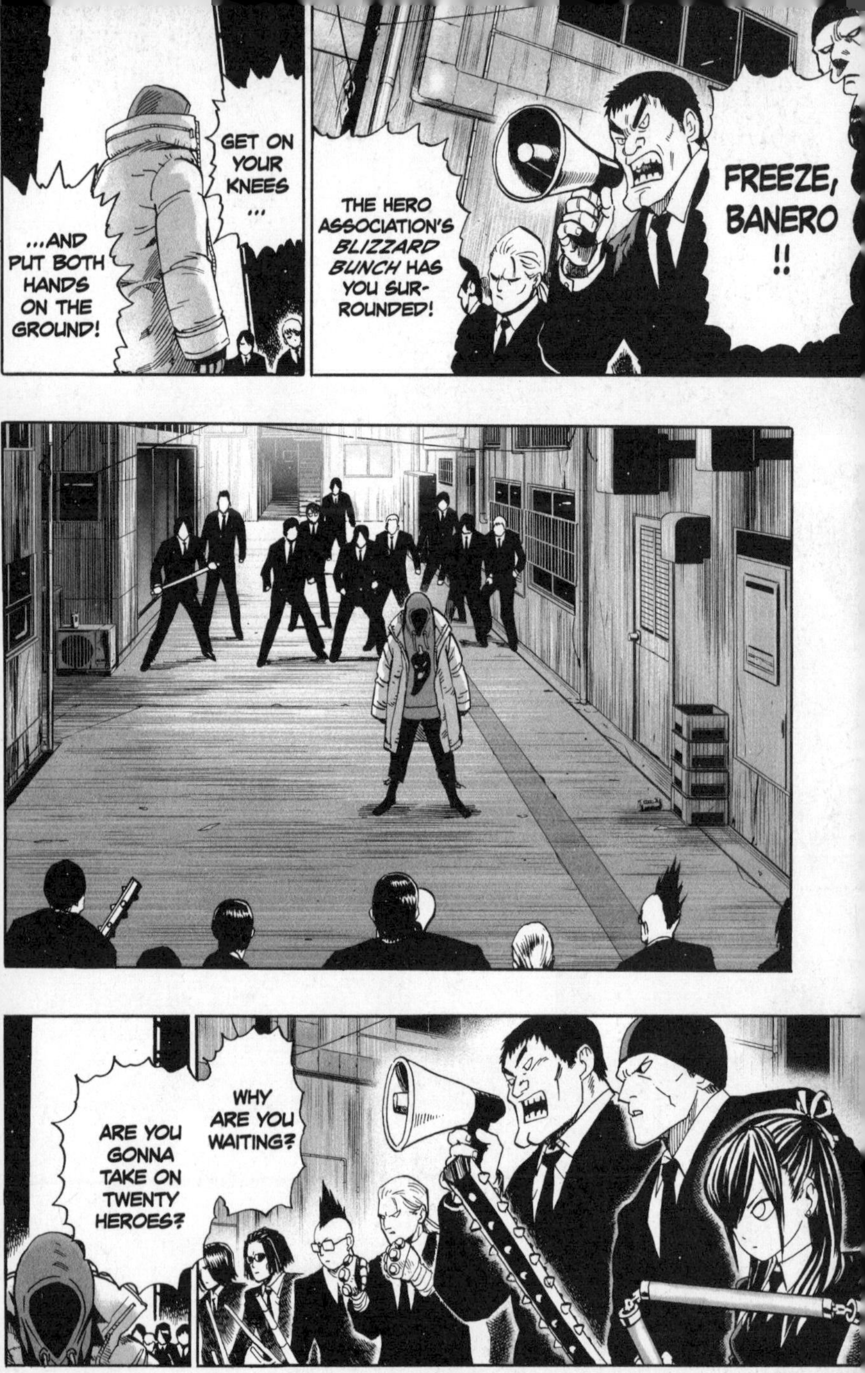
FREEZE, BANERO!!
THE HERO ASSOCIATION'S BLIZZARD BUNCH HAS YOU SURROUNDED!
GET ON YOUR KNEES...
...AND PUT BOTH HANDS ON THE GROUND!
WHY ARE YOU WAITING?
ARE YOU GONNA TAKE ON TWENTY HEROES?

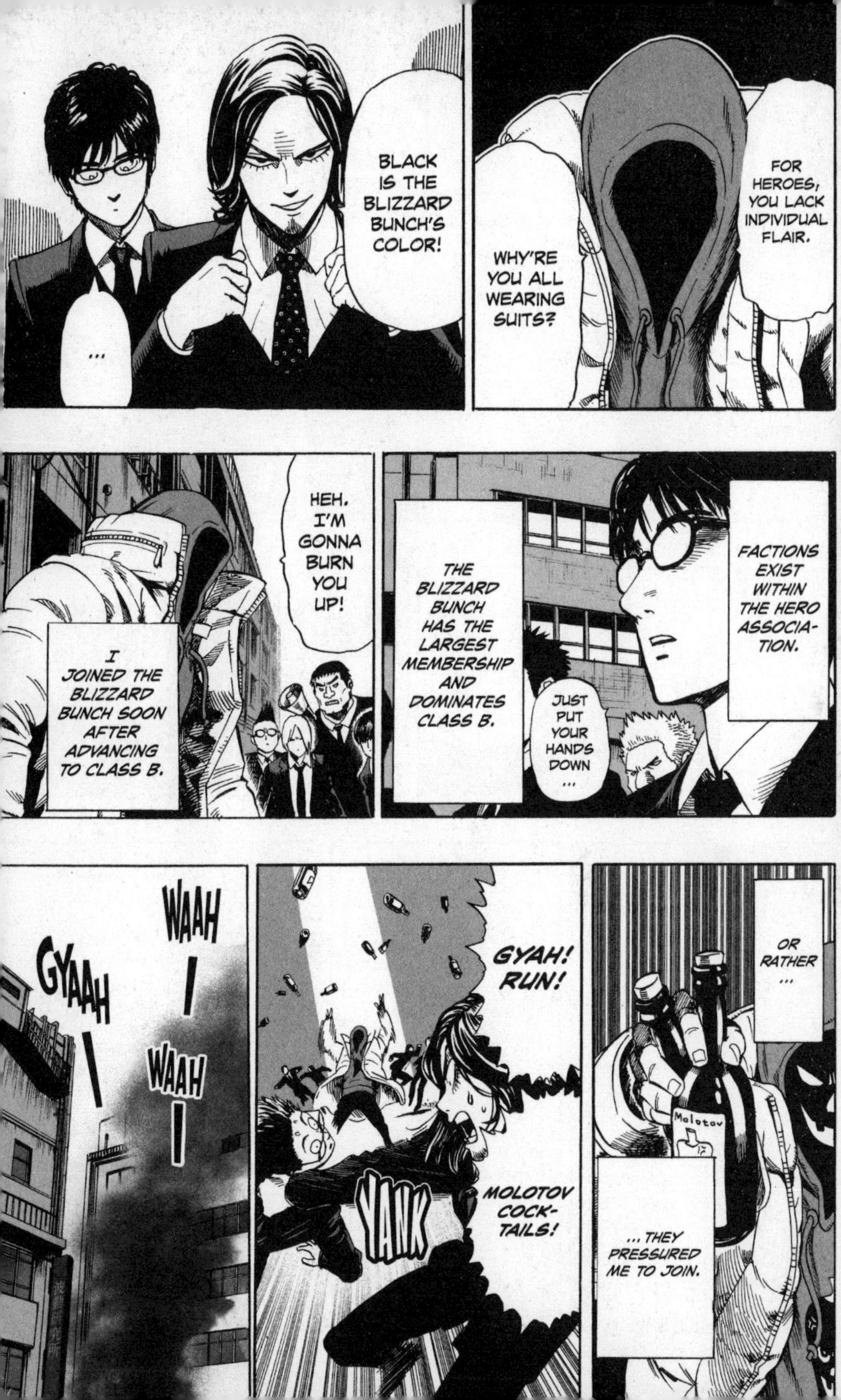

FOR HEROES, YOU LACK INDIVIDUAL FLAIR.
WHY'RE YOU ALL WEARING SUITS?
BLACK IS THE BLIZZARD BUNCH'S COLOR!
...
FACTIONS EXIST WITHIN THE HERO ASSOCIATION.
THE BLIZZARD BUNCH HAS THE LARGEST MEMBERSHIP AND DOMINATES CLASS B.
JUST PUT YOUR HANDS DOWN...
HEH. I'M GONNA BURN YOU UP!
I JOINED THE BLIZZARD BUNCH SOON AFTER ADVANCING TO CLASS B.
OR RATHER...
...THEY PRESSURED ME TO JOIN.
Molotov
GYAH! RUN!
MOLOTOV COCKTAILS!
YANK
GYAAH!
WAAH!
WAAH!

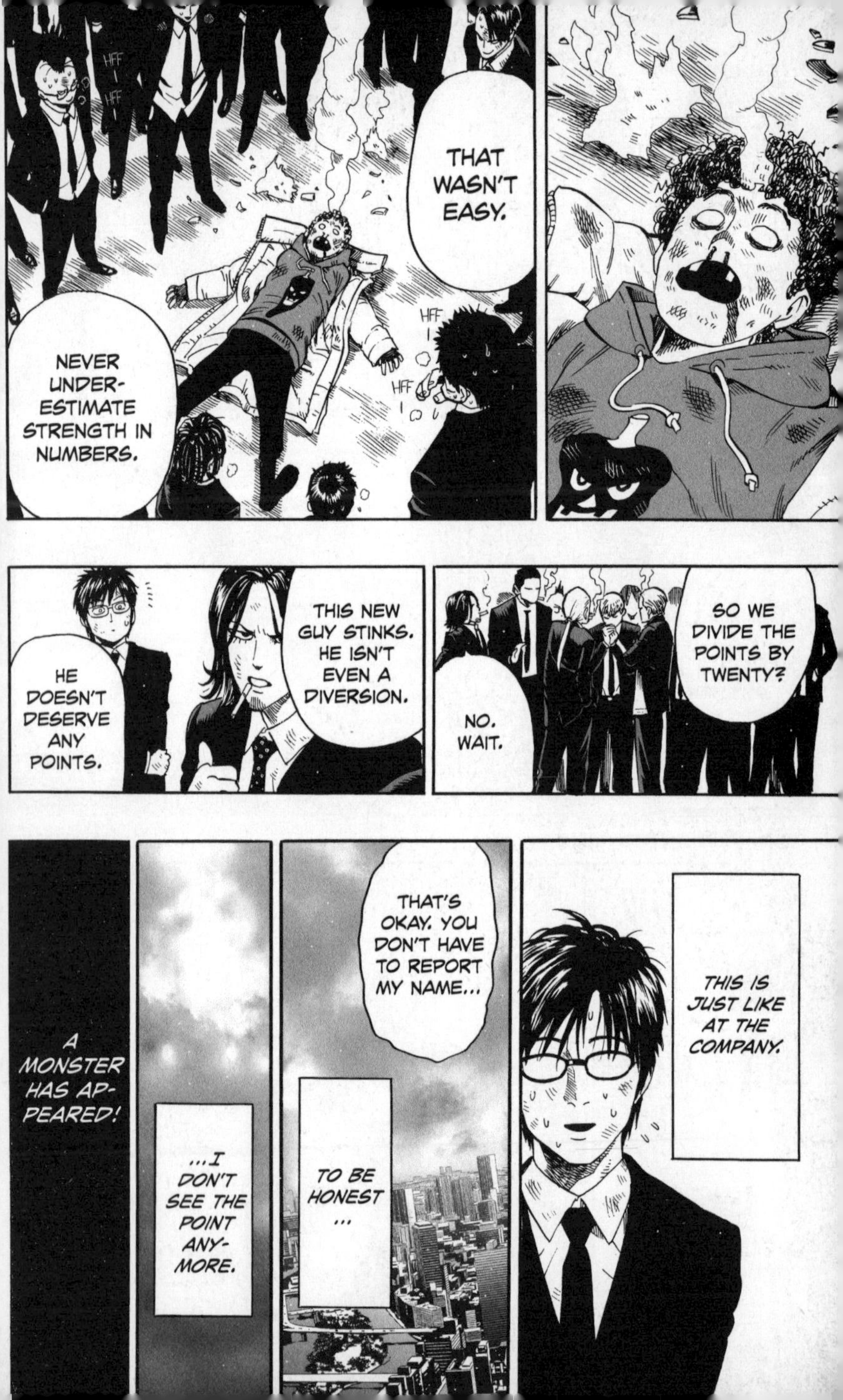
HFF HFF
THAT WASN'T EASY.
NEVER UNDER-ESTIMATE STRENGTH IN NUMBERS.
HFF HFF
SO WE DIVIDE THE POINTS BY TWENTY?
NO. WAIT.
THIS NEW GUY STINKS. HE ISN'T EVEN A DIVERSION.
HE DOESN'T DESERVE ANY POINTS.
THIS IS JUST LIKE AT THE COMPANY.
THAT'S OKAY. YOU DON'T HAVE TO REPORT MY NAME...
TO BE HONEST ...
...I DON'T SEE THE POINT ANY-MORE.
A MONSTER HAS AP-PEARED!

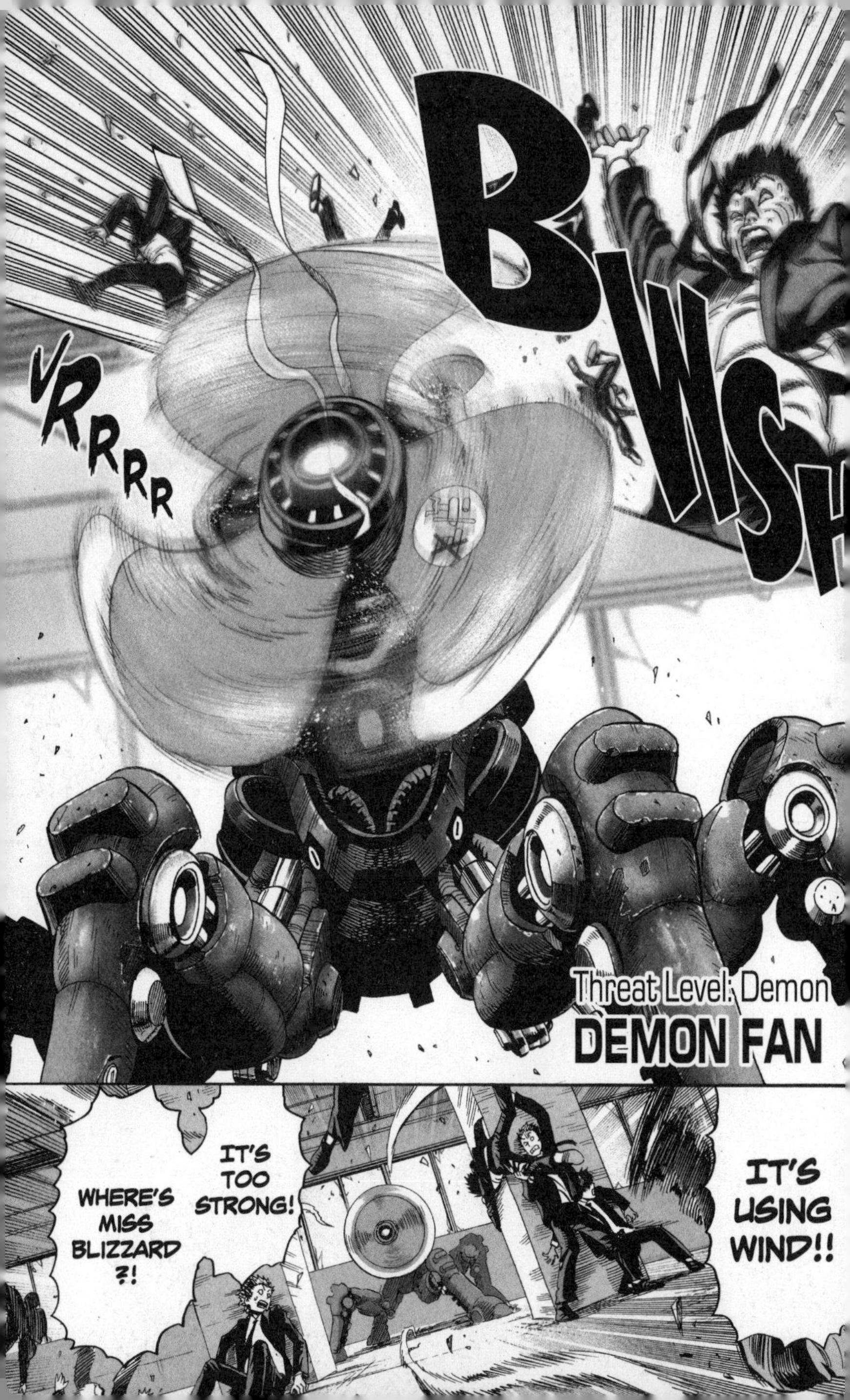
BWISH
VRRRRR
Threat Level: Demon
DEMON FAN
IT'S USING WIND!!
IT'S TOO STRONG!
WHERE'S MISS BLIZZARD ?!

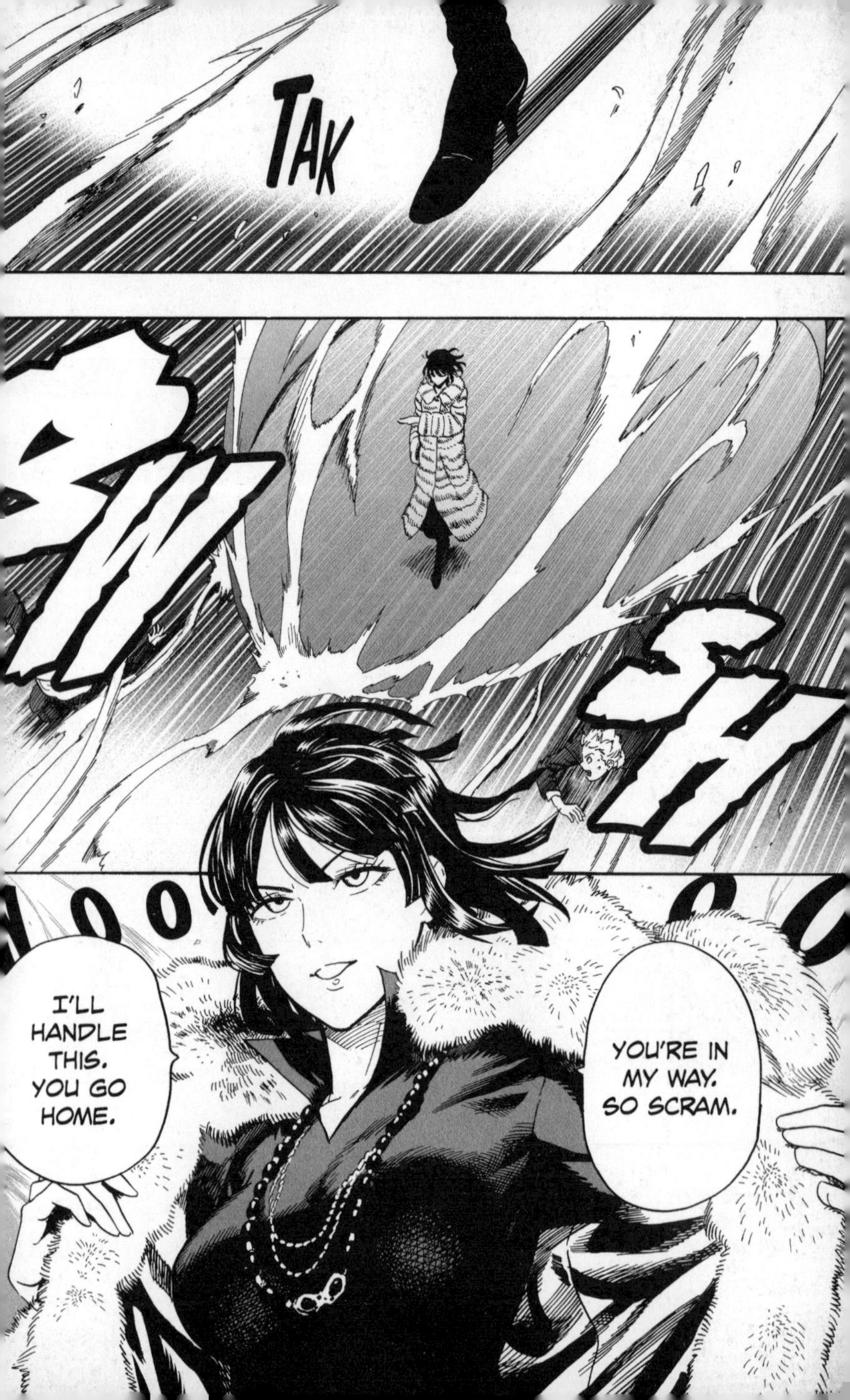
TAK
YOU'RE IN MY WAY. SO SCRAM.
I'LL HANDLE THIS. YOU GO HOME.

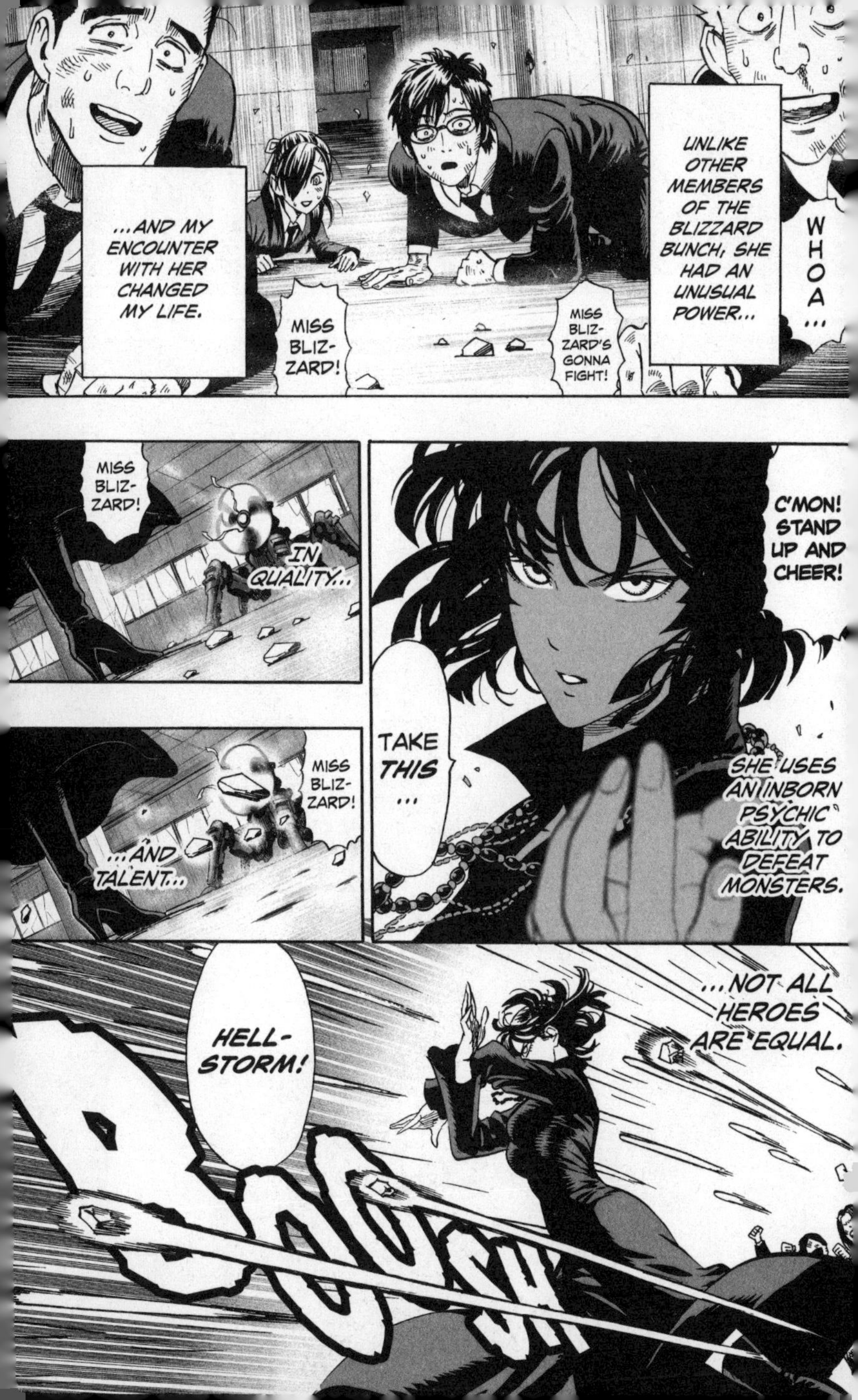
WHOA...
UNLIKE OTHER MEMBERS OF THE BLIZZARD BUNCH, SHE HAD AN UNUSUAL POWER...
MISS BLIZZARD'S GONNA FIGHT!
MISS BLIZZARD!
...AND MY ENCOUNTER WITH HER CHANGED MY LIFE.
C'MON! STAND UP AND CHEER!
SHE USES AN INBORN PSYCHIC ABILITY TO DEFEAT MONSTERS.
TAKE THIS...
MISS BLIZZARD!
IN QUALITY...
MISS BLIZZARD!
...AND TALENT...
...NOT ALL HEROES ARE EQUAL.
HELL-STORM!

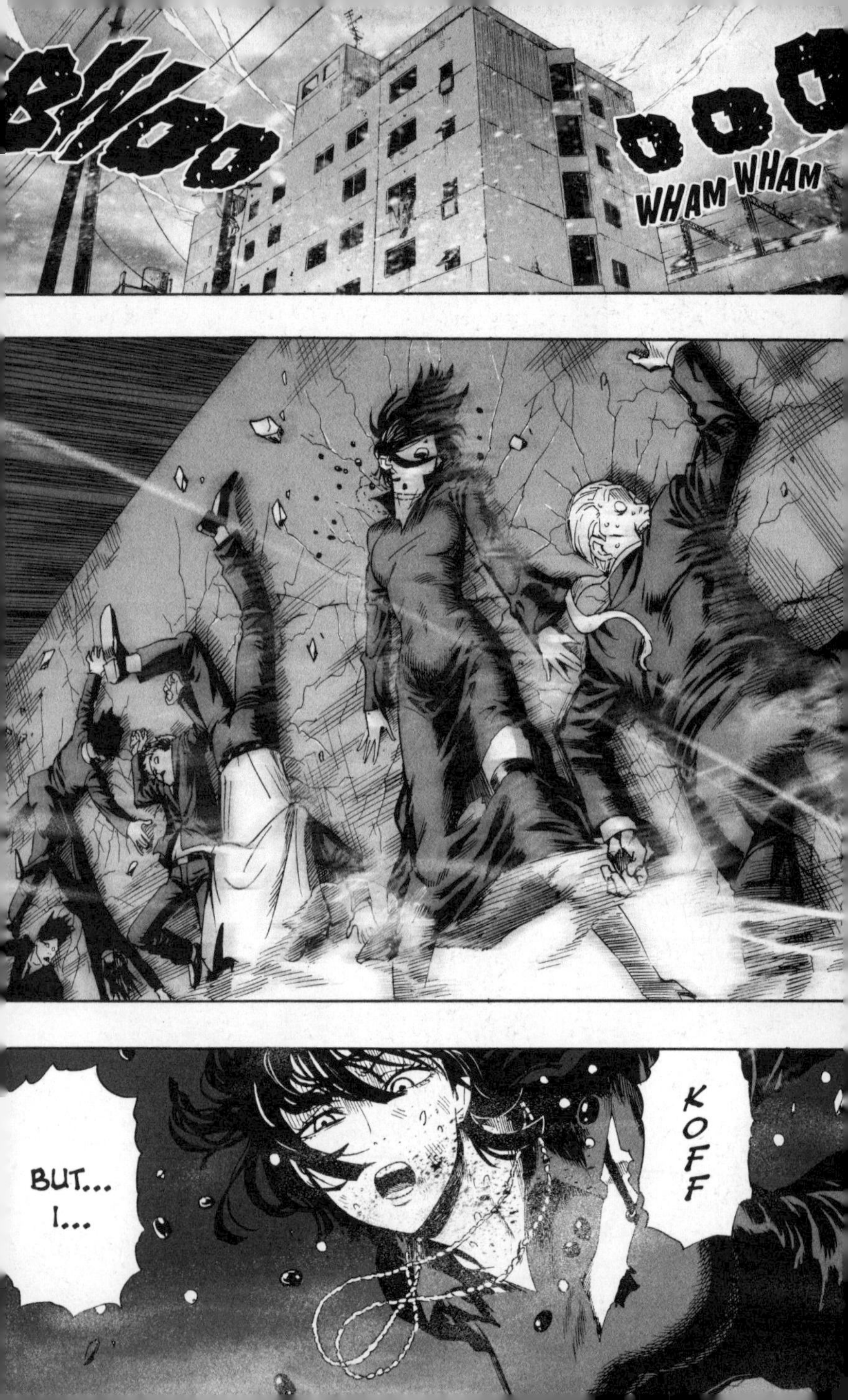
BWOO
OOOO
WHAM WHAM
KOFF
BUT... I...

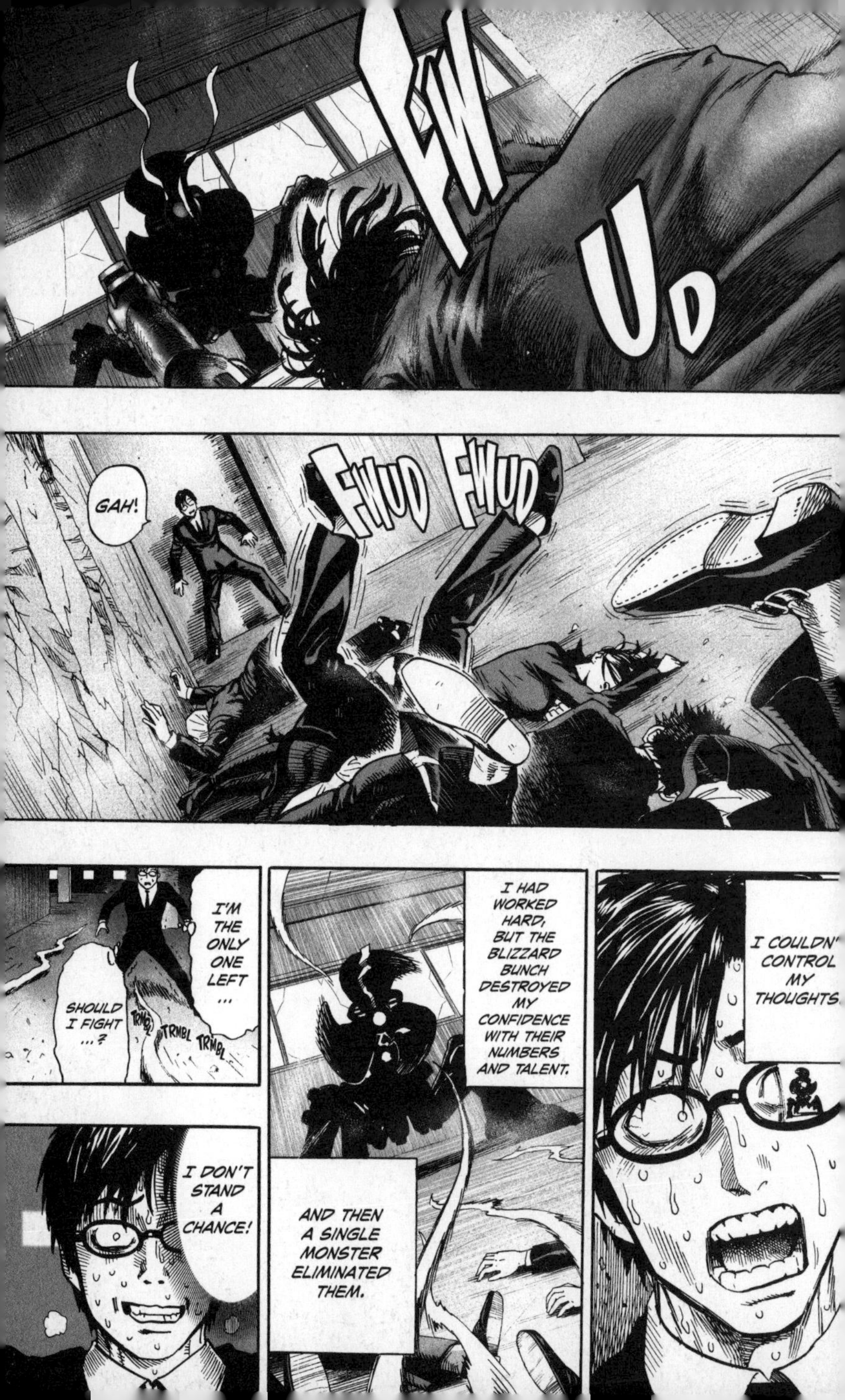

FWUD
GAH!
FWUD FWUD
I'M THE ONLY ONE LEFT...
SHOULD I FIGHT...?
TRMBL TRMBL TRMBL
I DON'T STAND A CHANCE!
I HAD WORKED HARD, BUT THE BLIZZARD BUNCH DESTROYED MY CONFIDENCE WITH THEIR NUMBERS AND TALENT.
AND THEN A SINGLE MONSTER ELIMINATED THEM.
I COULDN'T CONTROL MY THOUGHTS.

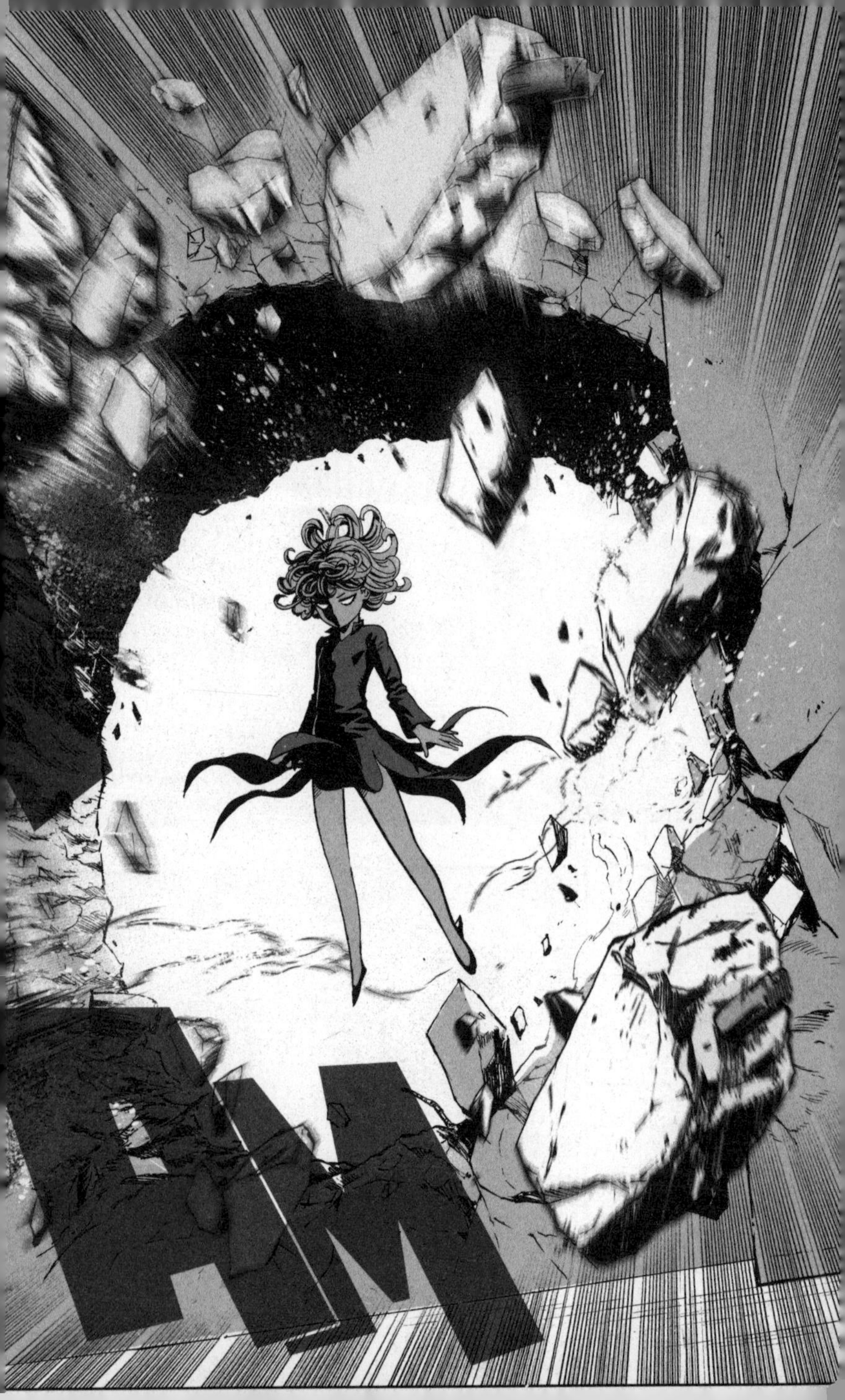
AM

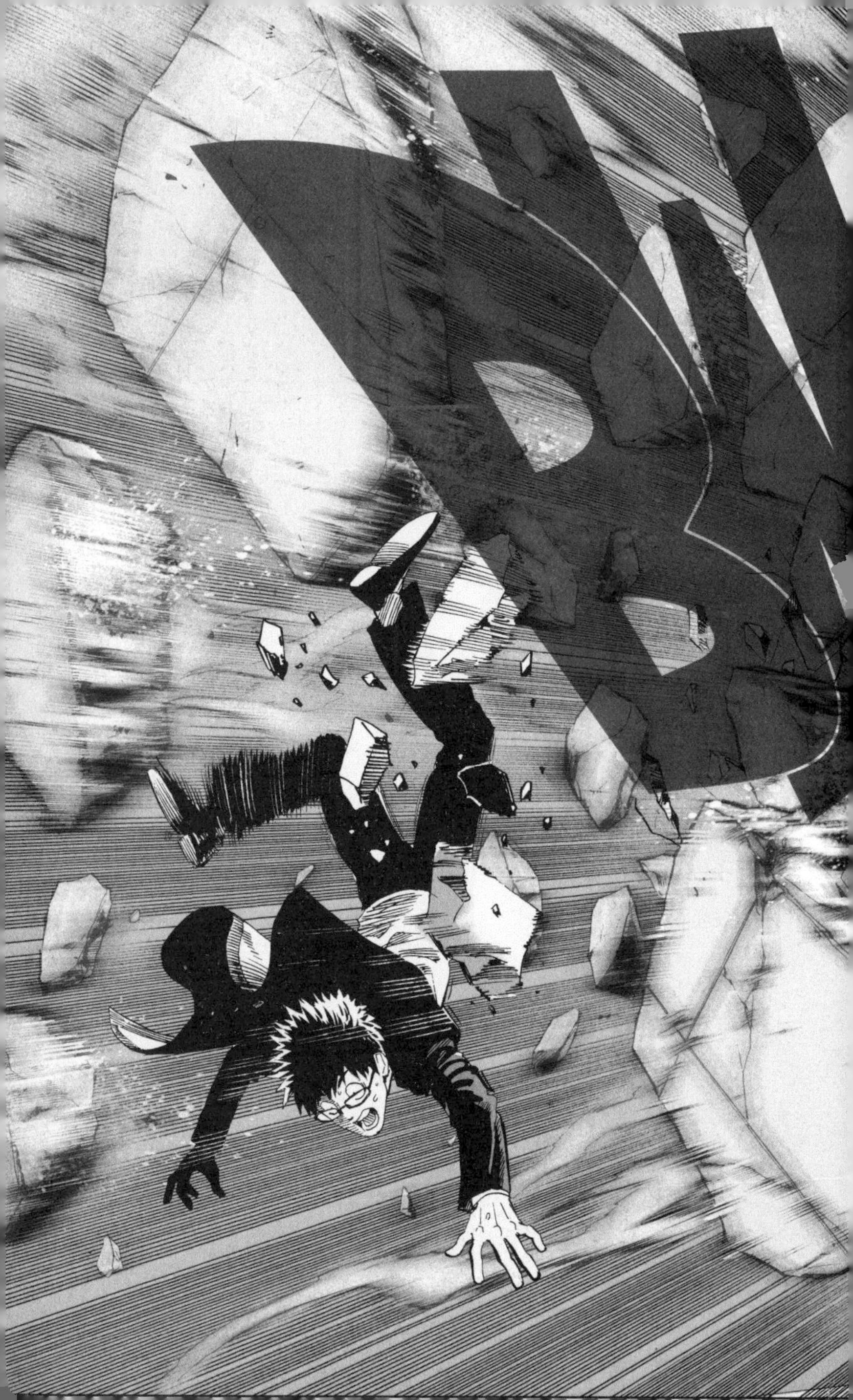

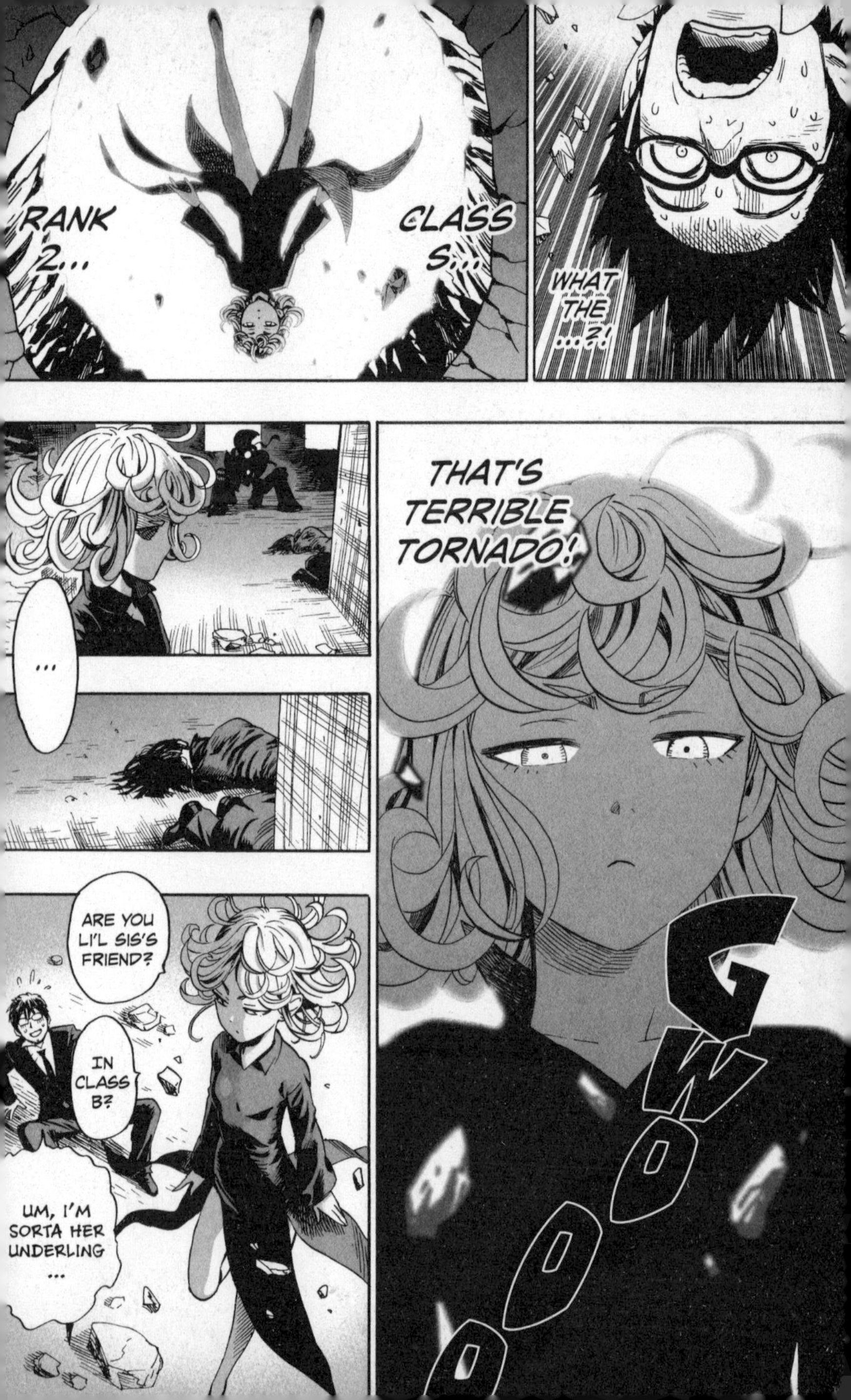
WHAT THE ...?!
CLASS S...
RANK 2...
THAT'S TERRIBLE TORNADO!
GWOOOOO
...
ARE YOU LI'L SIS'S FRIEND?
IN CLASS B?
UM, I'M SORTA HER UNDERLING ...

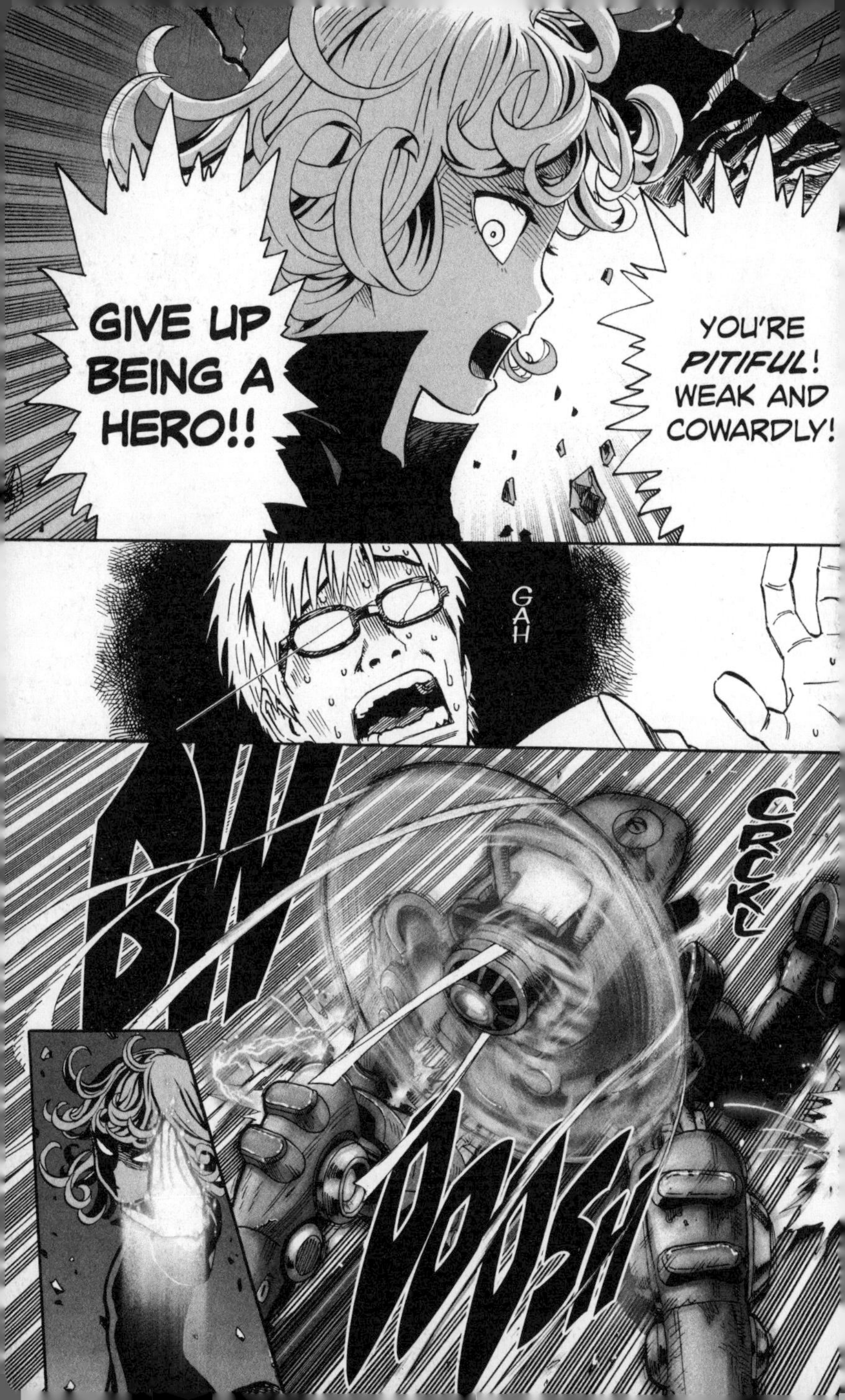

YOU'RE *PITIFUL*! WEAK AND COWARDLY!
GIVE UP BEING A HERO!!
GAH
CRCKL

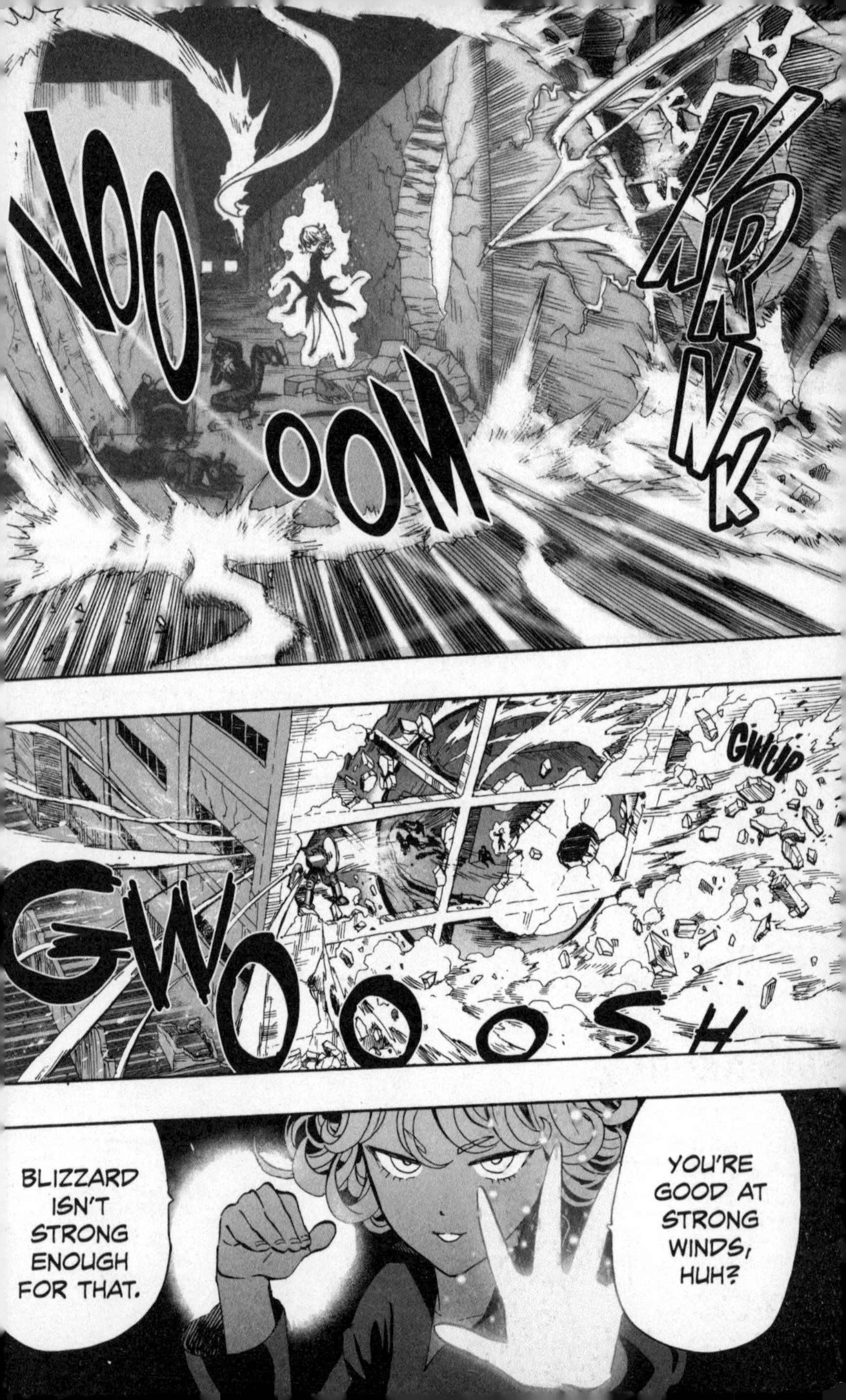
VOOOOM
KRNNK
GWUP
GWOOOOSH
YOU'RE GOOD AT STRONG WINDS, HUH?
BLIZZARD ISN'T STRONG ENOUGH FOR THAT.

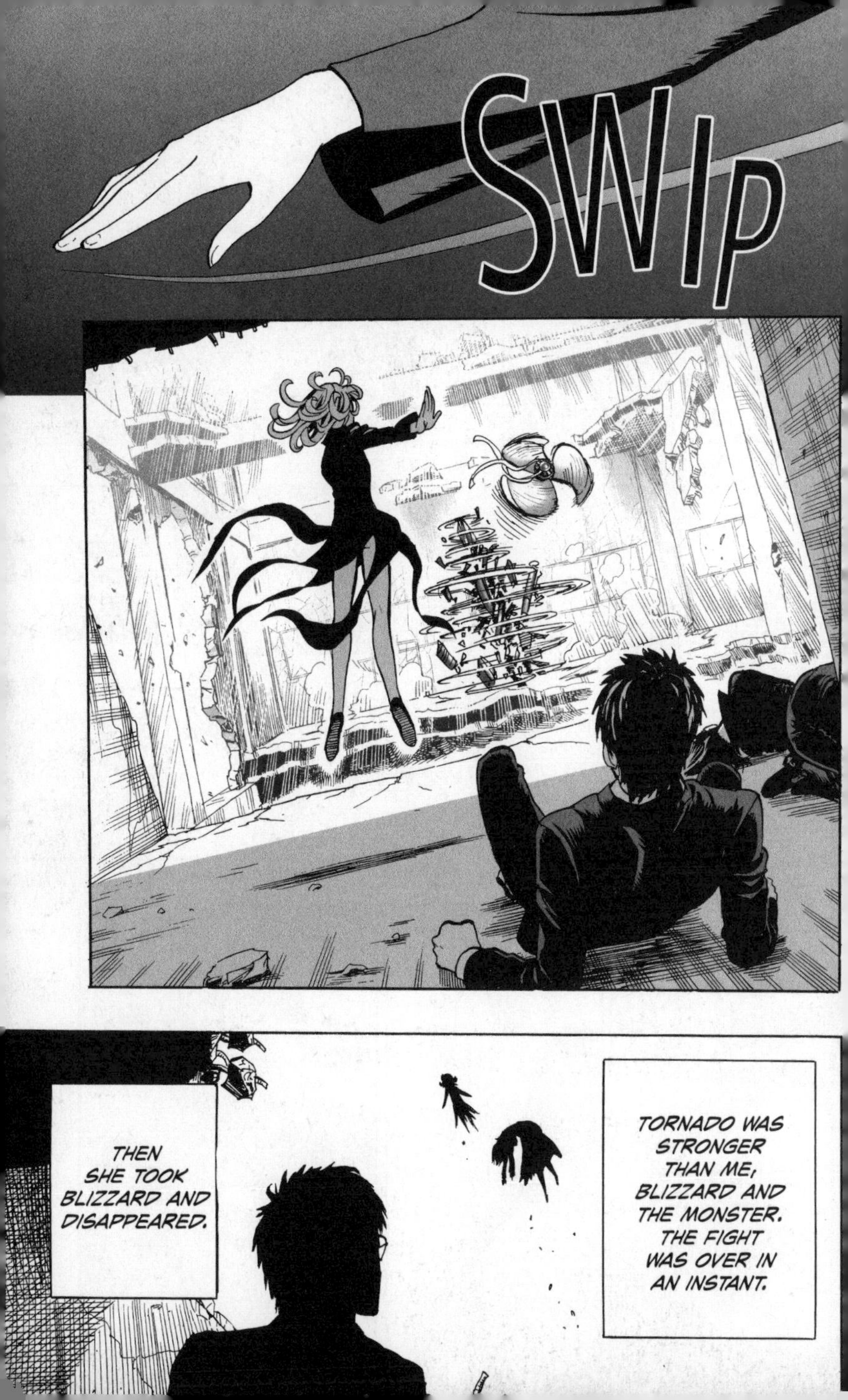
SWIP
TORNADO WAS STRONGER THAN ME, BLIZZARD AND THE MONSTER. THE FIGHT WAS OVER IN AN INSTANT.
THEN SHE TOOK BLIZZARD AND DISAPPEARED.

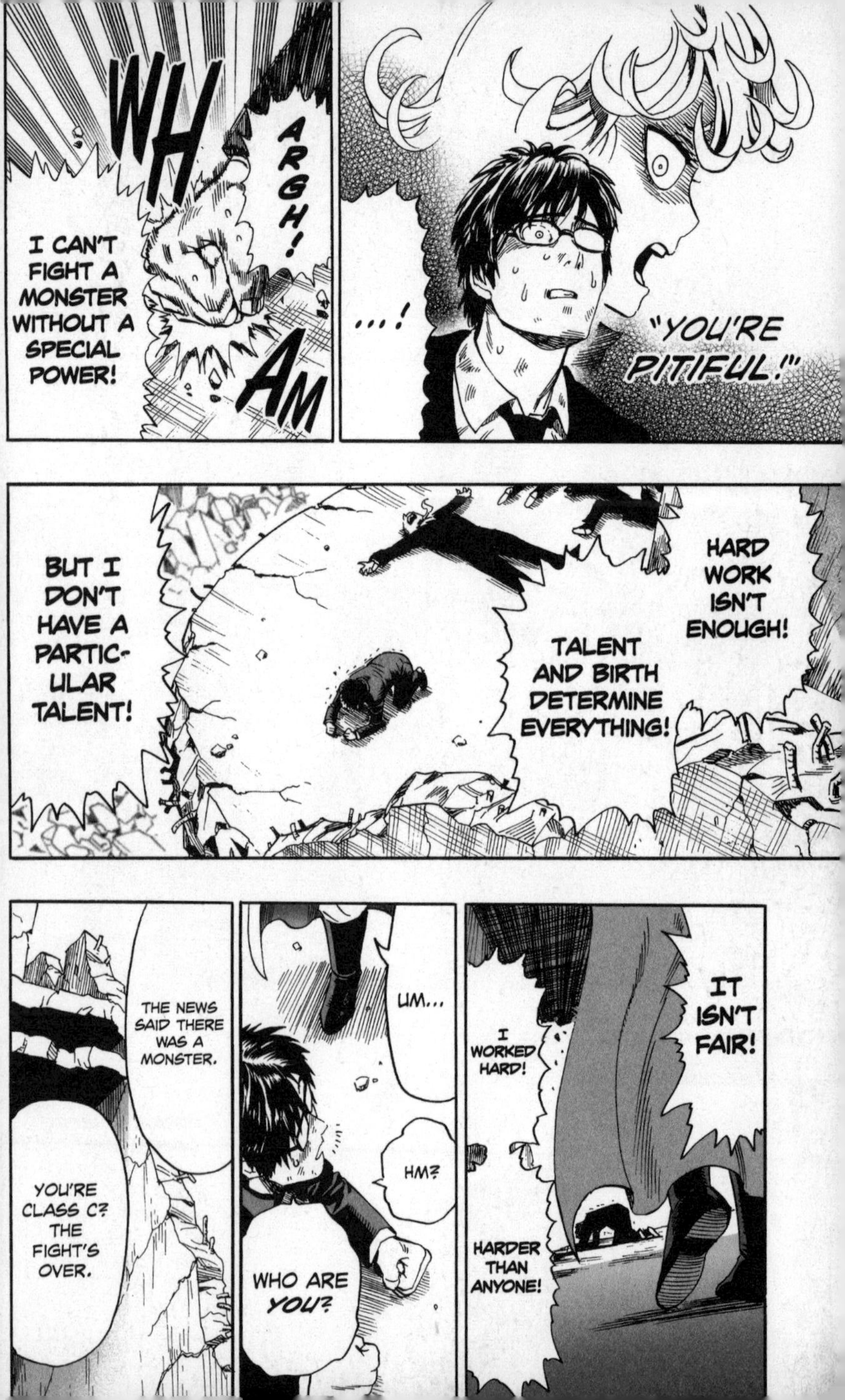
"YOU'RE PITIFUL!"
...!
WHAM
ARGH!
I CAN'T FIGHT A MONSTER WITHOUT A SPECIAL POWER!
HARD WORK ISN'T ENOUGH!
TALENT AND BIRTH DETERMINE EVERYTHING!
BUT I DON'T HAVE A PARTIC-ULAR TALENT!
IT ISN'T FAIR!
I WORKED HARD!
HARDER THAN ANYONE!
UM...
HM?
WHO ARE YOU?
THE NEWS SAID THERE WAS A MONSTER.
YOU'RE CLASS C? THE FIGHT'S OVER.

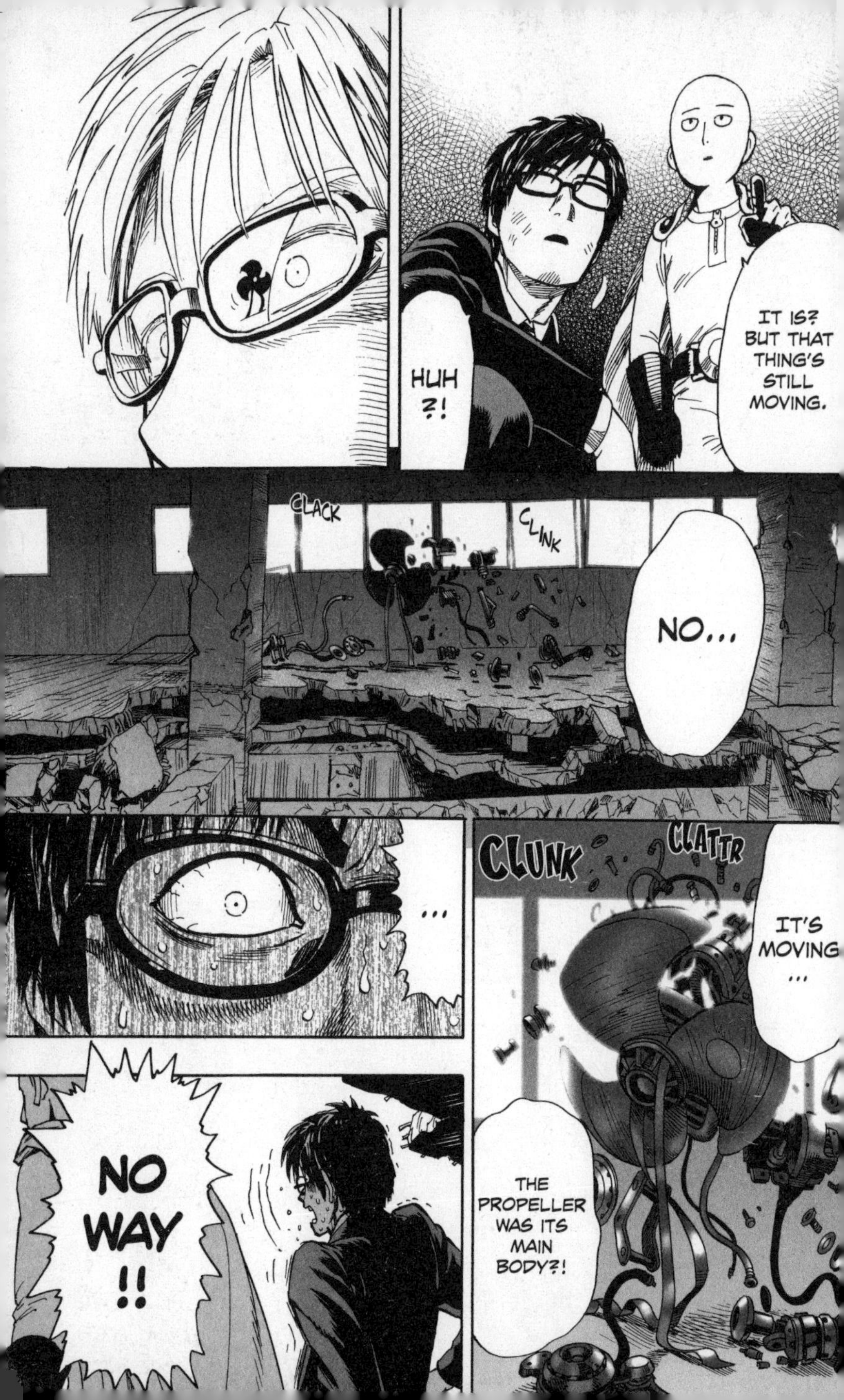

IT IS? BUT THAT THING'S STILL MOVING.
HUH ?!
NO...
CLINK
CLACK
IT'S MOVING ...
CLATTR
CLUNK
...
THE PROPELLER WAS ITS MAIN BODY?!
NO WAY !!

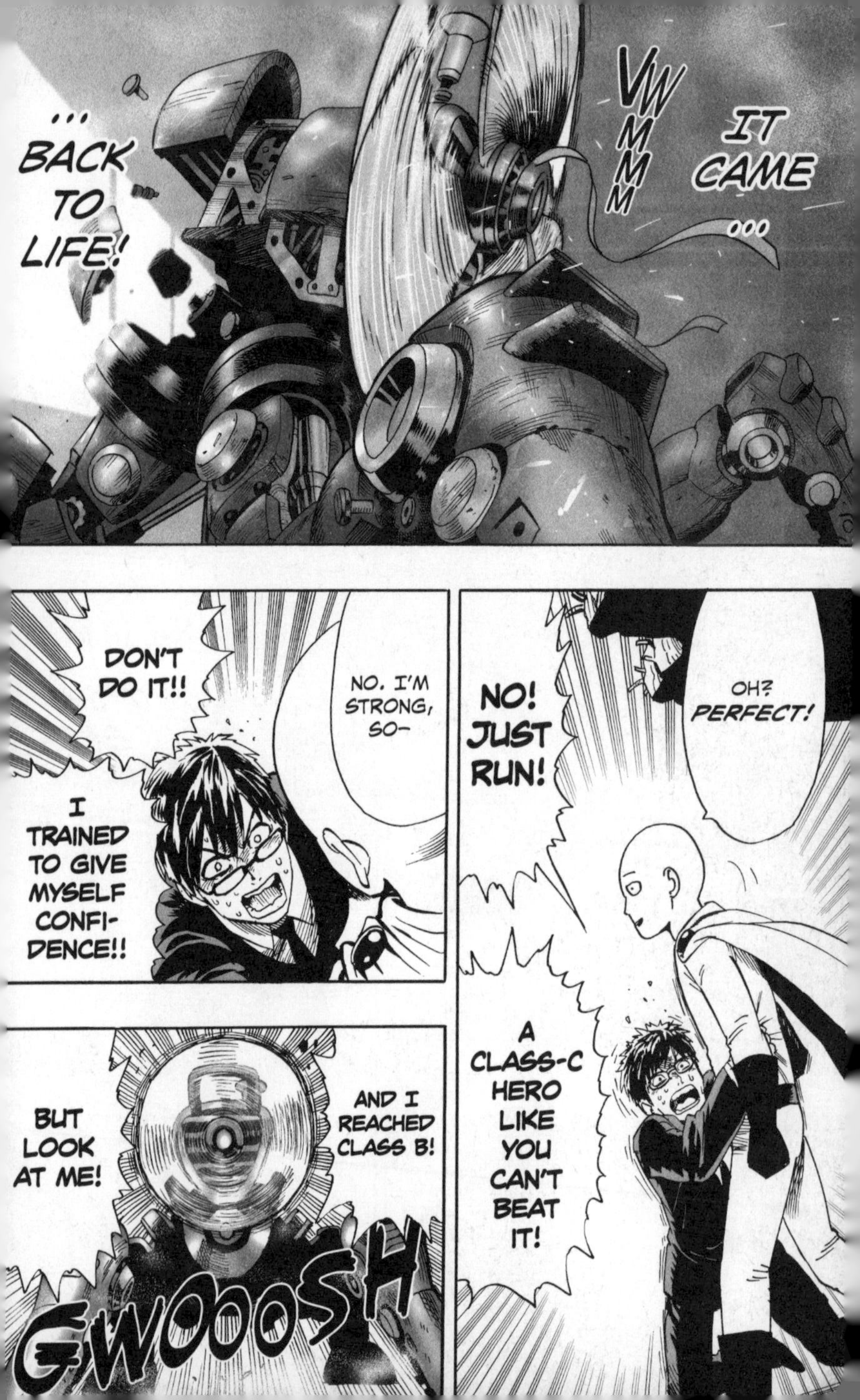
IT CAME...
VWMMMM
...BACK TO LIFE!
OH? PERFECT!
NO! JUST RUN!
A CLASS-C HERO LIKE YOU CAN'T BEAT IT!
NO. I'M STRONG, SO-
DON'T DO IT!!
I TRAINED TO GIVE MYSELF CONFIDENCE!!
AND I REACHED CLASS B!
BUT LOOK AT ME!
GWOOOSH

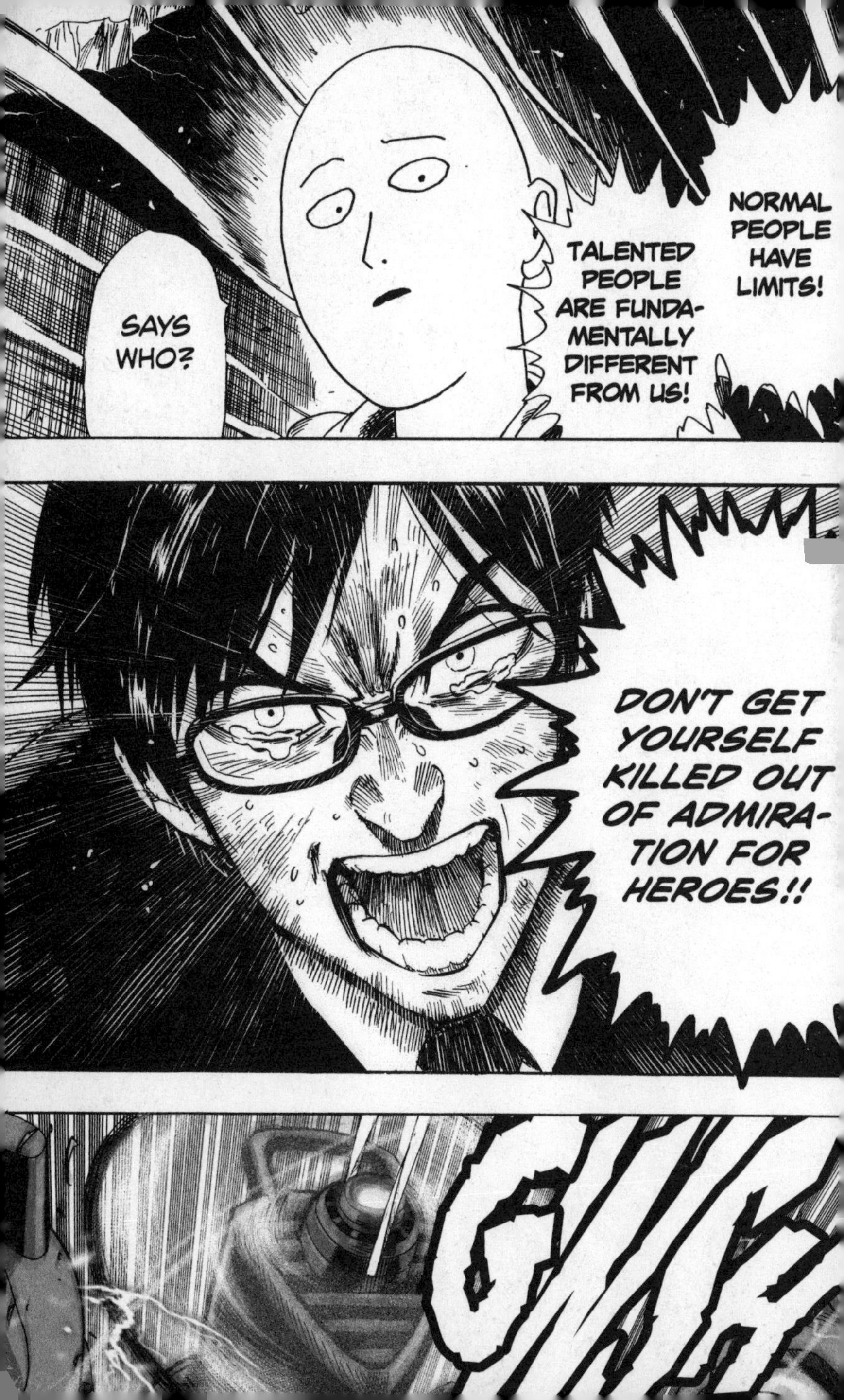
NORMAL PEOPLE HAVE LIMITS!
TALENTED PEOPLE ARE FUNDAMENTALLY DIFFERENT FROM US!
SAYS WHO?
DON'T GET YOURSELF KILLED OUT OF ADMIRATION FOR HEROES!!

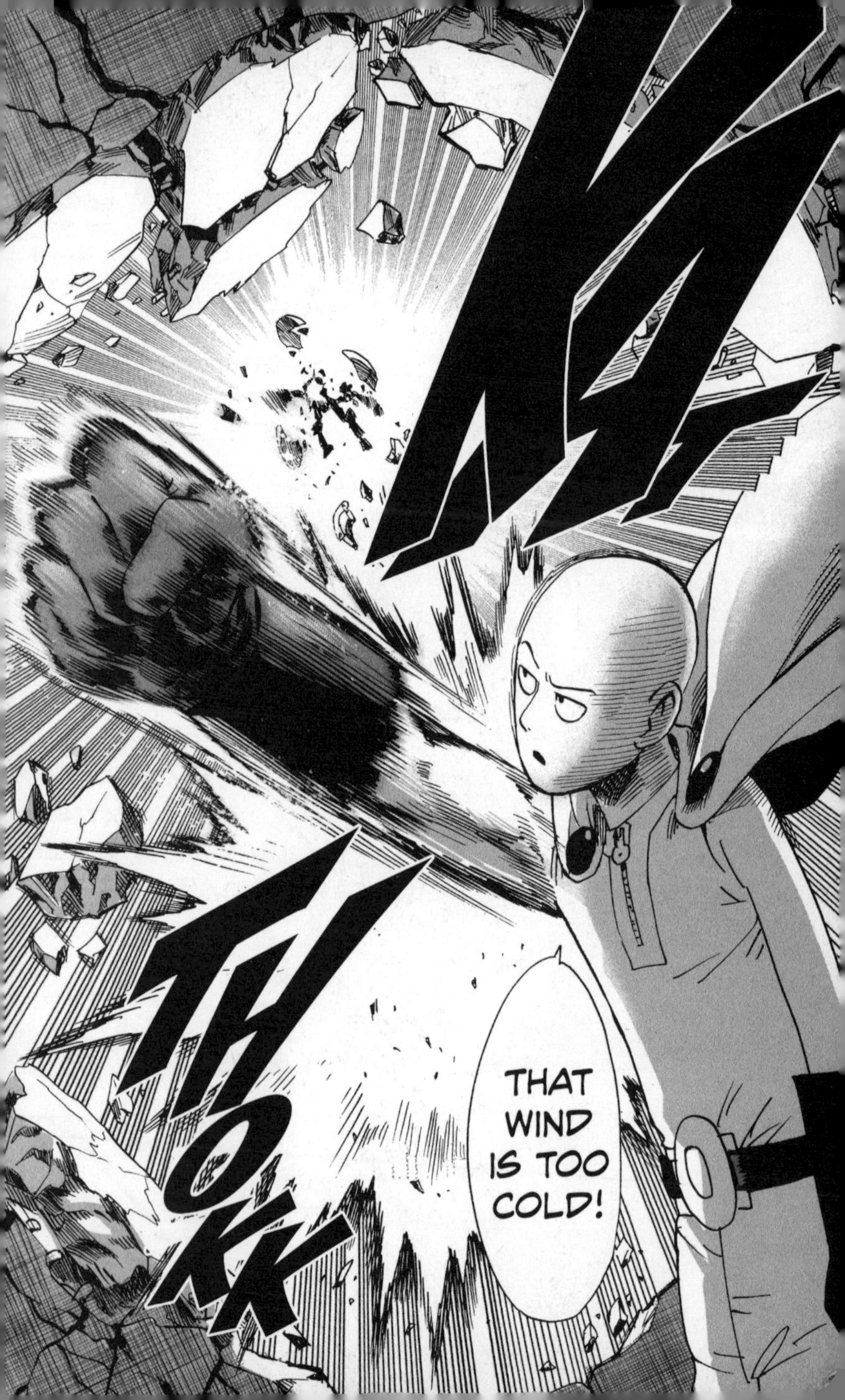
THOKK
THAT WIND IS TOO COLD!

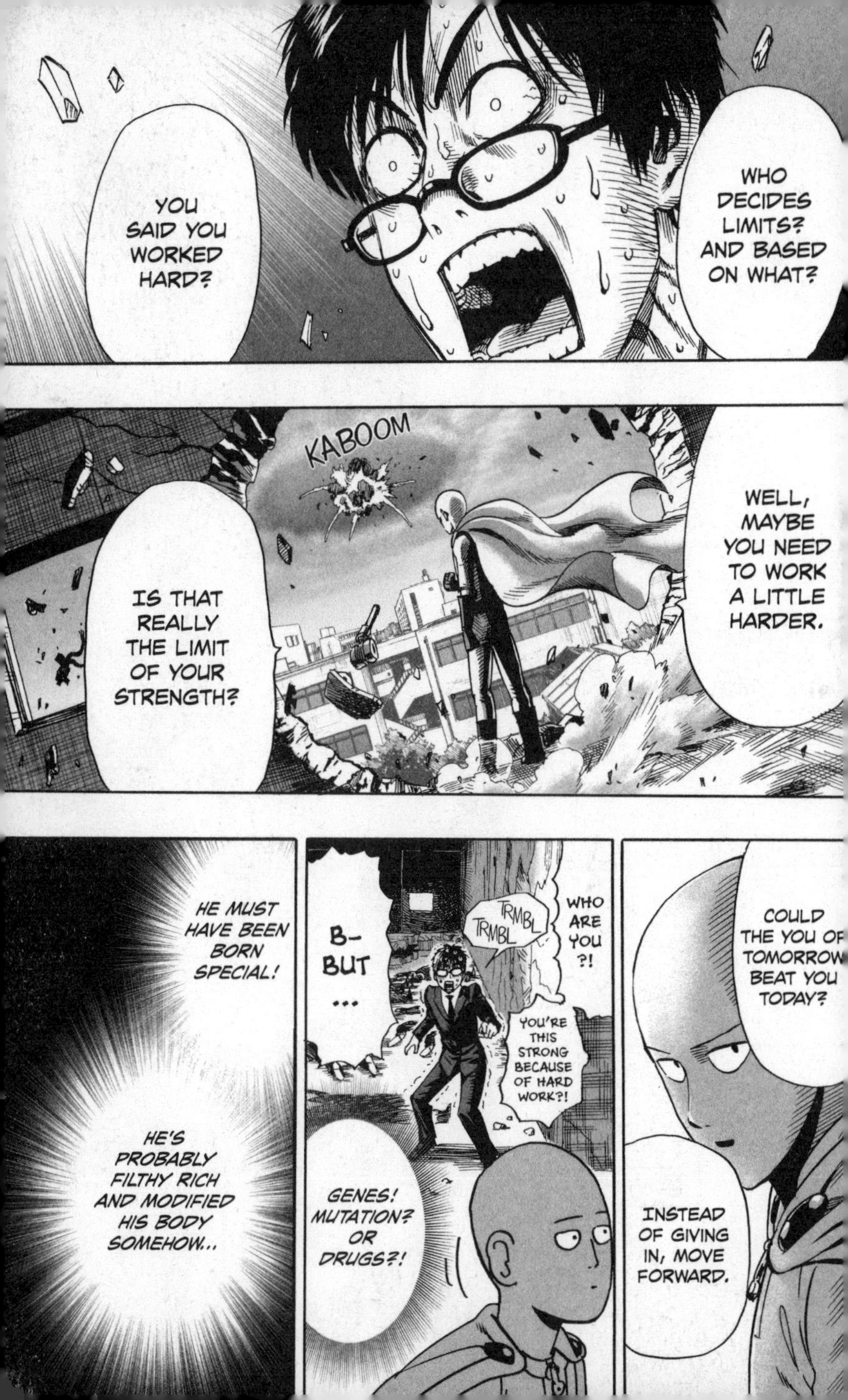
WHO DECIDES LIMITS? AND BASED ON WHAT?
YOU SAID YOU WORKED HARD?
WELL, MAYBE YOU NEED TO WORK A LITTLE HARDER.
KABOOM
IS THAT REALLY THE LIMIT OF YOUR STRENGTH?
COULD THE YOU OF TOMORROW BEAT YOU TODAY?
INSTEAD OF GIVING IN, MOVE FORWARD.
WHO ARE YOU ?!
TRMBL TRMBL
B- BUT ...
YOU'RE THIS STRONG BECAUSE OF HARD WORK?!
GENES! MUTATION? OR DRUGS?!
HE MUST HAVE BEEN BORN SPECIAL!
HE'S PROBABLY FILTHY RICH AND MODIFIED HIS BODY SOMEHOW...

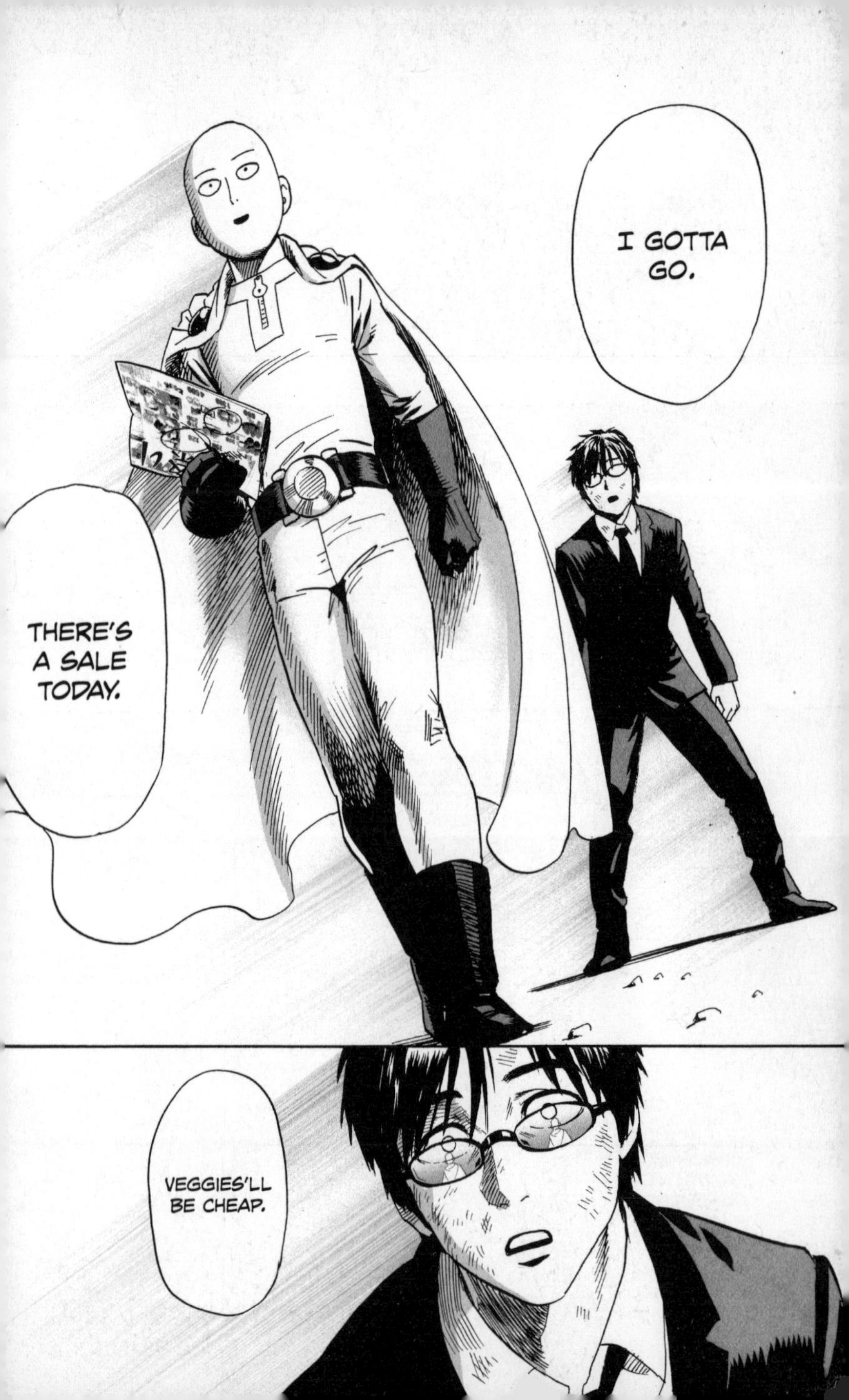
I GOTTA GO.
THERE'S A SALE TODAY.
VEGGIES'LL BE CHEAP.

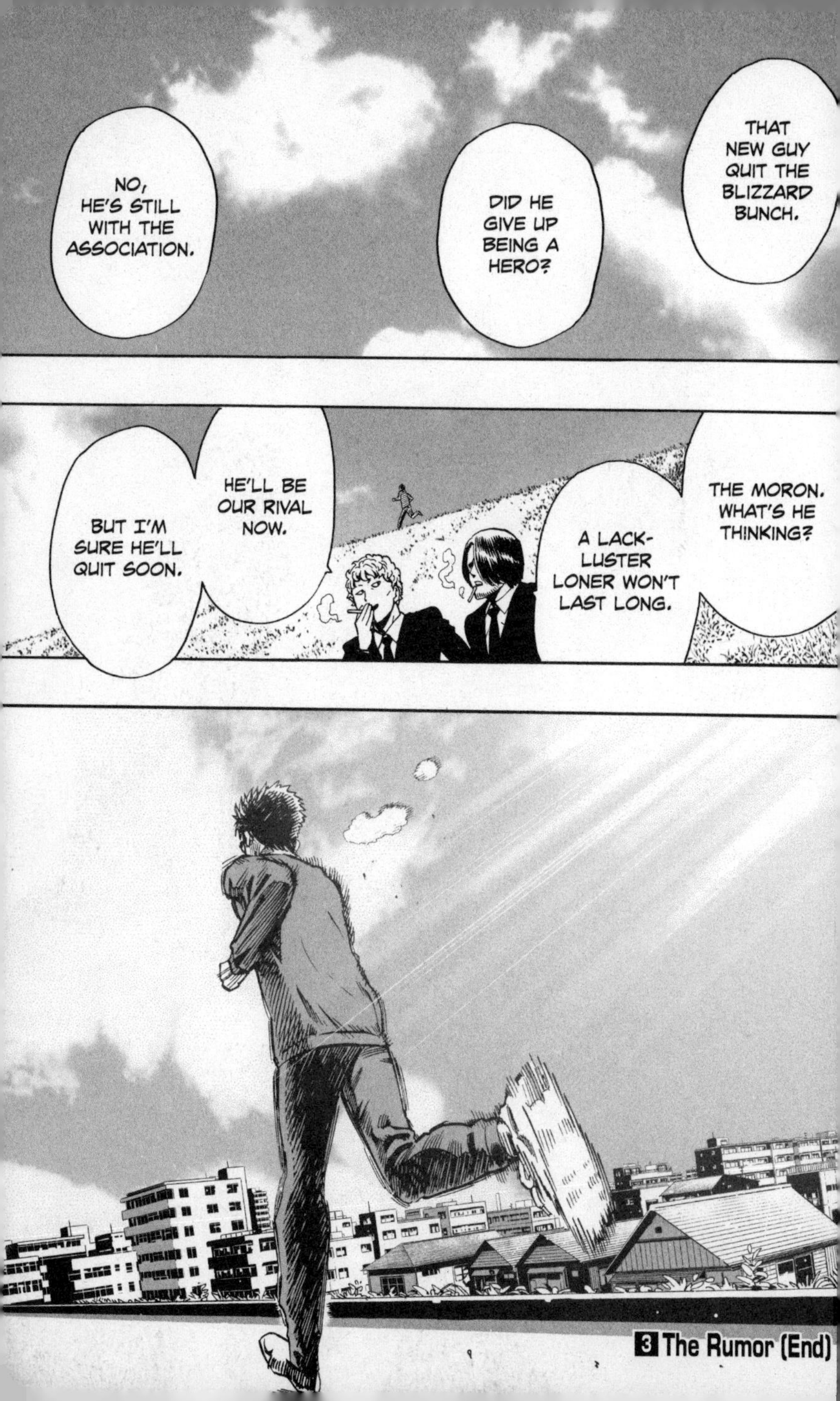
THAT NEW GUY QUIT THE BLIZZARD BUNCH.
DID HE GIVE UP BEING A HERO?
NO, HE'S STILL WITH THE ASSOCIATION.
THE MORON. WHAT'S HE THINKING?
A LACK-LUSTER LONER WON'T LAST LONG.
HE'LL BE OUR RIVAL NOW.
BUT I'M SURE HE'LL QUIT SOON.
3 The Rumor (End)

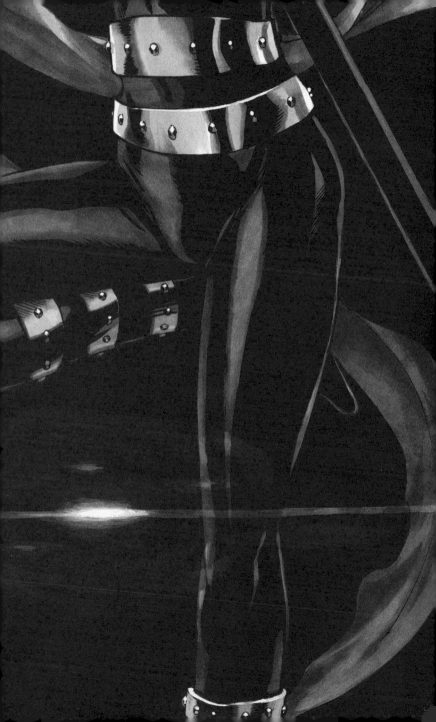

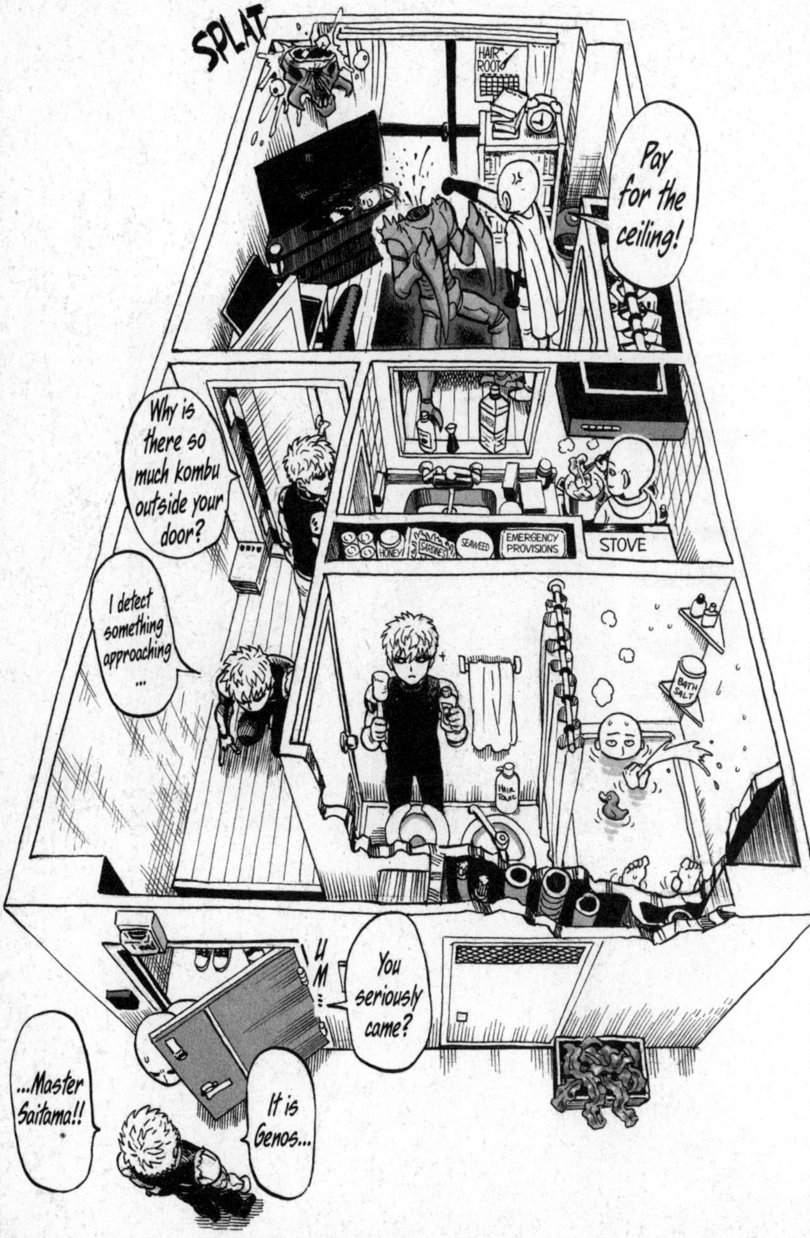
SPLAT
HAIR ROOT
Pay for the ceiling!
WATER
Why is there so much kombu outside your door?
HONEY!
SARDINES
SEAWEED
EMERGENCY PROVISIONS
STOVE
I detect something approaching ...
BATH SALT
HAIR TONIC
UM...
You seriously came?
...Master Saitama!!
It is Genos...

END NOTES

PAGE 142:
On the shopping bag Saitama is carrying,
Munageya's literal meaning is "chest-hair store."

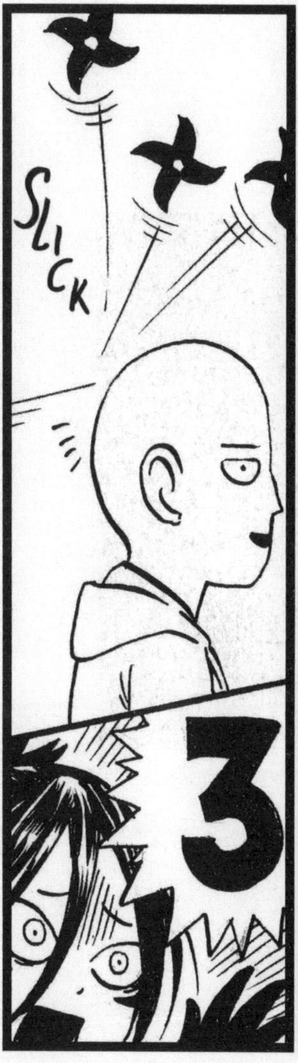
SLICK

ONE-PUNCH MAN
VOLUME 3
SHONEN JUMP MANGA EDITION

STORY BY | ONE
ART BY | YUSUKE MURATA

TRANSLATION | JOHN WERRY
TOUCH-UP ART AND LETTERING | JAMES GAUBATZ
DESIGN | FAWN LAU
SHONEN JUMP SERIES EDITOR | JOHN BAE
GRAPHIC NOVEL EDITOR | JENNIFER LEBLANC

First published in Japan in 2012 by SHUEISHA Inc., Tokyo.
English translation rights arranged by SHUEISHA Inc.

Printed in the U.S.A.

Published by VIZ Media, LLC
P.O. Box 77010
San Francisco, CA 94107

10 9 8 7 6 5 4 3 2 1
First printing, November 2015

www.viz.com

www.shonenjump.com

RATED T FOR TEEN

PARENTAL ADVISORY
ONE-PUNCH MAN is rated T for Teen and is recommended for ages 13 and up. This volume contains realistic and fantasy violence.

ratings.viz.com

★EYESHIELD 21

STORY BY **RIICHIRO INAGAKI**
ART BY **YUSUKE MURATA**

From the artist of *One-Punch Man!*

Wimpy Sena Kobayakawa has been running away from
bullies all his life. But when the football gear comes
on, things change—Sena's speed and uncanny ability
to elude big bullies just might give him what it takes to
become a great high school football hero! Catch all the
bone-crushing action and slapstick comedy of Japan's
hottest football manga!

VIZ media
www.viz.com

SHONEN JUMP
ADVANCED
www.shonenjump.com

RATED
T
FOR OLDER
TEEN
ratings.viz.com

EYESHIELD 21 © 2002 by Riichiro Inagaki, Yusuke Murata/SHUEISHA Inc.

A PREMIUM BOX SET OF THE FIRST TWO STORY ARCS OF ONE PIECE!

A PIRATE'S TREASURE FOR ANY MANGA FAN!

STORY AND ART BY EIICHIRO ODA

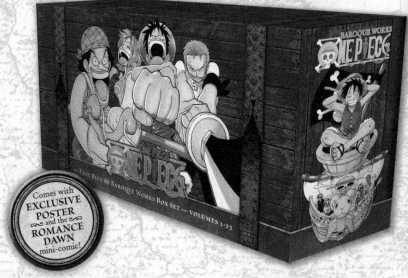

Comes with **EXCLUSIVE POSTER** and the **ROMANCE DAWN** mini-comic!

As a child, Monkey D. Luffy dreamed of becoming King of the Pirates. But his life changed when he accidentally gained the power to stretch like rubber...at the cost of never being able to swim again! Years later, Luffy sets off in search of the "One Piece," said to be the greatest treasure in the world...

This box set includes VOLUMES 1-23, which comprise the EAST BLUE and BAROQUE WORKS story arcs.

EXCLUSIVE PREMIUMS and GREAT SAVINGS
over buying the individual volumes!

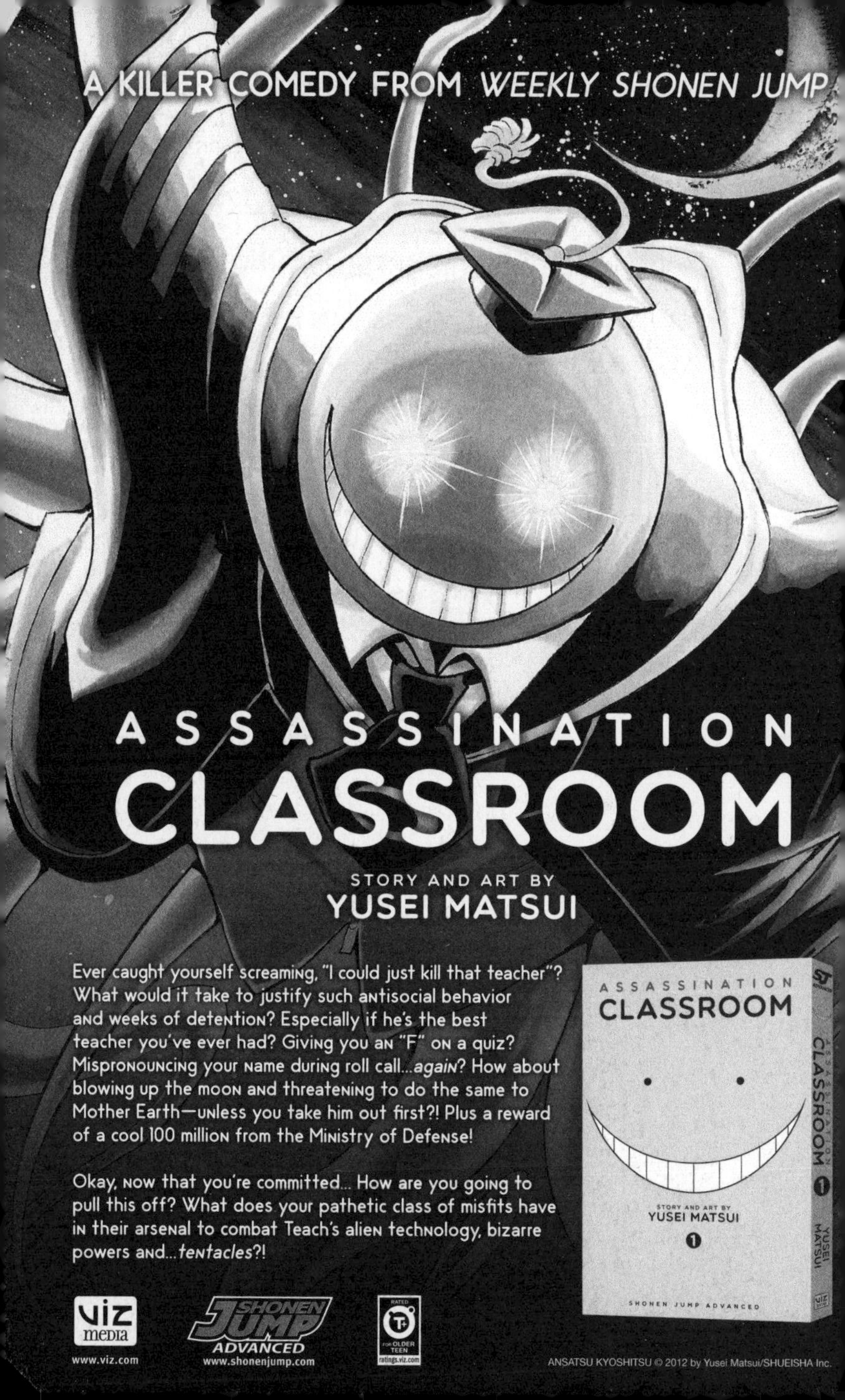

A KILLER COMEDY FROM WEEKLY SHONEN JUMP
ASSASSINATION CLASSROOM
STORY AND ART BY
YUSEI MATSUI
Ever caught yourself screaming, "I could just kill that teacher"? What would it take to justify such antisocial behavior and weeks of detention? Especially if he's the best teacher you've ever had? Giving you an "F" on a quiz? Mispronouncing your name during roll call...again? How about blowing up the moon and threatening to do the same to Mother Earth—unless you take him out first?! Plus a reward of a cool 100 million from the Ministry of Defense!
Okay, now that you're committed... How are you going to pull this off? What does your pathetic class of misfits have in their arsenal to combat Teach's alien technology, bizarre powers and...tentacles?!
ASSASSINATION CLASSROOM
STORY AND ART BY
YUSEI MATSUI
1
SHONEN JUMP ADVANCED
viz media
www.viz.com
SHONEN JUMP ADVANCED
www.shonenjump.com
RATED T+ FOR OLDER TEEN
ratings.viz.com
ANSATSU KYOSHITSU © 2012 by Yusei Matsui/SHUEISHA Inc.

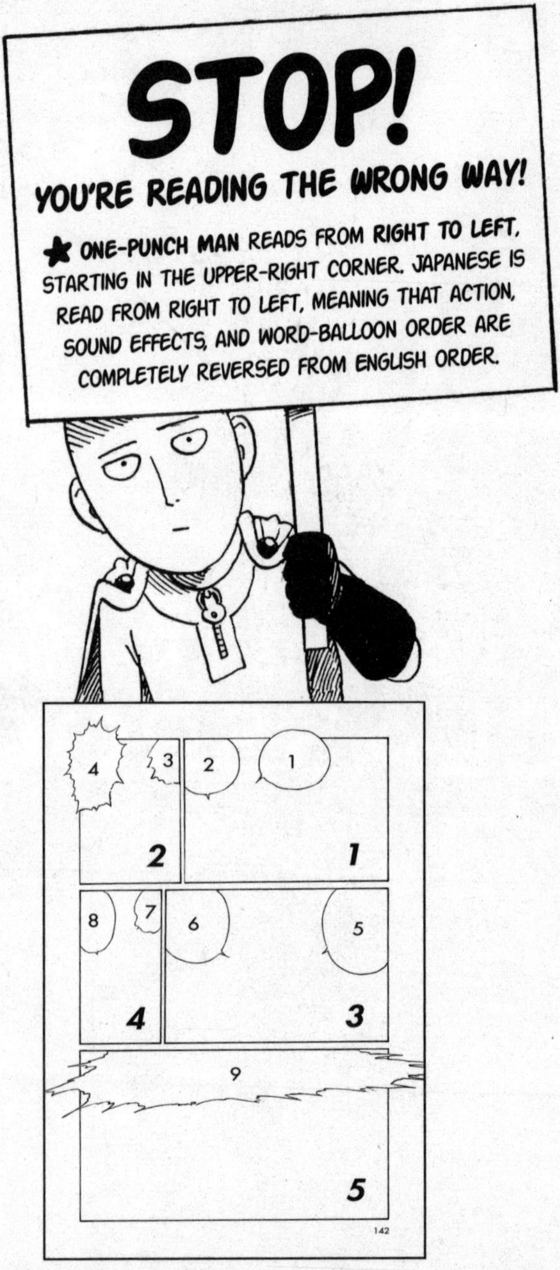
STOP!
YOU'RE READING THE WRONG WAY!
★ ONE-PUNCH MAN READS FROM RIGHT TO LEFT, STARTING IN THE UPPER-RIGHT CORNER. JAPANESE IS READ FROM RIGHT TO LEFT, MEANING THAT ACTION, SOUND EFFECTS, AND WORD-BALLOON ORDER ARE COMPLETELY REVERSED FROM ENGLISH ORDER.